WOLFE OF QUEBEC

Robin Reilly

James Wolfe's short but action-packed military career took him to Blenheim, where he served under Marlborough, to Scotland, where he fought against the Jacobites, and to Canada, where he died after wresting Quebec from the French. This is the stirring biography of the brilliant Major General, whose other foes — illness and jealous colleagues — were even more difficult to overcome, but whose courage and foresight changed the course of history.

WOLFE OF QUEBEC

ROBIN REILLY

CASSELL&CO

Cassell & Co
Wellington House, 125 Strand
London WC2R 0BB

Copyright © Robin Reilly 1960
First published by Cassell 1960
This edition 2001

British Library Cataloguing-in-Publication Data
A catalogue record for this book is available from the British Library

ISBN 0 304 35838 X

Printed in Great Britain by Creative Print & Design (Wales)

CONTENTS

CONTENTS

LIST OF ILLUSTRATIONS

Major-General James Wolfe
From a watercolour by George Townshend, drawn during the
Quebec campaign, 1759
   (*McCord Museum, McGill University, Montreal*)

James Wolfe
Painter unknown, *c.* 1742
   (*Major J. R. O'B. Warde and the National Portrait Gallery*)

Henrietta Wolfe
by Thomas Hudson
   (*Major J. R. O'B. Warde*)

James Wolfe
by Joseph Highmore
   (*Public Archives of Canada*)

Elizabeth Lawson
Artist unknown
   (*Webster Collection, New Brunswick Museum*)

Katherine Lowther
Miniature by Richard Cosway
   (*Lord Barnard*)

Major-General Sir Jeffrey Amherst
by Sir Joshua Reynolds
   (*National Gallery of Canada*)

Admiral Sir Charles Saunders
by Richard Brompton
   (*National Maritime Museum, Greenwich, Hospital Collection*)

Brigadier the Hon. Robert Monckton
From a mezzotint by James McArdell after a painting
by Thomas Hudson
   (*Webster Collection, New Brunswick Museum*)

Brigadier the Hon. George Townshend
From a mezzotint by James McArdell after a painting by
Thomas Hudson
(Webster Collection, New Brunswick Museum)

Brigadier the Hon. James Murray
Artist unknown
(National Portrait Gallery)

Attack of the French fire-ships on 28th June 1759
by Samuel Scott
(National Maritime Museum, Greenwich)

Attack of the French fire-rafts on 28th July 1759
by Samuel Scott
(National Maritime Museum, Greenwich)

View of Quebec from the Lévi shore
Engraving by P. Canot
(Webster Collection, New Brunswick Museum)

The Landing at the Anse du Foulon
Engraving by P. Canot after a drawing by Captain
Hervey Smyth
(Webster Collection, New Brunswick Museum)

MAPS

INTRODUCTION

IT IS a curious paradox that although most children know of James Wolfe as 'The Hero of Quebec', a first examination of the work of historians and of contemporary journals reveals that eminent scholars of all periods in common with eye-witnesses of the battle have entertained the gravest doubts about the accuracy of the title. From Wolfe's arrival in the Gulf of St. Lawrence in June 1759 to the capture of Quebec on 13th September scarcely an action of his is undisputed, hardly a motive unquestioned. There is, it is true, a thin, strong framework of undoubted fact upon which to build, but facts alone, even if they are proven beyond doubt, do not amount to history. It is the examination of the personalities involved and the interpretation of their characters that make events intelligible. For this reason, if for no other, the study of the life of James Wolfe is rewarding and necessary to the understanding of the Quebec campaign and the subsequent conquest of Canada.

The first part of this book is therefore devoted to Wolfe's early life in England, his battle experience in Flanders, his period of training and command in Scotland, and his emergence in the Rochefort and Louisbourg expeditions as a soldier of outstanding ability. In the second part are described the events from which Wolfe tore his claim to greatness and a permanent place in history, and which culminated in his death at the moment of victory on the Plains of Abraham. These are events the outline of which is well known: events of which all but the most conscientious historians and biographers have written with confidence. And yet they are events of which the truth is not, even now, known with any certainty, for the parts of the two journals which might have provided the whole truth were destroyed two hundred years ago. The strained relations between Wolfe and his brigadiers, and between Montcalm and Vaudreuil, discredit the writings of the senior officers who survived the battle as wholly reliable evidence, and those chroniclers whose impartiality seems unquestioned did not hold offices of sufficient importance to enable them to obtain first-hand knowledge of the commanders' conduct of the siege and defence of Quebec.

Faced with a mass of conflicting evidence, historians have been divided in their judgements. Some have accorded the merit of the enterprise to Wolfe and to Saunders, his naval commander. Others have been at pains to discover any reason for success but that of Wolfe's ability as a general: some awarding the laurels to one or more of the subordinate brigadiers; some attributing the victory to sheer good fortune; some even hinting that Quebec was betrayed by the French. Certain biographers have allowed a natural jealousy for the reputations of their ancestors to blind them to all evidence contradictory to their preconceived theories, producing work which is entertaining but historically valueless.

I make no claim to have made an impartial judgement, for I believe that neither impartiality nor the pronouncement of judgement are the function of the historian. His responsibility is the sifting and reasoned interpretation of evidence: to start without preconception, and to continue with honest research to an intelligible conclusion; but this does not preclude the forming of opinion as a gradual and reasonable process from which involvement and partiality may spring. Without this involvement a writer's work is unremitting drudgery lacking spirit or compulsion. My reason for writing this biography has been a desire to discover some of the answers to the many unsolved problems of the Quebec campaign and to know something of the man whose name is most closely associated with it. I make no apology if my researches have failed to uncover a new and different hero for there is no evidence to support such a discovery. If I have drawn a portrait of a man who, notwithstanding all too human frailties of character and great physical handicaps, overcame all obstacles to gain a deserved and lasting fame, I shall be well satisfied.

It is one of the faults inherent in biography that light must be focused on the figure of the subject alone, and others, often historically more important, must move in half-light or shadow. Political events and social changes, too, must be muted to leave the subject dominant against the background they provide. I have made no attempt to compromise with this problem. Such matters have been described in outline only where it seemed necessary for an understanding of the events which influenced Wolfe's actions.

Wolfe's life coincided almost exactly with the reign of George II, a period of intricate—and often futile—political intrigue, both at home and in European affairs, and of military inefficiency seldom equalled in the history of these islands. And yet, in the casual, almost indifferent, manner which has for so long been the envy and despair of her enemies, Britain produced, in her desperate need, men who would change her fortunes and lead her people towards a new golden period of prosperity and power.

Alone among the continuously changing factors in history, human nature, fortunately for the historian, changes little. This is not to say that Wolfe can be thought of as belonging to a certain category of human beings whose reactions in given circumstances can be calculated as a class. Wolfe was an individual faced with individual circumstances. His story, like that of so many great commanders, is one of trial and error, of planning and improvisation, of doubt and indecision, unsupported by a comfortable faith in his own infallibility. He conquered because he had in him the qualities of a great leader—a sense of duty, strength of purpose, great physical and moral courage, and the capacity to inspire faith, respect, and even devotion in those who followed him. A thorough military training, born of love of his profession, and a profound study of its theory and practice fitted him for command. Great opportunity gave him a place in history.

ACKNOWLEDGEMENTS

I wish to record my sincere thanks to all those who have generously given their valuable time to guide my researches and allowed access to manuscript or pictorial material, and in particular to Mr. Alastair Parker and Mr. Piers Mackesy, who read the manuscript and gave me the benefit of their advice and scholarship; Colonel G. H. G. Anderson, C.B.E., D.S.O., M.C., of Quebec House, and Major J. R. O'B. Warde of Squerryes Court, Westerham; and Mr. J. F. Kerslake, Assistant Keeper of the National Portrait Gallery, whose valuable advice on the difficult subject of Wolfe portraiture saved me from repeating old errors.

In Canada I was given hospitality and invaluable assistance by Mrs. Alice Turnham, Director, McGill University Museums, and Mrs. I. B. M. Dobell, Associate Historian, McGill University, Montreal; Dr. W. Kaye Lamb, Dominion Archivist of Canada; and Major G. Guimond, Museum Director at The Citadel, Quebec. If a similar welcome is extended to all historians visiting Canada, it is surprising that more do not find there a subject for their researches.

Permission for the use of manuscript or printed material was generously given by the Marquess of Lansdowne; the Earl Amherst; Colonel R. Campbell Preston; Major J. R. O'B. Warde; the Trustees of the British Museum; the Public Record Office; the National Library of Scotland; the Public Archives of Canada; and the McCord Museum, McGill University, Montreal. Unpublished Crown Copyright material has been used with the permission of the Controller of H.M. Stationery Office.

I am indebted to Lord Barnard; Major J. R. O'B. Warde; the National Portrait Gallery; the National Gallery of Canada; the Public Archives of Canada; the McCord Museum, McGill University; the Webster Collection, the New Brunswick Museum; the National Maritime Museum, Greenwich; and the National Trust for permission to reproduce photographs of portraits and pictures in their possession.

Permission for quotation from Beckles Willson's *Life and*

Letters of James Wolfe was given by William Heinemann Ltd.; from Mrs. Paget Toynbee's edition of *The Letters of Horace Walpole*, by the Clarendon Press; from Sir John Fortescue's *History of the British Army* and G. S. Kimball's *The Correspondence of William Pitt*, by Macmillan & Co. Ltd.; from *Augustus Hervey's Journal*, by William Kimber & Co. Ltd.; from R. H. Mahon's *Life of General The Hon. James Murray* and C. V. Townshend's *Military Life of Field-Marshal George First Marquis Townshend*, by John Murray Ltd.; from *The Private Correspondence of Lord Chesterfield and the Duke of Newcastle*, by the Royal Historical Society; and from *Wolfe in Scotland* by the representatives of the author, the late J. T. Findlay.

I must, also, acknowledge my debt to Sir Arthur Doughty and G. W. Parmelee, whose great work, *The Siege of Quebec and the Battle of the Plains of Abraham* is indispensable to any study of the campaign.

Lastly, my grateful thanks are due to my long-suffering family and friends who have given encouragement and help during the five years that this book has been in preparation; and in particular to Henrietta Gatehouse, who not only typed the entire manuscript twice but kept up a steady flow of candid, penetrating, and extremely valuable criticism which enabled me to correct innumerable faults of style and woolly description.

NOTE ON DATES

The change in this country, in 1751, from the use of the Julian (Old Style) calendar to the Gregorian (New Style) has caused the maximum confusion to historians. In this biography the dates are quoted according to the Julian calendar up to 1751 and according to the Gregorian thereafter except that all years have been assumed to start on 1st January and not—as in the Julian calendar —on Lady Day, 25th March.

'I am to act a greater part in this business than I wished or desired. The backwardness of some of the older officers has in some measure forced the Government to come down so low. I shall do my best, and leave the rest to fortune, as perforce we must when there are not the most commanding abilities.'

James Wolfe to Major Walter Wolfe
29th January 1759.

CHAPTER I

Childhood: Westerham and Greenwich

FOR England the year 1724 was not distinguished by great events. Under the rule of a German King who spoke little English and a Council of Ministers who spoke even less German, the country was uneasily at peace. In Whitehall, a Whig government led by Robert Walpole was concerned with the manipulation of affairs in Europe to create a period of stability during which the country could recover from the economic difficulties brought about by the long years of war and the recent South Sea Bubble crisis. At Eton, the sixteen year old William Pitt spent long hours with his books, and shorter hours with Grenville and Lyttelton friends bird nesting and playing cricket; in Yorkshire, the marriage, in the little church of Long Marston, of Henrietta Thompson and Edward Wolfe, Lieutenant-Colonel of His Majesty's Third Regiment of Foot Guards, passed almost unnoticed. There was, indeed, little in this event to create more than the local interest commonly aroused by an alliance of two well-to-do families in a parish church.

The Wolfes were of Welsh stock: with their cousins the Gouldsmiths they had emigrated to Ireland during the fifteenth century and settled in the south-west. There they had flourished, and by the sixteenth century members of the family had become leading citizens in the counties of Cork, Limerick, and Clare. Captain George Woulfe and his brother Francis, a Franciscan friar, distinguished themselves in the defence of the Catholic stronghold of Limerick in 1651 when, with an impartiality which argues that they had become truly Irish, they not only refused entry to the city to Ormonde's royalist troops, but, when he

I

retired in disgust to France, carried on a spirited but hopeless defence of the town against a Cromwellian force under Ireton. When Limerick fell, the Woulfe brothers were among those excluded from the amnesty terms. Francis was executed, but George somehow escaped to England and, settling in Yorkshire, married there, changed the spelling of his name to Wolfe, and prudently adopted the Protestant faith. Continuing the military tradition, his son, Edward, entered the army and served as a lieutenant in the Royal Regiment of Foot Guards in Ireland, but he too was to suffer for his religion and he was one of the Protestant officers removed from the regiment in 1688. In the same year, the revolution restored him to favour and, in May 1689, he was appointed by William III to be captain in Sir George St. George's Regiment of Foot, a commission confirmed by Queen Anne on her accession thirteen years later. In 1702 his son, also Edward, was appointed to Viscount Shannon's Regiment of Marines as second-lieutenant.

Three years later the younger Edward was promoted to captain in Sir Richard Temple's Regiment of Foot and, by 1710, when he was twenty-five, he had reached the rank of major. He served under Marlborough in Flanders and, though there is no evidence that he displayed military brilliance, his promotion, rapid for one with little means or influence, indicates that he was at least a capable officer. The Treaty of Utrecht, in 1713, all but put an end to his active career. He was put on half pay and was without employment until he was recalled to serve under Wade in the suppression of the 1715 rising in Scotland. Two years later he was promoted to the lieutenant-colonelcy of the 3rd Regiment of Foot Guards. He was to see no more of active service or promotion for more than twenty years. Much of his time was spent in York where no doubt he attracted some attention as a bachelor of good family and secure position. The Thompsons owned a town house in York in addition to the Old Hall at Long Marston, so it is probable that they were already well known to the Wolfes. Certain it is that the young Henrietta Thompson attracted the attention of Edward Wolfe, twenty years her senior, and they were married on 23rd February 1724, shortly before her twentieth birthday.

Henrietta Wolfe was tall and slender, and considered by some to be a beauty. Her portraits, painted some years later by Hudson and Thornhill, show her as handsome rather than beautiful: a commanding figure, dark hair drawn back from an oval face, her chin retreating precipitately from beneath a long and pointed nose, a divergence of features relieved by fine eyes and a good complexion. The Colonel, large-featured, bluff, and powerful, could have been taken for a country squire or parson.

After their marriage, the couple took up residence at the Thompson's house in York, where they lived for two years. In 1726, however, they decided to move south. Whether this decision was the result of a move by his regiment, or of the Colonel's natural desire to be nearer to the seat of government and patronage in Whitehall, is not known, but in the autumn they moved to Westerham in Kent. They chose for their first home a gabled Tudor house called Spiers, built on low ground at the eastern end of the village street and facing the Maidstone highway. It was not a grand house: it was, in common with other Tudor houses, dark, damp, and draughty; but it was not unsuited to their social position and, being but twenty-two miles from London, it was conveniently situated. The Wolfes must have found disadvantages in village life after two years in York, but Mrs. Wolfe was capable, energetic, and sociable, and she and her husband soon made friends among their neighbours. This was fortunate as the Colonel was often away on duty with his regiment, and the young Henrietta Wolfe was expecting her first child early in the new year. Among their closest friends were the vicar of Westerham and his wife, the Rev. George and Mrs. Lewis. The Lewises, with their large family, lived at the vicarage a few yards up the hill into Westerham, and during her husband's absences Mrs. Wolfe was a frequent visitor there. It seems likely that the Lewises invited her to stay with them during her confinement, but whether or not this was so, it was in a small bedroom at the vicarage that on 2nd January 1727 James Wolfe was born. Mrs. Wolfe remained at the vicarage for three weeks, until her son had been baptized and christened in the parish church; she then returned with him to Spiers and the duties of her own household. A year later a second son was born and was named Edward after his father and grandfathers.

The boys were delicate, suffering from colds and chest complaints, and Mrs. Wolfe engaged a nurse, Betty Hooper, to look after them. This Betty Hooper gained the lasting affection of both children, and her own sons were later to serve in the regiment of which James was lieutenant-colonel. It was customary for the mistress of a household to keep her own book of cookery and medical recipes, and these recipes for tonics, ointments, cordials, and nostrums of every kind were handed down with great care from generation to generation. That a remedy was old was judged an additional guarantee of its efficacy. Many of the prescriptions in common use seem horrible in the light of two centuries of medical research, but they were not considered extraordinary at the time and the patients often recovered from their ailments. Horse-dung posset, cockroach tea, and snail tea were much favoured. Snail tea being a popular remedy for chest complaints and therefore often needed at Spiers, Mrs. Wolfe had her own recipe for it.[1] 'Take', she advises, 'a peck of green garden snails, wash them in Bear put them in an oven and let them stay till they've done crying; then with a knife and fork prick the green from them, and beat the snail shells and all in a stone mortar. Then take a quart of green earth-worms, slice them through the middle and strow them with salt: then wash them and beat them, the pot being first put into the still with two handfulls of angelico, a quart of rosemary flowers, then the snails and the worms, the egrimony, bears feet, red dock roots, barbery brake, bilbony, wormwood, of each two handfuls: one handful of rue tumerick and one ounce of saffron, well dried and beaten. Then power in three gallons of milk. Wait till morning, then put in three ounces of cloves (well beaten), hartshorn, grated. Keep the still covered all night. This done, stir it not. Distil with a moderate fire. The patient must take two spoonfuls at a time.' As both Wolfe boys were consumptive it is to be feared that they were obliged to drink quantities of this brew, and it is sobering to think how much trouble and time were taken with the preparation of a recipe, the curative and palliative qualities of which were non-existent.

Mrs. Wolfe had a good stock of such remedies and set great store by them. She suffered from chest troubles herself, and from a number of other ailments, real and imagined, and she was thus constantly on the lookout for signs of illness in her husband and children. In later years her letters, filled with remedies and anxiety, were to pursue her elder son throughout his career and he, in his turn, was to use her interest in ill-health to distract her attention from his other human but less satisfactory frailties.

Little is known of the childhood of the young Wolfe brothers but it is not difficult to imagine how they spent their leisure. What they lacked in physique, they made up for in spirit. The country-side around Westerham is hilly and wooded; the house, Spiers, with its winding stairways, dim attic rooms and dark passages, stables and kennels, was a splendid place for children's games of adventure and make-believe, and a stream running through the grounds provided small-fry fishing and a sea for toy ships. In addition, the Colonel was at home for two years while his regi-ment was road-building in the vicinity—a task for which the small peacetime army was considered well qualified—and would tell the children stories of Marlborough's wars in Flanders and the Jacobite rebellion of 1715. Both boys were sent, with the sons of other local gentry, to a school in the village run by a Mr. Lawrence, and there they learned the rudiments of reading, writing, arithmetic and the classics. Five years after the arrival of the Wolfes in Westerham, the manor house, Squerryes Court, had been sold by the third Earl of Jersey to John Warde, a widower with several children, brother-in-law to the beautiful Countesses of Buckingham and Effingham. His second son, George, was just a year older than James Wolfe and the two boys began a friendship which was to endure until Wolfe's death. Both had ambitions for a military career and together they explored the countryside on horseback or with their dogs, discussing their plans for the future.

When James was eleven the Wolfes moved from Westerham to Greenwich, where they took a house in East Lane.* No doubt he was sorry to leave his friends and the familiar surroundings of his childhood but he was to make frequent visits to the Wardes at Squerryes; and Greenwich, with its fine buildings and view of the busy river traffic, must have provided exciting new sights and experiences for the boy. The reasons for the move are clear. In Greenwich there had recently been founded a school for the sons of officers in the Navy or Army, and conducted by the Rev. Samuel Swinden, a scholar and tutor of some repute and an

* Now East Street.

excellent judge of character. To this school went James and Edward Wolfe, and it is greatly to Swinden's credit that while recognizing the scholarly ability of the younger brother, he did not fail to discern the less obvious promise of the elder. He spared no effort to develop the qualities he saw in both boys and he was rewarded by their lifelong regard and friendship for him. The second and perhaps more urgent reason for the move was the strained relations between England and Spain. In the event of another war, new promotions and appointments would be made in the Army. Lieutenant-Colonel Edward Wolfe intended to be at hand to accept any appointment that might be offered. He could command little patronage, but his seniority in his rank and his presence at the source of preferment would lend weight to his request for an appointment. His decision proved wise, for within a year of the move to Greenwich England was at war with Spain.

The declaration of war on Spain, made on 8th October 1739 by a reluctant and apprehensive Walpole, was the culmination of many years of friction between the two countries. The War of Jenkins's Ear, as it has come to be known, was fought for trade. As Pitt had declared in the House of Commons in March,[2] 'When trade is at stake it is your last retrenchment; you must defend it or perish.' The fact that the trade in question was undeniably illicit and from a legal standpoint indefensible was obscured by the hereditary enmity of Britain and Spain and by the righteous indignation always aroused in the British by the brutalities of their enemies. The facts were simple: the great Spanish Empire in the New World was potentially a vast market for British goods; the Spanish colonists were anxious to trade with all-comers, and British traders were eager to explore the possibilities of the market; the Spanish Government forbade it. By the Treaty of Utrecht in 1713, certain concessions were wrung from Spain, and Britain obtained the right to traffic in slaves and to send one ship each year with merchandise for the Spanish colonies. It must have been clear to all parties that these concessions would not resolve the problem. British merchant seamen, smugglers by inheritance, carried on a brisk and contraband trade with the colonies; the Spanish Government took strenuous action to prohibit it by searching ships not only in Spanish territorial waters but also on the high seas, confiscating cargoes, and meting out imprisonment, torture, and death to the crews. This intolerable situation existed while Walpole carried out continuous and futile negotiations with the inflexible Elizabeth Farnese who had no thought of a compromise solution.

The Spanish monopoly of the trade of their colonies was unreasonable but not without precedent; it was a policy followed by all the great imperial powers in their time; but it is true that Spain possessed more territory in the New World than she alone could supply with European merchandise, and that her colonies would have welcomed and benefited from trade with British merchants. There were doubtless faults on both sides: the British disregard of Spanish rights can be accounted extreme provocation; the high-handed action of Spain outside her territorial waters, and the brutalities to which British crews, innocent or guilty, were subjected, was savage retaliation. Walpole clung to the fading hope of a peaceful settlement, but Pitt and the opposition voiced the wishes of the country in demanding action. The death of Queen Caroline in 1737 deprived Walpole of his most influential ally, and the King began to lose faith in his first minister. In 1738, the growing sense of exasperation received a stimulus and inspiration from the appearance at the bar of the House of Commons of Robert Jenkins, captain of a British sloop which had been engaged in trading from Jamaica. Jenkins related to a crowded House how Spaniards had boarded his ship to search it for contraband. Though they had found no proof of smuggling they had torn off his ear and, flinging it in his face, had told him to carry it to his King. He took them at their word and, wrapping the ear in cotton-wool, carried it with him wherever he went, awaiting a favourable opportunity. It was now some seven years since the event, but nothing could detract from the effect created by the production of this disgusting relic in the House of Commons. His version of his feelings at the time of the incident—'I commended my soul to God and my cause to my country'—had the simplicity and courage of a call to the nation. The popular clamour for war could no longer be ignored.

Walpole made one last bid for peace: in 1739 he concocted the Convention of Pardo, little more than an accountant's balance-sheet of merchant claims on both sides drawing a balance in favour of Britain. Before it was even signed, Spain had succeeded

7

in whittling down her debt to such an extent that it appeared negligible. Pitt denounced it as 'a stipulation for national ignominy'[3] and an 'illusory expedient'. 'Is this,' he demanded, 'any longer a nation? Is this any longer an English Parliament, if with more ships in your harbours than in all the navies of Europe, with above two millions of people in your American colonies, you will bear to hear of the expediency of receiving from Spain an insecure, unsatisfactory, dishonourable Convention? Sir, Spain knows the consequences of a war in America; Whoever gains it must prove fatal to her.' Walpole secured parliamentary assent to his Convention but his policy failed. On 8th October 1739 he declared war on Spain. His declaration was received everywhere in England with tumultuous joy. As the London crowds surged noisily exultant through the streets, Walpole saw the downfall of his policy and the approaching end of his power. He feared that a war with Spain in America might extend to a greater conflict with France in Europe. 'They may ring their bells now, but soon they will be wringing their hands.' He was to be proved right.

For England the war began with a spectacular success. One of the Government's most ardent critics in the Commons had been Captain Edward Vernon: with six ships, he had declared, he could capture Porto Bello itself, one of the most famous haunts of the *guarda-costas*. In July 1739, three months before war was declared, he was promoted vice-admiral and set out with eight ships under instructions to burn shipping in Spanish ports including Porto Bello. Two ships having been detached for other duties, Vernon reached his objective with the exact number for which he had asked. Ignoring strong fortifications, he carried out a bold and well-planned attack which resulted in the capture of the port on 11th November after only two days' fighting. News of this exploit was greeted with jubilation in England. In spite of Vernon's warnings it was obvious to the Ministry that only the deployment of a larger force was required for the capture of the entire Spanish Empire in America. Plans were made at once for a joint military and naval expedition to capture Carthagena, the port of New Granada, or Havana, or Vera Cruz—there was some doubt about the exact objective. Lord Cathcart was nominated to command the Army; the Navy would be commanded by Vernon. Lieutenant-Colonel Edward Wolfe was appointed colonel of the

8

1st Regiment of Marines and, in July 1740, was ordered to proceed to the Isle of Wight to take up the duties of Adjutant-General to the expedition.

This was the opportunity for which Colonel Wolfe had been waiting for so long; it was also the opportunity for which his son, James, had been preparing himself. It was customary for an officer of high rank to take with him volunteers as members of his private household. At his son's request, and against the advice and pleading of his wife, Colonel Wolfe agreed to take James with him in that capacity. The boy volunteer was thirteen years old, tall and lean, and constitutionally quite unfitted for the hardships of a long voyage and a military campaign, but he was determined to go. He was allowed to leave Swinden's school and, one day in July, he said good-bye to his mother and younger brother and set out with the Colonel on the Portsmouth coach to join the assembling army in Newport.

Hopes for the success of the expedition were everywhere high; a decisive blow was to be struck at Spain through her empire, and the outcome would surely be military glory and material gain for England. Nothing could have proved further from the truth. The success of the enterprise depended upon two factors: speed and secrecy. The assembly of the force was carried out with a conspicuous lack of both. When it finally sailed, nearly a year after orders for its preparation, the Spanish had been aware of its destination for many months and had taken the precaution of sending reinforcements to their naval forces and garrisons in the area. The original plan was sound enough but it was muddled through by senile incompetents; it began in confusion and ended in disaster. The troops were embarked in August but contrary winds and the unprepared state of the fleet prevented its sailing until October. Meanwhile the soldiers were cooped up in their cramped quarters aboard the transports in conditions far from ideal for troops embarked on a long and arduous campaign in the unhealthy climate of the Americas. On 2nd September Cathcart reported that he was ready to sail, but on the 14th he was still at Spithead and writing to the Duke of Newcastle,[4] 'The troops having now been six weeks on board, and upon salt provisions, and the prospect we have of being so much longer here, obliges me to represent to your Grace of what consequence it would be to the men's health if during our stay here they were ordered to be furnished with fresh provisions.'

It was inevitable that such conditions should take their toll of the strength of the army even before it sailed. The young James Wolfe wrote to his mother on 6th August:

'Dr Mamma,

I receiv'd my Dearest Mamma's Letter on Monday last, but could not answer it then, by reason I was at Camp to see the Regiments march off to go on board, & was too late for the Post but am very sorry Dr Mamma that you doubt my Love, which I'm sure is as sincere as ever any Son's was to his Mother.

Pappa & I are just now going on board but I believe shall not sail this fortnight, in which time if I can get ashore at Portsmouth or any other Town I will certainly write to you, & when we are gone, by every Ship I meet, because I know it is my Duty, besides if it was not, I wou'd do it out of Love, wh pleasure. I am sorry to hear that your head is so bad, which I fear is caus'd by your being so Melancholy, but pray, Dr Mamma, if you love me, don't give yourself up to fears for us. . . . I hope, if it please god, we shall soon see one another again which will be the Happiest day that ever I shall see. I will as sure as I live, if it is possible for me let you know everything that has happen'd particular, by every ship, therefore pray, Dearest Mamma, don't doubt of it. I am in a very good State of Health, and am likely to continue so. Pray my love to my Brother, and accept of my Duty. Pappa desires his Love to you & Blessing to my Brother. Pray my Service to Mr. Streton & his family,* & to Mr. & Mrs. Weston,† and to George Warde when you see him & pray believe me to be,

My Dearest Mamma
Your most Dutiful, Loving, and affectionate Son,
J. WOLFE

Harry gives his love to Margaret, & is very careful of me. Pray my service to Will and the rest. Pappa bid me tell you that Mr. Patterson will give Mr. Masterton two Hundred Pounds more.'

His spirits were high but his optimism about his health was

* Friends of the Wolfes in Greenwich.
† A master at Swinden's.

premature. He soon became so ill that his father had no alternative but to have him landed at Portsmouth and carried home to Greenwich. After his high hopes, and perhaps a little understandable boasting among his schoolfellows at Swinden's, it must have been a bitter disappointment and humiliation to the boy soldier to have to return so soon, weak and ill, to his home and his school. He lived to be thankful for his good fortune.

The fleet of transports sailed in October. Among those on board were a young second-lieutenant of Marines, James Murray, who was to serve under Wolfe on another more auspicious occasion, and an inexperienced surgeon's mate, Tobias Smollett, who in *Roderick Random* has left a detailed record of the miseries of the campaign. Many, including Lord Cathcart himself, died before Carthagena was reached; thousands died of fever, scurvy, and gangrene before the attempt was abandoned. Cathcart was succeeded as commander by Wentworth, an unimaginative, stupid, stubborn officer who would not co-operate with Vernon. As Smollett wrote,[5] 'It might be said of these great men . . . the one could not brook a superior, and the other was impatient of an equal; so that, between the pride of one, and insolence of another, the enterprise miscarried, according to the proverb, *Between two stools, the backside falls to the ground.*' Thus co-operation, the one vital support of a joint naval and military expedition without which it must fail, was lacking. By April the attempt on Carthagena had failed and the 3,500 survivors of the 8,000 troops disembarked for the attack were taken on board again. Two more attempts were made: the first against Santiago de Cuba, and the second on Panama from Porto Bello; both were miserable failures. In the autumn of 1741 both Wentworth and Vernon were recalled and no further operations on a grand scale were attempted. Just a year earlier, when the expedition was being assembled, Dr. Thomas Arne, with untimely optimism, had composed 'Rule Britannia'.

In England, the war was conducted by a Committee of the Privy Council led by Walpole and the Duke of Newcastle, who had neither the energy nor drive to direct operations nor the means to implement such action as they decided upon. During the previous twenty-five years the armed forces had been reduced and neglected. Officers, no less than their equipment, had grown old

— MANN —

NORWAY
(TO DENMARK)

SWEDEN

RUSSIA

BALTIC SEA

EAST
PRUSSIA

S E A

D
E
N
M
A
R
K

SCHLESWIG

EAST
FRISIA

HOLSTEIN

SW. POMERANIA

POMERANIA

MECKLENBURG

...nden

HANOVER

R. ELBE

R. ALLER

WESTPHALIA

R. EMS

MINDEN

×

BRUNS-
WICK

R. WESER

POLAND

Zorndorf

Kunersdorf

P R U S S I A

Leuthen

Vesel

Kreveld

Cologne

R. ELBE

Rossbach

SILESIA

R. RHINE

S A X O N Y

DETTINGEN
×

Mainz

R. MAIN

Chotusitz

...ALATINATE

BOHEMIA

MORAVIA

BAVARIA

E U R O P E
mid 18ᵗʰ century

VITZERLAND

TYROL

Miles

0   50   100   150   200   250

and out of date. Commanded to 'rule the waves', Britain had as
First Lord, Admiral Wager, and as Admiral of the Fleet, Norris,
whose combined ages totalled 152. These ancient mariners were
members of the Committee of the Privy Council responsible for
the vigorous prosecution of the war. Walpole now had to pay the
penalty for the exclusion from office of the ablest of his contemporaries, Pulteney, Carteret, Chesterfield, Townshend. Instead,
his colleagues were Hardwicke, an able but inactive Lord
Chancellor; Newcastle, the nervous genius of electioneering, for
guidance on foreign affairs; and Hervey, scented satirist and
erstwhile lap-dog to the Queen, as Lord Privy Seal. His task was
made no easier by the refusal of George II to abandon his frequent
visits to Hanover. The love of the King for his vulnerable
Electorate was the most powerful single influence on the framing
of British foreign policy from the accession of George I until Pitt
took office as Secretary of State in 1756. While Walpole struggled
with the problems of a war in America for which he had no heart,
his worst fears were being realized in Europe.

Since 1713 almost every ruler in Europe had agreed to the
Pragmatic Sanction which guaranteed the inheritance by Maria
Theresa of the Hapsburg possessions, then ruled by her father, the
Emperor Charles VI. Walpole himself had subscribed to this by
the Treaty of Vienna in 1731. Little more than a year after war had
been declared on Spain, Charles VI died and the rush for posses-
sion of the Hapsburg dominions, the War of the Austrian
Succession, began. Frederick of Prussia attacked Silesia; France,
Bavaria, Saxony, and Spain repudiated their guarantees; Spain
claimed the Hapsburg lands in Italy; Charles Albert of Bavaria
was nominated Emperor-designate, and plans were laid for the
partitioning of the Hapsburg possessions in Germany. Maria
Theresa called on Holland, Russia, Savoy, and England for help.
Russia was already engaged with a war against Sweden; Charles
Emmanuel of Savoy was venal and therefore undecided; the
Dutch were lethargic. England alone took active measures to
uphold the guarantee. In 1741, Walpole proposed a subsidy of
£300,000 and the contribution of a contingent of Danish and
Hessian mercenaries paid by England to support Maria Theresa's
claim. George II favoured this in the face of the strength of
Prussia and the consequent danger to Hanover. When, however,

the beloved Electorate was threatened by French troops, he hastily signed a treaty for the neutralization of Hanover and agreed to vote for Charles Albert of Bavaria, who was crowned Emperor in February 1742. Walpole then devised the convention of Klein-Schnellendorf by which Maria Theresa ceded Silesia to Frederick in return for peace with Prussia.

This expedient convention was Walpole's last manœuvre before his resignation in February 1742. Failures in the war against Spain, and the worsening situation in Europe had destroyed public confidence in the minister who had governed almost alone for fifteen years. The war was going badly and Walpole could no longer exercise control over the affairs of the nation. To the House of Commons he pleaded pathetically,[6] 'As I am neither general nor admiral, as I have nothing to do either with our army or navy, I am sure I am not answerable for the prosecution of the war.' His pleading was in vain; a scapegoat was needed and there was talk of impeachment. He escaped by bribing Pulteney, the leader of the opposition, with an earldom, and resigning his office. He was succeeded at the Treasury by Wilmington, a non-entity; but the conduct of foreign affairs went to Carteret, a brilliant scholar and diplomatist and a favourite of George II. His was a formidable task. Affairs in Europe went rapidly from bad to worse: Frederick, having repudiated the convention of Klein-Schnellendorf, attacked and crushed an Austrian army at Chotusitz; France invaded Germany, occupied Prague, and sent a naval force from Toulon to escort Spanish troops to northern Italy. Carteret applied himself with resolution to the problem. By the Treaty of Berlin in July he detached Frederick from the attack on Austria, and in November, by the Treaty of Westminster, procured his guarantee of the security of Hanover against the French; in December he concluded a treaty of mutual protection with Russia. England was now free to turn her attention to France and Spain. Neither England nor Maria Theresa were officially at war with France until 1744, but their armies could, none the less, meet in battle as auxiliaries of the Queen of Hungary or of the Emperor of Bavaria. This meeting was unlikely to be long delayed as French armies were already in action in support of the Emperor and, earlier in 1742, a 'Pragmatic army' composed of English, Hanoverians, and Hessians had been sent to the Low Countries under the command of the veteran Lord Stair. With this army went Ensign James Wolfe of the 12th Regiment of Foot.*

To William Weston, a young Oxford assistant master at Swinden's, Wolfe wrote in January 1742:[7]

'Last Sunday the Chapel being shut up we turn'd out in a Body to hear Dr. Skerret discourse on War, who has never come near us this twelvemonth. To show you how exemplary I am become I will give you an account of this Homily which was divided into four parts.

1   War as a Divine ordinance compatible with Humanity.
2   War as a means not of sund'ring but of binding Nations.
3   War as a just Punishment for Wickedness in both Parties in the State.
4   War as a moral discipline in the Individual.

Do I not deserve your Approbation for thus setting forth the Heads of our illustrious Sanctae Theologiae Professor? I wish I had not to add that the wicked Stretton fell fast asleep & that his snoring disturb'd our soldierly gravity.

You will be reliev'd to hear that by my father's last letter from the Havana that he is well. Although nothing could be worse than the Health generally of the Officers of this Expedition. Not only have they lost their leader, but they have met he says with the utmost discouragement in the country all from the want of simple Providence & unanimity.

As for me, I am sufficiently thankful that my carcase was not equal to my zeal else the good Collonel would soon have been put out of all anxiety on my account. It now looks as if I might get into Coll. Duroure's. If so I shall probably be off into Flanders by the middle of May to comfort her Hungarian Majesty. I hope this proceeding will not make Miss Patterson jealous. . . .'

* The Suffolk Regiment.

CHAPTER II

Active Service in Flanders

JAMES WOLFE'S appointment in 1742 as ensign in the Twelfth Foot was not his first for, while staying with the Wardes at Squerryes Court in the previous December, he had received a commission appointing him second-lieutenant in his father's regiment of marines. As this regiment was still in America, and there appeared to be small chance of his joining it there, Wolfe lost no time in making application for a transfer. One of his mother's sisters had been married to Lieutenant-General Thomas Whetham, until his recent death Colonel of the 12th Regiment of Foot, and this connexion probably served to obtain Wolfe's transfer to that regiment on 27th March. It was a fortunate choice; his new regiment was commanded by Colonel Scipio Duroure, a keen soldier who took an uncommon interest in the efficiency of his regiment and the welfare of his men. His new officer was fifteen years old, a six-foot, thin gangling boy with red hair and piercing blue eyes. His thin, sloping shoulders and long limbs gave the impression of exceptional height, but the figure was not commanding. He had inherited his mother's receding chin and pointed tilted nose but not her high complexion; he was a pale, fragile-looking boy, reserved, but with a charm of manner and expression which brought him many friends. It is a tribute to his character that his attention to duty and keen study of textbooks did nothing to diminish his popularity as a junior officer.

Enthusiasm such as Wolfe's was rare among officers in the Army of 1742. Indeed there was little inducement to officers or men to feel enthusiasm for their profession. It had long been a matter of deliberate political policy to exaggerate the dangers of a standing army, and, to enable the people to keep this danger in mind, barrack accommodation was provided only at the Tower, at the Savoy, in Edinburgh, and in Hull, with barrack quarters for the small number of 'invalid' gunners necessary to maintain the guns in a few garrisoned towns. The remainder of the Army was billeted on the civilian population, but widely dispersed in small detachments because inns were the only quarters permitted by the Mutiny Act, and the number of inns in any district was limited. Thus it was possible for units of one regiment to be scattered in six towns twenty-five miles apart without any method of communication other than mounted messenger. This alone would have made training and discipline difficult enough, but this was not all: the revolution had bred a dangerous indifference to authority, and the inadequacy and futility of the police made it necessary for troops to be used to suppress the frequent outbreaks of rioting, incendiarism, and lawlessness in the country. This brought the Army and the civil population into conflict and did nothing to dispel the suspicion and hostility felt by one for the other. Disputes were frequent, more often than not leading to violence and sometimes to bloodshed.

The system of political patronage and purchase of commissions merely added fuel to the flames. With the connivance of the civil population and the help of political influence, deserters went unpunished; officers might with impunity absent themselves from their regiments without leave, but might be deprived of their commissions for opposing the Government in Parliament;* officers and men falsely accused by a civilian, might be convicted and punished unheard. To add to the confusion, officers might be granted 'Secretary at War's leave of absence', without reference to their commanding officers, to enable them to vote for the Goverment candidate at a by-election, and vacancies in a regiment could be filled by the Secretary at War without consulting or even informing the colonel. When the road to advancement lay not through faithful performance of duty but through influence at Court and in the Government, it was not surprising that all sense

* In 1733 the Duke of Bolton, Lord Cobham, and William Pitt ('that terrible cornet of Horse') were among those deprived of their commissions for their opposition to Walpole's Excise Bill.

of military subordination was lost. The Duke of Argyll summed up the situation in 1739 when he said,[8] 'Our armies here know no other power but that of the Secretary-at-War, who directs all their motions and fills up all vacancies without opposition and without appeal.'

Against this system of nepotism and organized corruption, George I had exerted all his influence. He tried to abolish the purchase of commissions but succeeded, in 1720, only in the introduction of a tariff of prices which continued to appear until 1870. At the same time, he insisted upon certain qualifications of rank and length of service. He also took steps to prevent illegal deductions of pay, by the regulation of all such stoppages by warrant, and to check the abuse of false musters by which the colonel of a regiment might draw pay for men who did not exist or who were not serving. This was an advance on Queen Anne's permission to grant an ensigncy to a child 'for the support of his mother and family', but did not prevent commanders from regarding their regiments as a source of wealth. Colonels drew bounties for recruiting, and profits from clothing the men and from dealings with army contractors. Although officers' pay was relatively good, it was often necessary for them to recoup themselves for the cost of their commissions and this imposed a heavy burden on a young officer of slender means. As for the men, their pay at first sight appeared to compare quite favourably with the wages of civilians: a private in the infantry earned three shillings and sixpence a week and a sergeant seven shillings, while the equivalent ranks in the dragoon regiments earned nine shillings and elevenpence, and fifteen and ninepence. But with deductions for food, billets, farrier, and horse-provender, the net pay worked out at little more than sixpence and a shilling for the infantry, and one and twopence and seven shillings in the cavalry, and, even out of these pitiful sums, deductions could be made for medicines and clothing. Their quarters were abominable, as could only be expected when innkeepers were obliged to house, feed, and supply with small beer each man billeted on them for a beggarly fourpence a day. Recruitment was by voluntary enlistment and under such conditions none but the scum of the population could be expected to join. The officers were, for the most part, wealthy, idle, and corrupt, caring nothing for their profession or for the welfare of their men. Chesterfield described the Army of 1746 as 'the worst-officered in all Europe'.[9]

In drill and tactics, too, the British Army lagged behind other European countries, in particular Prussia, which owed its supremacy to Leopold of Anhalt-Dessau and Frederick the Great. By standardizing words of command and drill movements in all regiments, the Prussians had induced a precision and discipline into their formations which resulted in a rapidity and control of fire and movement unrivalled in Europe. In the British Army there was no such control; each regiment had evolved its own method, and the formations and orders in a regiment were largely a matter of the colonel's personal preference. The methods and discipline of the army which had triumphed under Marlborough were disregarded except by the few antique generals who had served under his command.

Punitive discipline, when civil interference failed to prevent it, was exercised with brutal severity. The spectacle of a deserter tied to a tree in Hyde Park to receive several hundred lashes was so common as to arouse little interest. The cat, the rod, cloak-straps, and stirrup-leathers were used for flogging, the executioners varying in numbers from drummers or the guard only to the whole regiment or several regiments in turn. Sometimes the culprit received instalments of a hundred lashes or more before the quarters of each detachment of his regiment, a military equivalent to the naval 'flogging round the fleet'. The *Weekly Journal* of 21st July 1739 quotes the example of a deserter who received fifteen hundred lashes from the three regiments of Foot Guards and was, in addition, whipped out of three regiments of the line. The penalty for repeated desertion was death. Other punishments included 'picketing', which consisted in hanging the offender by one wrist with only a pointed stake as support for his bare feet, and 'riding the wooden horse', a more entertaining punishment generally reserved for the correction of cowardice. The 'horse' was constructed of planks nailed together to form a sharp ridge about eight feet long and supported by four posts or 'legs' about six feet high, placed on a movable stand. A head and tail were affixed and the culprit, dressed in a petticoat and with his hands tied behind him, was mounted upon it and dragged round the regimental lines. This uncomfortable and humiliating punishment would continue for a specified period each day until the sentence was completed. The records of the Forty-Third Regiment cite the case of a 'notorious coward' completely cured of his timidity by this experience. In other offenders, however, it induced no more salutary a result than rupture and it was abolished in 1780.

Such then was the Army to which James Wolfe, a delicate boy of fifteen, was to give the rest of his short life. Horrifying though the conditions must have been to him, it is well to remember that no mother's care, however tender, could have hidden from him the sights and sounds of city and country life. Violence and brutality would be nothing new to him: in an age when a child could be hanged for stealing a handkerchief and men wagered large sums that they would stand a hundred lashes without flinching, he must often, as a child, have seen vagrants whipped through the streets and perhaps joined in the baiting of offenders in the stocks; in youth he could hardly have failed to see deserters flogged or shot and noted the bestial existence of the poor in London. His experiences had not perhaps made him indifferent to human suffering, but they must have mitigated the impact of military conditions on his young mind. His greatest hardship was to be the strain of campaign conditions on his frail constitution, his greatest obstacle his lack of wealth and influence.

Such also was the Army which, with the aid of the Austrians, a few thousand mercenaries, and the Dutch if they could be persuaded, was to oppose the combined might of France and Prussia. It was not an encouraging prospect. The command of the expedition to the Low Countries was given to Lord Stair who, although nearly seventy, was capable of vigorous and effective command. He had served with distinction under Marlborough as a regimental officer at Blenheim, as a brigadier at Ramillies, and on the Duke's staff at Oudenarde, and he had not failed to learn something of the art of war from his great commander. His force of 17,000 was assembled at Blackheath where, on 27th April the King, accompanied by his sons, Frederick, Prince of Wales, and William, Duke of Cumberland, held a ceremonial review. No doubt Mrs. Wolfe and her younger son, Edward, were among the crowds of spectators. By all accounts, the review was not an unqualified success, for His Majesty voiced his royal displeasure at the lack of precision and uniformity in the drill movements. The army marched off to Deptford where, Dutch objections to a British garrison in the Netherlands having been overcome by the crushing defeat of the Austrian army at Chotusitz, the troops were embarked in their transports for Ostend. They were not received on their arrival in Flanders with any demonstration of enthusiasm. After a day in Ostend, the army marched to Ghent where the populace were even less welcoming and it was a matter of extreme difficulty to find quarters for officers or men. There were frequent fights between soldiers and civilians and one of them developed into a pitched battle lasting for two hours in which several on both sides were killed. After this ugly incident, Stair commanded the burgomaster to issue an edict that 'whoever should offer the least affront to the subjects of the King of Great Britain should be whipped, burnt in the back and turned out of town.' This quelled open demonstrations of hostility but the undercurrent of suspicion and animosity was not stemmed. As one captain wrote home, 'They hate the English and we hate them.'[10] Nevertheless the army was obliged to remain in Ghent until Lord Stair could obtain the King's agreement to a plan of action, and this he was quite unable to do.

Stair has been unjustly blamed for the months which his army spent in discontent and idleness in Ghent while opportunities for striking effectively at the French armies were lost. It is clear from his correspondence with Carteret that these delays were imposed on him by the King and by the Austrian generals. The King appears to have been concerned primarily with the safety of his Electorate and of his precious Hanoverian troops which had, in the words of Pitt,[11] 'marched to the place most distant from the enemy, least in danger of attack, and most strongly fortified if an attack had been designed;' the Austrian generals favoured the use of the British Army in Germany to coerce the minor princes into alliance with Austria; neither would agree to Stair's plan of a direct and concerted attack upon France; both preferred to maintain the fiction that France was not at war with either country, being merely an auxiliary of Bavaria. Stair's plans were bold, imaginative, and sound. Had they been adopted the French would, at the very least, have been forced to retire within their own frontiers. But delay succeeded delay until the coming of winter banished all hope of a campaign in 1742. The army remained in its detested quarters until the following February.

Wolfe had obtained fairly comfortable lodgings and found plenty to occupy his time. He was intent upon learning all he could of his duties, and of those of his superiors, to fit himself for promotion. The old town with its massive fortifications, still bearing the marks of the siege in which his father had taken part, its ancient buildings and canals, was full of interest for him and he succeeded in making some friends among the citizens with whom he could air his French. He also bought a flute and engaged a master to teach him to play it. In August, George Warde, by then a cornet of dragoons, arrived in Ghent, and the two friends spent much time in one another's company, going to plays and talking with 'the Ladies, who are very civil, & all speak French.'[12] He wrote affectionate letters home, striving to dispel his mother's anxieties.[13] 'You desire to know how I live. I assure you, as to eating, rather too well, considering what we may come to, for drink I don't much care. But here's very good Rum and Brandy, in this Place, & cheap, if we have a mind to take a little Sneaker now & then at night just to warm us.' He evidently anticipated a long campaign, for as early as 27th August he wrote, 'My Shirts are in very good order, &, I hope will last me a great while; but I fancy (by what people say) not so long as we stay in Flanders.' He inquired often after his brother, who suffered from recurrent chest complaints, and wrote to him whenever he could. His father had at last returned from the disastrous campaigns in the West Indies, his health permanently impaired, and had been appointed Inspector of Marines. His employment as Adjutant-General to the Carthagena expedition had proved remunerative, and the Wolfes moved to a town house in Burlington Gardens, where the Wardes also had a house. There was an early prospect of the young Edward joining his brother in Flanders, and to this meeting James looked forward eagerly.

At last, in February, the army moved and James Wolfe, by then joined in Duroure's by his brother, started out on the long advance eastward into Germany. The Wolfe brothers suffered much on that march. On 12th February James was 'very much fatigued and out of order', and by the fifth day of the march admitted to having 'found out by Experience that my Strength is not so great as I imagin'd;' but added, 'however, I have held out pretty well as yet.' He decided to hire a horse to share with Edward, each riding one day and marching the next. Their hardships were the common experience of the whole army; the winter had been one of unusual severity and the march was long and arduous.

With extreme caution, and only after much hesitation and delay, George II had issued orders for the allied armies to converge on Mainz and occupy the heights commanding the junction of the Rhine and Main. The movement of the British Army was not accelerated by the absence of many of its officers on leave. With justifiable disgust, Stair wrote to Carteret,[14] 'I thought it hard to refuse them leave when they said that their preferment depended on the interest of their friends at Court. They had no notion that it depended on their exertions here.' In spite of these difficulties, the army bore with fortitude its weary march under icy conditions, and the junction with the Hanoverian and Austrian forces was effected. By 7th April, the army was within a few miles of the Rhine, but the coming of spring had made little change in the weather. Edward Wolfe writes to his father of 'a sad march last Monday in the morning. I was oblig'd to walk up to my knees in Snow, tho My Brother and I have a horse between us and at the same time I had it with me.' He had no bedding and little food. 'We are here at the worst time, for they kill no meat because it is Lent. They say there are many Wolves and wild Boars in the Woods; but I never saw any yet neither do I desire.'

The military significance of the allied armies' disposition is obscure; it would seem in fact to serve no military purpose whatever. Its function appeared to be to secure for the King's nominee the vacant Electorate of Mainz. The movement suited the French admirably. Marshal Noailles advanced with 70,000 men to a position on the upper Rhine, some forty miles to the south of the allied camp, to contain Stair's force while attempting to save Broglie's army which was in danger of being destroyed by the Austrians in Bavaria. Stair determined to prevent this, and crossed to the south bank of the Main to offer battle to Noailles, who advanced north from Darmstadt to attack him but withdrew again without firing a shot. Meanwhile King George, accompanied by Carteret and the Duke of Cumberland, had arrived in Hanover nearly frantic with anxiety lest his army should be engaged and defeated before he could join it. He wrote apprehensive and cautionary letters to Stair, at last nervously bidding him to recross the Main. Stair was convinced of the folly of this move as there was no forage to be had on the north bank and it could not be brought down by water with the French holding the south bank of the river, but he was obliged to obey his orders. The army was therefore forced up river and away from its magazines and Hessian troops at Hanau. When the King and the Duke of Cumberland, who at the age of twenty-four had been appointed major-general, arrived with the army on 8th June, they found it encamped on the north bank round Aschaffenburg, about six miles up river from the village of Dettingen. The position was bounded on the south by the river and to the north by the Spessart hills. Noailles lost no time in closing the trap: he threw two bridges across the river to the north to cut off the allies from reinforcements at Hanau, and at the same time seized a post further up river to intercept supplies sent down from the south. The King, after a week in command of a starving army, decided with great reluctance that only an immediate retreat to Hanau could save his forces from starvation or destruction. The way led across a narrow bridge which spanned a rivulet running through a boggy depression. Anticipating a withdrawal to Hanau, Noailles had posted batteries along the south bank to play upon the retreating army and when, at one o'clock on the morning of the 16th, he heard that the allies were on the march, he at once ordered Grammont to cross the Main with 28,000 men by the two bridges laid for that purpose and to take up a position by Dettingen; there he was to wait and destroy the allied army as it defiled across the bridge. Noailles himself took command of the remainder of his troops, sending a strong detachment of 12,000 men to cross the river at Aschaffenburg and cut off any retreat upstream. The trap was complete.

What followed was an unimaginable reversal of Noailles's plan. Had Grammont obeyed his general's orders, and waited in his position north of the rivulet, it is difficult to see how the allied army could have escaped annihilation; but the allies moved slowly and he was impatient to make an end of them. He advanced beyond the depression to a new position. George II, already warned of Grammont's presence, and after some confusion caused by harassing fire from the guns on the opposite bank and difficulty in disposing of the baggage train to safety on the right flank, drew up his army in line of battle. It was a warm, clear day and the two armies, drawn up to face each other, the French all in white, the allies in scarlet and blue and green, made an impressive show. The young Wolfe brothers were both in action with Duroure's, James performing the duties of adjutant which he had assumed some weeks earlier. He describes the battle vividly in a letter to his father written on 23rd June from Höchst, a personal eye-witness account which deserves to be quoted in full.

'Dr Sir This is the first time that I have been able or have had the least time to write, otherwise I should have done it when my Brother did. The Fatigue I had the Day we fought & the Day after, made me very much out of order, & I was obliged to keep my Tent for two Days. Bleeding was of great service to me, and I'm now as well as ever. The Army was drawn up this Day Sen'night, between a Wood & the Mayne, near a little Village, call'd Dettingen, in five lines 2 of Foot & 3 of Horse. The Cannon on both sides began to play about 9 o'Clock in the Morning, & we were expos'd to the fire of theirs, said to be about 50 Pieces, for near three Hours, a great part of which flank'd us Terribly from the other side the Water. The French were all the while drawn up in sight of us on this side. About 12 o'Clock we marched towards them, they advanced likewise, & as near as I can guess, the fight began about one. Their Gens D'Armes, or Mousquetaires Gris, attack't the first line, composed of 9 Reg^{ts} of English foot, & four or five of Austrians, & some Hanovarians. They broke thro' the Scotch Fusileers, who they began the attack upon, but before they got to the second line, out of 200 there was not 40 living, so they wheel'd and came between the first & second line (Except an officer with a standard, & four or five men, who broke thro' the second line & were taken by some of Hawley's Regt. of Dragoons), and about 20 of them escap'd to their army, Riding thro' an interval that was made for our Horse to advance. These unhappy men were of the first Families in France. Nothing, I believe, cou'd be more Rash than their Undertaking.

The Second attack was made on the left by their Horse against ours (who advanced before the first Line) & on neither side did much, for they both retreated, & our Horse had like to have broke our first line in the confusion. The Horse fir'd their Pistols which if they had let alone, & attack't the French with their swords, being so much stronger and heavier, they would certainly have beat them. Their excuse for retreating, they could not make their Horses stand the Fire!* The third & last attack was made by the Foot on both sides, we advanced towards one another, our men in high spirits & very Impatient for fighting, being elated with beating the French Horse, part of which advanced towards us (while the rest attacked our Horse) but were soon drove back by the great Fire we gave them. The Major & I (for we had neither Colonel nor Lt. Colonel) before they came near were employ'd in Begging and Ordering the men not to Fire at too great a Distance, but to keep it till the Enemy shou'd come near us, but to little Purpose. The whole Fir'd when they thought they could reach them, which had like to have ruin'd us, We did very little Execution with it, so soon as the French saw we Presented they all fell down, and when we had fir'd they got up & march'd close to us in tolerable good order, and gave us a brisk Fire, which put us into some Disorder & made us give way a little, particularly ours & 2 or 3 more Reg^{ts}, who were in the Hottest of it, however, we soon ralli'd again, & attack't them with great Fury, which gain'd us a compleat Victory, and forc'd the Enemy to retire in great Haste. 'Twas lucky that we did give way a little, for our men were loading all the while, & it gave Room for an Austrian Reg^t to move into an Interval, rather too little before; who charg'd the Enemy with great Bravery and Resolution. So soon as the French retreated, the line halted, & we got the sad news of the death of as good & brave a man as any amongst us, General Clayton, who was kill'd by a musquet ball in the last attack. His Death gave us all sorrow, so great was the opinion we had of him; & was the hindrance of anything further being done that Day. He had, 'tis said, orders for Pursuing the enemy, and if we had followed them, as was expected, it is the Opinion of most People, that of 27,000 men they brought

* A common fault in training. Both the King's and the Duke of Cumberland's horses bolted during the battle, and the King fought most of it on foot.

over the Mayne, they wou'd not have repassed with half that number. When they retreated, several Pieces of our Artillery play'd upon them, & made terrible Havock; at last we followed them, but too late, they had almost all pass'd the River. One of the bridges broke, & in the Hurry abundance were drown'd. A great number of their Officers and men were taken Prisoners. Their loss is computed to be between 6 & 7000 Men, & ours 3000.

His Majesty was in the midst of the Fight, & the Duke behav'd as bravely as a man could do. He had a Musquet Shot thro' the Calf of his Leg. I had several times the honour of speaking to him just as the Battle began, & was often afraid of his being Dash'd to Pieces by the Cannon Balls. He gave his Orders with a great deal of Calmness, & seem'd unconcern'd. The Soldiers were in high Delight to have him so near them. Captain Rainsford behaved with the greatest Conduct and Bravery in the World. I sometimes thought I had lost poor Ned, when I saw Men's Arms, Legs, and heads Beat off close by him. He is call'd Old Soldier & very deservingly. A Horse I rid of the Colonel's at the first attack was shot in one of his hinder Legs, & threw me, so I was obliged to do the Duty of adjutant all that and the next Day on Foot, in a Pair of heavy Boots.

I lost with the Horse, Furniture and Pistols which cost me 10 Ducats; but three Days after the Battle got the horse again, with the Ball in him, & he is now almost well again, but without any Furniture or Pistols.

A brigade of English and another of Hanoverians are in Garrison in this Town, which we are fortifying Dayly. We are detach'd from the grand Army, which is encamped between Frankfort and Hanau, about 12 miles off.

They talk of a second Battle soon. Count Kevenhuller and Marshal Broglie are expected to join the two armies in a few days. We are very well situated at Present, & in a Plentiful Country. Had we stayed a few days longer at Aschaffenburg we had all been starved, for the French would have cut off our communication with Frankfort. Captain Merrydan is killed. Pray mine and my brother's duty to my mother. We hope you are both perfectly well.

I am, dear Sir,

Your dutiful and affectionate Son,

J. Wolfe.'

28

Colonel and Mrs. Wolfe would already have received a letter from Edward, penned in haste on 19th June, to reassure them of their sons' safety and the successful outcome of the battle. To his mother he wrote, 'I take the very first opportunity I can to acquaint you that my Brother and self Escap'd in the Engagement we had with the French, the 16th of June last and thank God are as well as ever we were in our lives, after not only being cannonaded 2 hours and ¾ and fighting with Small Arms 2 hours and ¼ but lay'd the two following Nights upon our Arms, whilst it rain'd for about 20 hours in the same time yet are ready and as capable to do the same again. . . . Our Regiment has got a Great Deal of honour, for we were in the middle of the first Line, and in the Greatest Danger.'

The brothers had distinguished themselves in their first action, and official recognition was soon to follow. Meanwhile the beaten French army was allowed to escape. A volunteer on Lord Dunmore's staff, George Townshend, who was later to play an important part in Wolfe's greatest campaign, wrote in his journal,[15] 'The French, to the surprise of every one, were suffered to escape unmolested. The King halted and the scene of Action and military ardour was suddenly turned into a Court circle—His Majesty was congratulated by every military courtezan on horseback, on the glorious event—the Hanoverian Generals galloped up with their reports—questions innumerable were asked and reports made; the British Generals returning lamented the loss of so interesting a crisis and some of them ineffectually represented upon it, yet the Enemy was suffered to quietly repass their bridge over the Mayne! although 6000 Hassians were at Hanau in perfect order for Action—the greatest part of the British army with great solemnity then passed the Rivulet and encamped on the ground to the west of it. . . .' The most notable features of the engagement were the deadly accuracy of the British fire, the timidity of the French infantry, and the failure of the allies to follow up their fortunate victory and inflict a decisive defeat on the enemy. So urgent was the continued retreat to Hanau thought to be that the King succeeded, even in the moment of victory, in giving it the semblance of defeat by leaving his wounded on the battlefield to the care of the French. This gave rise to a satirical dialogue, by an unknown author, recorded by Horace Walpole in a letter to Horace Mann:[16] '. . . one can't get a copy; I must tell you two or three strokes in it that I have heard. Pierrot asks Harlequin, 'Que donne-t-on aux généraux qui ne sont pas trouvés à la bataille?' Harl. 'On leur donne le cordon rouge.'* Pier. 'Et que donne-t-on au général en chef, qui a gagné la victoire?' Harl. 'Son congé.' Pier. 'Qui a soin des blessés?' Harl. "L'ennemi".'

If Dettingen was not, for the allies, a glorious and deserved victory, it was at least a victory; but the fruits of it were thrown away. In torrential rain the allies withdrew to Hanau while Noailles gathered his beaten army into camp at Offenbach. There news soon reached him of the approach of the Austrian Army which had been operating in Bavaria under the command of Prince Charles of Lorraine, and he was obliged to withdraw in haste across the Rhine into Alsace. In spite of Stair's entreaties, the King and his advisers decided against pursuit and moved instead in leisurely safety to Worms where a new camp was formed. Wolfe writes as if another battle is daily expected:[17] 'We have a great deal of Sickness amongst us, so I Believe the Sooner we engage (if it is to be) the Better.' He is enthusiastic about the bravery and leadership of the Duke of Cumberland whom he describes as 'very brisk, & quite cured of his Wound.' He adds 'I hope some day or other to have the honour of knowing him better than I do now,' a wish that was soon to be gratified. His conduct during the battle had already earned for him two marks of royal approval: on 2nd July he was appointed adjutant of his regiment, and shortly afterwards he received his commission as lieutenant. He was not yet seventeen.

On 4th September, weary of the constant repudiation of his plans and advice, Lord Stair resigned his command, and the rest of the year thus passed quietly enough without any more troublesome suggestions of attacking the French or of active prosecution of the war. The King returned to London to enjoy his temporary popularity, and the army retired to winter quarters in Flanders.

Any hope of renewed activity in the following year was stillborn by the appointment, as Lord Stair's successor, of the septuage-

* The King created Generals Cope, Honeywood, Ligonier, and Campbell Knights of the Bath a few days after the battle.

narian Field-Marshal Wade, noted for his painstaking road-building in Scotland and for his deference to instructions.

Lieutenant Wolfe, with Duroure's, marched to Brussels and thence to Ostend. His brother, Edward, was granted home leave, but James remained at Ostend throughout the winter, carrying out his duties as adjutant and preparing himself for the campaign of the following year. Probably he could not have been spared to go on leave, and no doubt there were many officers with prior political claims, but his ambition would, in any case, have prevented him from pressing for it. In February he heard that his father had been promoted to brigadier-general, and in the following month he wrote an affectionate letter to Edward, gaily promoting his brother too by addressing him as 'Captain Wolfe at Brig. Wolfe's in Old Burlington Street':[18]

'Dear Ned,—I got yours yesterday from Dover by a Gentleman who was so good to take it up & bring it me from thence. I expected to have had my Box at the same time, for I thought our going to England (or rather the appearance of it) was entirely laid aside. I shall be oblig'd to you, if you'll take the first opportunity of sending it, I want it very much. I have not a pair of Boots I can wear. The Regiment will very soon be out to Exercise. You and I are to be tented together next Campaign. The Marquee is making & will cost us about £4. I shall send to Ghent very soon to bespeak a Cart, which with Harness for two Horses I'm told will come to ten Pounds or thereabouts. I shall get everything I find necessary for us, so you need not be in any Pain about your Equipage. I think Rainsford is not Brutal enough to send you, from England, who have done all his Duty this three or four months; sure he knows better. I have a better opinion of his Understanding.

I hear of no promotion in the Regiment, except Thickhead* has got his Father's Company. Stephens is certainly going out, he is to be surgeon to the 2 troop of Horse Grenadiers & sell his Employments with us, so you'll get a step by that. Ryder I believe will buy the Surgeonship. I am glad you find the Mantua-Maker pretty, I thought so, I assure you, I give up all Pretensions, Pray use her kindly. Doubtless, you love the Company of the fair

---

* 'Thickhead' was Lieutenant Romer whom Wolfe succeeded.

Sex. If you shou'd happen to go where Miss Seabourg is, pray don't fall in Love with her, I can't give her up tamely, remember I'm your Rival. I am also in some pain about Miss Warde. Admire anywhere else & welcome,—except the widow Bright. Miss Paterson is yours if you like her, and so is the little staring Girl in the Chappel, with twenty thousand pounds. Pray give my duty to my mother. I hope her cold is well. The Plum Cake she gave me was very good, & of singular service to me. I don't believe the Box wou'd hold any, they say 'tis particularly wholesome at Ostend.

I am, dear Ned, sincerely yours,
J. Wolfe.

N'oublie point mes Compliments à les adorables Femmes que Je viens de nommer.'

Wolfe's letters to his father and mother were penned with a care and formality which, even later in life, never entirely disappeared and which tends to obscure the affection and humour in them. In his letters to his brother and close friends Wolfe expresses himself without reserve and reveals his lack of priggishness or affectation. His popularity with his brother officers, with his men, and with 'les adorables femmes' seems to have suffered not at all from his unusual devotion to his profession.

While the army wintered in Flanders, the political game of seesaw to maintain the balance of power in Europe continued. Carteret juggled skilfully with the Emperor, the Queen of Hungary and Charles Emmanuel of Savoy, in the hope of isolating France; but his plans were doomed to failure. Frederick of Prussia was alienated by the strengthening of the allies, which he regarded as a possible Hanoverian threat to his conquests in Germany; France was thrown into the arms of Spain with whom she concluded a close alliance. On 31st January 1744, off Toulon, a British fleet under Mathews and Lestock failed to stop a combined Spanish and French fleet carrying troops to Italy. On the 13th, Roquefeuil's Brest fleet, and transports carrying Prince Charles Edward Stuart and Marshal Saxe, appeared off Dungeness but was dispersed by a storm. In March the absurd pretence of nominal peace with France was ended by formal declarations of war. Marshal Saxe was appointed to the chief command of the 80,000 French troops in Flanders which concentrated in April on the frontier between the Scheldt and the Sambre. The allied army was at last collected in May, close to Brussels. Field-Marshal Wade was, it is true, much hampered by disputes between the allies as to the disposition of their armies, but it is difficult to find excuse for his inactivity during the following months. The allied armies were frittered away in providing feeble garrisons while Saxe overran the Netherlands, taking Courtrai, Menin, and Ypres.

James Wolfe had received his commission as captain in Barrell's Regiment, the Fourth Foot,* and was therefore parted from Edward who had returned from leave as a lieutenant in Duroure's. Edward writes to his father in June to thank him for this promotion. 'We are here a Defensive Army and fewer in numbers than we were last Campaign still we never despair of coming off with Laurels whenever we meet our enemy. Our men keep up their spirits. The taking of these two towns and the number of men they imagine the French have does not in the least deject them, but makes them only wish for a Meeting.' At last, Wade received orders from the King, through Carteret, demanding that he should take the offensive and 'commence hostilities of all kinds forthwith.'[19] Meanwhile George II had begged Prince Charles of Lorraine to cross the Rhine with the Austrian Army and to take command of the entire allied force. This move, which might have put an end to the disputes of the allies and stirred Wade to long overdue action, was frustrated by the invasion of Bohemia by Frederick of Prussia in support of France in July. Nevertheless, Wade held a council of war and decided to try to bring Saxe to battle. Saxe was not to be tempted: the allies marched and counter-marched but, in spite of unusually determined efforts by Wade to induce the Austrians and Dutch to carry out offensive plans, no battle was fought and, in October, the army retired once more into winter quarters. Wade at once resigned his command and returned to England.

For the Wolfe brothers it must have been a wearisome and frustrating year. Neither was strong enough for the rigours of campaigning and, before the end of September, Edward, 'The

* The King's Own (Royal Lancashire) Regiment.

Old Soldier', became seriously ill. His old tubercular trouble had been much aggravated by fatigue and the chill autumn weather, and the return to the comparative comfort of winter quarters came too late. He died in October, some months before his seventeenth birthday. His mother wrote to James, desiring him to return to England on leave as soon as it could be obtained. He replied at once, in a letter the stilted, awkward reserve of which plainly shows his grief.[20]

'I receiv'd your letter this morning with a great deal of Pleasure, & have with this wrote to my father about coming to England. I hope he will be able to get the better of some Obstacles, and I shall be sincerely happy.

Poor Ned wanted Nothing but the satisfaction of seeing his Dearest Friends to leave this World with the greatest tranquillity, He often called on us; It gives me many uneasy hours, when I Reflect on the Possibility there was of my being with him some time before he died. God knows, it was being to Exact, & not apprehending the Danger the Poor Fellow was in, & even that wou'd not have hinder'd it, had I receiv'd the Physician's first letter; I know you won't be able to read this Paragraph without shedding Tears, as I do writing it. But there is Satisfaction even in giving way to grief now and then; 'tis what we owe the memory of a Dear Friend.

Tho' it is the Custom of the Army to sell the Deceased's Effects, I cou'd not suffer it, We none of us want, & I thought the best way would be to bestow them on the Deserving, who he had an esteem for in his Lifetime. To his Servant, the most honest & faithful man I ever knew, I gave all his old Cloaths, Linen, Stockings, & in short whatever I found in his Cloak bag. Except those sheets you mention'd, a Wig, a tall Hat, his Regimentals, the Towels, & a few Handkerchiefs that I had Occasion for. I gave his Horse to his friend Parry with the Furniture. I know he lov'd Parry, & I know for that Reason, the Horse will be taken care of. His Tent & Marquee I gave to another Friend of his in Duroure's Regt; his Regimental Waistcoat I gave young Rains-ford, & I believe shall do the same with the Coat. His other Horse I keep myself. I have his Watch, Sword, Sash, Gorget, Books, & Maps, which I shall preserve to his Memory. Everything else that

I have not mention'd shall be taken care of, or given to proper People.

He was an honest and a good lad, had liv'd very well, and always discharg'd his Duty with the Chearfulness becoming a good Officer, he lived and died as a Son of you two shou'd, which I think is saying all I can. I have the melancholy Satisfaction to find him regretted by his Friends and Acquaintances. His Colonel is particularly concern'd for him, and desired I would assure of it. There was in him the Prospect (when Ripen'd with Experience) of great understanding and Judgement, & an Excellent Soldier. You'll excuse my dwelling so long on this cruel Subject, but in relating this to you, Vanity and Partiality are banish'd, a strong desire to do justice to his memory occasions it. There is no part of his Life that makes him Dearer to me than that, where you have often mention'd,—he Pin'd after me. It often makes me angry that any hour of my Life should Pass without thinking of him, & when I do think of him, that tho all the Reasons I have to lament his Loss are now as forcible as at the moment of his Departure, I don't find my heart swell with the same sorrow as it did at that time; Nature is ever too good in blotting out the violence of affliction, for with tempers (as mine is) too much given to Mirth, it is often necessary to revive grief in one's Memory. I must once more beg you will excuse my tiresome length & manner of writing, but I know your Indulgence. I'm just now going to write to my Uncle Wolfe.* I am

Dearest Madam Your dutiful & Affectionate Son J. Wolfe.'

He did not obtain his leave. He remained in Ghent, applying himself with renewed vigour to his work in an attempt to blot out his sorrow.

The spring brought hope in the appointment of the Duke of Cumberland as commander-in-chief in Flanders and also in Great Britain, and, with his arrival, the welcome prospect of action. Saxe, having invested Tournai on 30th April, Cumberland marched at once to the attack. Barrell's Regiment remained behind to garrison Ghent so Wolfe was not present at the battle which followed. He gives a brief and second-hand account of Fontenoy in a letter to his father on 4th May. 'We attack'd a numerous

* His father's younger brother, Major Walter Wolfe, in Dublin.

Army, intrench'd; with a Multiplicity of Batteries, well plac'd both in Front & Flank. The Action began the 30th April, about 5 in the morning & lasted till 2 in the afternoon. There has been a great Slaughter, particularly among the Infantry, Officers more in proportion than Soldiers, the enemy's army were suppos'd to be seventy thousand, & ours about fifty. The Soldiery behav'd with the utmost Bravery & Courage during the whole Affair, but rather rash & impetuous. Notwithstanding the bravest Attempts were made to conquer, 'twas not possible for us to surmount the Difficulties we met with.' The words are those of Captain Field, who commanded Duroure's during the action and wrote to Wolfe of it. Wolfe speaks of the 'most unparrallel'd Bravery' of the Duke of Cumberland and the heavy losses sustained by his old regiment, Duroure's. He ends realistically. 'As it has turn'd out we may thank Providence we were not there.' Cumberland withdrew to Lessines and sent for reinforcements from Ghent. Among the regiments to join him was Barrell's. Shortly afterwards it became necessary to return two regiments to Ghent in the face of a threatened attack on the city. It was fortunate for Wolfe that Barrell's remained in Lessines. Ghent was surprised by the French at the end of June and forced to surrender. On 12th June Cumberland appointed Captain Wolfe brigade-major of Pulteney's Brigade.

The allied armies were soon in desperate straits. Outmanœuvred and outnumbered by the French, and failed by the Austrians and Dutch, they were forced to withdraw to the north of Brussels in order to preserve their communications with the sea and with Germany. When the position of the army was at its most critical, Cumberland received a letter from the Secretary of State with the news that the invasion of England was imminent and requiring him to release for home defence such troops as could be spared from Flanders without prejudice to his operations. An indignant reply, written for the Duke by Sir John Ligonier, was unavailing. By August the request had become an urgent order. First, ten battalions, among them Barrell's, were sent home; the rest of the foot soon followed; at last, almost the whole of the army, including Cumberland himself, was recalled. Prince Charles Edward Stuart had landed in Scotland.

CHAPTER III

The 'Forty-Five'

THE arrival in Scotland of Prince Charles Edward Stuart, son of the 'Old Pretender', and grandson and heir of the last of the Stuart Kings of England, was by no means unexpected. Walpole had given repeated warnings of the probability of such a landing, and Pitt had spoken openly of it in his speech criticizing Carteret's policy in December 1743.[21] 'In these circumstances,' he had said, 'I must desire the real friends of our present happy establishment to consider, what might be the consequence of the Pretender's being landed amongst us at the head of a French army? Would not he be looked upon by most as a third Saviour? Would not the majority of the people join with him, in order to secure the nation from those that had brought it into such confusion?' The warning was timely, but his estimate of the popularity of such an invasion was exaggerated. The Young Pretender's cause suffered from two major defects: in the first place, little as the Hanoverian dynasty was loved, the return of the Stuarts would mean a return to the Catholic faith, a change which would not be welcomed by the majority of the people; secondly, the return could be accomplished either with the help of French troops, which would give it the appearance of a foreign invasion, or by an unsupported landing in Scotland. If the landing in Scotland were chosen, it could only hope for any measure of success if it were accomplished while the greater part of the British Army was engaged against another enemy elsewhere, and this would give the rebellion an unpleasant aspect of treachery. Since the 1715 rising in Scotland, 'Jacobite' had become a convenient label to attach to the Tory opposition in Parliament. By making Tory motives supect, the Whigs could secure their position. It was an old political gambit, but it had the distinct advantage of being based on fact, for there was a sufficient number of Jacobite sympathizers among the Tories to lend verisimilitude to the charge against them. The Prince's welcome in Scotland was assured, and it seemed possible that in parts of England itself the resistance would be no more than half-hearted.

The first attempt was made with the support of 15,000 French under Marshal Saxe in February 1744, but Admiral de Rocquefeuil's fleet was broken up by a storm which wrecked many of the transports and drove them back to Dunkirk. The French victory at Fontenoy relieved them from the immediate necessity of creating a diversion in Scotland, and the Young Pretender was abandoned to fend for himself. This he did with some success. On 25th July 1745, he landed with seven companions at Loch-nan-Uamh, near Moidart, and sent messengers to the clans calling them to his support.

In England the situation was viewed with some anxiety, but there was little apprehension of real danger. Carteret's Ministry had fallen in the previous autumn—the result of a concerted effort by the Pelhams—and had been succeeded by what came to be called 'The Broadbottom Administration' consisting of the Duke of Newcastle, his brother Henry Pelham, Harrington as President of the Council, and their followers, with a small number of places filled by troublesome Opposition speakers. Pitt's uncompromising attacks on the King and his partiality for Hanover (which Pitt, with characteristic but improvident candour, had described as 'a despicable Electorate'[22]) effectively barred him from office in the new Ministry, but a number of his friends, including Lyttelton and George Grenville, received appointments. The Board of Admiralty was strengthened by the inclusion of Harrington's son-in-law, Anson, who had returned in June 1743 from his triumphant voyage round the world during which he had appropriated Spanish treasure worth £600,000. The change of government made little difference to policy. Something more was required to stir the people to an interest in their affairs. This much was for a short time achieved by the Jacobite rebellion of 1745. The time was well chosen: the King was in Hanover; the army, except for some 15,000 men, was in a critical situation in

Flanders; and the army in Scotland, numbering no more than 3,000 men, was commanded by Sir John Cope, an irresolute officer quite unequal to his task.

Rumours of Prince Charles's arrival reached Cope three weeks before the actual landing, but it was not until August that he realized that the rumours were true. His immediate decision to march northward was frustrated by delays in provisioning his small force, and it was not until 19th August that he moved from Edinburgh to Fort Augustus. He had, meanwhile, detached the Sixth Foot* and two companies of the Royal Scots to garrison the forts protecting the line of Fort William and Fort Augustus along Lochs Lochy and Ness. On the 16th, the two companies of the Royal Scots were intercepted by Macdonald of Keppoch and Cameron of Lochiel; twelve men were killed and the rest taken prisoner. On the 19th, as Cope began his march to the north, Prince Charles raised his red and white silk standard at Glenfinnan, less than two miles from Fort William, and within twenty-four hours had gathered an army of 1,600 men. Hearing of Cope's approach, he laid an ambush for him at Corry Arrack, but Cope was warned of the trap and turned north-east from Dalwhinnie to Inverness, leaving the roads to the south unguarded. Arrived in Inverness, he sent urgent messages to Edinburgh for transports to take his troops south by sea. Charles at once marched on Perth, where he was joined by Lord George Murray and James Drummond, titular Duke of Perth.† There he proclaimed his father King, appointed himself guardian of the realm, and instituted a system of levying tribute from the cities he captured to provide pay for his army. 'Though', read his proclamation, 'we acknowledge some obligations to the French Monarch, we shall not do anything that is not becoming to a King, and an English King. . . . You may rest assured that I put my faith in no other arm than the justice of my cause and in the justice and affection of my people.' By 16th September, the rebel army was in Edinburgh.

Cope, meanwhile, had moved in safety to Aberdeen, whence his army was shipped south, reaching Dunbar on the day of Prince Charles's entry into Edinburgh. Three days later, he marched north again and, sighting the Jacobite army near to the village of

* The Royal Warwickshire Regiment.
† 'A silly race-horsing boy' according to Horace Walpole.[23]

Prestonpans, took up what appeared to be an impregnable position, covered at the rear and flanks by walls, the sea, and a wide ditch, and masked in front by an apparently impassable marsh. During the night Charles crossed the unguarded marsh and, on the morning of the 21st, Cope and his army were routed in less than ten minutes' fighting. Four hundred were cut to pieces, more than 1,000 taken prisoner, and the 170 who succeeded in escaping fled south to Berwick where they found their commander already in safety. The effect of this defeat was quite disproportionate to its importance. By the end of October, Charles had gathered a force of 4,500 infantry and 400 horse with which to attempt the invasion of England. The British army in Scotland, beaten and dispirited, thought of the rebel army with superstitious horror. The annihilating onslaught of the Highlanders with their claymores at Prestonpans had filled them with unreasoning terror. Henry Pelham, writing to Robert Trevor at The Hague on the day of the battle, voices the misgivings of the Government:[24] 'I heartily wish the troops were arrived both Dutch and English, for though I look upon these Highland rebels as a sort of rabble, yet if there is no force to oppose 'em, they may come in time to be considerable. We have scarce any regular troops in the country, and between you and I, I don't find that zeal to venture purses and lives that I formerly remember. I don't care to look out for the reasons.'

Help was on the way: by 18th October Cumberland himself had arrived in London, and already some of his troops were marching to Newcastle to join a new force under Wade; Cope was removed from command in Scotland and superseded by General Handasyde. Among the troops to join Wade in Newcastle were Brigade-Major James Wolfe and his father, sixty and suffering from gout, on active service again for a short time as general of division. General Wolfe, unable to sit his horse, rode with the troops by post-chaise. On the 3rd November he wrote to Mrs. Wolfe:[25] 'My dear Wife—As I am about to begin a Journey north with General Handasyde in an Endeavour to dislodge the Remnant of the Pretenders Rabble who still linger at Edinborough I seize this occasion to assure you of my compleat Health & Safety. If I have a chance of sending you word from Berwick I will do so. My belief is that this Business is no very long duration & that you will see us both back at Christmas. James is well & eager for active service. He sends his love and duty.' A week later James writes to his mother of his meeting with the General. 'I was under some apprehension for him on the road to Berwick, & was even told he was made Prisoner, but not with Foundation to give much credit to, as it had fallen out. I really believe you need not concern yourself about my Father's safety, for 'tis the opinion of most men that these Rebels won't stand the King's Troops; & as to the marching North or South with the army in his post-chaise, it does him so much service that I never saw him look better. It is said the Pretender's people made an attack on Carlisle but have been repuls'd with loss, this, however is not to be depended upon.'

Wade set out to the relief of Carlisle, which was besieged by the rebels. Having feinted at Berwick, the rebel army advanced in two columns through the western counties, a part of England feebly garrisoned and sympathetic to the Jacobite cause. More important still, the western route lay along roads ill-suited to the movement of a regular army but perfectly practical for the lightly equipped Highlanders. To reach Carlisle Wade had to cross the Cheviot and Pennine watershed under arctic conditions. He set out on 16th November and covered ten miles in fifteen hours. The troops were marching in driving sleet and heavy snow and many dropped out from fatigue. On the 17th the march was continued to Hexham, where Wade received intelligence of the surrender of Carlisle. He decided to turn back to Newcastle. This return to quarters, which took four days and exhausted his troops, was a blunder on the grand scale. Had Wade persevered in his march, against the weather, he would have barred the way back to the north, and the rebellion must soon have been crushed. Prince Charles continued his unopposed progress through Wigan to Manchester.

By this time, Cumberland had mustered 8,000 men at Lichfield, while a still larger force, mainly of militia but strengthened by battalions of the Guards, was assembling at Finchley to guard the capital. Wade, also, began to move south. Lord George Murray now made a feint attack from Macclesfield towards Newcastle-under-Lyme; this drew Cumberland westward to Stone to intercept him, and Murray slipped past him, making a forced march eastward to Derby. There was now no regular army between

Prince Charles and London. The capital was panic-stricken: shops closed, all business was suspended; the King and his government prepared for flight, and the Bank of England only escaped ruin by paying out in sixpences to gain time. It seemed that nothing could prevent the Young Pretender from entering London. Cumberland and Wade were, it is true, moving south in pursuit, but their progress was slow in comparison with that of the Highlanders. The army assembling at Finchley was unlikely to be any match for them. On the night of his arrival in Derby, Charles was considering what he should wear for his ceremonial entry into the capital; but on the following day his officers persuaded him to withdraw to Scotland.

Opinions are divided about the wisdom of this advice. His force was dwindling fast as men returned to their homes and families; and every mile marched southward made his chances of a safe retreat more slender. On the other hand it may be argued that a victory over the Finchley army and the expulsion of the King might well have won over the Londoners to the restoration of the Stuarts. After a long day of argument Charles yielded to his advisers. It must have been a bitter decision for him, for there could never be another such opportunity. Pursued energetically by Cumberland, and with rather less enthusiasm by Wade, the Young Pretender succeeded, by a series of forced marches, in crossing the border in safety. Cumberland was recalled to London to command the army in the face of a threat of invasion from France, and the first danger from the rebellion was past. Prince Charles was still in the field, and a strenuous campaign was still to be fought before his army was finally crushed, but he was never again to cross the border into England.

If prospects of a successful invasion of England in 1746 had faded, hopes for the Jacobite cause in Scotland remained undiminished. The rebel army had outmarched and outmanœuvred the King's troops throughout the campaign of the previous year and, in their single engagement, had won a definite and deserved victory. Reinforcements, under Lord John Drummond, had arrived from France, and more than 4,000 new recruits had come in from the rebel clans. On his way to join them, Charles captured Stirling, but the castle held out under the stubborn command of General Blakeney. Wade had been recalled, General Henry Hawley being appointed by Cumberland in his place, and, under his command, the King's army marched to the relief of Stirling Castle. Hawley was a conceited and brutal man of mediocre ability and unbounded self-confidence. His partiality for gibbets, a couple of which he carried with him always as camp furniture for use whenever an opportunity arose, had earned him the felicitous title of 'Hangman'. He suffered under the grave misapprehension that he was conducting a campaign against an ill-disciplined rabble which would disperse at the first sight of regular troops. He was soon to be undeceived. Disdaining to attack the rebel forces assembled outside Stirling, he made camp at Falkirk on 16th January 1746 and rode off to dine with the Jacobite Countess of Kilmarnock, wife to one of the rebel leaders, at Callander House. General Huske, Hawley's second-in-command, was left to interpret the bewildering and contradictory movements of the Stuart army. Charles first manœuvred his men so that they had the winter wind at their backs and thus blowing directly into the faces of the King's troops. Then a body of men was dispatched towards Stirling, away from his main force, with colours flying for all to see; his standard, which had marked the site of his headquarters on Plean Moor, was left to fly over a deserted field. Under cover of these diversions, the rebels marched swiftly to take up a new position on the high ground of Falkirk Moor, a ridge overlooking the King's army from the south-west. Hawley, summoned from dinner at Callander House, galloped hatless to the scene and at once realized the danger. He ordered his dragoons to make for the ridge with all speed, to forestall the Highlanders, the infantry following with fixed bayonets. The ground was rough and had not been reconnoitred; in the race for possession of the ridge, Hawley's guns became hopelessly bogged down and were deserted by the Falkirk carters who drove them, the horses being cut loose to canter to safety. The south-west wind, carrying an icy rain, blew full in the faces of Hawley's men. The Highlanders won the race for the ridge, and Hawley was obliged to deploy on lower ground. The armies were drawn up for battle, about equal in numbers and both without artillery, and the action was begun at about four o'clock in the afternoon.

The first move came from the King's troops: the cavalry advanced in good order against the rebel right wing commanded by Lord George Murray. Murray held his fire until the dragoons were within pistol shot and then poured in a well-aimed volley. Most of the cavalry broke and fled; the remainder who came to close quarters with the enemy were dragged from their horses by the long skirts of their coats and finished with the dirk. The Highlanders then threw down their pistols and charged. The foot, demoralized by the fate of the cavalry and blinded by the rain in their faces, fired a ragged volley. One in four of the muskets failed to fire owing to the rain, and after a few minutes of hand-to-hand fighting in which the King's troops were much hampered by their heavy uniforms and equipment, the line crumpled. Within half an hour of the start of the battle, all but five of Hawley's regiments were in headlong flight towards Falkirk carrying Hawley with them. Wolfe's regiment, Barrell's, remained steady and was supported by the 14th and 48th Regiments,* the Buffs and the Royal Scots. These regiments, commanded by General Huske in person, made, with the 9th Dragoons, an orderly and even aggressive withdrawal, halting the rebels, and covering the retreat of the rest of the broken army. The gloom of the day soon merged into the midwinter darkness of evening and all attempt at pursuit was abandoned. Prince Charles was left in possession of the field, of the English camp with its quantity of military stores and booty, and of Hawley's bogged artillery. The English dead, stripped and plundered, lay out on the hillside through the night, in the words of an eye-witness, like a flock of quiet sheep among the heather.

Hawley, having blundered in his attempt to fire his military baggage in Falkirk, all of which, including regimental standards and quantities of ammunition, fell into enemy hands, withdrew in undignified haste to Linlithgow. There he paused to compose a blustering and mendacious account of the engagement: a report which was accepted, though with some exasperation, by the King. Whether or not he believed that the defeat was due to bad weather and misleading intelligence reports as Hawley alleged, it was at least clear to George II that a change in command was imperative. The Duke of Cumberland was appointed, with Hawley as his subordinate. 'The Hangman' continued his retreat

* The Prince of Wales's West Yorkshire Regiment and the Northamptonshire Regiment.

to Edinburgh where he whiled away his last days as commander of the army in Scotland justifying his nickname. On 29th January 1746 he wrote to the Duke of Newcastle, 'There are fourteen deserters taken, shall they be hanged? Thirty-one of Hamilton's dragoons are to be hanged for deserting to the rebels, and thirty-two of the foot to be shot for cowardice.' Perhaps the 'wooden horse' had been captured by the rebels at Falkirk.

Wolfe's part in the battle had been an honourable one. His regiment had behaved with exemplary coolness under circumstances of great difficulty and danger and, when at last obliged to withdraw, had done so in perfect order. He did not write to his parents of the battle, finding it undesirable, perhaps, to tell them the truth of the affair and impossible to tell them anything else. To his uncle, William Sotheron, he wrote from Edinburgh a laconic and guarded account, stressing the few good features of the army's behaviour and putting the best possible interpretation on the rest. 'If you have not seen the *Gazette*,' he writes,[26] 'you will have heard of our late encounter (for 'twas not a battle, as neither side would fight): and possibly it will be told you in a much worse light than it really is. Though we can't have been said to have totally routed the enemy, we yet remained a long time masters of the field of battle, and of our cannon, not one of which would have been lost if the drivers had not left their carriages and run off with the horses. We left Falkirk and part of our camp because the ammunition of the army—on which we can only depend—was all wet and spoiled; but our retreat was in no ways molested by the enemy, as affecting our superiority. The loss of either side is inconsiderable and we are now making all necessary preparations to try once more to put an end to this rebellion, which the weather has hitherto prevented, and in my opinion can at any time be the only objection.' Wolfe's personal feelings for Hawley were not frankly expressed until nearly ten years later;* but he was to have ample opportunity to study him during the following months, for on the arrival of the Duke of Cumberland in Edinburgh on 30th January, Wolfe was appointed to be Hawley's aide-de-camp.

After less than thirty hours in the Scottish capital, Cumberland followed his army, which had already marched westward, in a

* 5th November 1755. See p. 139.

coach and twelve. At Linlithgow he joined one of the columns and marched on foot to Falkirk at the head of the Royal Scots. On the following day he entered Stirling, relieved the castle, and congratulated its gallant defender, General Blakeney. The rebel army retreated before him, often less than a day's march ahead, to gather at the Highland capital of Inverness. Cumberland pushed on as far as Perth, but the severity of the winter made further progress impracticable and he halted to rest his troops and to await the arrival of 5,000 Hessians under his brother-in-law, the Prince of Hesse. Parties of soldiers were sent out to plunder the lands of local Jacobite sympathizers, and the Countess of Perth and Lady Strathallan were imprisoned in Edinburgh Castle. The Hessians, on their arrival, were posted to guard the Forth and Tay while Cumberland, with his army, marched north by the coast road to Aberdeen, a city staunch in its adherence and support to the Stuarts. Here Cumberland stayed for six weeks. He took up residence at 45 Guestrow, in the house of a certain Alexander Thomson, an advocate. Hawley, to be near his chief, installed himself in the next house, which belonged to a Mrs. Gordon of Hallhead and Esslemont, a lady of acknowledged Jacobite sympathies whose husband was at the time bearing arms with the rebel army as secretary to the aged Lord Pitsligo. The choice of these lodgings was to lead to a most discreditable incident which involved Wolfe in his capacity as aide-de-camp to Hawley. The incident was in itself trivial, and Wolfe's part in it was merely that of a subordinate carrying out orders, but it throws an interesting light on the behaviour of Cumberland and Hawley, and is one of the few surviving accounts of a conversation with Wolfe.

It appears that Hawley, after spending one night in Mrs. Gordon's house, sent to her for her keys. She tried to evade sending them to him but later received a more peremptory demand to which she yielded. 'That evening,' her statement continues,[27] 'One, Major Wolfe, came to me, and after asking if I was Mrs. Gordon, and desiring a gentleman who was with me to go out of the room, he said he was come to tell me that by the Duke of Cumberland's and General Hawley's order I was deprived of everything I had, except the cloaths upon my back. After delivering this message he said that General Hawley having

46

enquired into my character of several persons, who had all spoken very well of me, and had told him that I had had no hand in the Rebellion, and that I was a stranger there without any relations in that country, he, the General, would make interest with the Duke of Cumberland, and that I might have any particular thing that I had a mind to and could say was my own. I then desired to have my tea, but the Major told me it was very good, and that tea was scarce in the army; so he did not believe I could have it. The same answer was made when I asked for my chocolate. I mentioned several other things, particularly my china. That, he told me, was, a great deal of it, very pretty, and that they were fond of china themselves; but as they had no ladies travelled with them, I might perhaps have some of it. I then desired to have my pictures. He said he supposed I could not wish to have them all. I replied that I did not pretend to name any except my son's. He asked me if I had a son, where he was? I said I had sent him into the country to make room for them. To what place? said he. I answered, to Sir Arthur Forbes's. He asked, How old my son was. I said about fourteen. Fourteen, said he, then he is not a child, and you will be made to produce him. And thus we parted. This Major Wolfe was aide-de-camp to General Hawley. The next day a petition was drawn up and read to the Duke of Cumberland at his levee by Captain Forbes, who was also aide-de-camp to General Hawley and I was told the Duke said he would take care I should not be robb'd. That day Major Wolfe came to me again and told me that the Duke of Cumberland had sent him to let me know that my petition had been read to him, and that he would take care that every thing should be restored to me. Notwithstanding this, when I sent to the house to ask for anything, as, in particular I did for a pair of breeches for my son, for a little tea for myself, for a bottle of ale, for some flour to make bread, because there was none to be bought in the town, all was refused me. . . . I should have mention'd above that Major Wolfe did one day bring me my son's picture, but without the frame, and he then told me that General Hawley did with his own hands take it out of the frame, which was a gilt one and very handsome. This frame the General left behind him, and I afterwards found it in the house.' Notwithstanding the Duke's promise, Mrs. Gordon was robbed of everything she possessed—

everything from her prized china to the blankets from the beds; and her set of coloured table-china was dispatched to the Duke of Cumberland at St. James's Palace, so it is evident that the looting of the house was carried out at least with his approval and to his benefit. As a squalid sequel to this incident, some of the china was found later in the shop of a London antique dealer who admitted to having purchased it from a prostitute to whom it had been given by the Duke. Poor Mrs. Gordon was ruined.

There were, however, circumstances which to some extent explain the rapacity of the English commanders. Mrs. Gordon was married into a family of ardent and militant Jacobites. Her marriage had taken place in 1728 and it was therefore more than probable that her son was older than she said, and perhaps no more than two years junior to Wolfe. Her own list of the quantities of food stolen show that, even in days when it was customary to provision for the winter, there was ground for the suspicion that she was holding stores for purposes other than for her own consumption. As for her list of household goods, it is evident that Wolfe and his superiors suspected that these were not all her own property but that she was endeavouring to protect or conceal the possessions of proscribed friends.* On her own admission 'ten dishes, 40 plates, and 3 dozen of plates' did not belong to her but 'were sent in to me by two merchants to see if I would buy them.' These circumstances do not excuse Hawley's behaviour, but they tend to explain the ruthless manner of the theft. Cumberland was equally to blame, for it is evident that he did more than countenance the robbery, and his own behaviour in the house of Mr. Thomson was by no means exemplary. After six weeks' residence, for which he paid nothing and during which time he did much damage to the contents of the house and used all the available provisions, he left without a word of thanks to the owners and stole a quantity of sugar. Wolfe, while carrying out his orders, had found opportunity to return to Mrs. Gordon her son's portrait—some indication, perhaps, of unexpressed sympathy— but there is otherwise nothing to show where his own sympathies lay.

Cumberland's halt in Aberdeen was necessitated partly by bad

* See her statement 'any particular thing . . . I could say was my own', '. . . he told me was a great deal of it,' and '. . . he supposed I could not wish to have them all.'

weather and partly by the exhaustion of his troops. During the six weeks he remained there several hundred men rejoined his army from hospital and others 'recovered strength as well as spirit by the rest'.[28] Parties of troops were sent out into the surrounding country to pillage the estates of Jacobite supporters and to seek out and destroy rebel forces in the area. For those remaining in Aberdeen there were regular and long hours of drill each day. Meanwhile the rebels, by a series of daring and well-planned attacks, were clearing the central Highlands of the King's garrisons. While Cumberland stayed in Aberdeen, the country to the north and west was exposed to rebel intimidation, and the popularity of the cause grew daily greater. It was imperative that the King's troops should regain the initiative and bring the Stuart army to battle before it became large enough to constitute a second threat to England. On 6th April, the main body of the army advanced north-east out of Aberdeen to join the division commanded by Lord Albemarle which was already in Strathbogie. Wolfe remained behind in Aberdeen until the 8th, when Cumberland and Hawley moved out to join their troops at Oldmeldrum. Next day the march was continued to the coast town of Banff where a day's halt was ordered. On the morning of the 12th, the entire army, some 9,000 strong, forded the Spey, the infantry wading up to their waists in the swift current, one dragoon and a camp-follower being swept away and drowned in the crossing. By the 14th the army was in Nairn, sixteen miles from the rebel forces. There the Duke ordered another halt and the men celebrated his royal birthday with an allowance of brandy, cheese, and biscuit provided at his expense.

Prince Charles, meanwhile, had drawn up his army, a starving and disheartened force numbering no more than 6,000, in order of battle on Culloden Moor. When he learned that Cumberland was encamped on the 14th he decided on a night attack to surprise the royal army. The night was black and the Highlanders had miscalculated the time necessary to cover the intervening rough country in darkness; dawn was breaking before they arrived within striking distance; weary and dispirited, they were forced to fall back to their original position. The royal army moved early that morning, and before five o'clock it was on the march. There was a high wind and heavy rain which continued until noon, but soon after the battle began the sky cleared and remained fine for the rest of the day. Cumberland found the Jacobite troops drawn up in two lines, their right flank against a straggling line of park walls and huts, their left stretching towards Culloden House, where the Prince had spent the previous night. The King's army was formed in three lines, the ten guns of the artillery stationed in pairs between the regiments of the first line. Cumberland is reported then to have delivered a stirring address to his troops: 'I do not suppose that there are any men here who are disinclined to fight, but if there be, I beg them in God's name to go, for I would rather face the Highlanders with a thousand resolute men at my back than with ten thousand half-hearted.' As the cheers which greeted these words sounded across the moor, Hawley led the dragoons forward to break down the obstacles on the enemy's right flank. At about one o'clock the battle began with a salvo from the enemy's guns, a challenge immediately taken up by the guns of the royal army which raked the rebel line with an accurate and destructive fire.

Wolfe describes the battle that followed in a letter written on the 17th to Major Henry Delabene, from whom he had purchased his company in Barrell's.

'I have the pleasure to tell you' [he writes[29]] 'that yesterday about one in the afternoon we engaged the Rebel army, and in about an hour drove them from the field of battle; they left near 1500 dead, the rest (except prisoners) escaped into the neighbouring mountains; the action was three miles short of this place* on Lord President Forbes' land, and from thence the name of the battle of Culloden. I have never seen an action so general, nor any victory so complete. The Rebels had posted themselves so they imagined we could neither use cannon nor cavalry, but both did essential service. They waited till we came near enough to fire cannon on them, and were greatly surprised and disorder'd at it, and finding their mistake, they charged upon our front line in thick solid bodies, throwing down their arms without exploding them, and advancing furiously with their drawn swords. You must understand before the cannonading they were (I mean the clans) in a very extended thick line, with their right to some houses

* Inverness.

50

and a wall, their left and centre were supported in their rear by the Lowlanders and some few horse. Four pieces of cannon were in their front, which they often fired, but with little effect. The Duke's army had at the beginning six battalions in the first line commanded by Lord Albemarle and Lord Semple;* as many in the second under General Husk, and three regiments formed a third line or reserve, commanded by Brigadier Mordaunt; Cobham's Dragoons and two squadrons of Mark Ker's were on the left of the front line, where the ground was firmest; the other squadron and one of Kingston's Horse were on the right, and two pieces of cannon in equal intervals between the battalions of the first line. And a little after the Rebels begun their attack, the Duke observed they intended to extend their line beyond his right by breaking to the left from their centre, and instantly ordered Pulteney's from the reserve to form on the right of his first line, and brought the rest of that Corps towards the right of his second line to strengthen that wing; these movements obliged them to attack his front. The front line on the Rebels' near approach begun a most violent fire, which continued 8 or 9 minutes, and kill'd so many of their best men that they could only penetrate into our Battalion; that on the left of the line was Barrell's regiment; they were attacked by the Camerons (the bravest clan amongst them), and 'twas for some time a dispute between the swords and bayonets; but the latter was found by far the most destructive weapon. The Regiment behaved with uncommon resolution killing some say almost their own number, whereas 40 of them were only wounded, and those not mortally, and not above ten kill'd; they were, however, surrounded by superiority, and would have been all destroyed had not Col. Martin with his Regiment (the left of the 2nd line of Foot) mov'd forward to their assistance, prevented mischief, and by a well-timed fire destroyed a great number of them and obliged them to run off.

General Hawley, who commanded the five squadrons of Dragoons on the left, had, by the assistance of 150 Argyleshire, thrown down two stone walls, and was (when the fire of the Foot began) posted with his Dragoons opposite to the extremity of the enemy's right wing, and as soon as the Rebels began to give way and the fire of the Foot slacken'd, he ordered Genl. Bland to

* Sempill.

51

charge the rest of them with three squadrons, and Cobham to support him with the two. It was done with wonderful spirit and completed the victory with great slaughter. We have taken 22 pieces of brass cannon or near it, a number of colours, and near 700 prisoners, amongst which are all the Irish picquets, most of the remainder of Fitz James's Horse, and a part of Drummond's Regiment, great quantity of powder, muskets, bayonets, broadswords, and plads innumerable. All the troops acquitted themselves as troops worthy the command of a great and gallant General, and no individual corps has been wanting in their duty.

The Rebels, besides their natural inclinations, had orders not to give quarter to our men.* We had an opportunity of avenging ourselves for that and many other things, and indeed we did not neglect it, as few Highlanders were made prisoners as possible. Lord Kilmarnock is one, and Brigr. Stapleton, with some others you have a list of. The enemy, by their own order of battle, had 8300 men in the field, and our utmost was 7200. Our loss is inconsiderable. Poor Col. Rich had his left hand quite cut off, and a very bad cut in his right elbow, and six in his head, one or two very bad ones. Lord Robert Ker was killed fighting against numbers. . . . The Rebels are much dispers'd, and it is supposed will never be able to collect a body again. The Pretender was in their rear, but soon quitted the field. . . .'

In another letter, written on the same day, to his uncle William Sotheron, Wolfe gives a shortened version of the battle, much of it in the same words as the letter to Delabene, ending, with evident satisfaction,[30] 'I heartily wish you joy of the happy end of so horrid an undertaking. And may they ever be punished in the same manner who attempt the like!'

Wolfe's account contains a number of inaccuracies, due partly to his position as aide-de-camp to Hawley which allowed him only rarely to see more than one part of the battle in detail, and doubtless also to his acceptance of the confused impressions and reports of others. As to the numbers engaged, it is clear that Cumberland's army, the strength of which is given officially at 8,811, outnumbered the rebels by some 3,000 men. The strengths given by Wolfe were, however, probably those accepted at the

* Generally believed at the time, but now thought to be unfounded.

time. Barrell's suffered more heavily in the battle than any other regiment engaged, losing 120 officers and men killed or wounded, and it is perhaps fortunate that Wolfe was not with them. The hand-to-hand fighting was savage, most of the casualties falling to claymore and bayonet, and 'Barrell's regiment had not one but what was bent and bloody.'[31] Horace Walpole, in a letter to Horace Mann dated 25th April,[32] reports that Lord Robert Ker was 'cut to pieces with above thirty wounds.' Walpole continues, 'It is a brave young Duke! The town is all blazing round me as I write, with fireworks and illuminations: I have some inclination to lap up half a dozen sky-rockets, to make you drink the Duke's health. Mr. Doddington,* on the first report, came out with a very pretty illumination; so pretty that I believe he had it by him, ready for *any* occasion.'

The victory was decisive. The last hope of a Stuart restoration was crushed. All that remained to do was to hunt down the rebel fugitives, a task which was carried out with far more than necessary severity and which earned for Cumberland the name of 'Butcher'. One story survives of Wolfe's personal share in the day's events. It was never mentioned by him in any of his letters, but that is not in itself surprising for he was reticent about his own deeds and virtues. It rests on the single authority of Sir Henry Stewart of Allanton,[33] whose knowledge of it must have been at least second-hand as he was not born until thirteen years after the event described. It is said that after the battle, Cumberland, riding over the battlefield with some of his officers, discovered a young wounded Highlander lying in the heather. The Duke asked him to whom he belonged. 'To the Prince,' was the reply. Turning to Major Wolfe, riding at his side, Cumberland said, 'Wolfe, shoot me that insolent Highland scoundrel who dares look on us with such contempt.' Wolfe, so the story goes, answered, 'My commission is at your Royal Highness's disposal, but I can never consent to become an executioner.' Several other officers ordered to shoot the wounded man refused, and at last a common soldier carried out the execution. The young Highlander thus killed in cold blood was Charles Lovat, then acting as commander of the Master of Lovat's Regiment of Frasers. A

* George Bubb Dodington (1691–1762), Treasurer of the Navy in Pelham's administration.

little more than thirteen years later Simon Fraser, Master of Lovat, was to command the First Fraser Highlanders* with Wolfe at Quebec. Improbable as this anecdote may seem on the face of it, the actions described are not incompatible with what is known of the characters of Cumberland and Wolfe and it seems never to have been contradicted by any of those who were present.

On the evening of the battle, Cumberland marched his army into Inverness and at once began his campaign for the suppression by force of remaining Jacobite resistance. As Hawley's aide-de-camp, Wolfe was responsible for transmitting his orders to officers engaged in harrying the fugitives, burning their villages, and looting their possessions. An example of this correspondence is his letter to Captain Charles Hamilton, commanding Cobham's Dragoons in the Forfar district.[34] 'You know the manner of treating the houses and possessions of rebels in this part of the country. The same freedom is to be used where you are as has hitherto been practized, that is seeking for them and their arms, cattle, and other things that are usually found.' Cumberland remained in Scotland for three months after his victory. During that time he effectively stamped out the embers of the rebellion, but he did so by savage and ruthless methods which it is impossible to condone. Little attempt was made to differentiate between rebel and loyalist; the country was treated as enemy territory, the population as uniformly hostile and treacherous. Murder, transportation in coffin-ships to the colonies, indefinite imprisonment, and banishment were common; houses were set on fire, crops destroyed, and cattle confiscated. The 'Butcher' earned his name. On 18th July he left Scotland for London.

Hawley had resigned his command in June, and the Earl of Albemarle was appointed commander-in-chief in Scotland on 23rd August. Wolfe, his appointment as aide-de-camp automatically terminated by Hawley's resignation, rejoined his regiment in Linlithgow. From there he was soon detached to occupy the ruined fort at Inversnaid, in the heart of the rebellious MacGregor country. The fort, although in ruins, occupied a position of considerable strategic importance and it was thought imperative that it should be garrisoned. Wolfe remained there

* 78th Regiment.

54

until November when he received orders to rejoin his regiment after six weeks' leave. He reached London in time to spend Christmas and his twentieth birthday with his family in their new town house in Old Burlington Street. He had been away from home almost continuously for more than four years. He found his father crotchety with gout and the mortification of having to dun government departments for three years' arrears of pay as Inspector of Marines. As he wrote to the Duke of Bedford, in consequence of his office he was 'in a worse position than any other man who had the honour of having a regiment in His Majesty's service.'[35] However, he paid up, when the time came, for his son's new uniform, and in January 1747 Wolfe embarked again for the Netherlands. Early in the following month, Barrell's Regiment sailed from Leith for the same destination.

CHAPTER IV

Laffeldt

WHILE the greater part of the British Army was engaged in Scotland, the war in Europe dragged on with increasing complication and futility. The French, under the command of Marshal Saxe, captured Brussels and Ostend and overran the Austrian Netherlands. To offset this reverse, Maria Theresa profited by the death of the Emperor, Charles Albert, to make peace with Bavaria* and secure the election of her husband, Francis of Lorraine, as his successor. By the treaty of Dresden in December 1745, the final withdrawal from the war of Frederick of Prussia was purchased at the cost of Silesia. The Austrian troops set free by this manœuvre were sufficient to persuade Charles Emmanuel of Savoy against a proposed alliance with France, and he joined in the clearance of French and Spanish troops from northern Italy.

In England, the panic in London when the Highlanders reached Derby had produced a constructive change in the Government. The obvious weakness of their Ministry convinced the Pelhams of the need to include Pitt as Secretary at War and to reduce continental commitments until the rebellion was crushed. The King conceded the reduction of the continental army to a small contingent under Ligonier but declined to accept the appointment of Pitt; in this refusal he was actively supported by Carteret, now Lord Granville, and Lord Bath, who hoped thereby to obtain the fall of the Pelhams. The conspiracy failed: to the mortification of the King, the ministers of state, with unprecedented unanimity, resigned their offices, and after four days of fruitless attempts by Bath and Granville to form a new govern-

* Peace of Füssen, 1745.

ment, the Pelhams were recalled. Pitt prudently abandoned his claim to the post of Secretary at War and on 22nd February 1746 accepted office as Vice-Treasurer of Ireland; on 6th May he kissed hands on his appointment, as a privy councillor, to the lucrative office of Paymaster to the Forces.

Within a year of Pitt's appointment as Paymaster, the Duke of Bedford, First Lord of the Admiralty, proposed an expedition against the French in Canada. In June 1745 Shirley, the Governor of Massachusetts, had organized a force of New Englanders to attack Louisbourg, the French fortress commanding the entrance to the St. Lawrence river. Led by Colonel William Pepperell, and supported by a naval squadron under Commodore Warren, the colonials captured Louisbourg and Cape Breton Island, bringing to a standstill the rich French Newfoundland fishing industry and opening the way to a planned assault on the French colonial empire in America. Bedford advocated the immediate preparation of an expedition to capture Quebec and complete the conquest of Canada, and in this he was enthusiastically supported by Pitt. In theory the proposal was sound and might have achieved much: in practice it proved too much for the planning abilities of the Government. The expedition was delayed until it was too late and was then diverted to the Continent where, in the absence of any defined objective, a futile landing was made near L'Orient, on the Brest peninsula; little opposition was encountered, the troops were re-embarked with the trifling loss of about a hundred men, and the project abandoned. Its single achievement was the knowledge that landings could be made on the French coast with impunity, and the inference that these, if properly planned and led, might be used as diversionary tactics and to disrupt French offensive plans: a lesson which was to be remembered by Pitt for a future occasion.

The year ended with a brave show of renewed resolution: the sum of six million pounds was voted for the Army and Navy, and an army of 138,000, composed of Austrian, Dutch, Hanoverian, Hessian, and British troops was assembled in Holland under the supreme command of the Duke of Cumberland. It was his intention to open the campaign early in the year, while the main French army was still in winter quarters, by laying siege to Antwerp. This estimable plan was frustrated by wintry weather and by the Dutch surrender of Cadsand and Sluys which enabled Saxe to close the southern mouth of the Scheldt. Restricted to a landing to the north, which necessitated the overland transportation from Breda of all forage for his army, Cumberland was obliged to spend fourteen precious weeks in organizing his commissariat before he could attempt to take the initiative. Brigade-Major James Wolfe was as bored as his fellow officers with this enforced inactivity. 'There is', he writes from camp near Breda, 'such a dearth at present of everything new and entertaining, it seems no easy task to fill a letter; at least to give it such a turn as may please.' He whiled away the time by carrying on a lively and flirtatious correspondence with the daughter of a General Lacey, an Irishman in Austrian service. They were evidently old friends: 'You have left me in a doubt that is hurtful to my repose,' he writes on 11th June. 'Sure it must never happen that a soldier can be unhappy in his love; if so, what reward for great and glorious undertakings, or what relief from despair? Can we be forgot in the midst of danger and fatigue? But worse than this, shall I live to see an inhabitant of the bush succeed to my place and triumph in the frailty of my country-woman?' Writing later in a more sober mood, he adds flippantly, 'I write this in a moment of reflection; you'll pardon the style, 'tis unnatural. . . . I'm glad to catch myself in such a disposition and think it the beginning of reform.' If his qualities failed to impress Miss Lacey, they were not overlooked by his commander-in-chief: in May, Cumberland wrote to Lord Chesterfield recommending that Major James Wolfe, having served constantly and well during the past two years as major of brigade, and shown himself capable and desirous to do his duty, might be permitted to purchase the vacant lieutenant-colonelcy of the Eighth Foot. The recommendation was not accepted, and Wolfe had to wait another three years for a second opportunity.

Towards the end of May, Cumberland made an attempt to bring the French to a general action by concentrating his forces at Tilburg and advancing towards Louvain where the French army was strongly entrenched. Here he manœuvred for three weeks, trying to tempt Saxe from his position, but he declined to be drawn. Despairing of this stalemate, Cumberland moved eastward towards Tongres where he hoped to destroy the detached corps of 30,000 men under the Prince of Clermont before Saxe could reinforce him. Saxe immediately moved to concentrate his entire force at Tongres, and Cumberland decided to retire to a more favourable position to the north. This plan was frustrated by the speed of the French march from Louvain: covering nearly fifty miles in two days, Saxe confronted Cumberland at Laffeldt before his army had reached its chosen position, and the situation was only temporarily saved by the prompt action of Ligonier in drawing up his cavalry to bar the French advance while the infantry formed up in order of battle. Had they been able to give battle at once, the allies might still have snatched a quick victory: the French army was in an extended column, and weary after a long forced march; Saxe was unable to complete his dispositions until after nightfall, and was, until then, particularly vulnerable to attack; but the allied army was equally slow to concentrate, and the opportunity was lost.

On the following morning, 21st June, in the last major battle of the war, Cumberland was honourably but decisively defeated. The allied army was drawn up in a strong position, the core of which was formed by the villages of Laffeldt and Vlytingen, held by British and Hanoverian troops; to the right of them, and forming the centre of the line, were the Dutch; the Austrians, in a line thrown back towards Bilsen, protected the right flank and safeguarded the route for a withdrawal into Holland. At dawn Saxe, by doubling the left wing of his army behind his right, had massed a formidable column threatening the two villages from the south. Sending a strong force of cavalry and infantry to menace the allied left flank, he launched, simultaneously, six brigades with guns under the Marquis de Salières against Vlytingen, and five brigades supported by cavalry against Laffeldt. Salières, meeting with little success against the stubborn resistance of the brigade of Guards, turned some of his guns on Laffeldt but, in spite of this, both attacks were repulsed with heavy losses. Cumberland sent urgent instructions to the Austrians to create a diversion on the right flank but de Salières turned his guns against them and pinned them down. A second attack, reinforced by two fresh brigades and supporting cavalry, met with the same furious resistance and was beaten off. The third onslaught, with two more brigades and the Irish battalions, forced the British from their positions and the French swarmed into Laffeldt. Cumberland made a last gallant attempt to save the position, and ordered his entire line of infantry to advance; for a time they carried the French before them, but at a crucial moment some squadrons of Dutch cavalry in the centre took fright and galloped headlong into the British line, which suffered heavily and was thrown into confusion. By the time order could be restored, Laffeldt was lost and Saxe was gathering his army for a final crushing blow at the now retreating British infantry. Ligonier, realizing that only immediate action could avert disaster, gathered the Greys, Inniskillings and Cumberland's dragoons, and led them into a sacrificial attack upon the massed French cavalry. Hacking a path through to the French infantry, they inflicted heavy casualties upon them before being overwhelmed, Ligonier himself being unhorsed and taken prisoner. With the remainder of the cavalry Cumberland succeeded in covering the retreat of the army from the field.

The losses on both sides were heavy. The total of killed and wounded among the allies was about 6,000; the French, according to Saxe himself, lost not less than 10,000. Wolfe was among those wounded, having received a musket ball in the body early in the engagement, but refused to leave the field despite the entreaties of his servant, Roland. 'He came to me,' Wolfe writes some years later,[36] 'at the hazard of his Life in the last action with offers of his service, took off my Cloak & brought a fresh Horse, & would have continued close by me had I not order'd him to retire, & I believe he was slightly wounded just at that time, & the horse he held was shot likewise.' For his own gallant behaviour during the battle Wolfe received the official thanks of the commander-in-chief.

The allies retreated across the Meuse, and Saxe retired to his positions at Tongres, detaching, meanwhile, a corps for the capture of the fortress of Bergen-op-Zoom, the fall of which marked the end of the campaign. Horace Walpole gives news of the battle in his letter to George Montagu on 2nd July:[37] 'Though we have no great reason to triumph, as we have certainly been defeated, yet the French have as certainly bought their victory dear: indeed, what would be very dear to us is not so much to them. However, their least loss is twelve thousand men; as our least loss is five thousand. The truth of the whole is, that the Duke was determined to fight at all events, which the French, who determined not to fight but at great odds, took advantage of. His Royal Highness's valour has shone extremely, but at the expense of his judgement.' To Horace Mann, on the following day,[38] he adds caustically that Cumberland 'behaved as bravely as usual; but his prowess is so well established, that it grows time for him to exert other qualities of a general.'

The failures of the allied armies on land were offset to some extent by British successes at sea. News was received in London of French and Spanish plans for the recapture of Louisbourg, and for the relief of Pondicherry which was being threatened with blockade by a British naval squadron. In addition there were signs of preparations for large convoys under escort to the East and West Indies. On 3rd May, Anson, after a month's ceaseless vigil, sighted la Jonquière's fleet with convoys for the East Indies and Canada; immediate pursuit and a brisk action resulted in the capture of all the men-of-war and many of the ships under escort; the prize money amounted to more than £29,000. On 20th June, Captain Fox with eight ships captured forty-eight merchantmen bound for the West Indies. On 14th October, Hawke destroyed an escort fleet under Letanduère; the convoy escaped, but only to be gathered up by Pocock's West Indian fleet. These victories swept the French from the seas, paralysed her trade, and opened the way for further attacks upon her colonies. In such straits France could not afford to prolong the war. At best, she could hope to use her armies to dictate the terms of an early peace.

After a short time in a field hospital recovering from his wound, Wolfe returned on leave to England, reaching his parents' house in Old Burlington Street in time to celebrate his coming of age. This he did with characteristic thoroughness by falling in love. Recommendations from Sir John Mordaunt, under whom he had served in Flanders, gave him an introduction to a Miss Elizabeth Lawson, daughter of Sir Wilfred Lawson of Isel, niece to Mordaunt, and a maid of honour to the Princess of Wales. She was, if her portraits are true likenesses, very beautiful. Her mother, a niece of the Earl of Peterborough, enjoyed a reputation for sexual promiscuity which made her the envy of many but a subject of scandal among people of the Wolfes' respectability. It thus followed that Wolfe's choice of first love failed to satisfy his mother, and his enduring passion for Elizabeth Lawson was later to become the subject for a bitter family quarrel. There was, however, little time in the new year of 1748 for Wolfe to pursue his courtship. The spring campaign was starting, and in March Wolfe again sailed from Harwich under orders to join a Hanoverian detachment near Breda.

He arrived to find prospects of an early victory remote. The Duke of Cumberland was ill, and Saxe was exploiting his superiority in strategy and numbers to the full. Maestricht was invested by the French and it became increasingly apparent that the negotiations for peace which were already in train must succeed quickly if the war was to end on terms acceptable to the allies. Wolfe writes to his father from Osterhout on 12th April. 'I hear Maestricht is invested. Marshal Lowendahl pass'd the Maese with some troops at Namur, was join'd by those that winter'd at Louvain, marched through a Country that is almost impassable in the finest Seasons, seized Limbourg, and is (we are told) on the other side the River, where our Army lay the greatest part of last Campaign, while Mon^s de Saxe moves with the larger part of the French Army & invests Maestricht on this Side. If so, the body of Austrians there will be inferior to either of these Corps, and will certainly retire, or rather has retir'd, & leaves the unhappy Fortress to its Garrison and a Dutch Commander. I'm much at a loss to know whether that Place is thought of such worth as to risk a battle with disadvantage, especially in numbers.' Evidently it was thought not, for Maestricht fell to the French. He reports to his father a recent conversation in which Colonel Yorke, the Adjutant-General, 'proceeded to tell me that the Duke, in discourse with him, had expressed great concern at not having it in his power to serve me, but that his intention was just, and he would take an opportunity soon of making it appear.' There were plans for giving him a major's commission in Bragg's with the intention that he should succeed shortly to the lieutenant-colonelcy, but Wolfe adds philosophically, 'I'm sure the thing is yet far off, possibly may fail as heretofore, but with sincerity I assure you, I am out of the reach of disappointment.' In April he writes to his father of the peace congress at Aix-la-Chapelle which was being attended by Lord Sandwich and the Duke of

Newcastle:[39] 'The Conferences at Aix are rather languid, the warlike spirits conceive favourably, from the Interest or Intrigue perhaps of some mischievous particular, who may retard the general good, & keep our World in Arms. Sincerely I believe you'll think I'm crazy in the brain, in one letter I tell you all is at an end, and in the next that things have a fairer face; I'm sorry to say that my writings are greatly influenc'd by the state of my Body or mind at the time of writing, and I'm either happy or ruined by my last night's rest, or from the sunshine, or light & sickly air; such Infirmity is the mortal Frame subject to.' Already there were signs of the ill-health which was to dog him throughout the remainder of his life, aggravating the strain of campaigning and robbing him of the benefits of recuperation in quarters or on leave. Fortunately for him, the war was drawing to an end, and it would be nearly ten years before he would again be called upon to face the hardships of another campaign.

On 19th April the preliminaries of the peace were signed; and six months later they were expanded into the treaty of Aix-la-Chapelle. Long before the treaty was negotiated many of the countries engaged in the war would gladly have made peace. For England the continuance of the war meant the continuance of costly subsidies to her allies and the maintenance of an army on the Continent which, outgeneraled and outnumbered, would in all probability be destroyed; for France, the conquest of the Low Countries was as nothing compared with the loss of trade and the threat to her colonial Empire brought about by the destruction of her fleet; Frederick of Prussia was interested only in the annexation of Silesia and the freedom of the German states to regard him as their leader without domination from the Hapsburgs or from France, and his success in playing one enemy off against the other had assured the fulfilment of both aims. By the terms of the treaty, both England and France gave up their conquests, Prussia kept Silesia, the Austrian barrier fortresses in the Low Countries were handed over to the Dutch, and Spain obtained Parma and Piacenza. No settlement was made of English and French disputes in the East and West Indies or in America, and the original cause of the war with Spain—the right of search by *guarda-costas*—was ignored. For the allies the terms were humiliating, but the supremacy of the French armies in Europe left no choice. Pitt summed up the situation in a letter to George Grenville on 26th April:[40] 'I most heartily rejoice with you on this happy event; happy, I call it, because absolutely necessary to our very being.' The peace could at best be only temporary; little could be expected of a settlement which failed to determine the main issues in dispute between England and France: their conflicting colonial ambitions in America, India and the West Indies.

In England, however, the peace was greeted with public expressions of rejoicing. Walpole describes them in a letter to Horace Mann:[41]

'We have at last celebrated the Peace, and that as much in extremes as we generally do everything, whether we have reason to be glad or sorry, pleased or angry. Last Tuesday it was proclaimed: the King did not go to St. Paul's, but at night the whole town was illuminated. The next day was what was called "a jubilee-masquerade in the Venetian manner" at Ranelagh: it had nothing Venetian in it, but was by far the best understood and the prettiest spectacle I ever saw: nothing in a fairy tale ever surpassed it. . . . It began at three o'clock, and, about five, people of fashion began to go. When you entered, you found the whole garden filled with masks and spread with tents, which remained all night *very commodely*. In one quarter was a May-pole dressed with garlands, and people dancing round it to a tabor and pipe and rustic music, all masked, as were all the various bands of music that were disposed in different parts of the garden; some like huntsmen with French horns, some like peasants, and a troop of harlequins and scaramouches in the little open temple on the mount. On the canal was a sort of gondola, adorned with flags and streamers, and filled with music, rowing about. All round the outside of the amphitheatre were shops, filled with Dresden china, japan, &c. and all the Shopkeepers in mask. The amphitheatre was illuminated and in the middle was a circular bower, composed of all kinds of firs in tubs, from twenty to thirty feet high: under them orange-trees, with small lamps in each orange and below them all sorts of the finest auriculars in pots; and festoons of natural flowers hanging from tree to tree. Between the arches were firs, and smaller ones in the balconies above. There

64

were booths for tea and wine, gaming-tables and dancing, and about two thousand persons. In short, it pleased me more than anything I ever saw. . . . The next day were the fireworks, which by no means answered the expense, the length of preparation, and the expectation that had been raised: indeed for a week before, the town was like a country fair, the streets filled from morning to night, scaffolds building wherever you could or could not see, and coaches arriving from every corner of the kingdom. This hurry and lively scene, with the sight of the immense crowds in the Park and on every house, the guards, and the machine itself, which was very beautiful, was all worth seeing. The rockets, and whatever was thrown up into the air succeeded mighty well; but the wheels, and all that was to compose the principal part, were pitiful and ill-conducted, with no changes of coloured fires and shapes: the illumination was mean, and lighted so slowly that scarce anybody had patience to wait the finishing; and then, what contributed to the awkwardness of the whole, was the right pavilion catching fire, and being burnt down in the middle of the show.'

Our legacy from these junketings, Handel's *Music for the Royal Fireworks*, performed at Vauxhall and Green Park, justifies them all.

Wolfe was not in London for these celebrations. The peace negotiations dragged on for six months after the preliminaries had been agreed: the treaty was not signed until October, and the formal celebrations did not take place in England until the following May. During the summer of 1748, the armies of both sides remained in camp. The time passed slowly, and it being evident that active service was at an end at least for the year, Wolfe tried to obtain leave of absence to travel in Europe. His request was not granted. He writes, angrily, to his mother,[42] 'There will be difficulties in everything that contradicts a principle or settled opinion, entertained amongst us, that an officer neither can, nor ought ever to be otherwise employed than his particular military functions. If they could beat men's capacities down, or confine their genius to that rule (to be observed with the expected nicety, so as to exclude all other attachments), no man would ever be fitted for a higher employment than he is in. 'Tis unaccountable that who wishes to see a good army can oppose men's enlarging their notions, or acquiring that knowledge with a little absence which they can't possibly meet with at home, especially when they are supposed masters of their present employment and really acquainted with it. In all other stations in life, that method is usually pursued which best conduces to the knowledge every one naturally wishes to have of his own profession.' Mrs. Wolfe had expressed some anxiety about his health and had sent him fifty pounds to be used to augment his diet. He sets her mind at rest: '. . . what is there one may not be forced to do, where the health is concerned, however averse to inclination? To repel the vapours (as my friend justly terms them), Jemmy Donnellan and I are obliged to have recourse to a couple or three good things every day, and some Bordeaux; the management of all which he has solely undertaken, and calls for my weekly partition. If Mr. Fox* knew how well we feed, and that sometimes the table for four is crowded, he would be jealous of our emoluments and censure our extravagance, refuse perhaps our arrears, and cut off the non-effectives.' His sense of humour was unimpaired by his disappointment, but the months passed slowly and he could find little to occupy his time. He saw as much as possible of the armies of the allies, but his interest seems not to have been shared by his fellow officers. 'It is really surprising,' he writes,[43] 'that in the multitude of the idle & the curious, it shou'd not enter into any of their Heads to be for once spectators at a military show, and amuse themselves some little time with a view of the variety of Troops that compose the three separate bodies in the Country. The English should accustom themselves to such sights, that they may be less at a loss, & act like men when anything new or extravagant presents itself, & that a Plaid, Whiskers, or a ruff Cap may not be esteem'd by them altogether terrible and invincible.' He had not forgotten the lessons of Falkirk.

November came at last, and with it orders for his return on leave to England. He spent Christmas with his parents in London and lost no time in renewing his courtship of Elizabeth Lawson. Whether his addresses were well received is not known, but they were not prolonged, for his leave was once again cut short by

* Henry Fox, Secretary at War.

66

orders to join his regiment. He had been waiting, without enthusiasm, for instructions to rejoin Barrell's in Inverness in his permanent rank of captain; but on 5th January, and no doubt thanks to the influence of the Duke of Cumberland, he was gazetted major in Lord George Sackville's Regiment, the Twentieth Foot. * Towards the end of the month, he left London to join his new regiment in Stirling.

* The Lancashire Fusiliers.

CHAPTER V

Scotland: Command of a Regiment

AFTER the suppression of the '45 rebellion, the Government in London had enacted a number of repressive measures designed not only to destroy the feudal clan system but also to crush the spirit of the Scottish people. A stern determination to prevent a revival of Jacobite pretensions was both reasonable and prudent, but the measures taken were harsh and vindictive, and punishment was heaped indiscriminately upon innocent and guilty alike. The problem was one which has faced the conqueror in all periods of history: the destruction of old loyalties and the establishment of new in their place. In Scotland, success hinged on the enforcement of four principles: the forfeiture to the crown of the rebel estates; the oath of allegiance; prohibition of Highland dress and the bearing of arms; and the abrogation of the powers of the clan chiefs. This last was the root of all the troubles. Their power was vested in two accepted prerogatives: ward-holding and hereditary jurisdiction. By the first they could command military service as a condition of tenancy, and by the second they were empowered to judge and punish all offenders in their own courts without regard to the laws of the land. These powers were abolished by acts of parliament in May and June 1747. Of these Horace Walpole had written,[44] 'We are taken up with the Scotch bills for weakening clanships and taking away heritable jurisdictions. I have left sitting on it today, but was pleased with a period of Nugent. "These jurisdictions are grievous, but no body complains of them; therefore, what? therefore they are excessively grievous".'

The task was no easy one. For Wolfe it was made no easier by the fact that he found himself, at the age of twenty-two, virtually in command of his new regiment. The Colonel of the Twentieth was Lord George Sackville, third son of the Duke of Dorset, and at that time colonels of regiments seldom served with them; Sackville, unlike many colonels, was young, but he did not worry himself unduly with regimental duties and the welfare of his men. He adopted the accepted practice of leaving such work to his lieutenant-colonel, the Hon. Edward Cornwallis. At the time of Wolfe's appointment, Cornwallis was preparing to leave the regiment to take up the duties of Captain-General and Governor of Nova Scotia and, when he went, Wolfe would be left in command until a successor was named.

In his notebook, Wolfe recorded the General Orders, dated 22nd December 1748, which were to serve as his guide in implementing government policy in Scotland. The first was designed to suppress smuggling, and ordered the army to assist 'the Excise or Custom House Officer' in his duties by seizing 'run goods' and preventing 'an illicit trade being carried on, so prejudicial to His Majesty's Revenue and the fair trader.' In the three years since Culloden, the army in Scotland, reduced to a minimum because of commitments in Europe, had proved inadequate for the task of imposing law and order on the Scottish people. The turbulent state of the country was made clear in the orders for the apprehension of Jacobite supporters: 'As several disaffected and suspected persons are in the neighbourhood of your quarters, you are, as far as you are able, to enquire them out and keep a watchfull eye over all their motions, and if you should have any reason to suspect that they are carrying on any designs against His Majesty's Person or Government, you are, according to the urgency of the affair, to acquaint "the Commander-in-Chief" with the particulars you may be able to learn, either by express or the post.' The ministers of the church who refused to take the oath of allegiance or pray for the King in church were to be summarily dealt with: 'As the spirit of Jacobitism and disaffection is kept alive by Papist Priests and Non-juring Ministers, and as these people are originally and principally the cause of all the Evil proceeding therefrom, you are to be very alert in enquiring them out, and whenever you shall find any of them associating to more than the number prescribed by Act of Parliament,

69

immediately seize them, procure proof of their having so associated, and carry them before the Civil Magistrate, or next Justice
of the Peace, in order to their being committed to prison and
suffering as the Act directs.' The prohibition of Highland dress
and the carrying of arms was to be rigidly enforced: 'As the dis-
arming act was this summer carried into execution. . . . Whenever
you shall find any person carrying arms who is not qualified by
law, or by warrant by me so to do, you are immediately to seize
him and carry him before the Civil Magistrate. . . . The wearing
and use of . . . the plaid, philibeg, or little kilt, is absolutely
prohibited and abolished from and after the 25th day of this
instant December. . . . In obedience to these His Majesty's
commands, you are to seize all such persons as shall be found
offending herein, by wearing the plaid, philibeg, or little kilt, and
carry them before a Civil Magistrate in the same dress, that he
may be convinced with his own eyes of their having offended.'
Evidently some civil magistrates showed an unbecoming lack of
enthusiasm for their duties, for the orders continue: 'but in case
the magistrate before whom such offenders are carried shall refuse
or neglect putting the law into execution, in that case let me know
immediately the name of such magistrate, with the reason of his
not doing it.' But the occupying army was nevertheless reminded
that, 'In execution of all or any of the above orders, or any which
you may hereafter receive, you are to take care that no person be
injured either in his person or property, on pain of the severest
penalties the civil or military authorities can inflict on the person
offending.'* The orders end dryly, 'You may acquaint the
magistrates and justices of the peace in your neighbourhood with
the contents of this letter, since it may be the means of inciting
them the more readily to perform their duty.'

To Wolfe, on his first evening with Sackville's, as he looked
down over Stirling from the regimental headquarters in the castle,
the prospect must have appeared bleak. The dirty, dark and
narrow streets of the town with their squalid and too numerous
dram-shops, the instinctive reserve shown by officers to a new—
and young—commander, the difficulties of the army's task in

* The army in Scotland was experiencing the difficulties of the now familiar
semi-police role in 'aid to the civil power'. Neither the problems nor the methods
of dealing with them appear to have changed much in two hundred years.

70

Scotland, and, perhaps worst, the devitalizing cold, can have provided little that was friendly or welcoming for him. To his officers, the new major must have seemed something of an oddity: his tall and ungainly figure; the mop of red hair, crowning the ill-assorted features; the combination of extreme youth and veteran battle experience; and, strangest of all, his love of his profession; all combined to give them cause to wonder at the ineptitude of army appointments. Those who questioned his ability were not left long in doubt. Wolfe's standards were high, and it was soon made clear that the discipline and behaviour in the regiment fell far short of them. His first requirement was for a disciplined regiment; second only to that, and linked closely with it, was his care for the welfare of his men. The officers and non-commissioned officers were informed unequivocally of their duties, and were required to perform them with unaccustomed promptitude and efficiency. Extracts from Wolfe's orders from Stirling give some indication of his problems and his methods.

February 12th 1749.
'The Major recommends very particularly to the men to keep their quarters clean, as he is convinced that nothing conduces more to their health; the sergeants and corporals will in visiting the quarters daily give the necessary attention to this article.'

February 19th.
'In order to prevent all future attempts towards passing any false money the sentence of the court-martial to be put into execution against Samuel Hodgkinson, and Watkins the drummer. The major hopes it will effectively deter all men from such infamous and villainous practices; and he is determined to discourage as much as possible every act of knavery that may tend in the least to the discredit of the corps.'

February 24th.
'The soldiers are to avoid all kind of disputes with the inhabitants; and if at any time there should happen any tumult or riot, they are by no means to mix with the people of the town, or to be concerned with them. The officer of the guard is to order a detachment to seize any men who disobey these orders and to make them prisoners.'

71

March 27th.

'Every Subaltern Officer of a Company is to go round the Quarters of his Company at least once a week to see that they be kept clean and the orders obey'd. . . . When the Subaltern Officers have visited the Companies'. Quarters they are to report to the Captains, and if anything is wrong the Captains are desired to make it known to the Major. The Captains are likewise desir'd to enquire into the manner of the soldiers' messing and give orders that a sufficient part of their pay be laid out to provide victuals. . . .'

Unsuitable quarters were to be changed, guards to be properly regulated and supervised, regulations for dress were tightened up, and the old custom of allowing the soldiers to take part-time paid work to augment their pay was to be supervised by the officers so that the work should be suitable to the dignity of a soldier of Sackville's Regiment.

No doubt both officers and men deplored many of these changes, and the attention to detail demanded of them must have proved particularly irritating and arduous to officers accustomed to a normal, easy regimental life; but the new major, exacting as he was in matters affecting the welfare or efficiency of the regiment, showed himself to be also a human and likeable companion off-duty, with a keen sense of humour and a flair for putting people at their ease. By the time the regiment left Stirling his authority was established, but he had still much to do before the regiment would measure up to his standards, and officers and men accept him as their commanding officer.

Late in March, Sackville's was ordered to Glasgow. Wolfe welcomed this news; he was tired of Stirling and hoped to find in Glasgow more to occupy his men and his own mind. During the rebellion, the inhabitants of Glasgow had supported the Crown and had sent about five hundred men to join the royal army at Falkirk. This had been done not so much out of loyalty to the King as from practical considerations of their material welfare. Since the Union of Parliaments in 1707, Glasgow had benefited from the development of trade with the New England colonies: wool and linens from Glasgow in exchange for tobacco and other valuable commodities from Virginia and Maryland. This expansion of commerce had led to the growth of local industries and a significant increase in the population of the city which, at the time of Wolfe's arrival, numbered about twenty thousand. There were no barracks in the town and the regiment was consequently billeted out in private houses and inns. Wolfe lodged in a two-storey house in Camlachie which had been built in 1720 by John Walkinshaw, father of the Young Pretender's mistress.

As soon as the regiment was settled in its new quarters, Wolfe turned his attention to the improvement of his education. He had left school for the army at an unusually early age and was anxious to make up the resulting deficiencies in his knowledge. Already he had learned that an ill-educated officer was at a disadvantage among his fellows and also in the society in which he hoped to mix. There was a good college in Glasgow—since grown into the famous University—and Wolfe made arrangements for two hours' private tuition each day in Latin and mathematics. To his close friend, Captain William Rickson, then stationed in Ireland, he confides his view of Glasgow and its people:[45] 'The Men here are civil, designing & Treacherous, with their immediate Interest always in View; they pursue Trade with warmth & a necessary mercantile Spirit arising from the Baseness of their other qualifications. The women, coarse, cold & cunning, for ever enquiring after men's circumstances.' In the same letter he tells his friend of his feelings for Elizabeth Lawson:

'You shall hear, in justice, & in return for your Confidence that I am not less smitten than yourself: the Winter we were in London together I sometimes saw Miss Lawson, the Maid of Honour, G: Mordaunt's Niece, she pleased me then, but the Campaign in view, Battledore & dangerous, left little thought for Love. The last time I was in Town, only three weeks, I was several times with her, sometimes in Publick, sometimes at her Uncle's, & two or three times at her own house. She made a surprising progress in that short time, & won all my Affections: Some People reckon her handsome, but I, that am her Lover, don't think her a Beauty; She has much sweetness of Temper, sence enough, & is very civil & engaging in her behaviour; she refus'd a Clergyman with £1300 a year, & is at present address'd to by a very rich Knight, but to your Antagonist's* misfortune,

* Wolfe often used the word 'antagonist' to mean friend.

73

he has that of being mad added, so that I hold him cheap. In point of Fortune, she has no more than, at the Market, I have a right to expect, viz. £12,000; the Maid is tall & thin; about my own Age, & that's the only objection! I endeavour'd, with the assistance of all the Art I was master of, to find out, how any Serious proposal, wou'd be received by Mordaunt & her Mother. It did not appear that they wou'd be very averse to such a Scheme; but as I am but 22 & 3 months, it is rather early for that sort of Project, and if I don't attempt her, somebody else will; the Girl knows her own Interest, & I dare say, has very just notions of my Active Vigour. The General & Mrs. Wolfe are rather against it, from other more interested Views, as they imagine; they have their Eye upon one of £30,000.* If a company in the Guards is bought for me, or I should be happy enough to purchase any Lt. Colonel's commission within this twelve month, I shall certainly ask the question, but if I'm kept long here, the Fire will be extinguished. Young Flames must be constantly fed, or they'll evaporate. I have done with this subject, & do you be silent upon it.'

At a time when lack of money with which to buy promotion could ruin a peacetime army career, Wolfe's parents were inclined to view any proposed match for their son from the accepted financial standpoint. Wolfe was a realist, and honestly admitted the advantages of a good dowry, but he was not prepared to put such a consideration above all others.

From his orders to the regiment it is evident that there were still many problems on his hands. As he admits to Rickson,[46] 'These are all new men to me, and many of them but of low mettle.' He had some good officers, among them Captain Lewis Bouchetiere, Lieutenant 'Billy' Billing, Alexander McDowell, and Peter 'Bardolph' Hennis, with whom he made friends, but others needed constant reminders of their duties as extracts from his orders show.

April 9th.
'All officers are to examine every return brought to them with the greatest care, that they may not sign an improper one by

* Miss Hoskins of Croydon.

mistake. . . . When officers go round the quarters they are to observe the condition of the sick men, and if any thing is wanting, or that they are not kept clean, proper directions are to be given.'

June 1st.

'The major desires that none of the officers will oblige him by their behaviour to give out any orders that may relate particularly to them; and hopes they will avoid all quarrels and disputes with the inhabitants, which must necessarily tend to their discredit and create mischief; as may plainly be perceived from what has already happened.'

No detail escaped him; no fault in administration, if it affected the welfare of his men, was too trivial for his attention. Sport was encouraged, and the regiment kept its own pack of hounds. There was also some shooting and fishing to be had, but it was made clear that poaching was not to be countenanced: 'The soldiers are not to fish in gentlemen's ponds or locks without permission.' Wolfe, himself, found time for some hunting, and sent to London for his guns so that he could join in the local shoots. In June the regiment distinguished itself in a serious fire in the Gorbals district of the town and, besides fighting the fire and preventing the theft of property saved from it, subscribed generously to a fund for those who had lost their homes or possessions. The stern discipline exerted by Wolfe over the regiment and his evident desire to prevent trouble between his men and the inhabitants of the town soon brought him friends among the people of Glasgow. In April he was able to write to his mother, 'This place is very far from being so disagreeable as it appear'd at first. The Ladies are very civil, & in great numbers, and they are not so desperately afraid of a Soldier as formerly. The Inhabitants still retain all the Religion they ever had, I dare say, with rather less outward ostentation and mockery of Devotion, for which they are justly remarkable.' In religion, as in all things, he set an example to his men: 'I do several things in my character of Commanding Officer which I should never think of in any other, for instance, I'm every Sunday at the Kirk, an example justly to be admired. I would not lose two hours of a day if it did not answer some end. When I say lose two hours, I must explain to you that the generality of Scotch Preachers are excessive Blockheads, so truly & obstinately

75

dull, that they seem to shut out knowledge at every entrance; they are not like our good folks, ours are Priests, & tho' Friends to *venaison*, they are Friends to Sense.' It is clear, however, that he did not receive the support he expected from his officers, and when, in July, Lord George Sackville visited the regiment, he issued an order making the Colonel's wishes clear: 'It is hoped that decency and a proper sense of their duty will for the future prevail upon the officers to attend divine service, that the commanding officer of the regiment may not be obliged to order them to march to church with their respective companies.' As might be expected, the officers found these rare qualities latent within them, and no further encouragement was needed.

Lord George Sackville's visit to the regiment was opportune: the appointment of a successor to Cornwallis as lieutenant-colonel could not be much longer delayed, and although Wolfe, in letters to his parents, expected that he would 'certainly have a Lieutenant-Colonel put in', he must have hoped that his own qualifications would not pass unnoticed. Sackville stayed with the regiment for a month and, during that time, began a lasting friendship with Wolfe for whose abilities he came to have a high regard. He saw that the young officer was far from well and suggested that three months' leave in London in the autumn would do much to restore his health and keep him in the public eye. Much as Wolfe longed for a break from his duties and from the Scottish climate, he hesitated to accept the offer. 'Lord George,' he writes to his mother on 19th July, 'talks of the necessity of keeping up my present acquaintance amongst the Heads of our Trade and procuring new ones that may be of use. I have no turn that way.' Sackville's visit took much of the responsibility from his shoulders and he was sorry to see him leave, particularly as it appeared to be unlikely that he would return. Wolfe had little idea who would succeed him and feared that 'unless Col. Conway* falls to our share among many that solicit, none will be found that can in any manner make amends for the loss of him.'[47] He was conscious of the strain of command, and he dreaded the appointment of a colonel who would interfere with the regiment without being prepared to share the responsibilities of it. He was conscious

---

* Henry Seymour Conway (1721–1795), a protégé of Horace Walpole's and nephew to Sir Robert Walpole.

also of his youth and lack of experience, and he approached his own responsibilities with humility. 'You can't conceive,' he writes to his mother,[48] 'how difficult a thing it is to keep the Passions within bounds, when authority & immaturity go together; to endeavour at a character that has every opposition from within, & that the very condition of the blood is a sufficient obstacle to. Fancy you see one, that must do justice to both good & bad; reward & punish with an equal unbiass'd hand; one that is to reconcile the severity of Discipline to the Dictates of humanity; one that must study the Tempers & Dispositions of many men, in order to make their situation easy & agreeable to them; & should endeavour to oblige all without partiality; a mark set up for everybody to observe and judge of; & last of all, suppose me employed in discouraging Vice & recommending the reverse at the turbulent age of 23, when it is possible I may have as great a propensity that way as any of the men I converse with!' The wife of one of his sergeants wrote to him in Glasgow:[49]

'Collonel—Being a true Noble harted Pittiful gentleman and Officer yᵉ worship will excuse these few lines concerning yᵉ Husband of yᵉ under sign'd Sergᵗ White who not from his own fault is not behaving as Hee should towards mee and his Family although good and faithfull untill ye middle of November last
                                        Anne White.'

The letter is endorsed in Wolfe's hand, 'The writer of the above is a most respectable young woman & wife of a former servant of Cornwallis's whom I have since endeavoured to wean from his Evill ways!'

In October the regiment was again ordered to move, and on the 16th Wolfe led the march to new quarters in Perth. As in Glasgow, officers and men were billeted in the town in the absence of barracks to accommodate them. One of Wolfe's first orders after his arrival deals with the appointment of Sackville's successor: 'The King has been pleas'd to appoint the Right Honble. Lord Viscount Bury to be Colonel of this Regiment in the room of the Right Honble. Lord George Sackville promoted.' Wolfe cannot have welcomed this choice. Bury, son and heir to the second Earl of Albemarle, was an officer of fussy temperament

77

and no outstanding enthusiasm for his profession. As Cumberland's aide at Culloden he had shown himself to be not altogether without ability, but he owed his promotion to wealth and influence and it was unlikely that he would for long forsake the attractions of London for exile in Scotland. It was, in fact, the end of the following March before Bury ventured to visit his regiment and make the acquaintance of his officers. Until then he confined his attentions to letters of wearisome length and detail from the comfort of his house in London. 'My Colonel and I,' Wolfe writes on 31st January 1750, 'have a very exact correspondence. He is extreamly bent upon procuring all the knowledge of Regimental Affairs that the Distance between us will allow of, in order, I suppose, to make such alterations and amendments as seem requisite, & to be the better prepar'd against he comes amongst us. I answer his letters very punctually, & endeavour all in my power to satisfy him in such particulars as are properly within my Sphere; confining, however, my judgement of men & things to what is purely military & belonging to my office.'

In addition to his new colonel, Wolfe had other worries—his old servant, Roland, and the vacant lieutenant-colonelcy of his regiment. Roland had been with him for six years, behaving with great loyalty and courage at Laffeldt, but the Scottish climate had proved too severe for him: he became seriously ill, and after four months had passed without signs of improvement, Wolfe felt obliged to part with him.[50] 'At length we thought it would be better to get him into Chelsea, which I have endeavoured to do with the utmost of my power. . . . 'Twas death to me to part with him.' Later he writes[51] of him, 'He bore pretty well the warmth and uncertainty of my temper. . . . He has a wonderful calmness & quietness of disposition, that I sometimes thought degenerated into stupidity. I hardly ever knew him to give offence to any but myself—& then perhaps I was as much to blame as he.' The vacant lieutenant-colonelcy was always in his mind; there was a growing possibility that it might not be given to an outsider, but that Wolfe would himself be promoted. He thought that Cumberland would favour such an appointment, and his father and Lord George Sackville were using their influence with the Duke to bring it about. Lord Bury, as his new colonel, gave him little assistance. 'The words of Lord Bury's two last letters seem calculated to make me imagine his Lordship wishes me success, at the same time that they express his diffidence of it; I am not able to extract enough of his real opinion, to determine whether I am, or am not, to be his Lieu^{t.} Colonel, he says indeed, that the Duke is our friend, but does not affirm that he won't be prevail'd upon, to give up this point. Lord George Sackville sent me . . . the strongest assurances of his aid and service. As I know he is very sincere, I rely chiefly upon him. Whatever way the business turns, I shall be glad to know from you who the Persons are that seem the most to concern themselves in it; that I may thank them for their endeavours whether they succeed or not.' This letter was written on 23rd March. Less than a week later, Bury arrived on his first visit to the regiment, and on the 29th Wolfe was informed of his promotion to lieutenant-colonel in Bury's Regiment of Foot. Less than three months earlier he had celebrated his twenty-third birthday.

One other matter weighed on his mind: this was the disclosure of a major disagreement with his parents about Elizabeth Lawson. Mrs. Wolfe made her objections to the attachment abundantly clear in her letters, and impressed upon her son the suitability of Miss Hoskins of Croydon who could add to her other charms the useful sum of £30,000 as a dowry. Wolfe was unimpressed.[52] 'My Lieutenant Partridge came by here a few days since, & delivered Miss Hoskins's compliments. He is her neighbour at Croydon, he tells me he thinks her a compleat Woman, & advises me (as a Friend) to make up to her. This is his counsel and manner in which he offered it. But he did not know Miss Lawson, he confessed that.' Failing to achieve her object by admonition and advice, Mrs. Wolfe unburdened herself of a number of unworthy innuendos about the lady's family and morals, ending triumphantly with the assertion that only illness prevented her immediate marriage. Wolfe replied with renewed avowals of his constancy:[53] 'Your opinion of Miss Lawson has inflam'd me anew; & you have exactly hit upon that part of her Perfection (her behaviour) that worked strongest upon me; for I have seen a hundred handsomer women before, & never was in love with one; how could you tell me that you lik'd her, & at the same time say her illness prevents her wedding? I don't think you believe she ever touch'd me at all, or you could never speak with so much indifference of her ill-Health and Marriage,—the only things in relation to that Lady that cou'd give me the least uneasiness; except that I thought you were averse to her, & even that you have taken care to clear up, by your approbation of her manners & Person, & by that means have left me absolutely destitute of all Relief.' Baffled, Mrs. Wolfe called on the General to use his influence and authority. His blunt sincerity met with no better success than his wife's oblique methods. Wolfe replied to him with courteous resolution:[54] 'Though I have frequently given you occasion to blame either my neglect or levity, I am not however conscious of ever having intended to give you any uneasiness by obstinacy, or perseverance in an Error.' To his mother, who maintained a disapproving silence, Wolfe wrote in March: 'I hope your long silence does not proceed from the continuance of your Indisposition, I had rather it shou'd have any other cause, tho ever so unpleasant to myself; I desire you to think that I have undergone sufficient punishment, & judge, by the pleasure it gives me to hear from you. I'm sure you would not wish that the Penalty shou'd exceed the crime.' There the matter was allowed to rest until Wolfe went on leave at the end of the year.

Meanwhile the regiment once more claimed his attention. Wolfe was always concerned with the health of his men. Perth evidently provided many temptations, and it was clear that the too frequent recourse to dram-shops and the women of the town was having a demoralizing effect. With characteristic directness, Wolfe's orders provide for the imprisonment of soldiers' wives who 'sutle or sell liquor' without leave. He observes 'that the worst and idlest soldiers are those that are most frequently in venereal disorders, by which they are incapable of serving, and their duty is done by better men; he therefore thinks they should suffer for their intemperance; and orders that 6s. be paid for the cure of the pox, and 4s. for the clap; which sum of money is to be employed in providing necessaries and conveniences for the hospital.' In May he finds it necessary once again to remind his officers of their duty: 'The shameful drunkenness observed among the men, on pay-days in particular, is thought in a great measure to proceed from their not putting in a proportion of their pay regularly into their messes: the officers are to remember they have been more than once required to be very exact in this part of their duty, and that there is a standing order in the regiment for frequently visiting the quarters and messes; they are likewise desired to consider that any neglect on their part brings the men to disorders and crimes, and consequently to punishment, which would be avoided by a proper care of them, and watch upon their conduct.' Punishments were more lenient than in many regiments but included imprisonment in 'the black hole' on bread and water at a rate of twopence a day, and being 'put into the dungeon in irons'. Wolfe was careful that recruits should not learn bad habits from the start, and instructed that they should be 'taught all parts of their duty with the utmost care' and 'quarter'd and to mess with good and honest soldiers, and by no means suffer'd to associate with such as are of a different character and known to be infamous.'

Bury left the regiment again in June, having refused all Wolfe's requests for leave. Wolfe had, however, managed to obtain a few days away from the regiment, drinking goat-whey as a cure for scurvy, from which he had suffered in Glasgow and which had made an unwelcome reappearance on his hands. He received some hospitality from local landowners and spent a few days with Lord Glenorchy at Balloch Castle. Lady Glenorchy was an old acquaintance of Mrs. Wolfe's and entertained him 'with all imaginable civility'. This was an improvement on his laborious studies of Latin and mathematics in Glasgow, which he had discontinued, partly no doubt from lack of opportunity to pursue them but partly also from lack of faith in their worth. As he had written to his mother on 8th September, 'I don't know how the mathematics may assist the judgement, but they have a great tendency to make men dull; I, who am far from being sprightly even in my gayity, am the very reverse of it at this time; I'm heavier in discourse, longer at a Letter, less quick at apprehension; & carry all the appearances of Stupidity to so great a height that in a little time they won't be known from the reality; and all this to find out the use & property of a crooked Line, which, when discovered serves me no more than a strait one; & does not make me a jot more useful or more entertaining, but, on the contrary, adds to the weight that nature has laid upon the Brain, & blunts the Organs.' His old friend George Warde had paid him a visit and

Wolfe 'could not help being astonished at the strength of his understanding.'[55] He stayed for four days and the two young officers found that they still had much in common. Warde was, however, handicapped by a pronounced stammer and was lacking in ambition. Wolfe considered that these defects and his natural 'indolence of temper' made him 'unfit to bear a heavy part in life.' He underrated his friend.

At the end of September, detachments out working on the roads were recalled and the regiment moved out of Perth to take up new quarters in Dundee. On the eve of their departure, Wolfe issued to his men an order which must have given him much pleasure to write: 'The Colonel is very well pleas'd with the appearance of the men that are come from Work, and with their performance this summer at the Roads, and thanks the Officers for the care they have taken of them, their diligence and activity. The sobriety and industry of the soldiers of that Detachment are very much for the credit of the Regiment, and must meet with general approbation.' Wolfe's methods were beginning to show results.

CHAPTER VI

'Passion and Disappointment'

DURING October 1750 Wolfe busied himself with re-equipping
and clothing his men for the winter in Scotland and finding for
them quarters in Dundee where the housing shortage was already
acute. Evidently the Jacobite sympathies of the citizens had not
been entirely suppressed for within a week of the regiment's
arrival a sentry was knocked down and wounded, and a reward
of ten guineas offered for the discovery of his assailant appears
to have been without effect. Wolfe had some severe observations to make in his next orders about men who fell asleep at
their posts, but showed his customary concern for young recruits
by ordering that they were 'when on centry to be plac'd nearest
the protection of the Guard.' He professed himself 'extremely
well pleas'd with the behaviour of the Five Companies since they
came to Town,' yet another sign that the regiment was being
licked into shape.

He was also busy with preparations for his leave: at the end of
September he had despaired of obtaining any relief from his duties
in Scotland, which had occupied him for twenty-one months
without a break, and had written to his mother,[56] 'I am delighted
to hear you say my Father has been so well this Summer. Am I
never to eat figs with him in his own garden? How readily could
I resign my military authority, and lay down my Command, for
the pleasure of walking with him upon the dry ground and
gathering his Fruit.' He had plans, if leave were granted, to go
abroad, to winter in Metz, and return along the Rhine into
Switzerland and through France and the Netherlands. His hopes
were once again dashed by the refusal of the Duke of Cumberland
to allow him to leave England. He was bitterly disappointed, for

his health was much improved and he considered himself 'hard as flint' and fit to travel anywhere. Philosophically he turned his attention to other interests and wrote at length to his friend Rickson, by then arrived in Nova Scotia to serve under Wolfe's former lieutenant-colonel, Cornwallis. 'You are happy in a Governour,' he writes from Dundee in October, '& he'll be happy, to have one near him, that can be so serviceable to him as you have it in your power to be. I dare say you are on good Terms together, and mutual aid will confirm your former Friendships. . . . I look upon his Situation as requiring one of his very way of thinking before all things else; for to settle a new Colony, Justice, Humanity & Disinterestedness are the high requisites; the rest follows from the excellent nature of our Government, which extends itself in full force to its remotest Dependency.'

Wolfe's curiosity about the colonies was insatiable, and, writing with a map in front of him, he goes on to ask innumerable questions, besides making clear the fact that he has already formed some definite opinions of his own.

'In what a State of felicity' (he continues to Rickson) 'are our American colonies compared to those of other Nations; & how bless'd are the Americans, that are in our neighbourhood, above those that border upon the French & Spaniards; a Free People cannot oppress, but Despotism & Bigotry find enemies among the most Innocent. It is to the eternal Honour of the English nation that we have help'd to heal the wound given by the Spaniards to mankind by their Cruelty, Pride & Covetousness; within the Influence of our happy government, all Nations are in Security: the Barrier you are to form will, if it takes place, strengthen ourselves, & protect & support all our adherents. . . .

. . . I beg you will tell me at large the condition of your Affairs & what kind of Order there is in your Community, the Notions that prevail, the method of administering Justice, the Distribution of Lands & their cultivation; the Nations that compose the colony and who are the most numerous; if under Military Government, how long that is to continue; & what Sect in religious affairs is the most prevailing. If ever you advise upon this last subject, remember to be moderate. I suppose the

Governour has some sort of Council, and shou'd be glad to know what it is composed of. The southern colonies will be concern'd in this settlement, & have probably sent you some able men to assist you with their advice, & with a proper plan of administration. Tell me likewise what climate you live in, & what soil you have to do with; whether the Country is mountainous & woody, or plain; if well watered.'

In the light of later events Wolfe's letter is a revelation of his understanding of international affairs and the importance of the American colonies in the grand strategy of England and France: an understanding all the more remarkable in a young officer of twenty-three when statesmen of Pelham's experience were showing a lukewarm interest in affairs in the west. Rickson did not answer this letter until the following year; and meanwhile Wolfe had left his regiment for his long-awaited leave.

At the beginning of November Wolfe rode into Edinburgh where he spent a couple of days before taking the stage-coach to Belford. On the 5th he travelled to Durham in a storm of wind and rain which flooded the rivers and delayed the coach, and thence on to York arriving, exhausted, at seven o'clock on the evening of the 6th. There he visited his 'Uncle Tin'—his mother's brother Tindal Thompson—and other relatives nearby. It was not until the 14th that he joined his parents at their house in London.

Wolfe's leave at home was not a success. Whether it was that Elizabeth Lawson scorned the attentions of a lieutenant-colonel on short leave from Scotland, preferring the gallantries of more polished suitors who could afford to neglect their military duties in favour of fashionable court life, or that Wolfe's disappointment at being denied the opportunity to travel abroad temporarily deprived him of his normal self-restraint and good sense, will never be known. All that is certain is that he had a serious quarrel with his parents which drove him from their house; he took to the streets and taverns of the city and spent his passion in a round of dissipation which so damaged his health that he was obliged to take to his bed, where he lay for some weeks, weak and ill, his mind filled with thoughts of remorse and self-reproach.

The reunion with his parents in London had brought to the surface again the old disagreement about Elizabeth Lawson. No

85

doubt Mrs. Wolfe again urged her son to pay court to the rich Miss Hoskins, but in this design she was frustrated by the announcement, soon after Wolfe's arrival in London, of that lady's engagement to John Warde, eldest brother of Wolfe's friend George, of Squerryes Court. Wolfe, perhaps to occupy his time elsewhere as much as for the interest he hoped to gain from it, took to attending debates in the House of Commons, and was in the House to hear the debate on the colonies. He was quick to remark the absence of any move to send reinforcements to America, and deplored the lack of enthusiasm shown by Pelham. As he wrote later to Rickson,[57] 'a Minister cool in so great an affair, it is enough to freeze up the whole; but perhaps there might be a concealed manœuvre under these appearances, as in case of accidents, "I am not to blame", "I was forc'd to carry it on", & so forth; in the meantime I hope they are vigorous in supporting our claims.' His excursions to Westminster were not enough to make him or his parents forget their differences. After a violent quarrel, Wolfe left their house. London offered many temptations to a young soldier with time to waste and some money to spend. Wolfe's long period of service in Scotland and the frustration of his passions made them all the more inviting. The lack of an efficient police system, the absence of adequate street-lighting, and the warren of twisting narrow lanes among fetid slums, made the poorer districts of London the plague-spots of England. Government measures to control the sale of gin were ineffectual because they could not be enforced, and it continued to be sold at a price within the reach of the poorest labourer. Drunkenness was common habit; the rookeries of the area between the Haymarket and Holborn were filled with brothels and twopence-a-night lodgings, dram-shops and gambling dens. In the more prosperous quarters the coffee-houses, presided over by amiable bawds, and the fashionable gaming houses served the same purpose for the well-to-do. To this unfamiliar world Wolfe turned for relief from pent-up frustration and disappointment. The experience was painful but salutary: his health suffered but his understanding benefited. He knew now the temptations to which his men were subjected; and his own failure to resist them did much to temper his youthful intolerance and to mature his judgement.

Wolfe took formal leave of his parents at the end of March

1751 and rejoined his regiment, which had by then moved to the Jacobite centre of Banff. His health, although still far from good, was improving; the breach with his parents, however, was to take longer to mend. Banff pleased him no more than Stirling or Perth; the weather was bitterly cold and the population Jacobite and unfriendly. Wolfe had plenty of time for reading and for letter writing. To his parents he wrote lengthy apologies for his behaviour the previous winter. Evidently his father had written to him, pointing out the error of his ways in no uncertain terms, and Wolfe's reply leaves no room for doubt of his sincerity.

He writes on 12th June:

'Dear Sir,
I am very glad from the knowledge of your Sentiments (which in a case that concerns myself ought justly to be preferr'd to my own, & indeed in almost all other cases) to be able to make you some sort of apology for every particular instance of Vice or Folly that has very luckily fallen under your notice while I had the Honour to be near you. I say very luckily, for if you or some other perfect Friend had not discovered them, so as to make them known to me, I might have continued in the conceit of there being no such thing in my composition, & consequently they must in time have taken very deep root, & increased beyond the Power of any Remedy. Yours is a very lively picture of the Impertinence and Idleness that is often perceived in People of my years, so that it is not quite new & unexpected; and if I don't mistake, this is not the first time that you have observ'd the Seeds of Imperfections in me, that perhaps only wanted nourishment & proper occasion to break forth. I'm quite persuaded (tho' you express some indifference in the latter part of your letter) that you mean to recover me from the ill Habit of Mind you have seen me in, & with that View and that only, it is, that the just remarks you have made upon my conduct are put in their proper light. I am sure at the same time that your course of goodness & Indulgence to me is not entirely altered & that you are ready to make such allowances as may be expected from one who has so extensive a knowledge of mankind as you have.

The Respect I have for you & strong desire to be better in your opinion than I've been of late, will put me upon pursuing the

87

best means that you can devise, or that I can imagine for such an alteration of behaviour as may conduce to that end—I believe the first step to amendment is to acknowledge our Faults, a proof that we think them Faults. This I do very heartily & truly, tho' I must assert that most of them have arisen from inadvertency, & not from any ill Intention. I am very sensible that many things have appeared with an exceeding bad Grace; but am nevertheless quite clear and conscious that no offence ever was, or cou'd be, meant.

My Mother told me you intended to write, I was desirous to know your thoughts (which I am sorry to say I have been but too often unacquainted with) and that is one reason why I left such an Interval between asking your pardon in the short, tho' sincere manner in which I did it, when I came away, & making all the submission that can be made to one that I am very unwilling to disoblige. I hope the former part of my Life will in some measure make this appear; and I believe I may venture to say that my future conduct will help to convince you. . . .

. . . The warm Expressions that fell from me upon the Duke's refusing to let me go abroad, savour'd much of Ingratitude; & the words, it must be confess'd, were arrogant and Vain. I thought them so at the time of speaking; Passion and Disappointment produced them; Certainly H.R.H. could not have so truly convinced me of his kindness as by consenting to a reasonable & salutary request. For if Eternal Imprisonment and Exile is to follow Preferment, few will be thankful for the Favour.'

Mrs. Wolfe did not write again until July, and then only briefly. Wolfe writes to try to placate her.[58] 'I began to give up all hopes of hearing from you, & to think myself exiled to all intents and purposes without the consolation of being so much as thought of in this state of bondage & confinement. . . . Your letter, short as it is—unusually so, has nevertheless been of great aid & Relief—because it convinces me, that tho' deservedly neglected, I am not entirely forgot, alienated or divided from you, as of no further concern.' To these blandishments Mrs. Wolfe remained deaf.

Wolfe's one consolation at this time was his correspondence with Rickson, who had written answering his many questions about Nova Scotia and the American colonies. Within an hour of receiving Rickson's letter, Wolfe sat down to answer:[59] 'I have (as you justly acknowledge) a perseverance in Friendship that Time nor Distance, nor Circumstance can defeat—nay, even neglect can hardly conquer it; & you are just as warm & near me in North America, as you wou'd be upon the spot.' He acknowledges Rickson's congratulations on his promotion to lieutenant-colonel in the previous year and adds, 'I believe you are of opinion with me, that a great deal of good Fortune has fallen to my share already.' Wolfe has some prophetic observations to make on Rickson's answers to his questions about the settlement: 'I conclude your Post will be greatly improv'd; & instead of the shallow Works that you describe, something substantial will be erected, capable of containing a large Garrison, with inhabitants train'd to arms, in expectation of future Wars with France; when I forsee great attempts to be made in your Neighbourhood. When I say thus, I mean in North America.' 'Yours,' he continues, 'is now the dirtiest as well as the most insignificant & unpleasant branch of Military Operations; no room for Courage & Skill to exert itself, no hopes of ending it by a decisive blow, & a perpetual Danger of Assassination; these Circumstances discourage the firmest Minds; Brave men, when they see the least room for conquest, think it easy, & generally make it so; but they grow Impatient with perpetual disadvantages. . . . I shou'd imagine that two or three independent Highland Companies might be of use, they are hardy, intrepid, accustom'd to a rough Country, and no great mischief if they fall. How can you better employ a secret enemy than my making his End conducive to the common good? If this sentiment should take wind, what an execrable & bloody being shou'd I be consider'd here in the midst of Popery & Jacobitism, surrounded on every side as I am with this Itchy Race.'*

Whether, as seems likely, Wolfe was the originator of the scheme to raise the Highland regiments or not, it was adopted by Pitt at the outset of the Seven Years War in 1756; and ten years later Pitt was able to say, 'I sought for merit wherever it was to be found. It is my boast that I was the first Minister who looked for it and found it in the mountains of the North. I called it forth and drew into your service a hardy and intrepid race of men, who,

* A form of skin disease known as 'Itch' was very common in eighteenth-century Scotland among all classes of society.

when left by your jealousy, became a prey to the artifices of your enemies, and had gone nigh to have over-turned the State in the war before the last. These men in the last war were brought to combat on your side; they served with fidelity, as they fought with valour, and conquered for you in every part of the world.'

Wolfe's stay in Banff did nothing to change his dislike of the Scots, and he looked upon himself as an exile:[60] 'With respect to the inhabitants I am so, for I dislike 'em much.' He read widely to 'try to help an indifferent education and slow faculties' and offered to send books to Rickson. He refers to his rejected plan to go abroad for his leave: 'I got powerful people to ask the Duke no less than three times, for leave to go abroad, & he absolutely refus'd me that necessary indulgence—this I consider as a very unlucky incident, & very discouraging; moreover he accompanied his denial with a speech that leaves no hopes—that a Lt: Colonel was an officer of too high a Rank to be allow'd to leave his regiment for any considerable time: this is a dreadful mistake, & if obstinately pursued, will disgust a number of Men of good Intentions, & preserve that prevailing Ignorance of military Affairs, that has been so fatal to us in all our undertakings, & will be for ever so, unless other measures are pursued. We fall every day lower & lower from our real characters, & are so totally engag'd in everything that is minute & trifling, that one wou'd almost imagine the Idea of War was extinguished amongst us; they'll hardly allow us to recollect the little service we have seen: that is to say, the Merit of things seem to return into their old Channel, & he's the Brightest in his profession that is the most Impertinent, talks loudest, and knows least.'

His experiences in London are referred to with brief candour: 'I went to London in November & came back in the middle of April, in that short time I committed more imprudent Acts than in all my Life before. I lived in the idlest, dissolute, abandon'd manner that can be conceiv'd; and that not out of Vice, which is the most extraordinary part of it—I have escap'd at length, & am once again Master of my Reason, & hereafter it shall rule my conduct—at least I hope so.'

Wolfe's attempts to pacify his parents continued, and in this his health came to his aid. Mrs. Wolfe could never resist a call on her medicine chest, and Wolfe began once more to suffer from the gravel, a bladder complaint which caused him much discomfort and at times considerable pain. He drank the waters at Peterhead for three weeks and obtained some relief, but found that they affected him 'very violently in the lungs and stomach' and left him with a 'fixed pain' in his chest. He consulted a doctor who advised the much used but barbarous remedy of soap, to be taken internally. On 12th August he writes to his mother,[61] 'I know you wou'd be glad to contribute something towards the cure of a bad disease, & perhaps I may put it in your power. Honey is recommended to me—if you get any from Minorca, & can send such a jar as I devoured in London, it will be doing a humane & benevolent act.' He continues, 'Our winter is begun already. I am writing before a great Fire. Dreadful season that lasts from the beginning of August till the middle of May!'

By September it seemed that the reconciliation with his parents was complete. The Wolfes had moved from Burlington Street to a large house in Blackheath, and Wolfe took a lively interest in all the details of their new home. He asked humbly that there might be for him 'a very hard bed, upon which I hope to extend my long Limbs in 12 or 14 months, & take a little rest from care.'[62] He ends this letter to his mother on a note of light appeasement: 'I hope to hear from you now and then; you shall always be as short or as long as you please. Only remember that one side is very agreeable, but four sides, four times as agreeable, and so on in proportion.'

At the end of the month, the regiment was ordered to the Highland capital, Inverness, to make room for two regiments which had returned from Gibraltar. They came, as Wolfe told Rickson, 'from the hottest immediately to the coldest part of the King's dominions', bringing with them one of Wolfe's oldest friends, Captain Arthur Loftus who, with Rickson, had been wounded at Fontenoy six years earlier. Loftus was recovering slowly from a serious illness and with characteristic vagueness invited Wolfe to visit him at once from Inverness. Wolfe writes indulgently to his father,[63] 'it is about a hundred miles through the Highlands. One would think my friend Arthur did not know the carte du pays.' Quite evidently he did not. Wolfe was far too busy with his regiment to make the journey, and it was not until the following summer that the two friends were able to meet.

CHAPTER VII

Scotland: Inverness

WOLFE'S first impressions of Inverness were far from favourable. Always quick to praise or to condemn, he lost no time in passing judgement on the inhabitants of the Highland capital. 'A little while', he writes to his father[64] a few days after his arrival, 'serves to discover the villainous nature of the Inhabitants, and brutality of the People in its neighbourhood: those too, who pretend the greatest attachment to the Government, & who every day feed upon the public purse, seem to distinguish themselves for greater rudeness & incivility than the open and profess'd Jacobites.' Later in the month he adds, 'Besides the multitude of evils that this Town contains we have the additional mortification that the country about us affords very little relief; no hunting or shooting,—both healthy and manly diversions & that I take great delight in; instead of these, I ride about for the fresh air and motion; but when the Snows fall, we shall have little to do but to eat and sleep. I wonder how long a man (moderately inclined that way) would require, in a place like this, to wear out his Love for Arms, and soften his Martial Spirit. I believe the Passion would be something diminish'd in less than ten years; & the Gentleman be contented to be a little lower than Caesar in the list, to get clear of the Incumbrances of greatness.'

His rides took him to the scene of Culloden, and from his widened military experience he was able to draw some critical conclusions from the conduct of the battle as he remembered it. 'The Actors shine in the world too high and bright to be eclipsed; but it is plain they don't borrow much of their Glory from their performances upon that occasion, however they may have distinguished themselves in later Events.' But he is conscious of being wise after the event and criticizes only 'to exercise the faculty of judging. . . . The more a soldier thinks of the false steps that are gone before, the more likely is he to avoid them; on the other hand, the examples worthiest of imitation should never be lost sight of.'

Even the relaxation of riding was soon to be denied to him. The winter set in early and Wolfe warned his mother that his letters might be delayed:[65] ' 'Tis very possible that the snows will retard the march of our Highland Post Boy, who in the finest seasons, cannot pride himself on much expedition: the Winds sometimes drive the Snows with such violence that the roads are utterly impassable, & again, when it thaws, the rivers swell so prodigiously that there is no less danger & difficulty on that side.'

He tried to be cheerful about his new surroundings but he could find little to merit favourable comment: the weather was miserably cold, his food and lodging poor, and his fire inadequate. He writes soberly of 'these little evils', adding, 'whoever finds these inconveniences too hard to put up with will never be a match for a multitude of others that he is likely to meet with in his travel through life, especially if he has taken the trade of war.' Having little else to occupy his time, he wrote long letters to his parents, read what books he could obtain, and renewed his study of mathematics under the tuition of a Mr. Barbour. He spent an unfestive Christmas:[66] 'We had no other way of distinguishing Christmas than that we found it, as it commonly is, the coldest time of the year, & made a larger Fire than usual, & eat exceeding bad mince-pieces that our sutler's wife, who is a very religious woman, begg'd we might taste.' On his birthday he yielded to one of his recurrent moods of depression, and poured out to his mother the effects of his boredom and introspection:

'The winter wears away, so do our years, & so does Life itself; and it matters little where a man passes his days, & what station he fills, or whether he be great or inconsiderable; but it imports him something to look to his manner of Life. This day am I five-and-twenty years of age, & all that time is as nothing; when I am fifty (if it ever happens so) & look back, it will be the same; & so on

93

to the last hour. But it is worth a moment's consideration tha one may be called away on a sudden, unguarded & unprepared; and the oftener these thoughts are entertain'd, the less will be the dread or fear of Death. You'll judge by this sort of discourse, that it is the dead of night, when all is quiet and at rest, and one of those intervals wherein men think of what they really are, & what they really should be: how much is expected, & how little perform'd. . . . We are so mixed & compounded that tho' I think seriously this minute, and lie down with good intentions, it is likely I may rise with my old nature, or perhaps with the addition of some new Impertinence, & be the same wandering lump of idle Errors that I have ever been. You certainly advise me well. You have pointed out the one only way where there can be no disappointment, & comfort that will never fail us—carrying men steadily & chearfully in their journey, & a place of rest at the end. Nobody can be more persuaded of it than I am; but Situation, Example, the current of things, & our natural weakness draw me away with the herd, & only leave me just strength enough to resist the worst degrees of our Iniquities. There are times when men fret at Trifles, & quarrel with their Tooth-picks. . . .

You bid me avoid Fort William, because you believe it still worse than this place, that will not be my reason for wishing to avoid it, but the change of conversation, the fear of becoming a mere Ruffian, & of imbibing the tyrannical Principles of an absolute Commander, of giving way insensibly to the temptations of power, till I become Proud, Insolent, and Intolerable;—these considerations will make me wish to leave the Regiment before the next winter, and always (if it could be so) after eight months' duty; that by frequenting men above myself I may know my true condition; and by discoursing with the other sex may learn some Civility and mildness of Carriage; but never pay the price of the last improvement with the loss of reason—better be a Savage of some use than a gentle, amorous Puppy, obnoxious to all the world. One of the wildest of wild clans is a worthier being than a perfect Philander.'

It was not often that Wolfe permitted himself to set down his thoughts with such frankness. In the morning his natural reserve reasserted itself and he was tempted to burn his letter; but, after some thought, and an apology to his mother for his unusual gravity, he let it go.

To his father he writes, a week later, in a better humour, of his studies under Mr. Barbour:[67] 'I have read the mathematics till I am grown perfectly stupid, and have algebraically worked away the little portion of understanding that was allowed to me. They have not even left me the qualities of a coxcomb; for I can neither laugh nor sing, nor talk an hour upon nothing. The latter of these is a sensible loss, for it excludes a gentleman from all good company, & makes him entirely unfit for the conversation of the polite world.' With the state lottery he was more successful, and won a sum of money which enabled him to buy a French translation of Thucydides—'*our* historian—I speak as a soldier.'[68] This piece of good fortune, and the melting of the snows, raised his spirits and he wrote to his father, 'The spring that gives a new face to the whole creation, will enliven us all.' He had begun to make a few friends among the local population and speaks of an 'Assembly of Female Rebels every fortnight, entirely composed of Macdonalds, Frasers, & McIntoshes. I had the honour to dance last with the daughter of a chieftain who was kill'd at Culloden, the Laird of Keppoch;* they are perfectly wild as the Hills that breed 'em, but they lay aside their principles for the sake of sound and movement.' He was also a frequent visitor at Culloden House as the guest of John Forbes, only son of the famous Lord President of the Court of Session, Duncan Forbes. Mrs. Forbes, in spite of ill-health, was particularly kind to the young lieutenant-colonel and in later years he often asked his friends serving in Scotland for news of her.

He had also, as he confides to his mother,[69] 'fallen into the acquaintance (by mere chance) of two young Scotch ladies, with whose conversation I am infinitely delighted. . . . I speak of these ladies to show that we should not despair, and that some satisfaction may be found even where it is least expected.' But though he confessed[70] to 'a certain turn of mind that favours marriage prodigiously. . . . I love children & think them necessary to our latter days', he admitted that there was a 'great probability' that

* Alexander Macdonald of Keppoch was killed at Culloden advancing alone against the King's troops after his clan, with two others, had left the field without engaging the enemy and in revenge for the insult they had suffered by being placed at the left of the Jacobite line.

he would never marry: 'I shall hardly engage in an affair of that nature purely for money: nor do I believe that my infatuation will ever be strong enough to persuade me that people can live without it: besides, unless there be violence done to my inclinations by the power of some gentle nymph, I had much rather listen to the drum and trumpet than any softer sound whatever.'

The regiment, despite the lack of suitable recreation, behaved well in Inverness. Wolfe was quick to note this and to comment on it: 'It is with great satisfaction that the Lieut.-Colonel has receiv'd Reports from the Captains and Officers Commanding in the different Cantonments of the General good Behaviour of the Companies under their Order, of which he will not fail to acquaint Lord Bury when His Lordship joyns the Regim⁺ nor will he forget to mention how much reason he has to be pleas'd with the Companies at Inverness.' Bury's impending visit can have given little joy in anticipation to officers or men. His finicky mind and evident dislike for military service anywhere but in London had not gained him either popularity or respect. Wolfe had a low opinion of his colonel: 'Lord Bury professes fairly, and means nothing; in that he resembles his father, and a million other showy men that are seen in palaces and in the Courts of Kings.' He was expected in April. 'He'll stay six weeks,' Wolfe writes on 6th March, '& then swear there's no enduring it any longer, & beg leave to return.' There was some chance that he would stay until July for some shooting but this prospect was no more pleasing to his lieutenant-colonel than his early return to London:[71] 'Lord Bury likes his diversion, and so do I. He'll keep me to carry his powder horn and flints; and we shall ramble from post to post till he's tired and goes off, and then I shall retreat into Fort William and remain there until further orders.' He was mistaken: Bury could not bear to see so much of Scotland.

Bury's seniority rankled: Wolfe could see for himself how little promotion depended upon ability, and how much upon influence. As he wrote to his mother on 10th April: 'My success in that way depends upon events not to be wish'd or hoped for. I can only rise in War, by my willingness to engage in it—In these cooler times the Parliamentary Interest & weight of particular families annihilates all other pretensions; then I am amongst the youngest of my own Rank, and have had (as I mention'd before) as great

96

Favour shown me as I could with any modesty expect.' However, the weather had improved, and he was able to put away his books and get out into the country on horseback. He sent a large parcel of his books home: 'The weight grows too considerable for long journeys, & a few well chosen is a great Library for a Soldier.'

Bury arrived on 13th April and after reviewing his regiment, celebrated his second and last visit to the Twentieth in Scotland by an act of lunatic intolerance and arrogant discourtesy which did not endear him to the people of the Highland capital, who had been at some pains to receive him with a show of loyalty and goodwill. A deputation from the Provost and Councillors of the city waited upon him to request the honour of his presence at a celebration of the Duke of Cumberland's birthday on the 15th. Bury declined the invitation, saying that he was delighted to find the citizens so loyal and therefore had no doubt that they would wish, instead, to celebrate on the following day another occasion that would give the Duke even greater pleasure—the sixth anniversary of Culloden. The outraged deputation withdrew to consult their colleagues. The Council very rightly refused to celebrate the unhappy day on which so many of their townfolk and kinsmen had fallen, whereupon Bury refused to take responsibility for the behaviour of his men if they were disappointed by the cancellation of this celebration. The Council yielded to this brutal display of tyranny and the anniversary was duly commemorated. Wolfe can have felt small wish to rejoice at this setback to his patient and tactful handling of the predominantly Jacobite population.

Prospects of leave were uncertain: in his first letter since Bury's arrival, written on 23rd April to his father, Wolfe writes, 'His Lordship pays my attendance upon him with fair words & Promises, and he thinks it highly reasonable that my long confinement shou'd have an end, tho' he is far from being sure of the Duke's consent. I tell him the matter of fact; that when I feel any extraordinary restraint, & am kept longer with the Reg* than is equitable, I hate the sight of a soldier.' In May he was able to write to his mother, 'Lord Bury first advised me not to ask leave of absence; but afterwards he changed his opinion. I have reason to think that it will not be refused.' However disinclined Bury might

97

be to grant Wolfe's request, he had no wish to lose altogether so industrious and capable a lieutenant-colonel: he thought it prudent to recommend his leave, and it was granted.

Wolfe's health was much improved: better, indeed, as he told his mother, than it had been since he returned to Scotland in March of the previous year. He had been deaf in his right ear since his illness in London, but had now recovered his hearing and, but for breaking 'a fine large tooth all to pieces', was 'extremely well'. He talks of replacing the broken tooth:[72] 'At Paris they put in artificial teeth that are every way as serviceable as the natural ones, & perhaps they may do the same in London. I see no harm in repairing any loss of this kind, as we really can't eat or speak properly without them. . . . We have this comfort, that a Leg, an Eye, or a Tooth lost, does not necessarily carry away with it any one good Quality. We can be as Charitable, as Liberal, & as honest, wanting any of these members as with them. There is an old General mentioned in History that had but one left of what everybody else has commonly two; & yet with one leg, one arm, one eye and one ear, he was, for a drunken man, the best Officer of his Day.'*

About the middle of May, Bury and Wolfe led the Twentieth from Inverness to new quarters at Fort Augustus, arriving on the 18th. The fort had been built on the recommendation of General Wade after the suppression of the 1715 rising as a link between the old Fort George at Inverness and Fort William. After the '45 it had become customary to use it as summer headquarters for detachments patrolling the country. Soon after their arrival, Bury left for Fort William, on his way to London, and the companies were dispersed to outposts or on patrols, leaving Wolfe with about eight officers and less than a hundred men, of whom the majority were recruits. 'I can't find work enough to employ me here,' he writes to his father on 28th May, 'and as the weather is tolerably fair, will visit some of our Posts, & perhaps accept an invitation from the Laird of Macleod, who offers to show me a very extraordinary old castle in the Isle of Skye.' In the same letter he refers to what has since become known as one of the great unsolved crimes of history, the Appin murder. 'You have heard,' he writes, 'of the strange murder that was committed

* Josias von Rantzau of Holstein (1609–1650).

about a fortnight since by two Highlanders, at the instigation, it is believed, of a Lady, the wife of a banished Rebel. The Gentleman was an Argylshire man, and factor upon some of the Forfeited Estates. Several men are apprehended upon suspicion, but I'm sure it will be very difficult to discover the actors of this bloody deed. The Factor intended to remove the bad tenants & to plant others in their room, and this is suppos'd to be their reason for killing him.' The murder, used more than a century later by Stevenson for his novel *Kidnapped*, was another example of the unsettled state of the Highlands six years and more after Culloden. Further signs of unrest were to be uncovered later in the year, during Wolfe's absence abroad, by the betrayal of the Elibank plot to restore the Stuart succession.

Wolfe's leave was due towards the end of June, but before he left he had one task to carry out: this was nothing less than a plan to capture Ewen Macpherson of Cluny, appointed by the Young Pretender, in his flight from Scotland, to guard the French gold known as the Loch Arkaig hoard, and to act as paymaster to active Jacobite supporters. Wolfe's plan, revealed in a letter to Rickson written from Exeter nearly three years later, was ruthless and inhuman, and it is astonishing to find it coming from a man whose humanity and consideration for his men were to help to make his name known throughout the Army long before he achieved glory in battle. 'Mr. McPherson,' he writes on 7th March 1755, 'shou'd have a couple of hundred men in his Neighbourhood, with orders to massacre the whole Clan if they show the least Symptom of Rebellion. They are a warlike Tribe and he is a cunning, resolute fellow himself, they should be narrowly watch'd; and the party there shou'd be well commanded. . . . I tried to take hold of that famous man with a very small detachment—I gave the sergeant orders (in case he should succeed, & was attack'd by the Clan, with a view to rescue their chief) to kill him instantly which I concluded would draw on the destruction of the Detachment; and furnish me with a sufficient pretext (without waiting for any instructions) to march into their country ou j'aurois fait main basse, sans misericorde & Je l'aurois brulé d'un bout à l'autre. Wou'd you believe that I am so bloody? t'was my real intention: & I hope such execution will be done upon the first that revolt, to teach 'em their duty, & keep the Highlands in awe.

They are a people better govern'd by fear than favour.' His intention to 'draw on the destruction of the whole detachment' in order to make a pretext for pillaging the countryside which had sheltered Cluny is indefensible and unworthy of him. It is fortunate for his reputation that the plan failed, for success in such an operation would have disgraced even a Hawley. It was one of his last actions before his leave, and served to show how much he needed a break from duty in the disaffected Highlands and an interlude, however brief, in more civilized and congenial company.

CHAPTER VIII

On leave in Paris

WOLFE had decided to spend part of his leave in Ireland, visiting his uncle, Major Walter Wolfe, the favourite 'Uncle Wat' of his letters. He left Fort Augustus in mid-June and, inspecting the military post at Ruthven on his way, arrived on the 20th in Perth, where he spent four days with his friend Arthur Loftus. Earlier in the year Wolfe had commented on the preparation by Colonel Lafausille of 'a treatise of Discipline and Reflections upon the Government of Armies', and had remarked, 'I hope Loftus will add his Notes and Remarks, for the amusement of the public and great diversion of all his acquaintance.' Evidently illness had not affected his friend's high spirits, for Wolfe describes him as 'more humorous and pleasant than he used to be', and, failing to finish his letter to his mother from Perth, is obliged to cut it short in Glasgow because 'Loftus is by and makes such a noise that I must finish as quick as possible'.

During his three years in Scotland, little as he had enjoyed them, Wolfe had acquired some Scottish tastes: he had become particularly fond of outdoor pursuits, and, as he puts it,[73] 'nothing pleases me now but the rougher kind of entertainments, such as hunting, shooting and fishing; there's none of that kind near London, & I have distant notions of taking a little, very little house, remote upon the edge of the forest, or waste, merely for sport. . . .' He loved dogs, and had made arrangements, before he left Glasgow, for the delivery at Blackheath of a pointer, 'very ugly but very good', for which he asked his mother to find stable-room. He also asks 'another favour . . . and you'll think it an odd one; 'tis to order some currant jelly to be made in a crock for my use. It is the custom in Scotland to eat it in the morning with

bread; I find it not only a very pleasant custom but a very wholesome one.' Other preparations to be made for his return home
were the engagement of 'a good servant who can, or will learn to
dress a wig and save the prodigious expense in London,' and the
making of some more shirts which must be quite plain in order
to save the 'expense for fine ruffles'. It is clear that Wolfe was
finding it hard to make both ends meet without any income outside his pay. This can hardly have been due to extravagance: he
drank little, never gambled in the mess, and spent his leisure in
reading or in the outdoor exercise which he most enjoyed. No
doubt, also, he had been trying to save all he could to pay for his
leave, for he planned not only to visit Ireland and his parents at
Blackheath, but also to travel abroad. He had once more applied
for permission to visit the Continent and this time he planned to
stay in Paris. When he sailed from Portpatrick in Wigtown at the
end of June, he had still received no official reply to his request.

Wolfe arrived in Dublin on 12th July, after visiting Belfast and
Londonderry, and having examined the ground of the Battle of
the Boyne. 'I had,' he writes,[74] 'more satisfaction in looking at
this spot than all the variety that I have met with; & perhaps there
is not another piece of Ground in the world that I cou'd take so
much pleasure to observe.'

He found his uncle rheumatic or gouty—his physicians could
not decide which—but 'otherwise cheerful and well', and stayed
with him for four or five days. 'Uncle Wat' showed him the city,
and introduced him to Dublin society and his military friends in
Lucas's coffee-house. Wolfe was most favourably impressed:
'This appears to be a prodigious City & they continue to build,' he
writes on 13th July. 'The streets are crowded with People of a
large size & well limbed, & the women seem very handsome;
they have clearer skins, & fairer complexions than the women in
England or Scotland, and are exceedingly straight & well made;
you'll be surpris'd that I should know this so soon, but I have
seen a multitude already, for they take some pains to show themselves.' He went on to stay with relatives in Cork for a few days
and then sailed to Bristol, whence he made his way through the
west country to Blackheath.

His parents' neighbour in Blackheath, Lord Chesterfield, had
been active in promoting the change to the Reformed Calendar,

and it was during Wolfe's stay in Blackheath that the new method of dating was taken into use. By this change, England adopted the calendar used on the Continent: 3rd September 1752 became 14th September 1752 and the New Year was accepted as starting on 1st January instead of Lady Day, 25th March, as previously. Thus Wolfe, while staying with his parents, went to bed on the night of the 2nd and woke upon the morning of the 14th after no more than a single night's sleep. If this loss of eleven days' leave was a source of irritation to him, it was soon to be dispelled by the Duke of Cumberland's consent, given at the end of the month, to his application to go abroad. That Cumberland's permission, so long withheld, should suddenly be granted was probably due to the presence of Lord Bury's father, Lord Albemarle, in France as British Ambassador to the Court of Versailles. He could be relied upon to keep an eye on the young lieutenant-colonel and forestall any attempt that might be made to seduce him into the service of a foreign army.

On 2nd October Wolfe set out for Paris; he spent a night at Canterbury, and on the 3rd called on Lady Grey at Dover.* 'At her house,' he writes later to his father, 'I met a Miss Scott (whom my mother has heard of)—The good old lady diverted herself with us two, told each that the other was not married, offered her mediation, & thought it a very lucky Rencounter, for the Young Lady and I got to the house exactly at the same time. However, I escaped untouched, & left my old friend to make up matters as she pleased. . . .' He took the packet sailing at half past six on the 4th and reached Paris on the morning of the 7th after a rough crossing during which he was extremely sea-sick.

By the 9th he had already something to tell his father about his new surroundings: 'The People seem (as their Character is) to be very sprightly, & to deal largely in the exterior; for a man can hardly commit a greater crime than to be mal misé, ou mal coiffé. The Buildings are very magnificent, far surpassing any we have in London; I mean the Houses of the higher Nobility & Peers of France. The Gardens des Tuilleries, that you have heard so much of, is as disagreeable a sandy walk as one wou'd wish. They are indeed near the Seine & the Louvre, but have little else to recommend them. The Mall, or your Park at Greenwich, are infinitely

* Wife of Sir Henry Grey of Howick.

superior. There are no fortified towns between Calais & Paris; the Country is very beautiful in most Places, entirely in Corn, & quite open (where the woods allow it to be so) that is, there are few or no enclosures.' He wasted no time in calling on Lord Albemarle at Fontainebleau, where he was cordially received and when later in the month Albemarle visited his country-house near Paris, Wolfe was a frequent visitor. He met Philip Stanhope, natural son of Lord Chesterfield, and judged him ('not without some grounds') to be 'infinitely inferior to his father'.

He did not lack friends in Paris: Albemarle had introduced him to the young Duke of Richmond, who was later to serve in Wolfe's regiment, and they became firm friends. 'He promises,' Wolfe wrote of him to his father on 4th December, 'to make a considerable figure in our way, to which his genius seems to lead him, and what is uncommon at eighteen he is not entirely taken up with the outward appearances and gildings of soldiership but aims at the higher and more solid branches of military knowledge.' Lord and Lady Archibald Hamilton had also entertained him; and their son, William, who at the age of twelve was an ensign in the 3rd Regiment, and was later to become famous as a diplomatist and archaeologist and as husband of Nelson's 'Emma', was often in his company. When Lady Archibald died early in December, Wolfe did what he could to help and comfort her young family. His cousin, John Whetham, arrived in Paris in November and Wolfe describes him as 'the best tempered youth that I know.' They found many interests in common and spent much time together riding in the Academy and visiting the opera or the play-house.

Wolfe's way of life in Paris was—as he himself describes it[75] —'very singular for a young Man that appears to be in the world and in pleasure. Four or five days in the week I am up an hour before day (that is six hours sooner than any other fine gentleman ih Paris), I ride, & as I told you in a former letter, I fence & dance & have a Master to teach me French. These occupations take up all the morning I dine twice or three times a week at home, sometimes at Lord Albemarle's & sometimes with my English acquaintances; after dinner, I either go to the public entertainments or to visit, at nine I come home, and am in bed generally before eleven. I can't say I have any idle time; nor do I live in the most agreeable manner, but I get what I came here for, I take great care of my health. I succeed much better in fencing & riding than I do in the art of dancing, for they suit my genius better; & I improve a little in the French language. Lord Albemarle has done me the favour to invite me to his house when he has had the Foreign ambassadors and some considerable men of this country to dinner, but I have no great acquaintance with the French women, nor am I likely to have—it is almost impossible to introduce oneself amongst themselves without losing a great deal of money, which you know I can't afford; besides these entertainments begin at the time I go to bed, & I have not health enough to sit up all night and work all day.' He was restricted by lack of money, but none the less determined to gain as much benefit as possible from the visit. He had for long complained of his roughness of manner and lack of social accomplishments suitable to his position. He had had little opportunity to remedy these deficiencies and they had been underlined for him by his long exile in Scotland and his unsuccessful courtship of Elizabeth Lawson. While he had no ambition to become a Court sycophant, he had realized that an acquaintance in the right circles and the favourable disposition of powerful friends could raise him, as his military knowledge and ability alone in time of peace could not, above the common run of officers with greater fortunes.

He worked hard at his studies, and made good progress. After three months in Paris he wrote to his mother:[76] 'My exercises go on extremely well. Monsieur Fesian, the dancing-master, assures me that I make a surprising progress, but that my time will be too short to possess (as he calls it) the minuet to any great perfection: however, he pretends to think that I shall dance not to be laughed at. I am on horseback every morning at break of day, and do presume that, with the advantage of long legs and thighs, I shall be able to sit a horse at a hand-gallop. Lastly, the fencing master declares me to have a very quick wrist, and no inconsiderable lunge, from the reasons aforesaid. The General will explain the word *longe*, or lunge. I pronounce the French tongue, and consequently read it, better than when I came; but in the capital of this great Kingdom, I speak more English than French, and therefore don't do so well as I ought.' But he was not blinded to the superficiality of French society: 'There are men that only desire to shine, and that had rather say a smart thing than do a great one; there are others—rare birds—that had rather be than seem to be. Of the first kind this country is a well-stored magazine; of the second, our own has some few examples.'

In November he summoned a dentist to attend him, perhaps with the intention of having repaired the 'fine large tooth' he had 'broken all to pieces' while in Inverness. 'Some days ago,' he writes to his mother on 25th November, 'I sent for a Dentist to examine my teeth, he examin'd them; & told me they were much better teeth and in better order than was common to our Countrymen. However he found out that two of them stood in need of his art & he immediately applied himself to redress the evil and stuff'd lead where it was necessary. When the operation was over I told him that a Lady of my acquaintance whose welfare I had very much at heart, complain'd of her teeth; he asked me several questions concerning the condition of your gums & teeth, and what you had been accustomed to feed most upon, and what you had us'd to clean your mouth with, & what remedies you had hitherto us'd to preserve your teeth; as I could not satisfy him clearly, he told me that if you would get any surgeon to state the present case of your teeth & gums & omit nothing that could contribute to give him a thorough knowledge of your disorder, he would advise you how to proceed; but he seem'd to think by the description I gave him, that there is a scorbutick humour in your blood that discovers itself in the parts above mentioned. He talk'd of incisions in the gums and other operations that I did not understand.'

His health was much improved by regular exercise, and he was able to enjoy to the full the few leisure hours left to him by his studies. He saw tapestries being woven in the Gobelins workrooms and was out enough in Paris society to form his own opinions on the state of the country and the abilities of its rulers. Lord Albemarle took him with the Duke of Richmond to Versailles where Wolfe was 'a cold spectator of what we commonly call splendour and magnificence,' and later presented him at Court with his cousin, Whetham, and Lord Falkland. Wolfe was presented to the King and Royal Family, and also to Madame de Pompadour. He describes the scene in a letter written on 10th January: 'Madame la Marquise entertain'd us at her Toilette. We found her curling her Hair; she is extremely handsome, & by her conversation with the Ambassador & others that were present, I judge she must have a great deal of wit & understanding.' About the clergy he was less enthusiastic: 'The Ecclesiasticks have unluckily been the authors of almost all the mischief that has been done in Europe & in America since the first introduction of Christianity, & they do in some places continue their evil practices, it is surprising that there are so few Potentates in Europe that are able to keep them in any order, & the more surprising that the Example of these few has no effect upon the rest, notwithstanding the visible difference between a well-govern'd body of Clergy & the reverse.'

In January a new opportunity presented itself: Wolfe's young friend, the Duke of Richmond, was to be given a company in Bury's Regiment and to fit himself for this appointment he proposed to tour the fortified towns of the Low Countries under the guidance and instruction of a senior officer. Wolfe was asked to recommend a suitable man; he named his friend Guy Carleton.[77] 'It would,' he writes to his mother, 'have been as easy for me to hesitate about the question and afterwards to have offered my services; but, exclusive of my liking for Carleton, I don't think myself quite equal to the task, & as for the Pension that might follow, it is very certain that it would not become me to accept it.' His scruples against accepting money did not extend to his father, from whom he was obliged to ask for a loan, a request which brought down a sharp reprimand but also the required draft. Wolfe wrote at some length to thank his father, and to protest that his expenditure was no more than the barest minimum necessary to his continued stay in Paris and the attainment of those aims which he had set himself. He adds ruefully, 'The fortune of a military man seems to depend almost as much on his exteriors as upon things that are in reality more estimable and praiseworthy.'

He had received further news of Elizabeth Lawson from her uncle, Sir John Mordaunt, and also from his friend, Thomas Gage,* 'who,' he writes to his mother,[78] 'says the little Maid of Honour is as amiable, and alas (as he expresses it, poor gentleman) as cold as ever. What can that lady mean by such obstinate self-denial? or is she as much mistress of her own as of the hearts of all

* Thomas Gage (1721–1787), Commander-in-Chief in America 1763–72.

107

her acquaintance? Is she the extraordinary woman that has no weakness? or happily constructed without Passions? or lastly, and most likely, does she bid her reason chuse? She may push that matter too far, for common sense demonstrates that one should not be a Maid—of Honour too long. I writ a long letter to her uncle this post, & send him some books that he desired. I touched upon the tender string some time ago, as I told you; his answer was that he was sorry to find me so serious upon the old story; and there we rest for ever.' Elizabeth Lawson died, unmarried, six years later.

To his father, who may have expressed fears that he might involve himself in some unsuitable alliance during his stay in Paris, Wolfe writes:[79] 'By what you have said about matrimony, I judge you are averse to it, and, but that it is very difficult to live in any degree of temperance without a Wife, I shou'd join with you; however, there's a fit time, & 'tis commonly later with us Soldiers than with other men, for two reasons; the first is that in our younger days, we are generally moving from place to place, & have hardly leisure to fix; the other has prudence and necessity to support it. We are not able to feed our wives and children till we begin to decline. . . . Our tastes for pleasure and debauchery have an end, or should have, when the excuse or pretext of youth and warm blood is no longer allowed us; and one, terrible, frequent, and almost natural consequence of not marrying is an attachment to some woman or other & that leads to a thousand inconveniences. Marshal Saxe died in the arms of a little whore that plays upon the Italian stage,—an ignominious end for a Conqueror. Tho' I think much better of this condition than most young people . . . yet I may safely say that it won't produce any immediate consequence. My little experience has made me cautious. . . .'

The new year had brought with it a spell of icy weather and Wolfe had to forgo his morning rides. Towards the end of February, Lord Albemarle proposed to him that he should accompany the French Army into camp in the summer, and Wolfe wrote at once to Lord Bury to obtain permission. It was an unusual opportunity, for the Prussian and Austrian armies were also to assemble for manœuvres and there was a good chance that Wolfe would be able to see half the armies of Europe in the field. Albemarle's recommendation must have carried some weight with his son, but it was not enough to convince the Duke of Cumberland. Early in March, Wolfe received peremptory orders from Bury to return to his regiment before the official expiration of his leave. Due to return at the beginning of April, he had already asked to be allowed to stay until the 20th, but this request was refused. 'I dare not disobey openly,' he writes to his father on 9th March, 'but I will venture as far as a slight reprimand. There's an inconceivable obstinacy in this way of proceeding, a minute exactness that is quite unnecessary and excessively disagreaable. Everybody knows how difficult it is to get out of England, and yet they won't allow us to make use of the opportunity that offers, and that perhaps can never occur again. . . . "H.R.H. expects & orders me to tell you to be with the regiment by the time they assemble." These are the terms of his Lordship's letter, & he goes on to inform me that he believes the Companies will be collected towards the end of this month. Notwithstanding these hints, I shan't be in England before the 7th or 8th April, & the only thing that gives me any satisfaction or reconciles it to me is, that I shall have the pleasure of paying my duty to you and to my mother; & though the time that I shall be with you will be very short, those few days will make me some amends for the many disagreeable ones that are to follow.' His imprudent intention was frustrated by a second letter from Bury which caused him to set out at once: neglected by its colonel, and in the absence of the lieutenant-colonel on leave, the regiment had been allowed to fall into a pitiable state of indiscipline which had proved too much for its acting commander, a major, who had died of apoplexy.

After a few days in Blackheath to collect uniform and equipment, Wolfe took one of the 'new close post-chaises' to the north. He complains that he was 'beat to pieces' and describes these new machines as 'purposely constructed to torture the unhappy carcases that are placed in them.' He was obliged to take to post-horses which were 'accustomed to wear harness, and to be supported by stronger powers than my arms.' 'I was,'[80] he writes, 'every minute in danger, & fell twice at the hazard of my neck. Add to this that the movement of these brutes was so rude, that I bled to the saddle.' This was indeed a sad awakening to realities after his elegant horsemanship in the Academy in Paris, but it served as a timely reminder to Wolfe that his holiday was over; he must set to work at once to repair the damage done in his absence.

CHAPTER IX

A Move South

SELDOM can a commander have returned from leave to find his regiment in such a deplorable state as Wolfe found the Twentieth on his arrival in Glasgow. When he left the regiment at Fort Augustus in the previous June he had good reason to be pleased with the improvement in discipline and efficiency effected during his three years of command. The difference he saw on his return after an absence of nine months is best described in his own words from a letter written to his father on 22nd April. 'It is,' he writes, 'almost impossible to suffer more than I have done upon the road, & quite impossible to find a regiment in more melancholy circumstances than we are; Officers ruin'd, impoverish'd, desperate, & without hopes of preferment; the widow of our late Major & her daughter in tears; his situation before his death & the effects it had upon the corps, with the tragical end of the unhappy man in everybody's mouth . . . an Ensign struck speechless with the Palsy, & another that falls down in the most violent convulsions. . . . Some of our People spit blood, and others are begging to sell before they are quite undone; and my friend Ben will probably be in jail in a fortnight. In this situation we are, with a Martinet & parade Major to teach us the manual exercise with the time of the First Regiment.' He was particularly disgusted that the morale of the regiment should have fallen so low when he discovered that Lord Bury had received the official thanks of the King for the behaviour of the Twentieth while on duty in the Highlands. Bury had not thought fit to pass these on to Wolfe in Paris; nor had he considered his regiment worthy of another visit, even when the acting commanding officer had fallen seriously ill;

he was, it seemed, altogether too busy about the Court to concern himself with his regiment.

Wolfe set about the task with characteristic promptitude and ruthlessness. The problem was not so great as it at first appeared: under his firm hand, the regiment responded quickly to discipline, and a few sharp reminders to his officers were sufficient to set them about their duties. Those few who failed to aspire to his standards were removed from the regiment. The greatest obstacle was the weather which had turned bitterly cold, curtailing the rigorous training which officers and men so obviously needed, and retarding the recovery of the sick. 'We are all sick,' Wolfe writes despondently on 13th May, 'Officers and Soldiers. I am amongst the best, & not quite well. In two days we lost the skin off our faces, & the third were shivering in great Coats. Such are the bounties Heaven has bestowed upon this people & such the blessings of a northern latitude.' There were, however, compensations: his cousin, Goldsmith, had sent him a fine young pointer who, Wolfe claimed, eclipsed 'Workie', the pointer he had brought with him from Blackheath; and he had been sent two fishing-rods, and with these, his dogs and his guns, he hoped to enjoy some sport in the Highlands in June. There were also other entertainments: 'We have Plays; we have Concerts; we have Balls, publick and private; with Dinners and Suppers of the most execrable food upon earth, & wine that approaches to Poison . . . the men drink till they are excessively drunk; the Ladies are cold to everything but a bagpipe;—I wrong them, there is not one that does not melt away at the sound of an Estate; there's the weak side of this soft sex.' He had bought a horse for seven pounds, 'a horse that was never meant to move under the Dignity of a Commander of an old Legion . . . it was very near walking afoot, and yet can hardly be said to rise above the ground.'

These mixed diversions helped to occupy him for a time, and he was busy restoring order and discipline in the regiment, but Wolfe was unsettled. His visit to Paris, his dislike for Scotland, and his lately acquired knowledge that the work of years could be destroyed in a few months by the lethargy of officers whom he had himself trained and trusted, filled him with disillusionment. 'A man may serve long and well to very little purpose and make a sacrifice of all his days to a shadow,' he writes to his father on 24th May. No doubt the old general had some trenchant comments to make on this subject, but his own experience was hardly contradictory.

Wolfe had dined with the Duke and Duchess of Hamilton—the Duke had married the famous beauty, Elizabeth Gunning, in the previous year—but he seems not to have enjoyed it overmuch. He observes dryly that 'the lady has lost nothing of her bloom and beauty & is very well behav'd, supports her dignity with tolerable ease to herself and seems to be justly sensible of her good fortune.'

By June, the weather, though still changeable, was warmer and brought about the customary improvement in his spirits. 'Nature' he writes to his mother on 1st June, 'puts on her very best appearance at this Season & every production of the Earth is now in its highest beauty; the beasts have their new Coats, & the Birds their fine feathers; & even our Species, for whose pleasure all these seem intended, are properly dispos'd for the enjoyment of 'em.' Later in the month, detachments were sent out for road-making duties, and Wolfe encamped with five companies at Inveruglas, in country which he describes as 'wild as any that I have seen.' His stay was brief but he succeeded in returning to the Highlands for three weeks in July to supervise work on the roads near the head of Loch Lomond, and to dispel the constant headaches from which he was suffering, ascribed by him to the odours of the city.

Meanwhile, preparations were in hand for the movement of the regiment to quarters in England. Wolfe looked forward eagerly to the change: he was heartily sick of Scotland; but his pleasure in the prospect was tempered by apprehensions about the showing his regiment would make when reviewed in England by the commander-in-chief. The reputation he had built up with such care might suffer from the ragged appearance of uniforms used on road-making; and the drill of the regiment—changed by order of Lord Bury, as Wolfe angrily complains, 'from very quick to very slow, so that at present, in attempting to conform to his Lordship's directions, we are between the two, & can neither do one nor the other as they ought to be done'—left much to be desired. By 26th August he was back in Glasgow, and within a fortnight the first division of the Twentieth marched out of the city on the

Major-General James Wolfe
from a water-colour by George Townshend,
made during the Quebec campaign in 1759

James Wolfe
by an unknown painter, c. 1742

Henrietta Wolfe
by Thomas Hudson

James Wolfe
by Joseph Highmore

Elizabeth Lawson
by an unknown artist

Katherine Lowther
miniature by Richard Cosway

Major-General Sir Jeffrey Amherst
by Sir Joshua Reynolds

Admiral Sir Charles Saunders
by Richard Brompton

Brigadier the Hon. Robert Monckton
from a mezzotint by James McArdell after a painting by Thomas Hudson

Brigadier the Hon. George Townshend

from a mezzotint by James McArdell after a painting by Thomas Hudson

Brigadier the Hon. James Murray
by an unknown artist

Attack of the French fire-ships on 28th June 1759

by Samuel Scott

Attack of the French fire-rafts on 28th July 1759
by Samuel Scott

View of Quebec from the Lévi shore
engraving by P. Canot

The Landing at the Anse du Foulon
engraving by P. Canot after a drawing by Captain Hervey Smyth

road to the south. Wolfe remained behind for one day to finish up the business of the regiment and then followed to join his division, riding a horse which had belonged to his 'facetious friend' Arthur Loftus, who, to Wolfe's great grief, had died at Fort Augustus at the end of July. By the 17th Wolfe was with his division at Carlisle. He had crossed the border for the last time.

The march south was slow and wearisome, but Wolfe was in excellent spirits. Even the thought of the impending royal review could not spoil his pleasure in leaving Scotland. Everything seemed good to him: the season, 'the finest that ever was'; the countryside, 'every day . . . appears richer and more delightful'; the men, hard and fit, 'more tanned than the battalion from Minorca'. The regiment halted at Warwick for Bury to join it, and Wolfe was able to arrange a day's hunting and had 'exceeding fine sport'. By 2nd October they had reached Reading where the regiment was to be reviewed by the Duke of Cumberland. Its final destination was known to be Dover, where Wolfe would spend the winter. All his apprehensions had returned: 'The Duke reviews the Regiment on Saturday,' he writes on 22nd October, 'in their old Cloathes, & as I said before, they are thoroughly wore so that if H.R.H. piques himself upon finery of that kind, we shall inevitably be disgraced. It is true that we have numbers, for there's but five men wanting to compleat; but I cannot vouch for their beauty or fine performance; for many of 'em have been separated from the Regiment, & others ought to be sever'd from it for ever . . . the officers are loose & profligate & the Soldiers are very devils.' He need not have worried; the Duke was taken ill and the review postponed. 'I wish,' Wolfe writes on 4th November, 'his Royal Highness's martial spirit would submit itself to his state of health, in which case he wouldn't persevere in his resolution of seeing us.' It seems that his wish was granted for there is no further mention of the review in any of his letters, and on 7th November, the Twentieth moved out of Reading led by 'a tall thin officer astride a bay mare, his face lit up a smile and conversing pleasantly with the officers who rode by his side.'[81]

Bury left the regiment at Windsor, and at the end of the week Wolfe rode over to Blackheath to spend a day with his parents. He led the regiment into Dover Castle on 19th November. This gaunt pile was to house Wolfe and six companies for the winter;

the remainder of the regiment was quartered in Maidstone. It is clear from his first letter from Dover that the new quarters were not luxurious:[82] 'As soon as ever I cou'd get my green Cloath spread upon the Barrack table, and pen, ink, and paper out of my Baggage, I sett down to write to you to inform you that the remainder of our march was as fortunate in point of weather as the former part had been; and here our Labours end—I can't say comfortably or warmly, but in a Soldier-like starving condition. The Winds rattle pretty loud & the Air is sharp, but I suppose healthy for it causes great keenness of appetite. I lye at the foot of a Tower supposed to be built by the Romans, & cannot help wishing sometimes that they had chosen a snugger situation to erect their fortress upon; or that the moderns, who demolish'd a good part of the works of antiquity, had been so kind to us, their military posterity, as not to leave one stone upon another. . . . Here's a ready deliverance down the perpendicular Cliffs to such as are tir'd of their existence. They need not run far to get out of this world; one bold step frees 'em from thought.'

Wolfe remained at Dover until the following March. Time lay heavily on his hands during the winter, the cold and rain confining him to his quarters, and Christmas being enlivened only by the sutler's mince-pies and the ghosts of the castle. Boredom produced in the men the usual effect: they went off to the taverns, gaming-houses, and brothels of the town, and behaved with such offensive abandon that the citizens complained to their commanding officer. On 23rd December, Wolfe issued an order which for sheer bluntness can seldom have been surpassed: 'The lieutenant-colonel has had complaints from the people in the neighbourhood of this castle against some women of loose disorderly conduct, supposed to belong to the garrison; which however is not true. . . . The colonel is likewise informed that the soldiers have in an open, indecent, and scandalous manner frequented these same women to the great dishonour not only of the corps they belong to, but to mankind in general: he therefore desires they may be informed, that he considers this sort of commerce with the sex as the last and most dangerous degree of brutality, ignominy, and vice; and that he cannot but entertain an exceeding contemptible opinion of those who have been concerned in it.'

In the same orders from Dover, Wolfe gives a vivid picture of his difficulties with deserters: 'Hazle, of Capt. Maxwell's company, is not hereafter to be suffered to go without the castle gates; the lieutenant-colonel does not mean by this to prevent his deserting, but to punish him for his insolence: but he desires that Hazle, and Findass the grenadier, who has already been condemned for treason, may know, as well as all those who have been in the service of France, or desire to be there, that he sets no sort of value or estimation upon them, and that he had much rather they were in the Irish Brigades than in the army of Great Britain; but if ever he hears that any deserter shall dare hereafter to threaten to desert, he'll be immediately whipped out of the regiment, with every mark of infamy, contempt, and disgrace, as unworthy to continue in it, and as a fit recruit for the rebel battalions, hired by the French to serve against their country. As there is reason to believe that recruits are embarked at Dover Castle for the French army, and that deserters from our troops escape in the same vessels, any soldier of the regiment who can make discovery of such recruits, or apprehend any of these deserters, shall be rewarded over and above the allowance granted by act of parliament.' This was a recurrent problem for officers commanding the Dover garrison throughout the wars with France, and early in 1754 Wolfe had to witness the public execution of a deserter from his own regiment.

With the coming of the new year, Wolfe became resigned to the discomforts of the castle, and began to enjoy the amenities offered by the town and the surrounding countryside. He rode over the downs between Dover and Deal, and shot some pheasant, quail, and partridge. The quail he sent home to his parents, but the larger birds were protected by the Game laws and he dared not run the risk of disposing of them. In his letter dated 6th January, he deplores these restrictions: 'It is a misfortune for a man that likes this sort of sport preferable to any other to be liable to law & fine, or to be obstructed in the pursuit of a very innocent and wholesome diversion. Over the water 'tis death to shoot without license; here 'tis prosecution, damages, and costs.' He encouraged his officers to frequent the local dances and social gatherings: 'Commonly I go along with 'em,' he writes, 'to see how they conduct themselves. I am only afraid they shou'd fall in Love and marry. Whenever I perceive the symptoms, or anyone else makes the discovery, we fall upon the delinquent without mercy, till he grows out of conceit with his new passion; by this method we have broke thro many an amorous alliance and dissolv'd many ties of *eternal* love and affection. My experience in these matters helps me to find out my neighbour's weakness and furnishes me with Arms to oppose his Folly. I am not however always so successful as could be wish'd; two or three of the most simple & insensible in other respects have triumphed over my endeavours, but are seated upon the stool of repentance for the remainder of their days.' His mood of depression had evidently left him.

In February there was an epidemic of plague in the town, but a hard frost helped to stamp it out before the garrison of the castle was affected. Meanwhile the regiment was expecting to be moved at any time to other quarters. It was rumoured that the Twentieth would be sent to the East Indies but, as Wolfe writes to his mother on 2nd February, 'Lord Bury's rank & employment exempts him from these undertakings, & I do suppose he would not think it consistent to let his regiment embark without him; so we are reserved for more brilliant service.' He was eager to lead the Twentieth into action; he knew that he had created a regiment capable of distinguishing itself in battle, and it was crippling to an officer of his restless energy and enthusiasm to remain inactive in barracks while prospects of action were offered to others. In February he was appointed to preside at his first general court-martial, and in a letter to his father on the 13th he wisely observes, 'These courts of justice should not be assembled too frequently; lest the troops should forget or lose the respect and veneration that they ought to have for such courts.' In March the regiment moved to Sittingbourne, whence five companies were to march on to Guildford to be reviewed by Lord Bury, while the remainder moved to Bristol in answer to appeals from the magistrates for troops to keep order in the town where there had been some rioting among seamen and colliers. Wolfe went with the companies for review. He left Dover without regret: 'I am sure,' he writes on the 24th, 'there is not in the King's Dominions a more melancholy dreadful winter station than what we have just left; & the neglect of the board of Ordnance adds considerably to the natural horror that the situation & buildings raise in men's minds; and even makes it dangerous to reside in it in the cold weather; & so much for that vile Dungeon.'

The review passed off satisfactorily, and Wolfe went on leave until the end of September. He stayed at Blackheath, where he spent three happy months with his parents. His dogs, of which there were now six, gave him plenty of exercise in the park and on the heath, and from time to time he rode over to Westerham to see the Wardes at Squerryes Court. In July he accepted an invitation from Sir John Mordaunt, Elizabeth Lawson's uncle, to visit Freefolk near Whitchurch in Hampshire, and there he stayed until the end of the month. Elizabeth Lawson did not visit her uncle during Wolfe's stay, but her portrait hung on the wall of the dining-room to prove to Wolfe that he was not cured of his old passion. 'It took away my stomach for two or three days, & made me grave,' he writes to his mother on 14th July, 'but time, the never failing aid to distress'd Lovers, has made the semblance of her a pleasing, but not a dangerous object. However, I find it best not to trust myself to the lady's eyes, or put confidence in any resolutions of my own.' He returned to Blackheath for August and September and then set out to join his regiment in Bristol, but his time there was brief: early in October the Twentieth took up new quarters in Exeter.

The new station presented to Wolfe problems with which he was already familiar: Exeter was renowned as the Jacobite capital of the west country—a stronghold of Tories, who had little sympathy for the Hanoverian dynasty in London and were open in their support of the lost cause of the Stuarts. The choice of the 20th Regiment to garrison the town was an unusually wise one; long service in Scotland had given both officers and men some experience of similar situations, and Wolfe's tactful handling of the Scots made him eminently suited to command the garrison. From Exeter on 25th October he writes to his father, 'I begin to flatter myself that we shall soften the rigorous proceedings of our adversaries here, & live with 'em on better terms than hitherto; it is not our interest to quarrel with any but the French; and those must be devilish minds that take a pleasure in disputing.' A week later he writes to his mother, 'Will you believe that no Devonshire squire dances more than I do? What no consideration of pleasure or complaisance for the sex could effect, the Love of peace &

harmony has brought about. I have danc'd the officers into the good graces of the Jacobite Women here abouts, who were prejudiced against 'em. . . . We were upon such terms with the people in general that I have been forced to put on all my address, & employ my best skill to conciliate matters. It begins to work a little favourably but not certainly, because the perverseness of these folks, built upon their disaffection, makes the task very difficult.'

One first-hand impression of Wolfe in Exeter remains. Mrs. M. Deverell, author of *Miscellanies in Prose and Verse* published in 1781, writes: 'I remember the great General Wolfe to have been much admired for his talent in this science likewise; but he was generally ambitious to gain a tall, graceful woman to be his partner, as well as a good dancer; and when he was honoured with the hand of such a lady, the fierceness of the soldier was absorbed in the politeness of the gentleman. When thus innocently animated, the General seemed emulous to display every kind of virtue and gallantry that would render him amiable in a private character. Such a serene joy was diffused over his whole manners, mien and deportment, that it gave the most agreeable turn to the features of the hero, who died for his country.' The impression was no doubt enhanced in her memory by later events, but it is evident that Wolfe had profited by his training in Paris.

His task was not easy, but by a judicious mixture of firmness and tact, by the good behaviour of his men, and by his obvious friendliness towards the local population, Wolfe succeeded in keeping the peace. He even made friends with the ardently Tory mayor of the town. He writes on 16th November, 'The Right Worshipful the Mayor of Exeter and myself are hand & glove—we drink Church and King together upon extraordinary occasions at the Guildhall—but when he does me the honour to dine, we leave out the Divine part of the toast, which makes him suspect my religion, and he cannot help thinking that the officers of the Army are no better than they should be. The People seem to be tolerably well disposed towards us at present, how long they will continue in such good humour it is quite uncertain; I hope it will last our time, for as the town has nothing in it either inviting or entertaining, the circumstances of a civil war would make it intolerable.'

In December Wolfe rode over to Bath to spend Christmas with his parents who were taking the waters, and it was there that he received news of the death of Lord Albemarle. Lord Bury's succession to the earldom would certainly induce him to give up the colonelcy of the Twentieth. Wolfe had been the Lieutenant-Colonel for five years and could therefore, in spite of his extreme youth, reasonably expect to be considered for promotion to fill the vacancy. He had little time to consider such a possibility, for on his return to Exeter he found orders awaiting him to proceed at once to Bristol to preside at a court-martial on board the fleet. The weather was particularly severe; the icy east winds, and the disagreeable duty of sentencing several men to death chilled his spirit. 'Folks are surpris'd', he writes to his mother on 19th January, 'to see the meagre, consumptive, decaying figure of the son, when the Father and mother preserve such good looks; & People are not easily persuaded that I am one of the Family. The campaigns of '43, '4, '5, '6 & '7, stripped me of my bloom, and the winters in Scotland and at Dover have brought me almost to old age & infirmity, and this without any remarkable intemperance. A few years, more or less, are of very little consequence to the common run of men, & therefore I need not lament that I am perhaps somewhat nearer my end than other of my time. I think & write upon these points without being at all moved.' He was already aware that his feeble constitution was unlikely to support a long life, and he was impatient for great opportunity, the prerequisite of great achievement. This awareness is again made apparent by his resistance to a suggestion by Mordaunt that General Wolfe should give up his colonelcy in his favour. This, he points out, would leave his mother without support if she should outlive them both. To his father he writes on 7th February, 'Some security there should be for my mother if she should outlive you, & me, and the public credit,—a thing, in my mind, not altogether impossible.'

His uncle, Major Walter Wolfe, had plans for obtaining for him an appointment in the East India Company but Wolfe was opposed to this also. He was expecting orders to embark the regiment for service in America, and had no wish to miss such a chance. Already a hundred men had been transferred from the Twentieth to Dunbar's Regiment for service in America under General

Braddock. Wolfe's father was doubtful of the wisdom of another expedition to America; he had not forgotten the dismal failure of the Carthagena campaign, and he was loath to see his son engaged in a similar venture. Wolfe writes to his mother on 19th February, 'May I be permitted to say that my father's apprehension (and consequently yours) are not well founded? He was on board the fleet in the beginning of the war, preceded by a peace of thirty years, in which the sea officers as well as ours had almost forgot their trade. Matters are not so circumstanc'd now & there are many commanders in the fleet who are men of high courage & spirit.... It is no time to think of what is convenient or agreeable; that service is certainly the best in which we can be most usefull.... I hope I shall have resolution and firmness enough to meet every appearance of danger without great concern, & not be over-solicitous about the event.'

Since the Treaty of Aix-la-Chapelle in 1748, England and France had been nominally at peace, but the struggle for supremacy in America and India had continued unimpeded. Clearly that struggle must soon spread again to Europe. At the end of January Wolfe had, in his orders, warned the regiment of the approach of war, and he had intensified the programme of training. There were more outside exercises under arms, more practices in firing by platoons, and even greater attention was paid to the training of recruits.

Writing on 7th March to Rickson, who had returned from Nova Scotia and was now stationed at Fort Augustus, Wolfe confides his suspicions that a new war with France might lead to further unrest in the north. He criticizes the conduct of the campaign of 1745 and puts forward his own plan for the prevention of another rising: 'Such a succession of errors, & such a strain of ill-behaviour as the last Scotch War did produce, can hardly, I believe, be match'd in History; our future annals will, I hope, be fill'd with more shining events. What if the Garrisons of the Forts had been under the orders of a prudent, resolute man (yourself for instance) wou'd not they have found means to stifle the Rebellion in its birth ? & might not they have acted more like Soldiers & good subjects than it appears they did? What wou'd have been the effects of a sudden march into the middle of that Clan who were the first to move? What might have been done by means of Hostages of Wives and Children, or the chiefs themselves? How easy a small body, united, prevents the Junction of distant Corps; & how favourable the Country where you are for such a manœuvre if, notwithstanding all precautions they get together; a body of troops may make a diversion, by laying waste a country that the male inhabitants have left, to prosecute rebellious schemes; how soon must they return to the defence of their property (such as it is) their wives, their children, their Houses & their cattle? But above all, the secret, sudden, night march into the midst of 'em; great Patrols of 50, 60, or 100 men each, to terrify 'em; letters to the chiefs, threatening fire & sword, & certain destruction if they dare to stirr: movements that seem mysterious to keep the Enemy's attention upon you, and their fears awake. . . .' He details the preparations necessary to strengthen the Highland forts against attack, and goes on to advise musket practice: '. . . Let me recommend the practice, you'll soon find the advantage of it. Marksmen are nowhere so necessary as in mountainous Country; besides, firing Balls at objects teaches the Soldiers to level incomparably, makes the Recruits steady, & removes the foolish apprehension that seizes young Soldiers when they first load their arms with Bullets.'

In March the regiment moved from Exeter to Winchester, and on the 8th April Lieutenant-Colonel Philip Honeywood was gazetted Colonel of the 20th Regiment. Wolfe was dismayed; he had been prepared for the appointment of a senior officer, and there had been rumours that the colonelcy would be given to General Fowke, but the promotion of an officer of his own rank was a bitter blow. This disconcerting news came at a time when he was particularly irritable; he was again suffering from scurvy, and needed to go to Southampton to try a salt water cure. He now had to wait for Honeywood to join the regiment before he could leave. His old friend Sir John Mordaunt reviewed the regiment in April and was favourably impressed. Wolfe also was satisfied, as his orders show: '. . . The lieutenant-colonel takes this opportunity to thank the officers and soldiers of the companies here for their extreme handsome behaviour under arms, the knowledge and diligence of the officers, and the obedience and attention of the soldiers was very conspicuous.' It was just a year since Wolfe had returned from Paris to find his regiment in a pitiable state of ill-health and indiscipline at Fort Augustus.

He still expected that the regiment would be ordered on board the fleet which lay at Portsmouth under the command of Sir Edward Hawke, and he issued instructions for the training of his men in the use of their muskets on board ship. Some of the marine regiments had been disbanded in 1748 and until they could be re-formed their duties were assigned to the infantry. By the end of June, however, 800 Marines had been drafted to the Spithead fleet from Chatham and Portsmouth, and the Twentieth was no longer required to stand by for this service. Wolfe concentrated again on normal infantry training.

Winchester provided some welcome diversions from drill and manœuvres; Wolfe had friends in the neighbourhood, and his easy manner and fondness for dancing made him a welcome guest at their houses. He visited Southampton to 'wash away' his scurvy in salt water, and spent a few days in Lymington. From there he wrote again to Rickson to give him further advice for the organization of the army in Scotland, where, he was certain, there would be more trouble in the event of war with France: 'If the French resent the affront put upon 'em by Mr. Boscawen, the War will come on hot & sudden; & they will certainly have an eye to the Highlands. Their Friends & Allies in that country were of great use to 'em in the last war, that famous diversion cost us great sums of money & many lives, and left the Pais bas to Saxe's mercy. I am such of your opinion, that without a considerable aid of Foreign Troops, the Highlanders will never stirr.' The French might well resent the capture by Boscawen, in time of peace, of two of their ships, the *Alcide* and the *Lys*, off Cape Breton, carrying the Governor of Louisbourg, four other officers, and treasure worth £30,000.

Wolfe visited his aunt, Anne Burcher, and her husband, at their house in the New Forest. It was not a happy meeting; the Burchers were impoverished and their house, 'a lonely miserable mansion in the forest', had 'the look of indigence and decay'. They were pathetically pleased to see their celebrated nephew, but he did not stay long. He promised to return 'if our march is not too sudden.' He can hardly be blamed for his indifference. He had many things on his mind: the approaching war, the training of the regiment, the absence of his colonel, the diminishing prospects of promotion or chance of active employment. Such considerations tended to obscure the problems of poor, grateful Aunt Anne and her insignificant husband. At the end of August came news which banished the Burchers from his mind altogether: General Braddock's army had been all but annihilated at Monongahela.

CHAPTER X

Rivalries in America

W<small>HILE</small> Wolfe served in Scotland his apprenticeship for command in war, the British and French Governments watched, with growing anxiety, the collapse of the Treaty of Aix-la-Chapelle. The terms of the treaty had left all the countries concerned, with the exception of Prussia, dissatisfied: Austria had lost Silesia to Prussia; France had been forced to withdraw from the Austrian Netherlands in order to regain the vital fortress of Louisbourg; England had sacrificed the New Englanders' conquest of Louisbourg to prevent the French from acquiring naval stations beyond the Dover Strait and an outlet in the North Sea. The preservation of the Dover defile had formed the crux of British foreign policy for a century. It had been reinforced in the Treaty of Utrecht in 1713 and again at Aix-la-Chapelle by insistence on the destruction of the port and defences of Dunkirk and the creation and maintenance of the 'Barrier Fortresses'. These fortresses, erected by Austria on the frontier between France and the Netherlands and garrisoned by Dutch troops in Austrian pay, were intended to secure the Low Countries—and thus the North Sea ports— against sudden conquest by France. They had not at any time secured this object, and by 1754 the defences were crumbling and the garrisons unpaid. Holland was left unprotected, and but for her defensive alliance with England, which provided for mutual assistance in case of aggression by another nation, might be expected to look to France or Prussia for some guarantee of her security. The family ties of the Bourbons were likely to unite France and Spain against England, particularly in the event of a colonial war. Prussia, also, might seek in alliance with France the counterpoise to the threat of action by her enemies, Austria and

Russia. Frederick, it was true, despised Louis XV; but his strained relations with the Tsaritsa Elizabeth, the Empress Maria Theresa, and his uncle, George II, made the preservation of friendly relations with France imperative. Austria, in her turn, led by the Emperor and his shrewd adviser, Kaunitz, looked to France as a possible ally in the overthrow and partitioning of Prussia and the recovery of Silesia. Isolated among these great European Powers, and vulnerable to attack on all sides, lay the Electorate of Hanover. However much British statesmen might deplore the King's preference for his little German state, its problems could not be shelved entirely. The ports of the Elbe, the Weser, and the Ems, and the control of the German seaboard from Holland to Denmark could not lightly be allowed to fall into the hands of an enemy; and any British conquest in a future war would have to be sacrificed at the peace in return for Hanover. The British problem in Europe was therefore twofold: to preserve the security of the Straits of Dover and the North Sea ports of Europe; and to protect Hanover. If these two objects could be achieved, England could safely turn her attention to the colonies where events threatened to precipitate a war which must at all costs be prevented from spreading to Europe. If there must be war, it must be confined to the colonies and to the sea, where Britain had a clear superiority.

The uneasy truce which had lasted in Europe since 1748 did not extend to India or America. Plenipotentiaries of England and France had met in Paris and wrangled for three years, but nothing had been achieved and the colonies had been left, as before, to fend for themselves. This they did with far-reaching results. It had long been customary to regard limited military action in the colonies as something apart from European politics. Thus a minor clash between the forces of England and France in colonial territory did not necessarily constitute an act of war, and some of the most significant actions in America and India were fought during a period when France and England were nominally at peace. In India, the rivalry between the two East India Companies had led to open warfare. Dupleix, the French Governor of Pondicherry, had evolved a grandiose scheme for bringing the whole of the Carnatic and the Deccan under French control by supplanting the rulers of these territories by his own nominees and supporting the change by force. This policy was strenuously resisted by the British under Clive and Stringer Lawrence. Clive's capture of Arcot, the capital of the Carnatic, and his subsequent victories at Arni and Coveripak, Lawrence's defeat of Chanda Sahib, and the restoration of Mohammed Ali as Nawab of the Carnatic, so alarmed the French that in 1754 Dupleix was recalled in disgrace and, by the agreement of both parties, all military action was suspended.

In America the clash of interests was even more marked. The New England colonies stretched along the Atlantic seaboard from Newfoundland to Georgia. The colonial ambitions of France were based on her claim to the whole of the Mississippi basin, and her possession of Acadia and the islands in the Gulf of the St. Lawrence in the north and a sickly settlement at New Orleans in the south. Her aim was the connexion of these possessions by a chain of forts which would, in theory, give her the effective occupation of the vast hinterland to the west of New England, confining the British colonies to their narrow Atlantic strip. This would reserve to France the monopoly of the valuable fur trade centred on the Great Lakes and the Ohio valley. The design was impressive; but it took no account of practical considerations. The French colonies were an artificial creation, under-populated, heavily subsidized, and entirely subservient to centralized administration in France. In spite of their unification and their provision for compulsory military service,* the French colonies were weak. The retention in France of the power to make all decisions affecting their development and welfare had robbed the people of their vigour and initiative. In marked contrast, the New England colonies, founded haphazardly and left by ignorant or indifferent statesmen to look after themselves, bred a hardy race of healthily independent people, proud, jealous, stubborn and unrepresentative; difficult to weld into a cohesive body for any purpose, but potentially formidable. They had already shown something of their mettle in the capture of Louisbourg in 1745, and they viewed with disgusted resentment the return of their conquest to France under the provisions of the Aix-la-Chapelle Treaty. They had not the smallest intention of giving up the fur

* The governor of a colony had the right to conscript all men between the ages of fourteen and seventy for military service.

trade, and they saw the building of a line of French forts round the Great Lakes as a threat to their very existence. The half-hearted but lengthy attempt in Paris to settle disputes in America had left the frontier between Nova Scotia and Canada undefined, and had set up a theoretical buffer of Indian territory between Canada and New England. As the extent of this territory was not clearly defined either, its boundaries were unlikely to be respected, They were, in fact, ignored.

There were two weak links in the chain which the French proposed to forge from the St. Lawrence to the Gulf of Mexico: the British settlement of Nova Scotia which, in spite of the strengthened fortifications of Louisbourg, constituted with New-foundland a threat to the Gulf of the St. Lawrence; and the unguarded territory bounded by Lake Erie, the Alleghany mountains, and the head waters of the Ohio river, where the British colonies of Pennsylvania, Maryland, and Virginia pene-trated most deeply towards the Great Lakes. The rebuilding of the Louisbourg fortifications had aroused some misgiving in England, and in 1749 Lord Halifax, the energetic President of the Board of Trade, obtained the King's permission for the establish-ment of a fortified port in Nova Scotia which he named after himself. The population of Nova Scotia was predominantly French. Incited by a fanatical Jesuit priest, the Abbé le Loutre, they ignored the oath of allegiance and agitated for the union under French rule of Nova Scotia and the neighbouring French province of Acadia. The Canadian Government encouraged this movement and established a fort, Beauséjour, on a hill dominating the isthmus between the two settlements, which acted as a base for Indian raids. In April 1750, Edward Cornwallis, the Governor of Nova Scotia and Wolfe's predecessor as lieutenant-colonel of the 20th Regiment, dispatched a force of 400 men to occupy Beaubassin, a village in British territory a few miles south of Beauséjour. Spurred on by le Loutre, who fired the parish church with his own hand, the population razed the village to the ground. On the site, Major Lawrence, commander of the British force, raised a new fort. From then on the situation deteriorated rapidly until in 1755 Lawrence, who had become governor, took the drastic step of expelling 5,000 of the French population from the colony.

Meanwhile, the Marquis Duquesne, who had succeeded in 1752 to the governorship of French Canada, was putting into operation the plan to link the St. Lawrence with the New Orleans settlement. The first step was to secure the head waters of the Ohio and to this end he dispatched, in the spring of 1753, an expedition to occupy the Ohio valley and to build forts necessary to its protection. It did not achieve its main objective, but a fort was established at Presque Isle on the shores of Lake Erie, and another, Fort le Boeuf, on French Creek, a tributary of the Alleghany river. By that time illness had taken its toll of the troops and they could only continue south a few miles further to capture a small English trading station at Venango, which they made into a military outpost. In their advance they had driven off or captured a' number of traders from the newly formed English Ohio Company, which had obtained a concession of the Indian trade from the Crown and was busily engaged in opening up a route to the fur country round the Great Lakes. The principal shareholders were men of considerable influence in Maryland and Virginia.

Dinwiddie, Governor of Virginia, was confronted by a most dangerous situation. Instructions had already arrived from England urging him to build forts on the line of the Ohio river and to effect the withdrawal of foreign troops from Virginian soil —instructions that presupposed, quite erroneously, Virginian right of ownership to the disputed territory. As the French were already in occupation of the territory, their withdrawal would have to be compelled by force, and this would entail an open act of war. Furthermore it was at least debatable whether a sufficient force could be raised for the task. Help from England had not been forthcoming in over-generous measure (thirty light pieces of cannon and eighty barrels of powder) and it seemed unlikely that the other colonies would co-operate in any plan for united action. Dinwiddie tried bluff: he sent a formal protest to the French, expressing his astonishment that they should have violated territory so indisputably the property of Great Britain. To carry this protest he chose a young and inexperienced major of militia, George Washington. Washington delivered the message to the commander at Fort le Boeuf, and returned with the unsatisfactory reply that it would be forwarded to Duquesne. But his journey was not without value: he was by profession a surveyor, and he was quick to appreciate the suitability of the junction of the Ohio and Alleghany rivers as a site for a fort of considerable strategic importance. Dinwiddie agreed.

Early in 1754 Washington set out again, this time with 150 men, to build a fort on the site he had recommended. The force was too small to achieve its object, and Washington destroyed any chance of success by dividing it. He led his men to a fortified trading post at Wills Creek, and from there dispatched a pathetically small detachment to the Ohio fork where he intended to join them when reinforcements arrived. It was not long before the French heard of this move and Duquesne lost no time in sending a force of 500 men to compel the Virginians to withdraw. On the site of their inconsiderable fortifications the French set to work to build Fort Duquesne as the last link in their chain. It is improbable that Washington understood the full importance of the fort in the French strategic plan; but he understood the value of the site to the colonists and resented the destruction of his work. He sent at once to Dinwiddie for reinforcements, but without waiting for them to arrive set out with his small detachment to attack the French position. The attack was ill-advised for he was hopelessly outnumbered and his men were suffering from shortage of food and ammunition. After forcing a minor action, he was compelled to retreat and surrender at a hastily improvised defensive position on the western slopes of the Alleghanies which he had aptly named Fort Necessity. He and his men were released on condition that they returned to Virginia and undertook not to build any more forts west of the Alleghanies for a full year. War with France had begun.

It was at this stage that the American war became the concern of the Government at home which, owing to the unexpected death of Henry Pelham in March 1754, was led by the Duke of Newcastle. Since the peace, Newcastle had busied himself with affairs in Europe, trying by a series of complex manoeuvres to solve the dual problems of the security of Hanover and the North Sea ports. His efforts were further complicated by an extraordinary plan for the election of the Emperor's son, Joseph, as King of the Romans to ensure his succession as Emperor on the death of Francis of Lorraine. This entailed the canvassing and bribery of a number of German states whose reliability was, to say the least, questionable, and whose help in war, even if it were forthcoming, would be of small value. Newcastle's policy was founded on what he called the 'old system'—the alliance of Britain, Holland, and Austria against France—which had proved effective enough in Marlborough's time but was now outmoded and impracticable. He underestimated the importance of Prussian strength in European affairs. Austria no longer looked upon France as her most dangerous enemy; her main concern had become control of the German states, and in this ambition her rival was not France but Prussia. France was, indeed, her most likely source of support in a war to partition Prussia, regain Silesia, and restore the Hapsburg domination of Germany. Such was the view taken by Kaunitz, the Emperor's chief adviser, and the *renversement des alliances*, which was to follow, grew from it. Newcastle had received little support for his schemes from Pelham, who regarded the subsidies as useless and extravagant at a time when he was trying, and with considerable success, to balance the nation's economy. The fact that not even Maria Theresa or the Emperor were whole-heartedly in favour of Newcastle's intrigues for the election of their son branded the whole plan as absurd.

Pelham's death left two vacancies in the Government: the posts of First Lord of the Treasury and Chancellor of the Exchequer. The first was promptly filled by Newcastle, who thus became the King's first minister, but this left vacant the post of Secretary of State for the North. It would also be necessary to find a leader for the House of Commons. For these positions, Newcastle sought for obedience rather than brilliance; he wanted no rivals. To the Exchequer he appointed Henry Legge, a younger son of the Earl of Dartmouth and a friend of Pitt. The transfer of Lord Holdernesse, Secretary of State for the South, to the more important northern province, lessened the significance of the vacancy, but there was still the leadership of the House to be assigned. The obvious candidates were Murray, the Solicitor-General; Henry Fox, the Secretary at War; and Pitt, Paymaster to the Forces. But none of these was suitable from Newcastle's point of view: Murray was too weak and would be browbeaten by Pitt; Fox and Pitt were too strong and might challenge his own authority. Pitt would not be accepted by the King and could therefore be ruled out, but Fox had the support of the King and the Duke of Cumberland and his claims could not be ignored. By a piece of outrageous political chicanery Newcastle succeeded in persuading Fox to accept the post and then to resign from it within two days. This left the field open for his own nominee, Sir Thomas Robinson, a portly and long-winded diplomat without parliamentary experience, who could be relied upon to do as he was told.

The danger of an alliance between Pitt and Fox was still to be overcome, and as soon as the new Parliament met they launched a concerted attack upon Murray, promoted to Attorney-General, which reduced him to nervous prostration. This could not be allowed to happen to Robinson. Fox was promptly muzzled by the bribe of a seat in the Cabinet Council and the promise of the effectual leadership of the House with Robinson as figurehead. Newcastle now felt free to pursue his policy of subsidy treaties, and the King bustled off to Hanover where he persuaded Russia and Hesse Cassel to accept heavy bribes in return for promises of aid in the event of an attack being made on the precious Electorate. These treaties were to be ratified by Parliament in the autumn session, due to open on 13th November 1755. Newcastle made frantic efforts to win Pitt over to his side, but he could not offer him the seals of Secretary of State, and nothing else would do. The only alternative was to secure the active support of Fox, and this he did by promising to pension off Sir Thomas Robinson and appoint Fox to succeed him. To Pitt this was the last straw. When Parliament met, he made his famous Rhône and Saône speech in which he compared the alliance of Fox and Newcastle to the junction of the two rivers, 'the latter a gentle, feeble, languid stream, languid but not deep: the other a boisterous and overbearing torrent.' The treaties were ratified, Fox received his promised reward for his support of the Government, and on 20th November Pitt was dismissed from his office of Paymaster to the Forces. Newcastle had rid himself of his most dangerous rival; but not for long.

Meanwhile, in America the situation had deteriorated still further. In the autumn of 1754, it had been decided to send out an expedition as a reprisal for French action in the Ohio valley. It was imperative that Fort Duquesne should be destroyed and, at the same time, Newcastle was persuaded to sanction plans for action elsewhere in America. Two regiments were to be sent from Ireland, two colonial regiments were to be raised by Shirley and Pepperell, and the command of the expedition was to be given to Major-General Edward Braddock, a stubborn, un-imaginative officer of great personal courage, whose experience as a commander in the field was limited to an unsuccessful attempt to raise the siege of Bergen-op-Zoom nine years earlier. It is not quite fair to blame him for what followed: as the commander of an army to be engaged in a set-piece battle in Europe he might well have proved to be an excellent choice; for unconventional forest warfare, where flexibility of thought and action was the first essential, the choice of Braddock to command could hardly have been worse.

The expedition was, in theory at least, defensive and retaliatory; in practice the operations which Braddock was authorized to conduct looked suspiciously like a deliberate offensive. The operations were to consist of four thrusts against French forts in disputed territory: the first and main objective was the capture of Fort Duquesne and the destruction of French outposts on the south shore of Lake Erie; a second force would attack Fort Niagara, which the French had established to control communica-tions between Lakes Erie and Ontario; a third column was to capture Crown Point, a fort which the French had built at the head of Lake Champlain, described by Newcastle in 1751[83] as *'built upon His Majesty's Territory in the Province of New York, very near the Town of Albany & very obnoxious to His Majesty's Planta-tions;'* the plan was completed by a fourth attack, from the sea, on Fort Beauséjour, commanding the isthmus between Acadia and Nova Scotia.

Strategically the plan was excellent. Bearing in mind the necessity for making France fire the first shot in any new war—for on this depended the defensive alliances with Holland and Austria—the four thrusts were all aimed at 'illegal' French for-tifications in disputed neutral territory. In theory, the French could not condemn these attacks without condemning their own previous actions in the same territories. In practice, the success of the four operations would put an end to French control of the Ohio valley, break the chain which linked the colonies of the north and south, and open the way for an attack on French possessions which might well end in the expulsion of the French from Canada.

From the beginning the preparations were handled with an all too familiar lack of foresight and discretion. Fox, as Secretary at War, rightly doubted Newcastle's resolution to put the plan into operation, in spite of the personal direction of the Duke of Cumberland. He therefore released certain details to the *Gazette* which published them on 8th October 1754. Newcastle was appalled, and wrote in haste to Albemarle in Paris that[84] 'a most ill-judg'd Advertisement from the War Office has set all the Foreign Ministers on Fire, and made them believe that We are just going to War, which is, I hope, the furthest from our Thoughts.' He begged Albemarle to reassure the French, and to 'give Such a Turn to all these necessary Defensive Measures, as may make the French Ministers asham'd to complain of them; and willing to avoid taking Such Notice of them as may bring on Such Consequences as They don't seem at present to wish.' The French, much as they wished at that time to avoid war, viewed these 'necessary defensive measures' with scepticism, and laid their own plans to thwart them.

In January 1755 Braddock sailed from Cork to his inglorious death in America. Within a few weeks of his departure a copy of his orders was being studied by the French Government, and by the middle of February it was known in England that the French proposed to send 3,000 regulars to Canada. Clearly the arrival of such a force would lead to the destruction of British hopes. The 'Inner Committee' of the Cabinet met on 18th March to discuss counter-measures to be taken. On the 24th another meeting was called, and it was resolved to send a squadron not exceeding seven of the line to cruise off Louisbourg with instructions to engage any French ships attempting to land troops in Nova Scotia, Cape Breton, or Quebec. Command of this squadron was given to Vice-Admiral the Hon. Edward Boscawen. France promptly presented to the British Government an ultimatum in which she claimed the right of possession over all disputed territory in Nova Scotia and the Ohio Valley. This was as promptly rejected, and on 27th April Boscawen sailed with his squadron supplemented by three more ships of the line and a frigate of fifty guns. He was instructed to make for Halifax, where he would take under his command Keppel's squadron which had escorted Braddock's force to America. He was to cruise off Louisbourg, and if he fell in with any French warships or other vessels carrying troops or stores he was to capture or destroy them. On 3rd May the French put to sea with two squadrons: one, under Dubois de la Motte, to escort the transports to America; the second, under Macnamara, to act as additional protection into the Atlantic. This escort was greatly superior to the combined squadrons of Boscawen and Keppel, and a further six of the line under Rear-Admiral Francis Holburne were therefore dispatched on 11th May to reinforce Boscawen off Louisbourg. On 10th June, Richard Howe in the *Dunkirk*, acting on Boscawen's orders, sighted and engaged the French ship *Alcide* and forced her to strike her colours; two more ships were sighted, and after a chase lasting two hours, the *Lys* was captured with four companies each of the La Reine and the Languedoc Regiments on board. From these prisoners it was learnt that Macnamara's escort had turned back. By the 21st, Boscawen and Holburne had assembled their squadrons at Louisbourg, but only to find that de la Motte had eluded them and sailed into the Gulf of St. Lawrence with his convoy.

Boscawen's news was received in England with alarm: it seems not to have occurred to anyone that the convoy could escape, and while even the irresolute and cautious Newcastle was prepared to accept the dangers of a worthwhile action in which the French convoy would be destroyed, none of the Cabinet had envisaged an open act of aggression with so little material advantage. It would be unjust to blame Boscawen, for his instructions gave him no hint that he should only attack if he could be certain of dealing a blow which would offset the diplomatic consequences inseparable from such action. By the end of July, diplomatic relations with France had been formally broken off and Hawke had put to sea with sixteen ships of the line. His orders were to prevent the junction of the French Mediterranean and Atlantic fleets and to bar the return of de la Motte's fleet to Brest.

Newcastle's predicament was further complicated by the disaster which overtook Braddock in July. Four commanders had been chosen to lead the operations: Braddock himself was to lead the attack on Fort Duquesne; Shirley commanded the troops to capture Niagara; William Johnson, with a force of colonials was to take Crown Point; and Colonel Robert Monckton, with 2,000 New Englanders, was to lead the assault by sea on Beau-séjour. Braddock stubbornly ignored the advice and experience of the colonial soldiers and chose as his adviser the officer least qualified to advise him, George Washington. On 10th June, Braddock led his army into the forest. Progress was slow: his men fell sick, his horses died; in a week they covered thirty miles. Washington advised him to leave baggage and artillery behind and to push on with a small lightly equipped force. Braddock accepted this advice and thus repeated Washington's error of the previous year: he divided his force, leaving nearly half his men behind under Colonel Dunbar, and hurried on to disaster. On 9th July some eight miles from Fort Duquesne, his force was all but annihilated in an ambush and Braddock himself was mortally wounded. The remnants of his detachment fled to Dunbar's camp. The heavy baggage and artillery were fired and Dunbar led the survivors in a panic-stricken flight into Philadelphia.

Of the three other operations, only one succeeded. Shirley and Johnson never reached their objectives, Niagara and Crown Point: Shirley never even brought his men into action; Johnson fell into an ambush, fled into camp, and beat off the attack which followed, but he failed to take advantage of this success and marched home to receive, incomprehensibly, a baronetcy and a vote of £5,000 from Parliament. Monckton's assault on Beau-séjour succeeded. A younger son of Lord Galway, and Colonel of the 2nd Battalion the Sixtieth Foot, Monckton had seen service in the previous war, and had shown himself to be an officer of considerable ability. Beauséjour was inadequately garrisoned, and commanded by Captain Duchambon de Vergor, an unsavoury character who owed his position to his services as procurer to François Bigot, the notorious Intendant of Canada. Vergor was a spineless creature whom not even the fire-eating Abbé le Loutre could rouse to action. A short cannonading was sufficient to convince him of the need for surrender, and within a few days the whole of Acadia was in British hands. Five thousand of the French were deported, and the problem of Nova Scotia was solved. Louisbourg was now isolated, and it was a foregone conclusion that as soon as war was declared an attempt must be made to restore the fortress to the New Englanders who had captured it during the previous war and so reluctantly parted with it at the peace.

With British prestige in America destroyed by the defeat of Braddock, and the prospect of more trouble there in the near future, with the two East India Companies preparing to renew hostilities, and with the threat of Austrian and Dutch defection from their alliances, it was vital for Newcastle that the Russian and Hessian treaties should be ratified to prevent the total isolation of Hanover. By the end of the year his aim had been achieved and, more important, the Russian treaty had been shown to Frederick of Prussia. With one of his characteristic swift changes of policy, Frederick abandoned his French alliance, and in January 1756 signed the Convention of Westminster by which Britain and Prussia mutually guaranteed the security of their possessions in Germany against attack. It is difficult to see how this could be made to accord with the recent treaty with Russia; 55,000 Russian troops were already massed on the Livonian frontier ready to march into Prussia on the smallest provocation— a moment which the Tsaritsa was eagerly awaiting. There could be only one logical outcome: the complete reversal of Newcastle's 'old system'. France must either allow herself to be isolated, or turn to her old enemies, Austria, Holland, and Russia. By May 1756 Austria and France had concluded the Treaty of Versailles. Austria agreed to remain neutral in any war between Britain and France, and both signatories mutually guaranteed their possessions and frontiers against invasion.

Newcastle was left to contemplate the shattered ruins of his elaborate structure of alliances; he had not the wit to understand that he had destroyed it himself.

CHAPTER XI

War with France

NEWS of Braddock's defeat and the ignominious flight of Colonel Dunbar with the survivors reached Wolfe while he was at Southampton. On 4th September he writes to his father: 'The accounts of Mr. Braddock's defeat are not yet clear enough to form a right judgment of the cause of it—but I do myself believe that the cowardice and ill behaviour of the men far exceeded the ignorance of the chief, who though not a master of the difficult art of war, was yet a man of sense & courage. I have but a very mean opinion of the Infantry in general. I know their discipline to be bad, and their valour precarious. They are easily put into disorder, and hard to recover out of it; they frequently kill their officers, thro' fear, & murder one another in their confusion.' He goes on to speak of the 'extream ignorance of the officers, & the disobedient & dastardly spirit of their men' and severely criticizes methods of training: 'We are lazy in time of Peace, and of course want vigilance & activity in War—our military education is by far the worst in Europe. . . .' To his uncle he wrote,[85] '. . . You know how readily the Infantry under the present method of training are put into Disorder even on the Battlefields of Europe. How much more then when they are led on to encounter a horde of Savages ambush'd behind Timber in an Unknown trackless Country! Some day we will learn the Lesson; meanwhile we can only look on & marvel at the insensate Stupidity which tollerates this laxity in our affairs.'

He applied himself more closely than ever to his military studies. It was obvious that the declaration of war with France could not be much longer delayed, and there were already reports

137

of French preparations for invasion. 'I intend,' Wolfe writes to his mother on 28th September, 'to devote myself this Winter to my profession, & shall read without ceasing. . . . I have been very idle all this summer—if a man may venture to say so who has given up much of his time to the ladies—If there is to be war, we should be prepared for it; if not, I am entirely at their service.' In the same letter he mentions that he has discarded his wig in favour of 'the covering nature has given me'. He wore his red hair short, and though he covered it with a wig on formal or ceremonial occasions, he preferred to be bare-headed and never again wore a wig in battle.

In October Wolfe returned to Winchester to prepare for reviews of his regiment by Sir John Mordaunt and the Duke of Cumberland; 'Our whole military business seems to be confined to reviews,' he writes, thinking no doubt with envy of the chances of action in America. By the 19th he was constantly expecting war to be declared: 'When two nations have arm'd themselves to the highest pitch of their strength, I suppose they will try which is the strongest. The French are getting their fleet into order & threaten an invasion; we equip all our ships and increase our Army to oppose 'em—We have begun hostilities both in Europe & America—in these circumstances is it to be suppos'd that a War with such a nation as France can be avoided? I think it cannot.' He is full of exhortations to his parents: they are to avoid government bonds, and invest in land; give money to the state; and sell their plate for the public benefit. The old General may be forgiven if he found his son, at the age of twenty-eight, a little too ready with advice. But it was well-intentioned; Wolfe had a nagging fear that his mother would be left without sufficient provision for her old age. His father was unlikely to live to any great age, and if Wolfe himself was killed his mother would have no means of support except her capital and the doubtful bounty of the Government. His fears were not unfounded.

At the end of October Wolfe issued orders for the regiment to move to Canterbury 'to assist in the defence of the country'. 'If,' his orders read, 'the enemy lands (as they seem to intend) the lieutenant-colonel does not doubt that the officers and soldiers will act against them with the resolution and courage of men who mean to distinguish themselves in the defence of their King and country, and with the spirit of a free people.' The threat of invasion was very real: frequent and detailed intelligence reaching the Duke of Newcastle at the end of the year[86] via Stockholm served to confirm previous reports that French troops were being concentrated in Normandy and Brittany. British troops were accordingly moved to stations along the Channel coast.

At Canterbury there were two regiments of foot and a regiment of dragoons. Wolfe writes on 5th November, 'General Hawley is expected in a few days to keep us all in order; if there is an invasion, they could not make use of a more unfit person. The troops dread his severity, hate the man, & hold his military knowledge in contempt.' 'The Hangman' had not improved his reputation in the nine years since Culloden. Wolfe's reputation, on the other hand, was growing steadily: the 20th Regiment had reached a state of efficiency which had not passed unnoticed in military circles and it was common knowledge that its young lieutenant-colonel was held in high esteem by the commander-in-chief. In Cumberland, Sackville, Albermarle and Mordaunt, Wolfe now had powerful friends at Court, and even his extreme youth could not be expected to retard his promotion much longer. He was quite conscious of the reputation he had created for himself; but he was also honest enough to admit that competition—if merit was to be the first consideration—was slight. This he explains to his mother in a letter from Canterbury on 8th November: 'The officers of the Army in General are Persons of so little application to business and have been so ill-educated, that it must not surprise you to hear that a man of common industry is in reputation amongst 'em. I reckon it a very great misfortune to this country that I, your son, who have, I know, but a very moderate capacity, and some degree of diligence a little above the ordinary run, should be thought, as I generally am, one of the best Officers of my Rank in the service; I am not at all vain of the distinction. The comparison would do a man of genius very little honour, and does not illustrate me,* by any means; & the consequences will be very fatal to me in the end, for as I rise in Rank People will expect some considerable performances, & I shall be induced, in support of an ill-got reputation, to be lavish

* Wolfe often used the word 'illustrate' as meaning to make illustrious or add lustre to.

of my life, and shall probably meet that Fate which is the ordinary effect of such a conduct.' A modest enough summary of his capabilities, and one which has been snatched up greedily by some biographers as a convenient prophecy.

The proposal, made earlier, to promote Wolfe to his father's colonelcy was again discussed in the New Year; but, once again, he was lukewarm. He could not accept the scheme unless some guarantee of income could be made to his father in the event of his own death, and there were too many obstacles to such an arrangement. Furthermore, it was clear to him that if the emergency continued, or war were declared, more regiments would be raised and his own just claim to a colonelcy would be strengthened.

Meanwhile, the regiment exercised and drilled rigorously under Wolfe's critical eye. It was about this time that he issued his famous 'Instructions for the Twentieth Regiment'. The discipline of the line about to receive a charge was always one of his chief concerns. A line which would stand firm and silent under enemy fire would hear the commands of its officers and shoot, when the time came, with precision and maximum effect. This was the discipline which would win battles, and extracts from his 'Instructions' show clearly that this, above all, was his aim and it was to be achieved at all cost: 'Neither officer, non-commissioned officer, or soldier, is to leave his platoon or abandon the colours for a slight wound; while a man is able to do his duty, and can stand and hold his arms, it is infamous to retire. . . . The battalion is not to halloo or cry out upon any account whatsoever, although the rest of the troops should do it, until they are ordered to charge with their bayonets; in that case, and when they are upon a point of rushing upon the enemy, the battalion may give a war-like shout and run in—A soldier that takes his musket off his shoulder and pretends to begin the battle without order, will be put to death that instant: the cowardice or irregular proceedings of one man is not to put the whole in danger—A soldier that quits his rank, or offers to fly, is to be instantly put to death by the officer that commands that platoon, or by the officer or sergeant in the rear of that platoon; a soldier does not deserve to live who won't fight for his King and country.'

By February it was known that the French plan for invasion

devised by Marshal Belleisle had been adopted. A detailed account of this plan had been acquired by Colonel Joseph Yorke, the British envoy to The Hague, and transmitted at once to the Duke of Newcastle. This was later confirmed by another intercepted dispatch from Stockholm. The major problem, as always, was to transport an invading army across the Channel without inviting its destruction by the British Navy. This problem Belleisle proposed to solve by four simultaneous thrusts: three at the British Isles, at widely separated points in Ireland, Scotland, and England, of which two would be feints; the fourth at the island of Minorca. The main force would be kept in reserve to support and drive home the most successful of the first three. The fourth attack, on Minorca, would be made in sufficient strength and with sufficient warning to force a division of the British naval forces between the Channel and the Mediterranean. If it failed as a diversion it could be hammered home as a secondary offensive. The plan was ingenious and practicable. It was unlikely to achieve complete success, but the effect of such bold action on a weak and vacillating British Government was certain to be worth while; moreover the immense prize to be gained by success far outweighed the loss to be expected from failure.

At the beginning of 1756, therefore, Newcastle's administration was faced with a problem of strategy the solution of which was of vital importance and could not be postponed. The French plan was known in detail; Newcastle's dilemma was to choose between the three possible methods of frustrating it. By concentrating the greatest available naval strength in the Channel, he could probably prevent the invasion fleet from sailing, but this would mean leaving Minorca to its fate. Alternatively, he could order an offensive against the invasion fleet which was still in the vulnerable state of preparation. Thirdly, he could prepare a counter-attack which would not be launched until the French were fully committed to their plan; this would have the immeasurable advantage of disrupting the French attack and forcing them to fight a defensive action on unfavourable ground. This was the course most likely to crush French hopes altogether but it required courage and strategical insight, qualities which were sadly lacking in the Cabinet. It is, perhaps, as well that Newcastle decided against this adventurous design. The pitiful lack of planning ability made evident by previous attempts to launch even the simplest expedition would surely have blighted its chances long before it was put into operation. He chose, instead, a compromise of bewildering futility. After several months of nervous indecision, he sent to Minorca a fleet too small to accomplish anything and too late to be of use to anyone. The unlucky commander of this detachment was Admiral John Byng.

The choice of Byng to command the Mediterranean fleet was unfortunate; he was a man of unquestioned personal courage and progressive ideas about naval tactics, but these qualities were strangled by a fatal indecision of mind which he was quite unable to overcome. This had already shown itself in his action—or rather lack of action—in Mediterranean waters during the previous war. He could always see, with terrible clarity, the difficulties and obstacles in an operation, and in the Mediterranean enterprise he was now called upon to undertake he did not have far to look in order to find them. He was allotted ten ships which, with the three already under Commodore Edgecombe's command, were considered sufficient to prevent the French from sailing out of Toulon; they were certainly not too many. Moreover all priority in fitting out and manning the ships available was given to Hawke, whose fleet was to blockade the French Channel ports and prevent the sailing of the invasion fleet. It was April before Byng could sail, and May before he arrived off Gibraltar. His instructions were complicated by uncertainty at home whether the French Toulon Squadron was intended for the attack on Minorca or to convoy reinforcements to Canada. Byng was therefore ordered to call at Gibraltar to find out whether the Toulon squadron had passed through the Straits: if it had, he was to pursue it into the Atlantic; if it had not, he was to blockade Toulon or sail to the aid of Minorca, whichever proved to be necessary.

Meanwhile a squadron of six of the line crept out of Brest, eluded Hawke and sailed for Canada. It carried Montcalm, the new governor, his lieutenants, de Lévis and de Boulamaque, and his aide, Bougainville, the four principal commanders of the French army during the ensuing campaigns in Canada.

Byng arrived at Gibraltar on 3rd May, only to learn from Edgecombe that a French army of 14,000 men with supporting artillery was already in possession of Minorca, except for the castle of St.

Philip, where the garrison, under the octogenarian General Blakeney, was besieged. Byng took counsel with General Fowke, then Governor of Gibraltar. To do so was only to take counsel with his fears. Fowke was a man of timid disposition, and together he and Byng indulged in an orgy of apprehensive indecision. When at last he sailed for Minorca on 8th May, Byng was already convinced of the certain failure of his mission. He was not destined to be disappointed.

Unknown to the British Government, the French had abandoned the invasion project and had concentrated for the attack on Minorca a force nearly four times the size of that intended by Belleisle and protected by a strong naval escort under the Marquis de la Galissonière, who as Governor of Canada had been the progenitor of the plan to strangle the New England colonies by a chain of forts from the Mississippi to the St. Lawrence, and who was one of the most capable officers in the French Navy. To command the land forces, Louis XV had appointed the Duc de Richelieu, a veteran roué more distinguished for his exploits in the bedroom than on the battlefield. He was supported by a galaxy of the French military aristocracy including two lieutenant-generals, five 'marshals of the field', and twelve brigadiers. The landing on Minorca had been unopposed and the army had advanced rapidly to Port Mahon; but there the attack had been halted. The ground was too rock-strewn for trenching and a galling fire was poured down upon the attackers by the besieged garrison in St. Philip's Castle. On 17th May, Byng's fleet was sighted, threatening Richelieu's lines of communication. On 20th May a long and indecisive naval action was fought, after which the French fleet stood away. Byng decided against giving chase and cruised indeterminately for three days without bringing the French to action. On the fourth day he summoned a council of war at which he succeeded in convincing himself that he could achieve nothing further and that the right course of action was to withdraw to Gibraltar. This decision was to cost him his life.

Early in May a dispatch was received in England from the Hon. Augustus Hervey, captain of one of Edgecombe's frigates, giving fresh details of Richelieu's force, and this was quickly followed by news of the landing in Minorca. On 18th May war was declared on France and four ships of the line were ordered to sea to reinforce Byng. By the end of the month Byng's anxious dispatches, written before he sailed from Gibraltar, had been received. Anson wrote to the Duke of Newcastle,[87] 'You won't be much pleased with his letter, and less with the Governor of Gibraltar's, who has sent no troops for the relief of Port Mahon, and for a very extraordinary reason, viz. because he then would have had fewer at Gibraltar.' Urgent action was required to retrieve the situation, and it was decided to supersede all the commanders concerned. Hawke was sent to replace Byng; Lord Tyrawly to take over from Fowke at Gibraltar; and Captain Charles Saunders, one of Anson's brilliant band of lieutenants on his famous voyage round the world,* was promoted to flag rank as Hawke's second-in-command.

Byng arrived at Gibralter on 19th June, collected his reinforcements, landed his sick who numbered a thousand, and set about repairing his fleet for a return to Minorca. On 4th July, before his preparations were completed, Hawke arrived to supersede him. Meanwhile Richelieu had received reinforcements of five battalions and had launched a successful attack on the citadel on 27th June.

Wolfe had followed the course of events with interest. On 1st June he wrote to his mother, 'The Lisbon mail is arrived, so you may expect some account of the Siege of Fort St. Philips, and of Admiral Bing's feats in the Mediterranean. . . . If things take a bad turn, & by our management I don't know what other to expect, this war may rout the funds & destroy our public credit root & branch.' The Twentieth were on their way from Canterbury to Devizes. From Bristol he writes on 7th June, 'Are the measures taken for the safety or relief of Minorca, or the proceedings of our Admiral most to be admired?' By 27th June, he knew of Byng's withdrawal and wrote to his father who was once more laid up with gout, 'I wish you joy of Admiral Bing's escape, and of the safe arrival of our fleet at Gibraltar. General Blakeney has no great obligations to the Navy upon this occasion. They have left him in an ugly scrape, out of which, I am persuaded, he will only be delivered by a Cannon Shot. . . . You are happy in your infirmity, for 'tis a disgrace to act in these dishonourable times.'

* Others included Augustus Keppel, Piercy Brett (whose sons, Charles and Timothy, were close friends of Wolfe's) and John Campbell.

His temper was doubtless not improved by the appointment of another colonel of the regiment to succeed Honeywood. This time, however, the choice was a worthy one; the new colonel was William Kingsley, who later commanded the regiment with distinction at Minden, and died, a lieutenant-general, in 1769. Wolfe accepted the appointment as reasonable and just—and a great deal more suitable than many that might have been made—and was soon on good terms with his new commander. The failure of British arms at Minorca had made clear to him the faults in administration, and the lack of decision at command level: 'So,' he writes to his father on 17th July, 'upon summing up the whole of our conduct in this affair, both as to project & execution, it does appear to me that we are the most egregious Blunderers in War that ever took the Hatchet in hand.'

A heavy responsibility for the Minorca fiasco lay on the Duke of Newcastle's shoulders and he lost no time in finding a scape-goat for his failure. He wrote at once to his friend Hardwicke, the astute Lord Chancellor, urging that Anson should prepare a defence of the Government, and demanding the 'Immediate Tryal & Condemnation of Admiral Byng'.[88] The unfortunate Admiral landed at Portsmouth on 26th July, where he was ceremoniously arrested and brought to London under armed guard. Incited by a planned campaign of vilification, the mob of the city howled for his blood, and he was burnt in effigy in towns all over England. His trial was ordered, and to a deputation from the City of London a trembling Newcastle promised abjectly, 'Oh! indeed he shall be tried immediately—he shall be hanged directly.'[89] Byng was fairly tried, and as fairly condemned, on the charge of having failed to do his utmost against the enemy. Under the Articles of War then in use, the only penalty for this crime was death. The court strove to have the sentence reduced, and they were supported by Pitt and by protests from Voltaire and Richelieu himself. The protests were unavailing; Byng was shot on the quarter-deck of the *Monarque* in Portsmouth Harbour on 14th March 1757. 'Dans ce pays-ci,' wrote Voltaire,[90] 'il est bon de tuer de temps en temps un amiral pour encourager les autres.' Towards the end, public opinion had veered in Byng's favour, but Wolfe was inflexible: 'The public papers seem to have taken a turn in favour of our Admiral,' he writes from Stroud in

November; 'but I, who am an eye-witness of the consequences of his fatal conduct shall never be brought to soften towards him. . . . Alas! our affairs are falling down apace. The country is going fast upon its ruin, by the paltry projects & more ridiculous execution of those who are entrusted.'

The public anger was not exhausted by the return and arrest of the unhappy Byng. Grave mistakes had been made and it was clear that they had their roots in the Government itself whose pusillanimity had been exhibited too openly to be ignored. Newcastle sought frenziedly for any excuse to retain his high office; but Fox and Murray had deserted him to save themselves, and even Pitt, to whom he had turned as the last resort, had refused to take office under his leadership. The wily Granville, with whom Newcastle had offered to exchange offices, had replied, 'I will be hanged a little before I take your place, rather than a little after.'[91] Meanwhile the news from abroad was daily more depressing; in America the fort of Oswego had fallen to the French; on 8th September Frederick of Prussia had marched into Saxony, plunging into the continental war which Newcastle had been at such pains to avoid; the Russian alliance was crumbling; and in India, Calcutta had fallen to Siraj-ud-Daula and the inhabitants had been murdered in the 'Black Hole'. Newcastle realized that where intrigue had failed only discretion could save him and he resigned. With great reluctance the King called upon Pitt to form a Ministry.

While Newcastle had been rummaging among his political acquaintances in fruitless search of a friend, Pitt, who had no direct access to the King, had been making his opinions known to him through Lady Yarmouth, the King's mistress. To Queen Caroline's dying suggestion that he should marry again George II had replied, 'Non, j'aurai des maîtresses'; Amalie Wallmoden, created Countess of Yarmouth in 1740, showed that the King was a man of his word. Pitt's unequivocal refusal to serve under Newcastle had left George II no option but to accept the loss of Newcastle and resign himself to the disagreeable prospect of a Government which included Pitt as Secretary for the South. The Duke of Devonshire replaced Newcastle as First Lord of the Treasury, and Temple, Pitt's brother-in-law, took over the Admiralty. Holdernesse remained as Secretary for the North, and

Granville as Privy Seal. The new Ministry was short-lived. Pitt's support of Byng had lost him some popularity, but the real causes of his fall were the King and Newcastle: the King had not wanted him and looked for an early opportunity to get rid of him; Newcastle wielded, by wealth and influence, a political power against which it was impossible to stand alone. In April 1757 the final blow was struck when Cumberland refused to take up his command in Germany while Pitt was in power. On 6th April the King ordered Pitt to return his seals of office.

Pitt, so easily dismissed, was not so easily replaced. If no one could stand against Newcastle, no one, it seemed would stand with him. For nearly three months, while England was engaged in a crucial struggle with France, the country was virtually without a Government, and it was not until 29th June 1757 that a solution to the problem could be found.

Throughout the year, Wolfe remained with his regiment, hoping for orders that would send him on active service to Europe, America, or India. He waited in vain. He was destined never to take into action the regiment which he had brought to such a high degree of fitness for battle. Meanwhile he had busied himself with his military studies and the continued training of his men. His advice was sought frequently by young officers, and he spared himself no trouble in helping them. Thomas Townshend, the future Lord Sydney, sought his advice for his younger brother, Henry, and Wolfe wrote at length to recommend a course of study for the young officer.[92]

'Your brother, no doubt, is master of the Latin and French languages, and has some knowledge of the mathematics; without the last he can never become acquainted with one considerable branch of our business, the construction of fortification and the attack and defence of places; and I would advise him by all means to give up a year or two of his time now while he is young, if he has not already done it, to the study of mathematics, because it will greatly facilitate his progress in military matters.

As to the books that are fittest for this purpose, he may begin with the "King of Prussia's Regulations for his Horse and Foot", where the economy and good order of an army in the lower branches are extremely well established. Then there are the "Memoirs" of the Marquis de Santa Cruz, Feuquières, and Montecucculi; Folard's "Commentaries upon Polybius"; the "Projet de Tactique"; "L'Attaque et la Défense des Places", par le Maréchal de Vauban; "Les Memoires de Goulon"; "L'Ingenieur de Campagne". Le Sieur Renie for all that concerns artillery. Of the ancients, Vegetius, Caesar, Thucydides, Xenophon's "Life of Syrus", and "Retreat of the Ten Thousand Greeks". I do not mention Polybius, because the Commentaries and the History naturally go together. Of later days, Davila, Guicciardini, Strada, and the "Memoirs of the Duc de Sully". There is an abundance of military knowledge to be picked out of the lives of Gustavus Adolphus and Charles XII, King of Sweden, and of Zisca the Bohemian; and if a tolerable account could be got of the exploits of Scanderbeg,* it would be inestimable; for he excels all the officers, ancient and modern, in the conduct of a small defensive army. I met with him in the Turkish History, but nowhere else. The "Life of Suetonius" too, contains many fine things in this way. There is a book lately published that I have heard commended, "L'Art de la Guerre Pratique"—I suppose it is collected from all the best authors that treat of war; and there is a little volume, entitled "Traité de la Petite Guerre", that your brother should take in his pocket when he goes upon out-duty and detachment. The Maréchal de Puységur's book, too, is in esteem.

I believe Mr. Townshend will think this catalogue long enough . . .'[93]

Hugh Lord, a nephew of his friend William Rickson, also received a lengthy discourse, only part of which remains, filled with detailed advice on the behaviour of a young ensign:[93]

'Dear Huty,—By a letter from my mother, I find you are now an officer in Lord Chas. Hay's Regiment, which I heartily give you joy of, and, as I sincerely wish you success in life, you will give me leave to give you a few hints which may be of use

* George Castriota (1403?–1468), Albanian national hero, 'The Albanian Alexander'. Known as Scanderbeg (Turkish: Iskender Bey).

to you in it. The field you are going into is quite new to you, but may be trod very safely, and soon made known to you, if you only get into it by the proper entrance.

I make no doubt but you have entirely laid aside the boy and all boyish amusements, and have considered yourself as a young man going into a manly profession, where you must be answerable for your own conduct; your character in life must be that of a soldier and a gentleman; the first is to be acquired by application and attendance on your duty; the second by adhering most strictly to the dictates of honour, and the rules of good breeding; and be most particular in each of these points when you join your Regiment; if there are any officers' guard mounted, be sure constantly to attend the parade, observe carefully the manner of the officers taking their posts, the exercise of their espontoon, etc.; when the guard is marched off from the parade, attend it to the place of relief, and observe the manner and form of relieving, and when you return to your chamber (which should be as soon as you could, lest what you saw slip out of your memory), consult Bland's *Military Discipline* on that head; this will be the readiest method of learning this part of your duty, which is what you will be the soonest called on to perform. When off duty get a serjt or corporal, whom the adjutant will recommend to you, to teach you the exercise of the firelock, which I beg you to make yourself as much master of as if you were a simple soldier, the exact and nice knowledge of this will readily bring you to understand all other parts of your duty, make you a proper judge of the performance of the men, and qualify you for the post of an adjutant, and in time many other employments of credit.

When you are posted to your company, take care that the serjeants or corporals constantly bring you the orders; treat those officers with kindness, but keep them at a distance, so will you be beloved and respected by them. Read your orders with attention, and if anything in particular concerns yourself, put it down in your memorandum book, which I would have you [keep] constantly in your pocket ready for any remarks. Be sure to attend constantly morning and evening the roll calling of the company; watch carefully the absentees, and enquire into reasons for their being so; and particularly be watchful they do not endeavour to impose on you sham excuses, which they are apt to do with young officers, but will be deterred from it by a proper severity in detecting them.'

These letters provide striking evidence of his own studies and of the unusually high standards he demanded from his officers.

In July, the regiment moved into camp on the downs near Blandford. Wolfe hoped it would not be for long: 'If there is an ounce of resolution left, we shan't lye long idle,' he writes on 26th July, 'but I am afraid we have not spirit enough for an undertaking of any great moment. The Duke of Belleisle's name makes our pusillanimous tremble, and God knows there was never less cause.' He describes Kingsley, his new colonel, as 'a sensible man, & very sociable and polite.' The army which assembled on the downs consisted of six battalions with six squadrons and two troops of light horse, and 'twelve small pieces of artillery', but Wolfe reports 'a great scarcity of gun powder in the camp, so 'tis like we shall be obliged to do business without noise.' On 7th August, Wolfe writes[94] of the forthcoming addition of second battalions to every regiment of foot and his first care is to remind Lord Albemarle of a previous promise of a commission for a young friend, James Adeane, who many years later was to become a lieutenant-general and Gentleman of the Bedchamber to George III. He does not mention his own chances of promotion which were greatly strengthened by the addition of fifteen battalions to the army. At the beginning of September he accompanied the Duke of Richmond to Goodwood where he helped to entertain the Prince of Nassau and took the opportunity of watching the manœuvres of the Hessian troops which had recently arrived in England to strengthen the defence of the island against invasion. He was impressed by their exhibition of Prussian discipline and, according to another spectator, they made[95] 'a fine appearance, being generally straight, tall and slender. Their uniform is blue, turned up with red & faced with white, & their hair plaited behind hangs down to the waist.'

October brought the regiment the chance of action, but it was not of a kind to please men trained for war: orders were received by Wolfe on the 19th to march with six companies into Gloucestershire to assist in the suppression of riots among the weavers. From Sodbury on the 24th Wolfe writes of them with sympathy: 'I write you this short letter to inform you that the Gloucestershire Weavers & I are not yet come to blows nor do I believe we shall. The expedition carries me a little out of my road & a little in the dirt, but I believe there never was a more harmless piece of business—for I have men enough to beat the Mob of all England collected. I hope it will turn out a good recruiting Party, for the People are so oppress'd, so poor & so wretched, that they will perhaps hazard a knock on the pate for bread and cloaths, and turn Soldiers through sheer necessity. Tomorrow I enter the Enemy's Country, and disperse my Troops into their Winter Quarters, myself to a straggling dirty village, over the ankles in Mud. Bad accommodation & bad company are so familiar to me, that I am almost in danger of losing the taste for anything better.' He remained in Stroud throughout November and succeeded in avoiding the use of force in spite of some mob violence. The rest of the regiment had moved down to Plymouth, and with it had gone Richard and William Hooper, the sons of Wolfe's childhood nurse at Westerham, 'two of the finest soldiers in the camp at Shroton.' 'Richard,' he writes, 'has behaved so well that he has hopes of preferment; the other is an exceedingly able fellow, & strong as ten common men. I furnish'd them for their march to Plymouth, & gave them hopes of many good things in the profession.'

Wolfe's disagreeable assignment in Stroud brought on one of his moods of depression, and his thoughts turned again to his own ambitions: on 6th December he writes to his mother: 'It may happen that the 2nd Batt$^{ns.}$ of these Reg$^{ts.}$ may have Colonels appointed to them without including your Son in the number. A man who never asks a favour will hardly ever obtain it. I persuade myself they will put no inferior Officer (unless a Peer) over my head, in which case I cannot complain; not being able to say that I have ever done more than my duty; and happy if I came up to that. If any Soldier is preferred when my turn comes, I shall acquaint the Secretary at War that I am sensible of the injury that is done me, and will take the earliest opportunity to put it out of his or any man's power to repeat it. Not while the war lasts; for if 500 young officers one after another were to rise before me I should continue to serve with the utmost diligence, to acquit myself to the Country, & to show the Ministers that they had acted unjustly. But I flatter myself that I shall never be forced to these disagreeable measures.'

He was right: later in the same month he was able to report from his new headquarters in Cirencester that Sir John Mordaunt had taken the opportunity to recommend his name to the King, and by the following February Wolfe was writing to the Duke of Bedford* to thank him for the offer of the appointments of Barrackmaster-General and Quartermaster-General of Ireland, both of which, by custom, carried the rank of Colonel. Wolfe suspected, however, that in his case the promotion might be overlooked. To his father he writes on 6th February, 'But I shall give it up immediately & come back to the Battalion, if the rank of Colonel is omitted; & I had rather see the King of Prussia's operations the next Campaign than accept of this employment with all its advantages.' Bedford was, in fact, soon prevailed upon to give the office of Barrackmaster-General to someone else. Wolfe accepted the post of Quartermaster-General, but with reservations which he confides to his father. 'I am far from being pleased with it otherwise than as a mark of the Duke of Bedford's friendship & good opinion, being too much a Soldier to desire any but military employments, which this can hardly be reckon'd.' Nor was he shy of acquainting the Duke of Bedford with his doubts: 'The only circumstance,' he writes on 19th February, 'that could at all lessen my satisfaction on this occasion is, to be in some measure distinguished from the officers who have held this employment before by a rank inferior to theirs, and which seemed to be annexed to this office.' Nevertheless, by the end of March he was in London to attend a royal levee at St. James's and to kiss hands on his appointment. Among those who watched the young lieutenant-colonel as, with mixed feelings, he formally accepted his new office, was the Secretary of State for the South, William Pitt, who was to be dismissed from office eight days later only to return in triumph to direct the conduct of the war in which Wolfe was to achieve his highest ambition.

* John Russell, 4th Duke of Bedford (1710–1771), Lord-Lieutenant of Ireland, 1756–7.

CHAPTER XII

The Rochefort Expedition

ON 29th June 1757, Pitt again kissed hands on his appointment as Secretary of State for the South. After nearly three months of fruitless search for an alternative, the King had been forced to agree to a coalition of the Pitt and Newcastle factions. Pitt, as Secretary of State, would be responsible for the conduct of the war; Newcastle, as First Lord of the Treasury, would direct administration at home. The King was far from satisfied with the arrangement, but all attempts to form any kind of government without Pitt had failed. Moreover there had been an embarrassing demonstration of public affection for Pitt after his dismissal from office: London had presented him with the freedom of the City in a gold box worth a hundred pounds; and, as Horace Walpole wrote on 5th May,[96] 'Bath, Exeter, Yarmouth and Worcester have followed the example of London, and sent their freedoms to Pitt and Legge: I suppose Edinburgh will, but instead of giving, will ask for a gold box in return. . . .' For some weeks 'it rained gold boxes.' Even Newcastle could not afford to ignore such clear expressions of public opinion, and without his support no ministry could stand for long. George II gave his new ministers a cool reception: some, according to Bedford's secretary, Rigby, were 'not in the Closet long enough for the door to be shut,'[97] and Pitt was only allowed about five minutes.

In spite of the royal displeasure, the new Government was strong: Anson, one of the ablest of all naval administrators, returned to the Admiralty; Holdernesse remained as Secretary for the North and Barrington as Secretary at War; Legge became Chancellor of the Exchequer; and Fox accepted the office of

Paymaster-General, 'professing great content, and that he should offend neither in thought, word, nor deed.'[98]

Seldom has a new government been faced with problems of such urgency and magnitude. In Europe, on 11th June, Frederick the Great had sustained a crushing defeat at Kolin, news of which reached England on the day Pitt took office; Russia and Sweden were preparing to attack Prussia; and the fleet under Admiral Holburne which, during his first ministry, Pitt had ordered to fit out for an attack on Louisbourg to relieve pressure on the New England colonies, had not yet sailed.

Pitt at once made clear the strategic principles upon which his direction of the war was to be founded. Britain, he argued, was a maritime and mercantile power; her strength lay not in her armies—which could not be raised on the continental scale—but in her fleet and her wealth from trade. War on the Continent was of secondary significance:[98] 'The distant operations in America are of at least as much consequence to what ought to be the King of Prussia's ultimate end in the measures he had pursued, viz. a safe and honourable peace.' Frederick was to be supported but he must be made to realize that[100] 'it is the result of the great struggle between England and France that will determine the conditions of the future peace.' Frederick was pressing for a British fleet to be sent to the Baltic to guard his rear, but to this demand Pitt could not yield. The priority tasks for the Navy were to blockade the French fleets in Brest and Toulon, thus securing the Channel and the Mediterranean and preventing the flow of reinforcements to the colonies, and to support our land forces in India and America. Any ships that could be spared from these duties could be best employed in covering combined land and sea attacks on the French coast. This had, in fact, been suggested by Frederick himself in the previous year. 'If,' he had written,[101] 'France strips her channel coasts to form her army, the English fleet can profit by it and make descents on the naked coasts spreading the alarm throughout Brittany and Normandy.' This was exactly what Pitt now had in mind. Our armies were not in sufficient strength to exert any dramatic influence as land forces in Germany, but if the Navy could immobilize the French fleet a decisive blow could be struck in America, and harassing raids could be made on the coast of France which would force the

French to withdraw a substantial part of their army from the field against Frederick.

Plans for such a raid were put in hand without delay. Frederick's plight was desperate, and unless he could be offered some relief there was a distinct danger that either his army would be destroyed or he would sue for a separate peace. As a first step, therefore, the Hanoverian and Hessian troops, brought over by Newcastle—to the disgust of the people—to defend the country against invasion, were sent back to the Continent to join Cumberland's army, and a militia force was raised to replace them. Pitt then set about planning a combined naval and military operation against the French coast. The objective he chose was the naval fort of Rochefort. Intelligence had been received that the port was weakly defended on the land side, and it was of sufficient intrinsic importance to the French to make an attack upon it a threat which could not be ignored. The urgency of the operation was increased by the unwelcome news that Cumberland's army had been defeated by the French under D'Estrées at Hastenbeck on 24th July. Fortunately the French chose that moment to supersede D'Estrées by the Duc de Richelieu, and, although by 11th August, Hanover had fallen, the advantage was not fully exploited. One of the principal reasons for Richelieu's failure to follow up the victory at Hastenbeck was his anxiety about his exposed coastal flank. News had already reached him of preparations for the embarkation of an army from England, but nothing was known of its objective. It might appear at Emden, or at Stade on the Elbe, or even in the Netherlands. Richelieu's advance was halted until further information could be acquired, and the Austrian garrisons in the Netherlands were reinforced. Already Pitt's plan to relieve the pressure on Cumberland's and Frederick's armies was having effect.

The expedition against Rochefort was to consist of about 8,000 men and almost the whole of the home fleet. Command of the fleet was given to Hawke, and Wolfe's friend and patron, Sir John Mordaunt, was nominated to command the army. The choice of Mordaunt was ill-judged: in his youth he had acquired a considerable reputation for bravery and daring, but he was now sixty and had lost his nerve; he was, as Horace Walpole wrote, 'much broken in spirit and constitution, and had fallen into a nervous disorder.'[102] Pitt had originally chosen Lord George Sackville, but he had declined the appointment; Pitt's second choice, Conway, had been refused by the King on the grounds that he was too young. Conway was therefore appointed second-in-command with Cornwallis as third. Cornwallis had been among those who, with General Fowke, had shared the lesser responsibilities for the Minorca fiasco and his determination was therefore suspect. Both Mordaunt and Conway viewed the whole project with apprehension.* The one army officer who could be counted upon to bring energy and enthusiasm to the task was the Quarter-master-General to the expedition, Lieutenant-Colonel James Wolfe. It is clear, however, that at first even Wolfe had his doubts, for on 21st July he wrote to Rickson, 'We are about to undertake something or other at a distance; and I am one of the Party. I can't flatter you with a lively picture of my hopes as to the Success of it—the reasons are so strong against us (the English) in whatever we take in hand; that I never expect any great matter—the Chiefs, the Engineers, & our wretched discipline, are the great & insurmountable obstructions.' None the less he was glad to be offered active service at last and he wrote to the Duke of Bedford to give him news of his new employment. His commission as colonel had not been granted for the Irish appointment and it was evident to him that a landing on the French coast offered more opportunities for distinguishing himself than the post of Quartermaster-General in Ireland.

By the middle of August the troops for the expedition were assembled in the Isle of Wight, but difficulties in obtaining sufficient transports delayed their sailing. Pitt, who was only too conscious of the resistance to his plan both from within the Cabinet and from the commanders concerned, issued brusque orders to Hawke to take troops on board his battleships if necessary but at all costs to sail. Up to the last moment Pitt was under pressure from the King, from Newcastle, and from the rest of the Cabinet, to divert the expedition to Stade, but he resolutely refused to change his plan, even offering to resign rather than do so. The urgency was all the greater as Pitt had been forced to yield to

* 'Mordaunt & Conway, are both full of apprehension, that the intended expedition may be hazardous, in the greatest Degree.'[103] Newcastle to Hardwicke, 21st July 1757.

156

Hardwicke's insistence that the army should be back in England by the end of September. When he heard that contrary winds had further delayed the departure of the expedition, he wrote curtly to Hawke ordering him to sail, and instructed his messenger to wait until he could return with the news that this order had been carried out. Hawke sailed on the following day, 6th September.

The instructions given to the commanders were clear enough and, in the light of the events that followed, merit some attention: Rochefort was given as the primary objective, where docks, magazines, arsenals, and shipping were to be destroyed. Whether this attack succeeded or not, the expedition was to continue along the coast and operate against any suitable harbour or landing-place from Bordeaux to Havre.

The fleet arrived at last off the French coast on the 20th, but was blown out to sea again and could not anchor between the islands of Rhé and Oléron until the 22nd. Mordaunt and Conway had, according to Hawke, by then made up their minds that if they were to be back in England by the end of the month as instructed it was already too late to attempt anything. Wolfe had had a wretched voyage: 'I have not myself been one hour well since we embark'd,' he wrote on the 17th from aboard *Ramillies*, 'and have the mortification to find I am the worst Mariner in the whole Ship. . . . If I make the same figure ashoar, I shall acquire no great reputation by the Voyage.' On the 21st he wrote to his father, from a position off the Isles of Rhé and Oléron, to tell him of the fleet's arrival at its destination: 'Yesterday morning the Fleet made the Land of the Isle of Rhé, & in the afternoon Vice-Admiral Knowles was detached with his Division to go within the Pertuis d'Antioche & see what anchoring there was for the fleet; and I suppose he had orders to attack any fortifications or Batteries of the Enemy that might incommode us at an anchor, or prevent our Landing. While the Vice-Admiral was getting on to put these orders in Execution, a large French Man of War bore down into the middle of the Fleet, (a ship supposed to be homeward bound from the East or West Indies), upon which three ships of his division were directed to chace. They did so, & drove the French ship Close in with the Shoar above the river of Bordaux; & there our great ships were obliged to leave her. This chace put an end to the operations of yesterday. As soon as the chasing Ships return'd this morning, it was resolved that the whole fleet should go down & anchor in the Basque Road, from whence we may attack either of these two Islands, Rochelle or Rochefort. A disposition was made, & the Vice-Admiral's division led in. Just as the whole Fleet was getting within the Pertuis the wind took 'em short, and they were oblig'd to stand out again, & here we now are, beating on & off, waiting for a better day & a more favourable Gale.' On the 22nd and 23rd he adds to his letter: '22nd.—we are now at an anchor within the Pertuis d'Antioche, between the isles of Rhé & Oléron, waiting for a breeze of wind to go down upon the Isle D'Aix, which is in sight; but it is a perfect calm, and our whole force is unmovable. 23rd., in the morning,—All still at an anchor, the inhabitants of Rhé working hard at their entrenchments along the Shoar, to prevent our landing. The Medway, Achilles, and a fire-ship order'd to burn a French Ship of War behind the Isle D'Aix as soon as Admiral Knowles' division begins the attack.' The *Magnanime* which led the chase of the French ship was then commanded by Captain Richard Howe with whom Wolfe struck up a friendship 'like the union of a cannon and gunpowder.'[104]

The attack on Rochefort necessitated the sailing of the fleet through the Basque Roads between the islands of Rhé and Oléron and on into the Charente estuary. It was not until the 22nd that Hawke succeeded in manœuvring the fleet into the Roads, which were then seen to be far wider than he had been led to believe; this permitted the entire force to anchor out of range of the batteries on the islands. Nevertheless it was considered that the small island of Aix must be reduced before any troops could be landed. Howe therefore led Knowles's division into the attack, and brought his ship to within forty yards of the fort; *Barfleur* followed his courageous lead, and the flag on the fort was promptly hauled down in surrender.

There was now apparently nothing to hinder an attack on the mainland. If further encouragement were needed, it had arrived in the form of dispatches from Pitt extending the time limit of the operation. The fort at Fouras, defending the mouth of the river, was weakly held, and the French garrison considering that all was lost concerned themselves with saving their personal property.

As soon as Aix had surrendered, Wolfe had gone ashore to reconnoitre. He climbed to a bastion commanding a view of the mainland and made a careful examination of the coast near the mouth of the Charente. Then, pausing only to gather a handful of grapes ['exceedingly delicious, especially to a sick stomach'] he hurried back to report to Mordaunt.

Wolfe's report took the form of an outline plan of attack.[105] He proposed the bombardment of Fouras, a diversionary demonstration by the fleet against La Rochelle, and a landing in force at Chatellaillon Bay; and he added that to ensure success no time should be lost in putting the plan into operation. Hawke consulted his Huguenot pilot, Thierry, and agreed to all but the Rochelle diversion. The generals being also in agreement, Hawke's rear-admiral, Brodrick, was sent with three captains to find a suitable landing-place. No military officer accompanied them, as Mordaunt in his ignorance considered the choice of a landing-place purely sailors' business. No single omission of all those for which he was responsible so clearly demonstrates Mordaunt's abysmal failure to comprehend the first principles of a combined operation. On the afternoon of the following day, the 24th, Brodrick returned to report that he had found a place in Chatellaillon Bay where he could land 'without wetting his shoes'. Hawke assumed that a landing would be attempted immediately; but instead, a council of war was summoned for the morning of the 25th. At this meeting the generals debated for several hours whether or not Rochefort was protected by a wet or dry ditch and whether or not it could be taken by escalade. Deciding that an escalade might fail, they asked Hawke for an assurance that their retreat would be covered by the Navy. Hawke could only reply that troops could not be embarked in a heavy surf. Fortified by the news that Hawke's ships detached to bombard Fouras had run aground, the generals clung to their one safe decision: they agreed to do nothing.

Wolfe describes the events which followed in a letter to his 'Uncle Wat' written on 18th October:[106] 'The 25th,—this famous council sat from morning till late at night, and the result of the debates was unanimously not to attack the place they were ordered to attack, and for reasons that no soldier will allow to be sufficient. The 26th,—the Admiral sends a message to the General, intimating that if they did not determine to do something there, he would go to another place. The 27th,—the Generals and Admirals view the land with glasses, and agree upon a second council of war, having by this time discovered their mistake. The 28th,—they deliberate, and resolve to land that night. Orders are issued out accordingly, but the wind springing up after the troops had been two or three hours in the boats, the officers of the navy declare it difficult and dangerous to attempt the landing. The troops are commanded back to their transports, and so ended the expedition! The true state of the case is, that our sea-officers do not care to be engaged in any business of this sort, where little is to be had but blows and reputation; and the officers of the infantry are so profoundly ignorant, that an enterprise of any vigour astonishes them to that degree that they have not strength of mind nor confidence to carry it through.'

At daybreak on the 29th, Wolfe and Conway together carried out a further reconnaissance; but by this time Hawke, who had given up any pretence of co-operation, had lost all patience. 'Sir,' he wrote to Mordaunt, 'should the officers of the troops have no further operations to propose considerable enough to authorise my detaining the squadron under my command longer here, I beg leave to acquaint you that I intend to proceed to England without loss of time.' Mordaunt pleaded feebly for another joint council, but this request was dismissed by Hawke who made it plain that he would brook no further delays. Mordaunt meekly agreed to abandon the entire project and return to England. He returned to an official inquiry and a general court-martial.

Wolfe writes in his letter to 'Uncle Wat', 'I look upon this as the greatest design that the nation has engaged in for many years, and it must have done honour to us all, if the executions had answered the intentions of the projector. . . . If they would even blunder on and fight a little making some amends to the public by their courage for their want of skill; but this excessive degree of caution, or whatever name it deserves, leaves exceeding bad impressions among the troops, who, to do them justice, upon this occasion showed all the signs of spirit and goodwill.'

By 17th October he was back in Blackheath, and writing to his mother in Bath:[107] 'As to the expedition, it has been conducted so ill that I am asham'd to have been of the party. The Publick could not do better than to dismiss 6 or 8 of us from their service.

No Zeal, no Ardour, no care or concern for the good & honour of our Country.'

It was to Rickson that Wolfe poured out his true feelings about the failure of the expedition, and his letter remains to this day one of the classic utterances on the principles of amphibious warfare, of which he was to make himself one of the great exponents. He writes from Blackheath on 5th November:

'Dear Rickson,

I thank you very heartily for your welcome back—I am not sorry I went, notwithstanding what has happen'd; one may always pick up something useful from amongst the most fatal errors. I have found out that an Admiral should endeavour to run into an enemy's port immediately after he appears before it, that he shou'd anchor the transport ships & frigates as close as he can to the land, that he shou'd reconnoitre & observe it as quick as possible, and lose no time in getting the troops on Shoar—that previous directions shou'd be given in respect to landing the troops, & a proper disposition made for the Boats of all sorts, appointing Leaders and fit Persons for conducting the different divisions. On the other hand experience shows me that in an affair depending upon vigour & despatch—the Generals shou'd settle their plan of operations, so that no time may be lost in idle debates and consultations when the Sword shou'd be drawn—that pushing on smartly is the road to success, & more particularly so in an affair of this nature; that nothing is to be reckon'd an obstacle to your undertaking which is not found really so upon tryal—that in War, something must be allowed to chance & Fortune—Seeing it is in its nature hazardous, and an Option of difficulties—that the greatness of an object should come under consideration, opposed to the impediments that lye in the way; that the honour of one's Country is to have some weight & that in particular circumstances & times, the loss of 1000 men, is rather an advantage to a Nation than otherwise—seeing that Gallant attempts raise its reputation and make it respectable, whereas the contrary appearances sink the Credit of a Country, ruin the Troops & create infinite uneasiness & discontent at home. I know not what to say, My Dear Rickson, or how to account for our proceedings—unless I own to you—that there never was People collected together so unfit for the business they were sent upon—Dilatory, ignorant, irresolute, & some grains of a very unmanly Quality, & very unsoldierlike or unsailorlylike. I have already been too imprudent. I have said too much, & People make me say ten times more than I ever utter'd; therefore, repeat nothing out of my letter—nor name my name as author of any one thing. The whole affair turned upon the impracticability of escalading Rochefort, & the two Evidences brought to prove that the Ditch was wet (in opposition to the Assertions of the chief Engineer, who had been in the Place) are Persons to whom in my mind very little Credit shou'd be given; without these Evidences we should have landed, & must have marched to Rochefort, and it is my opinion that the place would have surrender'd, or have been taken, in 48 hours.

Little Practice in War, ease & convenience at home, great incomes . . . with no ambition to stirr to action are not the instruments to work a successful War withal; I see no Prospect of better deeds. I know not where to look for them, or from whom we may expect them. Many handsome things would have been done by the troops had they been permitted to act. As it is, Captain Howe carried off all the honour of this enterprise. . . .'

It is to Wolfe's undying credit that the clarity with which he saw the appalling shortcomings of his commanders did not affect his loyalty to them. No word of criticism of their inaction was spoken in his evidence at the inquiry or at Mordaunt's court-martial. But his apprenticeship was ended: he was now fitted for command, and the opportunity for which he had prepared himself was not long to be delayed.

CHAPTER XIII

Design for Conquest in America

WHEN Pitt returned to office at the end of June 1757, he was confident that under his direction England could regain the initiative in the war with France, and at the same time give material assistance to Prussia in her struggle with Austria, Russia and Sweden. His strategy was founded on four essential aims: the security of England as a base; the continuance of the alliance with Prussia; command of the sea; and the conquest of Canada. The Militia Bill made provision for adequate defence at home, and released the Hanoverian and Hessian troops in England for service under Cumberland in Germany; the presence of Cumberland's army would help to sustain the Prussian alliance, but further assistance could be given by combined operations which would force the French to withdraw part of their army in Germany to defend their own coastline; command of the sea was already within our grasp; and Admiral Holburne was preparing to sail to Halifax, where he would join Lord Loudon, who had replaced Shirley as colonial commander-in-chief, for an attack on Louisbourg and Quebec.

By the end of October, the whole structure of this strategic plan had disintegrated. On 16th September it was learned in London that Cumberland, driven into a corner by Richelieu, had signed the Convention of Closterseven under the terms of which it was agreed that his army should be disbanded; no concessions to Hanover were offered in return. The Rochefort expedition returned on 7th October having, as it seemed, achieved nothing. At the end of the month, there arrived news from Canada: Montcalm had profited by Loudon's move to Halifax to attack

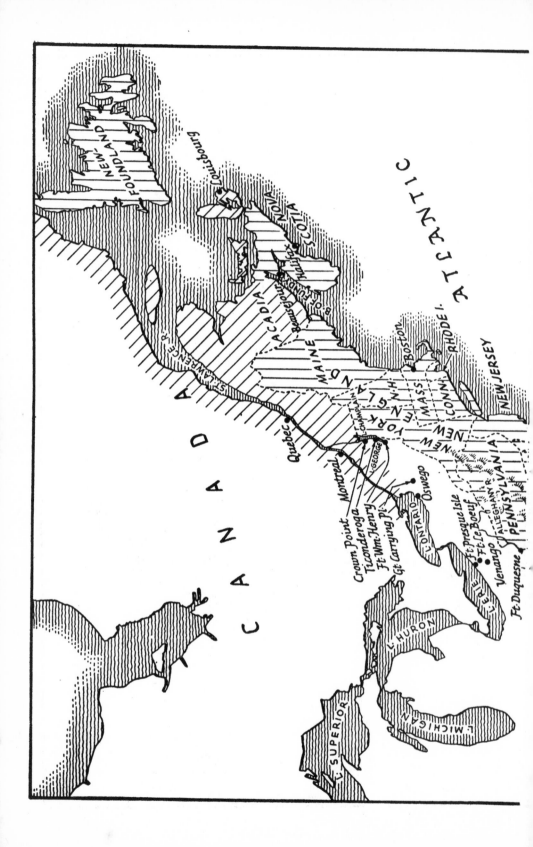

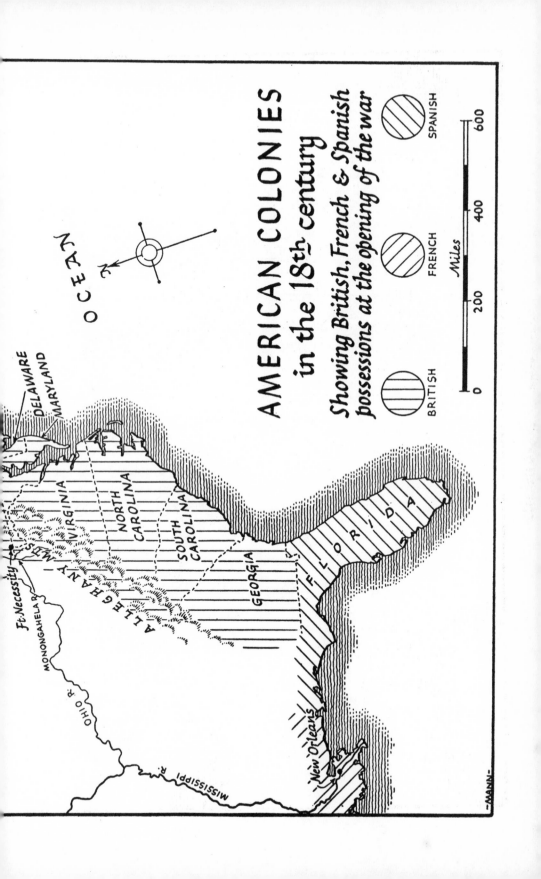

AMERICAN COLONIES
in the 18th century

Showing British, French & Spanish
possessions at the opening of the war

BRITISH   FRENCH   SPANISH

Miles

0   200   400   600

OCEAN

DELAWARE
MARYLAND

VIRGINIA
NORTH CAROLINA
SOUTH CAROLINA
GEORGIA

ALLEGHANY MTS.

Ft. Necessity
MONONGAHELA R.
OHIO R.
MISSISSIPPI R.

New Orleans

FLORIDA

—MANN—

Fort William Henry at the end of Lake George. On 9th August the fort had surrendered, and Montcalm had apparently been powerless to prevent the massacre of almost the entire garrison by his Indians. Further news was to follow: Holburne had arrived in Halifax too late to persuade Loudon to attempt the attack on Louisbourg, and the project had been abandoned. As if this were not enough, attempts to enforce the Militia Bill had resulted in widespread riots throughout the country. 'I fear,' wrote Pitt with unusual but commendable restraint, 'we do not stand in the smile of heaven.'

On 13th July, before he set out for Rochefort, Wolfe had written to his friend Lord Fitzmaurice,[108] '. . . the Tide seems to set strongly against us, every where, & I know not the Man to stop it: However there are still some remains of Vigour in the Army, which indeed breaks out now & then, a little irregularly; an Officer of Cornwallis's Regt. at the Camp of Amersham has committed a rape, for which (to avoid being hang'd) he has fled— I hope Billy Nugent will abstain.' On his return he wrote again to Fitzmaurice,[108] 'We shall never Muster up resolution enough to make another attack, the disappointments of this Campaign, (which I reckon by this time are compleated with the safe return of the Squadron from Louisbourg) will put us out of humour with offensive measures, & we shall continue to tremble here at home, under the fluttering of the Duke of Newcastle's wings.'

Only in India had there been any sign of success. There, Clive and Admiral Charles Watson had recaptured Calcutta and avenged the disgrace of the 'Black Hole'.

Immediate action was required to retrieve the country from the disasters into which it was falling. The Convention of Closterseven must be refuted and the Prussian alliance revived; and a new expedition must be fitted out to take Louisbourg and Quebec. Closterseven proved to be easier to break than to keep: Pitt persuaded parliament to subsidize the whole of Cumberland's army in Germany if the King would reject the convention, but no sooner had George II agreed to this than Richelieu, ignoring the provisions of the treaty, threatened to disarm the Hessians. George II promptly repudiated the convention; Cumberland was recalled; and the army was reconstituted under the command of Prince Ferdinand of Brunswick. The problem of the Prussian alliance was more difficult. Pitt was determined that Frederick should sign a convention by which, in return for a large subsidy, he would agree not to make peace with France except by mutual agreement with England. Frederick was equally determined to obtain the subsidy without the convention, and to force Pitt to send a British army to Germany. Several months passed before the stalemate could be broken. There remained America: before any preparations for another expedition could be made Pitt had to settle with the King the vital issue of the choice of commanders.

The failure of the Rochefort expedition had filled Newcastle and the other members of the Cabinet with apprehension. This, they thought, was another Minorca. Already the people were shouting for punitive action to be taken against the leaders of the expedition, and the frightened ministers were thankful to have Mordaunt at hand to be sacrificed. But Pitt had no intention of allowing Mordaunt to discredit the Government by becoming another Byng. He had failed in his command, but he could still be useful. There would be an official inquiry into the failure of the expedition, and from the findings of the court it would become apparent that the fault lay not with the plan but with the leaders. By this method Pitt hoped to gain further support for his strategy and to obtain complete control over the appointment of commanders in the field. The first step in that direction was taken, unwittingly, by the King himself. Anxious to prove that Cumberland had exceeded his brief in signing the Convention of Closterseven, George II had recalled him from Germany. It was, in fact, clear to Pitt and to the Cabinet that Cumberland's action, however unjustifiable from a military standpoint, was within the scope of the power delegated to him by the King. But George II was not above disgracing his own son to exculpate himself. Cumberland resigned, and on Pitt's recommendation Ligonier was appointed commander-in-chief. Pitt could now undertake the organization of another expedition against Canada confident of the support of a commander-in-chief whose ability, experience, and prestige were beyond dispute. To Ligonier, whom he had knighted on the field of Dettingen, the King would listen with attention and respect.

The next step was to confirm public confidence in Pitt's direction of the war by clarifying the reasons for failure at Rochefort. In November a Board of General Officers was convened to inquire into the conduct of the expedition. It consisted of the Duke of Marlborough, Lord George Sackville, and General Waldegrave. Before them appeared Mordaunt, Conway and Cornwallis; and among those called to give evidence was Colonel James Wolfe.

Wolfe's promotion to Colonel of the Sixty-Seventh Foot* had been announced during October, while he was at his parents' house at Blackheath. The General and Mrs. Wolfe were in Bath, and he wrote at once to give them his good news. He was conscious of the significance of his promotion at a time when the conduct of all those who had been engaged in the Rochefort operation was under critical examination, and he had little doubt that it was to Hawke that he owed this public recognition of his services. On 8th November he wrote to his mother that he had been summoned to give evidence at the inquiry. It was a summons which he obeyed without enthusiasm. There was no doubt in his mind where the blame for failure should be laid, and he expressed his opinions with great freedom in letters to his parents and to Rickson. But Mordaunt and Cornwallis were his friends. Faced with the conflicting interests of his duty to the Army and loyalty to his friends, he gave his evidence on the 14th without prevarication; but he deliberately minimized the importance of his plan for a landing, and depreciated its chances of success. He even gave it as his opinion that the landing could have been prevented by so small a force as a thousand foot and three or four hundred horse. The fort at Fouras, he admitted, had seemed vulnerable, and Howe had offered to take it with his ship alone. On the 21st the board informed the King of their findings: the expedition had, in their opinion, failed principally because the plan of attacking Fouras simultaneously by sea and land had not been carried out. Wolfe's plan, they recorded, 'certainly must have been of the greatest utility towards carrying your Majesty's instructions into execution.' Wolfe had done what he could, but nothing he could say or leave unsaid could disguise the incompetence and faint-heartedness of the military commanders concerned. Mordaunt was sent for court-martial. Fortunately nothing could hide the resource and energy which had been displayed by both Wolfe and Howe.

* 2nd Battalion The Royal Hampshire Regiment.

Wolfe was tied to London until Christmas, dividing his living between his parents' house at Blackheath and lodgings in the city, while his evidence at the inquiry and Mordaunt's court-martial was being heard. Mordaunt was in a miserable state of health, and Wolfe doubted if he would be able to stand up to the strain of lengthy court proceedings. Towards the end of December, the court acquitted him, and after a week of hesitation the King was persuaded to approve the verdict. Wolfe was thus freed to join his parents in Bath for Christmas.

The year ended in a sudden blaze of renewed hope: Frederick, 'the Protestant Hero' of Europe, routed a French army under Soubise at Rossbach on 5th November, and, turning swiftly back to Silesia, on 5th December crushed a force of 80,000 Austrians at Leuthen with an army less than half as strong. Pitt, when he heard the news of Rossbach, wrote thankfully to Grenville,[109] 'Heaven be praised for this great event. And now to dinner with a better appetite.' But Frederick's successes revived the old clash of rival interests. British interests, in Pitt's view, demanded the support of Frederick's army to contain French and Austrian strength in Europe until the conquest of Canada could be completed; British prestige required the support of the mixed army under Prince Ferdinand to regain the Electorate of Hanover. Frederick's strategy, on the other hand, took little or no account of conquests in India or America, but focused on the defeat of France and Austria and the permanent recovery of Silesia. The danger to England lay in the possibility that these more limited aims might be achieved by one or two more victories of Rossbach or Leuthen proportions and might then become the terms of a separate settlement. Pitt's negotiations with Frederick were lengthy and delicate; the care with which each instruction to Mitchell, the British Ambassador to Prussia, was drafted drove Holdernesse to distraction; but Pitt was determined to extract a definite undertaking from Frederick that no separate peace would be concluded, and he succeeded. He was prepared to pay any price except the deployment of a British army on the Continent. The price he paid was a subsidy of the unprecedented figure of £670,000.

On 26th December, Pitt wrote to the Duke of Newcastle urgently requesting his presence in London for a meeting of the

Cabinet to approve new plans for an American campaign. New-castle declined this invitation; it was, he explained, impossible for him to leave home so soon after Christmas and at a time when he was entertaining the Bishop of Durham. He would, he felt sure, concur with anything upon which Pitt might decide. Pitt's reply was cool:[110] 'I hope,' he wrote on the 27th, 'Your Grace will not think me unreasonable or improper in wishing to have the sanction of a meeting of the Cabinet and particularly of your Grace present there, concerning so important and extensive a scene as the campaign in America, where England and Europe are to be fought for. . . . I cannot, however, after the desire your Grace has expressed not to break the agreeable engagements of Claremont, press any further your Grace's taking the trouble to come to Town.'

No time was wasted. On 7th January, Wolfe received in Exeter a letter calling him at once to London. He had already ridden thirty-three miles the previous day, and now had to ride a further hundred and seventy almost without a halt. He rode through the night, leaving Exeter at five o'clock on the 7th and arriving in London at one on the following day. He writes to his father on the 8th:[111] 'It was pretty dark last night, & I was obliged to have lights all over Salisbury Plain. About midway our Candle went out, & we seem'd at a stand; when the provident François produc'd a Tinder box, struck a light, & we proceeded happily to our Journey's end. He offers his services to go along with me, which I am glad to accept of, and so my Equipage stands compleat. I was hurried from Exeter by a letter, intimating the sudden departure of our forces for North America.'

Pitt's plan, which was outlined to Wolfe on his arrival in London, followed lines similar to those of previous plans to conquer Canada but with two essential differences: adequate forces were to be allotted to the task, and they were to be led by men whom Pitt and Ligonier had chosen for command. Loudon was to be recalled; he was altogether too slow and irresolute. His place was to be taken by Abercromby, who with a mixed regular and provincial force of 15,000 was to advance by the Hudson route to Montreal and Quebec. Meanwhile, Amherst, with 14,000 regulars was to take Louisbourg, and then, if there was still time before winter put an end to operations, follow the St. Lawrence to attack Quebec from the east. This pincer movement against the main objective, Quebec, would be indirectly assisted by a third force of 4,000 men under Forbes, which was to capture Fort Duquesne and regain control of the Ohio valley. Of the three operations, clearly the most important was that directed against Louisbourg and the St. Lawrence. Amherst's force was composed entirely of regulars; his three brigadiers were to be Colonel Whitmore in command of the New York contingent, Colonel Lawrence, Governor of Nova Scotia, and Colonel James Wolfe of the Sixty-Seventh Foot.

Pitt's choice of commanders for the expedition was not faultless. Abercromby, appointed to succeed Loudon as commander-in-chief in America, had not previously shown the outstanding qualities of command which would fit him for such an operation; but he was an able administrator, and he had on his staff Colonel Lord Howe, elder brother of the young captain who had distinguished himself at Rochefort, who was reputed to be the most promising young officer in the Army. Jeffery Amherst, who at forty-eight was to be recalled from Germany to conduct the Louisbourg operations, was a capable and conscientious soldier, but it was at least arguable whether he possessed the daring and resolution to succeed in unfavourable circumstances. Wolfe was to be his spur. Of the three commanders, Brigadier John Forbes was the best qualified for his command. Although suffering from an agonizing disease of the stomach, he was a man of youthful vigour and enthusiasm, and his experience of colonial troops and warfare was second to none. The plan was ambitious in conception—planned on a grand scale—and it was not surprising that Pitt should have needed the assistance of Newcastle and the Cabinet. Without that assistance he staggered alone under the colossal burden of work entailed in the preparation of the expedition. Orders poured from his pen, astonishing in their volume and clarity, and by 11th January the plan had been completed and all the necessary instructions issued.

The orders to the fleet indicated a new departure from the accepted strategy for a naval force in support of a military expedition. Pitt and Anson believed that the battle fleet should be free to operate unhampered by escort duties and to concentrate on seizing and denying to the enemy the lines of sea communication and the use of vital ports and anchorages. This theory had already been tried at Rochefort and it was now extended to transatlantic operations. There was to be no great concentration of naval and military forces in home waters. Instead, separate convoys of troops and stores from England, Ireland, Nova Scotia, and Boston, were to gather at the three sea bases of operations at Philadelphia, New York, and Halifax. The troops and stores from England and Ireland would sail in detachments, as they were ready, under minimum naval escort, while the main battle fleet under Boscawen made for Louisburg with all possible speed to cut off communications between France and her American colonies. Several ships of the line were already in Halifax, having wintered there on Pitt's instructions after the previous attempt on Louisbourg. Sir Charles Hardy, Boscawen's second-in-command, was sent out at once to command this squadron and to prevent French reinforcements from reaching Louisbourg. On 5th January, sixteen of the line were ordered to be made ready for immediate service in Boscawen's fleet. From this force, with its attendant frigates, Boscawen was ordered to provide escort for the various convoys. This done, he found himself with a battle fleet of ten of the line and five frigates, which should be more than a match for any enemy force he might encounter in the Atlantic.

Meanwhile, the army for America was being assembled and embarked in detachments. Wolfe was to sail with Boscawen, and was busy putting his affairs in order. On 17th January he writes to his mother, 'The Publick affairs are pretty much fix'd, & my private matters are so far advanc'd that I reckon to be ready at least as soon as the Squadron, which will hardly be in a condition to put to sea till the latter end of next week, or the beginning of the following one. . . . I don't deserve so much consideration or concern as my Father & you are so good as to express for me; he wishes Rank for me, & you my preservation. All I wish for myself is, that I may at all times be ready & firm to meet that fate we cannot shun, & to die gracefully & properly when the hour comes, now or hereafter. A small portion of the good things of this world will fully satisfy my utmost desire. I wouldn't be tempted to set an unjust value upon life, nor I wouldn't wish to be thrown in the way of those trials which nature has not provided for. I mean that it would give me some concern to rise into a station that I knew myself unequal to. . . . Upon recollection, it costs me dear to serve. £200 the last affair; & 5 or 600 now; and an employment that I am about to resign, so that if we should miscarry, my condition will be desperate, & my Finances exhausted. The ladies, too, will despise a beaten Lover, so that every way I must be undone; and yet I am run readily, heartily, & cheerfully into the road of ruin. . . . If my thoughts would be greatly diverted from their present object, the youngest of your neighbours might rival my Lady Bath.* My duty to the General. I wish you both all happiness.' The Wolfes' 'youngest neighbour' was a Miss Katherine Lowther, whose brother, Sir James Lowther, was one of the richest young men in the country—'master', according to Walpole, 'of £40,000 a year.'[112] Wolfe had met her during his brief visit to his parents at Christmas, and, but for his Louisbourg appointment, he would have arranged to renew the acquaintance at an early opportunity. It was nearly a year before they would meet again.

On 21st January he wrote a long letter to 'Uncle Wat' to describe his new appointment and to tell him, at the same time, of his promotion to the rank of brigadier in America. His commission was signed by the King two days later. To his uncle, also, he explained his fears for his parents. He had felt obliged to resign from the lucrative post of Quartermaster-General in Ireland, to which he had been appointed by the Duke of Bedford, 'not being able to give that attention to it which the Duke had reason to expect.' 'I am,' he continues,[113] 'totally ignorant of the state of our private concerns here, and have taken no precautions in case any accident should happen in my absence. I trust you will give the best advice to my mother, and such assistance, if it should be wanted, as the distance between you will permit. I mention this as the General seems to decline apace, and narrowly escaped being carried off in the spring; and that proceeding from a cause which still subsists and will in time work its natural effects,—I mean his excessive indolence and inactivity. On my mother's side there is no friendship or connection, nor do I know anybody to whom she can apply but yourself. She, poor

* Anne Maria Gumley (1694–1758) married William Pulteney who was created Earl of Bath in 1742. See p. 15.

woman, is in a poor state of health, and needs the care of some friendly hand to prop up the tottering fabric. She has long and painful fits of illness, which, by succession and inheritance, are likely to devolve on me, since I feel the early symptoms of them. I wish you health and peace.'

Mrs. Wolfe chose this unfavourable moment to press her son to exert his influence in favour of one of her nephews, a son of Tindal Thompson, who sought to obtain a commission. Wolfe's opinion of his cousin is made amply clear in his reply written on 25th January: 'You cannot doubt,' he writes, 'my readyness to oblige you in anything that is of immediate concern to yourself, but you must not put me upon actions that I shou'd blush to engage in, and that my Uncle shou'd blush to ask. I never can recommend any but a Gentleman to serve with Gentlemen. There is little prospect of a low Dog's doing any shining act to cover the obscurity of his Birth. When such a thing does happen a reward is due to merit, so unexpected courage alone is no sort of recommendation to put a private Soldier upon the footing of an officer. I don't apprehend that Mr. Thompson addresses himself to me, or that he has any just right to expect that I shou'd interest myself in behalf of an Idle Vagabond; for such he must be, by the expression in the letter. "Unhappy Man", meaning the Uncle, that has such an Heir to His Estate. I will write a civil letter to my Uncle, which may serve for an apology for the General & myself.' In the same letter he mentions his 'very great grief and disappoint-ment' that the King had refused permission for Carleton to join him on the expedition. Another young friend, Lord Fitzmaurice, who had served under Wolfe in the 20th Regiment, had applied to go with him but was also refused permission to do so. Wolfe was well aware of the reasons: 'Prejudice against particular people often hurt the common cause. Misrepresentations, falsities, injustice, are too frequent to create any degree of surprise. Princes, of all people, see the least into the true characters of men.'

By 1st February he was in Portsmouth waiting to sail. Before he left London he had written to his old friend George Warde:

'My dear Major,—As the time of my sojourning in North America is uncertain, accidents may happen in the Family that may throw my little affairs into disorder, unless some kind

Friends will take the trouble to inspect into them. Carleton is so good as to say he will give what help is in his power. May I ask the same favour of you, my oldest Friend, in whose worth & integrity I put entire confidence. I believe there shou'd have been some powers drawn out & some formality in this business—all which I am a stranger to: but I am no stranger to the good will & honour of the two Persons to whom I recommend my concerns. I wish you much health and Prosperity and am, my dear Major,
Your faithful & affectionate servant,
Jam: Wolfe.'

From Portsmouth on 7th February he wrote at some length to Lord George Sackville, his first colonel in the Twentieth, with whom he had kept up a friendly correspondence during the previous nine years. Sackville had become Master-General of Ordnance, and Wolfe had some trenchant observations to make to him concerning the forthcoming operations: 'It is,' he writes,[114] 'of consequence, my Lord, not to confine the Admirals and Generals too much as to the number of men to land with; five or six thousand men are sufficient for the preparations; it is of vast importance to get on shore before the fogs come on, and still more not to lose time. Amherst . . . will tell your Lordship his opinion of Carleton, by which you will probably be better convinced of our loss. I shall begin to write to your Lordship the day we sail, and continue writing until the end of the campaign.' Portsmouth and its garrison did not appeal to him: 'The condition of the troops that compose this garrison (or rather vagabonds that stroll about in dirty red clothes from one gin-shop to another) exceeds all belief. There is not the least shaddow of discipline, care, or attention. Disorderly soldiers of different regiments are collected here; some from the ships, others from the hospital, some waiting to embark—dirty, drunken, insolent rascals, improved by the hellish nature of the place, where every kind of corruption, immorality, and looseness is carried to excess; it is a sink of the lowest and most abominable of vices. Your Lordship could not do better than to get the company of Artillery moved out of this infernal den, where troops ought never to be quartered.' He also takes the opportunity of recommending the claims of Rickson to be confirmed in his appoint-

175

ment as Deputy Quartermaster-General of Scotland with the customary rank of lieutenant-colonel. He writes, 'Your Lordship, I think, is persuaded that I never did, nor ever will, undertake to establish any man in your good opinion but from a thorough conviction that he deserves your esteem.' In a postcript he adds, 'Our Admiral is arrived, and is in haste to sail. I wish the voyage was over and that we struck soundings upon the Banks. Take care to reinforce the fleet if it be necessary; don't let us be beat. Barré,* who knows Whitmore better than anybody, assures me that he has no health nor constitution for such business as we are going upon; he never was a soldier, but otherwise, a very worthy gentleman. I pray you beware how you employ him near the top; this prevented, we may jog on tollerably.'

Wolfe was more and more concerned to see that men with previous experience of war in America should be attached to the expedition. He wrote to Sackville recommending several of them by name—Cheshire, Carden, Adam Livingstone, and Delaune†— and asking that they should be employed. He had not forgotten the lessons of Braddock's disastrous march.

On 11th February he wrote to his mother his last letter before he embarked:

'Dear Madam,—When any matter of importance to a Country is resolved on, the sooner it is carried into execution the better. Delays are not only productive of bad consequences, but are very tiresome & very inconvenient, as every unhappy Person, whose lot it is to be confined for any length of time in this Place can certify. The want of company & of amusement can be supplied with Books and exercise, but the necessity of living in the midst of the diabolical citizens of Portsmouth is a real & unavoidable Calamity; it is a doubt to me if there be such another collection of Demons upon the whole Earth. Vice, however, wears so ugly a Garb, that it disgusts rather than tempts. The weather begins to be more moderate than it has been for some days past, & I fancy we shall go on board this afternoon, to be ready to get under sail with the first favourable turn of the Wind. I shou'd be glad if we were at sea, tho' I have no very agreeable prospect before me; however, I

* His brigade-major.
† Delaune had served under Wolfe in the 20th Regiment.

hope to overcome it, & if not, have a mind strong enough to endure that, & still severer trials, if there are any more severe.

I heartily wish you all the benefit that you yourself can hope for from the Bath—the General will be kind enough to put up with some inconveniences for your sake. I beg my duty to him, & am, Dear Madam,

Your obedient and affectionate Son,

Jam. Wolfe.

P.S. You shall hear by all the opportunities that offer.'

On the following day he went on board the *Princess Amelia*, ready to sail for Halifax, but it was too much to expect that the fleet should sail at once. The winds were unfavourable and on the 18th Wolfe was able to send off another letter to his father: 'Our Captain sends me word that a Boat is just going ashoar, and I have time to write three or four lines. Mr. Boscawen, impatient to get out to Sea, left Spithead the 15th, & brought his Squadron here to be ready for the first favourable change of wind—which has blown for some days directly against us, & with great violence. The weather is now mild, & the moon old enough to light us in the night, but our mariners see no immediate prospect of sailing. We are extreamly well in this Ship, have great room, & much kindness & civility from the commander, and hitherto the motion has not had any very great effect upon me.' On the 22nd the fleet had anchored in Plymouth Sound, one ship, the *Invincible*, having been driven aground and wrecked at St. Helen's. At last, on 24th February, Boscawen's battle fleet cleared the Channel and set sail for Halifax.

CHAPTER XIV

Louisbourg

ON 9th May 1758 Boscawen's fleet entered Halifax harbour. Brigadier Lawrence, the Governor of Nova Scotia, had already assembled there three battalions from England, and Boscawen had picked up two and a half battalions of the Philadelphia contingent on his way; but there was no sign of Whitmore or the regiment from Ireland, and it was known that Amherst was far behind.

On the eve of sailing from England, Boscawen had received additional instructions from Pitt: as soon as a force of 8,000 men could be collected, and without waiting for Amherst's arrival, he was to assist Lawrence in an attempt to land and establish a footing on Cape Breton Island, either in Gabarus Bay to the south of Louisbourg or in Miré Bay to the north. On 10th May Boscawen wrote to Pitt, 'We shall be disappointed as to numbers though I think we shall have enough to carry out the first part of His Majesty's orders.' The passage across the Atlantic had been slower than anyone had anticipated, gales and fog having driven the convoy off its course. One of those on board records that[115] 'On the night of the 5th *May* we had so severe a Frost, that the next Morning all our Rigging was cased over with such a thick *Ice*, that it was not capable of being worked till the Ice was beaten off from the Ropes. . . . Our Officers computed the Quantity of Ice beaten off from the Rigging of our single Ship, between 6 and 8 Tun Weight . . . we were for 16 days together without Sight of Land, on Account of the Thickness of the Fog though we were every Day within a proper Distance to see it, had the Air been tolerably clear.' These delays had made it more than ever essential that a landing should be made with all possible speed if Louisbourg

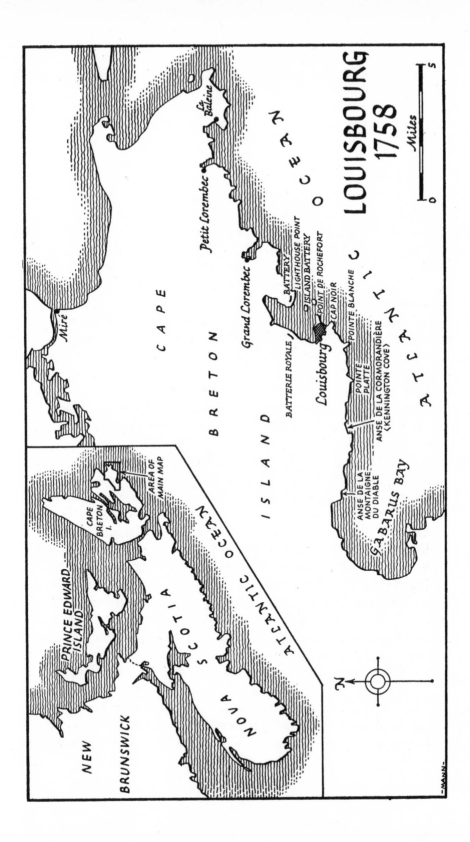

LOUISBOURG
1758

Miles

La Baleine

Petit Lorembec

Grand Lorembec

BATTERY
LIGHTHOUSE POINT
ISLAND BATTERY
POINT DE ROCHEFORT
CAP NOIR
POINTE BLANCHE
BATTERIE ROYALE

Louisbourg

POINTE
PLATTE

ANSE DE LA CORMORANDIÈRE
(KENNINGTON COVE)

ANSE DE LA
MONTAIGNE
DU DIABLE

GABARUS BAY

Miré

C A P E

B R E T O N

I S L A N D

ATLANTIC OCEAN

N

N

AREA OF
MAIN MAP

CAPE
BRETON I.

PRINCE EDWARD
ISLAND

NEW
BRUNSWICK

NOVA SCOTIA

ATLANTIC OCEAN

—MANN—

was to be taken and the attack pressed forward to Quebec before the winter put an end to operations.

Wolfe writes on 12th May to Lord Sackville,[116] 'From Christopher Columbus's time to our days there perhaps has never been a more extraordinary voyage. The continual opposition of contrary winds, calms, or currents baffled all our skill and wore out all our patience. A fleet of men of war well mann'd, unincumber'd with transports, commanded by an officer of the first reputation, has been eleven weeks in its passage. . . . Two or three of the ships are sickly, the rest are in very good condition. The Admiral, who has omitted no care or precaution to advance the service, is labouring to fit the fleet for the sea with all possible despatch.' While the fleet watered and provisioned, Boscawen and the brigadiers laid their plans. They were well informed about the fortifications of Louisbourg, for it was little more than ten years since the New England garrison had been withdrawn, and in November 1757 Brigadier Samuel Waldo had drawn up a detailed plan of attack which he had entrusted to Pitt.[117] Boscawen and the brigadiers exercised their men frequently in practice landings and manoeuvres on land under conditions similar to those likely to be encountered on Cape Breton Island.[118] This appears to be the first occasion in history when troops were trained in assault landings before a combined operation. Whitmore had arrived with the Irish regiment and there was no reason for delay. On the 21st they embarked, but once more the weather was against them and there was an exasperating delay of a week while the fleet battled with winds and tide.

On the 24th Wolfe wrote a long letter to Sackville:[119] 'The latter end of May and the fleet not sail'd! What are they about? Why are they not landed at Louisbourg? The troops have been all embark'd these 3 or 4 days (except Bragg's and two hundred men from Lunenburgh, who we suppose to be at hand), but the war ships are not quite ready, and if they were, the wind, rain, and fog of this last week would have kept us here. The Admiral means to sail with the first fair breeze and leave some of the ships of war to follow.' He then gives a brief outline of the plan of attack: 'The enemy we are told has entrenched the shoar of the Bay of Gabarouse and has planted his artillery upon the beach thereof. If we find him strong in that part, we must try him at a greater distance, and where perhaps he is less prepared. Our present notions are to land 3000 men at Miré and march towards Gabarouse, attack at the same time the further L'Orembeck and La Balleine, get footing in one or other of those little harbours, land a considerable body and march to the nether L'Orembeck which is not above a mile from the end of the North East harbour. A small body of men (by way of diversion) are likewise to be detached to the bottom of Gabarouse Bay, there land and entrench themselves. While these operations are carrying on the Admiral threatens them at the harbour's mouth with the gros of his squadron and makes all possible show of attack with the rest in that part of the Bay of Gabarouse where the Americans landed. If neither of these succeed we must fall upon some other method for we must get on shoar or perish all together in the attempt. It will be my part to command the body that goes round to Miré (3 battalions of the Light Foot). Monckton has L'Orembeck with 2 battalions, and M. Lawrence manages the rest. Nothing, however, is yet fix'd upon or can be fix'd till we see the object, and perhaps General Amherst may arrive in the meanwhile time enough to improve the present plan. When the troops, &c. are landed we shall possess the Light House Point, canonade and bombard the Island Battery and destroy the shipping; then we proceed to open the trenches. . . .' There is nothing to show that the plan was Wolfe's but it bears a striking resemblance to his Rochefort plan in its use of feint attacks and naval diversions to confuse the enemy and it seems most probable that he inspired it. It was not, however, attempted as Amherst arrived before it could be put into operation.

Wolfe's letter to Sackville contains some severe criticism of the equipment and provisioning of the army: 'General Abercrombie has withheld the haut-vitzers that were at New York amongst the stores intended for the siege of Louisbourg last year, and comprehended in the preparations of this year by which we shall be great sufferers. I hope Mr. Abercrombie has sufficient reasons to give for depriving us of so essential an article. We ought to have had a dozen of the largest sort for this business. I am told, too, that his Excellency had a great mind to keep the tools, in which case there was an end of the siege of Louisbourg altogether, and I believe it will now be found that we have not one pick axe too many. . . . The army is undone and ruin'd by the constant use of salt meat and rum. They might often be provided with fresh meat as cheap as the other. . . . Some of the regiments of this army have 3 or 400 men eat up with scurvy. All of them that are wounded or hurt by any accident run great risk of their lives from the corrupted state of their blood. . . . There is not an ounce of fresh beef or mutton contracted for even for the sick and wounded, which besides the inhumanity, is both impolitick and absurd. Mr. Boscawen, indeed, has taken the best precautions in his power by ordering 600 head of live cattle for the fleet and army the moment he arrived. . . . I think our stock of provisions for the siege full little, and none of the medicines for the hospitals are arriv'd. No horses or oxen for the artillery, &c. . . . Our cloaths, our arms, our accoutrements, nay even our shoes and stockings are all improper for this country. Lord Howe is so well convinc'd of it that he has taken away all the mens breeches.' He also commends to Sackville's attention Rogers, of the Rangers, and Bradstreet, a colonel of militia from Maine, whom he describes prophetically as an 'extraordinary man' most fitted for 'Battues and for expeditions.'

At last, on 28th May, the expedition again put to sea, but just out of Halifax it fell in with Rodney's ship, the *Dublin*, carrying Amherst who immediately assumed command. Bragg's Regiment had also come in, bringing the expedition up to a full strength of fourteen regular battalions of infantry, 500 Rangers under Major Scott, and a detachment of artillery and engineers, a total of nearly 12,000 men to which could be added almost as many again in seamen and marines of the fleet. Sir Charles Hardy's squadron had been cruising off Louisbourg to prevent the reinforcement of the garrison. In spite of his vigilance four French men-of-war and some smaller supply vessels had succeeded in entering the harbour, but even including the 3,000 sailors on board the ships in the bay the effective garrison only numbered about a quarter of the British force sent against it.

Five days after leaving Halifax the fleet sighted Louisbourg. The first impression was not encouraging. The fortress was built upon a craggy promontory dominating the harbour from the south-west. Protected on the harbour side by cliffs and water, and by strong batteries erected on the far side of the harbour and on Goat Island which commanded the entrance, the city had been strongly fortified against land attack by a series of four connected bastions. Only on the right, nearest to the harbour, was the ground outside the defences high enough to be of use to an attacking army. The rest of the line looked over a pond and an extensive marsh. Strong and forbidding as the fortress appeared, there could be little doubt that if an army could be landed in overwhelming strength either to the south-west or to the north-east of the harbour Louisbourg would fall. Strong defensive positions had therefore been dug along the shore at the few points where it was accessible. When, on 1st June, the long-expected white cloud of canvas which heralded the arrival of the British expedition appeared over the horizon, Drucour, Governor of Louisbourg, sent the greater part of his small garrison to man the shore defences and prevent a landing.

The fleet anchored in Gabarus Bay, and, in spite of a heavy swell, Amherst, Lawrence and Wolfe set out immediately in a small boat to reconnoitre. They found that the enemy had[120] 'a chain of posts along the shore from Cape Noir to Flat Point and irregulars from thence to the bottom of the bay with works and batteries where it was probable or practicable for any troops to land.' Amherst decided that too much time had already been lost to try the brigadiers' plan for turning the defences of Gabarus Bay and he therefore proposed a frontal attack on them, supported by two feints at points nearer to the city. On 3rd June he issued orders accordingly, but it was 8th June before any landing could be made; gales had whipped up a dangerous surf which drove one of the frigates on to the rocks and seriously threatened the transports at anchor close to the shore. The troops were ordered into the boats on the 4th, but after being tossed about for several hours the attempt to land was abandoned and they were re-embarked, drenched and bruised, in their transports. There was talk of a council of war, but Rochefort was fresh in the minds of the commanders and its lessons had not been entirely forgotten.

By 8th June the sea had calmed a little and it was considered possible to make the attempt. At about four o'clock in the morning Wolfe led his division, which consisted of 600 Light Infantry, four companies of Grenadiers, and the battalion of Highlanders, towards Kennington cove, while Whitmore and Lawrence made diversionary attacks to the east. As the boats neared the shore it became clear that the chances of success were negligible: a high sea was running, the approaches to the shore were well protected by rocks, and the 3,000 French irregulars and Indians had entrenched themselves behind defences strengthened by cannon and by abattis—fallen trees whose tops pointed towards the shore, their branches interlaced to prevent men passing between them. The position looked impregnable. As soon as Wolfe's boats came within range the French opened fire. This was a fatal error. Had the troops been allowed to land before the hidden strength of the defences was revealed scarcely a man would have escaped. Wolfe gave the signal to withdraw eastward, but hardly had he done so than he noticed that a landing-place on the eastern shore of the cove and sheltered from the fire of the defenders had been found by two young subalterns, Hopkins and Brown. The approach was made hazardous by jagged rocks and a boiling surf but Wolfe decided without hesitation to press home the landing at that point. The angry sea broke over the boats, crushing many of them against the rocks and flinging the men into the sea where a number were battered to death or drowned; but the landing was made. Wolfe, whose flag-staff had been shot away, leapt into the water, cane in hand, and waded ashore. His lead was quickly followed by his men and he was able to form a line to withstand the attack of a detachment of enemy Grenadiers who rushed down upon them from the hills above. The French were flung back and, as Lawrence followed in to the landing-place with his division, Wolfe led an attack on the main shore defences. The French, seeing their retreat to the city threatened, broke and ran. An eye-witness writes, 'The enemy fled with great precipitation, and Brigadier Wolfe pursued them almost to the gates of the town.'

Why no better resistance to the landing was offered remains a mystery. Less than seventy landing barges were used, each holding at the most fifty men. A properly controlled fire from the safety of the strong defensive position on the hills above the shore would have broken up the attack before a footing could have been gained. But the French, seeing the feint attacks to the east and fearful that their retreat to the town would be cut off, fled to the temporary safety of its walls. Wolfe's and Lawrence's brigades pursued them for about four miles until they came under fire from the guns in the city. This cannonade conveniently

184

marked the range of the defenders' guns and showed Amherst how near he might encamp in order to invest the fortress.

Amherst set about the task of landing the rest of his army and stores, but the sea was so rough that communication with the fleet was made impossible for several days. The men already ashore were encamped without tents and there was an acute shortage of provisions and ammunition. On the 11th, deserters from the Regiment of *Volontairs Etrangers* brought intelligence that the French were abandoning their batteries at Lighthouse Point and on the far side of the bay, and Wolfe was immediately ordered to march his brigade round the bay to take possession of them. At two o'clock on the morning of the 12th, Major Scott and his Rangers with 500 Light Infantry set off towards Lighthouse Point, followed by Wolfe with four companies of Grenadiers and 1,200 men detached from the line. By four in the afternoon Wolfe and his men had encamped on the position, and Scott led the Light Infantry and Rangers back to the main camp.

Wolfe lost no time in setting up his own batteries to fire on the French ships in the harbour and the batteries on Goat Island, but he encountered considerable difficulties: the guns had to be man-handled through marshy land, there was not enough suitable wood for platform mountings, and every move had to be made under heavy fire from the citadel and Goat Island. To add to his worries he had to compete with rain and fog, and a large proportion of his detachment had to be employed constantly to guard his camp against sorties by the garrison and raids by Indians. But he succeeded in setting up several batteries of 24-pounders, 12-pounders, and howitzers, and on the 19th he opened a vigorous cannonade. The ships in the harbour turned their guns on him and joined the guns of the citadel and Goat Island in subjecting his position at Lighthouse Point to a heavy counter-bombardment. This artillery duel continued almost without pause for a week. Wolfe's guns did little damage to the French ships, but by the 25th the batteries on Goat Island had been silenced and there no longer seemed to be any reason why Boscawen should not force the harbour, destroy the French ships, and open the way to an attack on the thinly fortified harbour walls. But he made no attempt to do so. Pitt had written to Boscawen on 23rd February 1758:[121] 'His Majesty, relying on your Zeal for his Service, is persuaded, tho' no particular Order is given, by your Instructions, to that purpose, that you will not omit attempting to force the Harbour of Louisbourg, in case you shall judge the same to be practicable, as the Success of that Operation will greatly tend to shorten and facilitate the Reduction of that Place.' On land he displayed great activity, supplying Wolfe with guns from the fleet, and relieving his troops with marines, and Wolfe was full of praise for his co-operation; but he was in no hurry to use the fleet in an attacking role in the enclosed waters of the harbour and under the guns of the fortress, even with the support of Wolfe's batteries. When, therefore, Goat Island had been silenced, and it became evident that no move was to be made to force the harbour, Wolfe decided to leave the batteries under the command of a subordinate and return to the main camp.

While Wolfe was busy at Lighthouse Point, Amherst had not been idle. He had been fully occupied in landing his siege train and entrenching his army before the city bastions. An officer describes the work in a letter to Captain John Knox:[122] 'We have an incredible deal of labour on our hands, cutting and making fascines,* gabions† and hurdles; intrenching our camp and posts, erecting blockhouses, throwing up redoubts, making roads for our artillery through vile country, partly rough (worse, if possible, than the ground we encamped on last year at Halifax) but in general swampy; advancing our lines of approaches, constructing batteries, and skirmishing continually with the rabble in the woods round our camp, who are very troublesome neighbours: such are the employments of the army, often by night as well as by day; such the toils we have to encounter, in the progress of this enterprise; yet with inexpressible pleasure I behold the zeal of the troops surmounting every difficulty, in all which they have noble examples before them in our General Officers.' It was slow work assembling an army for a set-piece siege, and Amherst was showing a caution and lack of enterprise oddly at variance with his precipitate frontal attack of the 8th. He seems to have been overawed by the reputation for impregnable strength with which the Louisbourg fortifications had been credited. It is clear

* Long faggots used singly or in bundles for lining trenches and setting up batteries.
† Wicker cylinders filled with earth.

that the French garrison, on the other hand, expected the city to fall soon after a landing in force had been made.

On 1st July, after repelling an enemy sortie, Wolfe succeeded in setting up a new battery of guns on the hills overlooking Louisbourg from the north, and began to bombard the city. The Governor, Drucour, sent a message to Amherst complaining that women and children were being slaughtered and asking that the bombardment should cease. Wolfe writes to Amherst,[123] 'When the French are in a scrape they are ready to cry out in behalf of the human species; when fortune favours them, none more bloody, more inhuman. Montcalm has changed the very nature of war, and has forced us, in some measure, to a deterring and dreadful vengeance.' The French were already showing signs of a shortage of ammunition, and one account lists a startling variety of ironmongery used as shot:[124] 'It is remarkable, that they discharged great Quantities of old Iron of several Kinds (such as *Shovels, Tongs*, and the like, besides a most destructive Sort of Square Iron-bars of about 5 or 6 Inches long, and about an Inch and a half square, several of them cased in Plates of Tin,) which they call *Mitraille*, by way of Grape Shot—the Wounds they give are very difficult, if at all, to be cured, from their being made with such angular, ragged Weapons.'

On the 16th, Wolfe led a detachment of Highlanders and Grenadiers to the heights in front of the fort and poured down a destructive fire on the defenders on the city walls. Five days later a lucky shot set on fire *L'Entreprenant*[125] in the harbour, and the explosion from her magazine fired two of the remaining ships. As four frigates had already been sunk by the French to block the entrance to the harbour, there were now only two ships left: the *Prudent* of seventy-four guns, flagship to the squadron, and the *Bienfaisant*. By the 23rd the barracks in the city had been destroyed, and Wolfe's fearless energy had brought the siege so near to the fortifications that the enemy gunners were within range of musket fire from the forward trenches. One observer writes of Wolfe: 'There is no certainty where to find him—but, wherever he goes, he carries with him a *Mortar* in one Pocket, and a 24 *pounder* in the other.'

Boscawen at last decided to force the harbour. His plan was so bold that it makes his previous hesitancy the more incomprehensible. On the night of the 25th, while every available gun bombarded the city, two divisions of the fleet under Captains Laforey and Balfour crept into the harbour under the guns of the fortress and seized the French ships. The flagship *Prudent* ran aground and had to be fired, but the *Bienfaisant* was towed triumphantly away to the shelter of Wolfe's battery at Lighthouse Point.

The way was now open for a frontal attack, and Boscawen went ashore to inform Amherst of his willingness to send six ships of the line into the harbour. He found the commander-in-chief engaged in negotiations for the surrender of the city. The terms he imposed were stern, and they were at first refused, but Drucour was obliged to yield to the demands of the garrison and citizens of the town, and on the 26th Louisbourg surrendered, and with it the whole of Cape Breton Island and the Isle of St. Jean (Prince Edward's Island). Captain Knox's informative correspondent writes: 'Eleven stands of colours are taken into our hands, which, with all the prisoners, are to be sent to England: they amount (I am told) to almost 6000 men. We have got immense quantities of stores of all kinds, with some ammunition and provisions, and a respectable artillery: the enemy have now, both by sea and land, sustained a fatal blow in America. Mr. Amherst has displayed the General in all his proceedings, and our four Brigadiers are justly entitled to great praises; Mr. Wolfe being the youngest in rank, the most active part of the service fell to his lot; he is an excellent Officer, of great valour, which has conspicuously appeared in the whole course of this undertaking. The troops behaved as British troops should do, and have undergone the fatigues of this conquest chearfully and with great steadiness; the light infantry, who are inconceivably useful, did honour to themselves and to that General who first saw the necessity of forming these corps. The troops have suffered considerably by sickness; but though I am told so, I find upon inquiry, the loss has been mostly among the rangers and New England artificers, to whom the small-pox has proved very fatal; the greatest unanimity has subsisted throughout this whole armament both naval and military, and Admiral Boscawen has given us all the assistance that could be asked for.'

The gateway to Canada had been forced. It remained to be seen whether it would be used again for the building of a new empire or sold as the bargain offer for peace.

CHAPTER XV

In the Gulf of St. Lawrence

ON the day Louisbourg was surrendered to Amherst, Wolfe wrote three letters. The first, to his mother, tells little of the siege except to say that the operations have been 'slow but sure, & at length have brought things to a very good conclusion with little loss'. He hopes to be home for Christmas, though he admits that he would 'much rather besiege a place than pass four weeks at sea'. He gives news of friends known to his family serving at Louisbourg and is particular to mention a young officer who was later to become one of his aides: 'If you are acquainted with Mrs. Bell of the Hospital, I beg you will signify to her that her Son has been of great use to me during the siege, has carried on business with great spirit & dispatch, & is an excellent Officer—got a slight scratch upon his Right Arm, but is quite recovered, tho' I have forbid his writing for fear of any inflammation.' To his father he writes a very brief account of the siege, making no mention of his own part in it. He again complains of the slowness of the operation and adds, 'but still I hope there is fine weather enough left for another blow, & as our Troops are improved by this Siege, the sooner we strike the better.'

The third letter, to his uncle Walter, is more revealing. 'It is,' he writes,[126] 'impossible to go into any detail of our operations, they would neither amuse nor instruct, and we are all hurried about our letters. In general, it may be said that we made a rash and ill-advised attempt to land,* and by the greatest of good fortune imaginable we succeeded.' His criticism of the landing is

---

* Monckton recorded in his journal:[127] 'Gen! Wolfe who opposed this Attack in Council was the most vigorous to animate the Execution of it, & begun this Campaign with the same bravery Activity & Judgment which the whole Army have been a Witness to in the Continuation of it.'

fair: the defensive position was one of great strength; and the incompleteness of the reconnaissance, the lack of any element of surprise, and the vulnerability of the boats to rough seas and rocks and to concentrated fire from the shore, made the undertaking hazardous and even unjustifiable. On the other hand, Amherst knew that time was the all-important factor; and he was careful not to commit his entire force before a reasonable chance of success was assured. Furthermore, he had confidence in his subordinate commanders and in the courage of his men. He knew that Wolfe, whom he had appointed to lead the first assault, would not be deterred by danger and that no opportunity to succeed would be neglected. The good fortune, without which no commander can succeed, helped to justify his confidence. But this was his last confident action in the operation. For the rest of the campaign he was painstaking and methodical to the point of tedium, and he seemed in no hurry to follow up his success. 'I do not,' Wolfe continues, 'penetrate our General's intentions. If he means to attack Quebec, he must not lose a moment. If we have good pilots to take us up the River St. Lawrence and can land any tolerable Distance from the Place, I have no doubt of the event.' Of the Indians he writes, 'They attacked one of my posts (for I commanded a detached corps) and were repulsed, and since that time they have been very quiet. I take them to be the most contemptible *canaille* upon earth. Those to the southward are much braver and better men; these are a dastardly set of bloody rascals. We cut them to pieces wherever we found them, in return for a thousand acts of cruelty and barbarity.' News had come in from Abercomby's army: 'There is a report that Abercombie's Army has attacked the Enemy's detach'd posts, and forced 'em,—that my Lord Howe is killed. If this last Circumstance be true, there is an end to the Expedition, for he was the Spirit of that Army, and the very best Officer in the King's service. I lament the loss as one of the greatest that could befall the Nation.'

Wolfe wrote, also, on 30th July, to Lord George Sackville. His letter is long and—even by his standards—uncommonly frank. He is critical of Amherst's caution (except in the landing), describes Brigadier Whitmore as 'a poor old sleepy man',[128] and makes no attempt to disguise his impatience to follow up the success at Louisbourg by laying siege to Quebec. His letter is not, however, entirely taken up with criticism. He commends Lieutenant-Colonel the Hon. James Murray, who he says 'has acted with infinite spirit. The public is indebted to him for great services in advancing by every method in his power the affairs of this siege. Amherst no doubt will do him all manner of justice, and your lordship will get him a regiment or the rank of colonel.' He also praises the work of 'little Smith', whom he describes as 'a most indefatigable, active spirited man and has a just claim to your favour and friendship.' Captain Hervey Smith was to share with Bell the duties of aide-de-camp to Wolfe in the following year. Wolfe is also particular to stress what was perhaps the most singular achievement of the entire campaign—the close and amicable co-operation of Army and Navy at all levels: 'The Admiral and the General have carried on public service with great harmony, industry and union. Mr. Boscawen has given all and even more than we cou'd ask of him. He has furnish'd arms and ammunition, pioneers, sappers, miners, gunners, carpenters, boats, and is I must confess no bad *fantassin* himself, and an excellent back-hand at a siege. Sir Charles Hardy, too, in particular, and all the officers of the navy in general, have given us their utmost assistance and with the greatest cheerfulness imaginable.' The one element of Amherst's army which seems to have been entirely unworthy was the engineers, and Wolfe again laments the King's refusal to allow Carleton to accompany the expedition. But for this, he writes, 'we might now be ruining the walls of Quebec, and compleating the conquest of New France. So much depends upon the abilities of individuals in war that there cannot be too great care taken in the choice of men for the different offices of trust and importance.'

Wolfe's patience was quickly exhausted, and he wrote to Amherst respectfully inquiring when he might expect to sail for Quebec, and pointing out that no time was to be lost if the city was to be taken before winter. Amherst replied on 6th August: '*La belle saison* will get away indeed; what I most wish to do is to go to Quebec. I have proposed it to the Admiral, who is the best judge whether or no we can get up there, and yesterday he seemed to think it impracticable.' Amherst had already had three meetings with Boscawen[129] to urge a move against Quebec, but each time met with a firm refusal. The Admiral merely repeated his statement that the plan was impossible to execute and even tried to dissuade Amherst from his intention to send three regiments up the St. Lawrence with a squadron under Sir Charles Hardy.

The truth was that Boscawen's fleet was in no condition to support a second siege. There was no doubt in the minds of Amherst or Wolfe that unless Quebec could be taken before winter the French would reinforce the garrison and strengthen the fortifications to an extent which might make its capture not only costly but even impossible. But a successful attempt required the maximum co-operation of the fleet, and this Boscawen felt unable to promise. The transports and ships of the battle fleet had taken a severe battering from the gales, the fleet was short of provisions, and some 5,000 prisoners from the Louisbourg garrison had to be embarked and sent to England. The arguments against continuing the campaign to Quebec were strong and reasonable; only Wolfe realized that this was no time for reason, that all arguments were far outweighed by the urgency and importance of the task. His restless energy alone could have surmounted the obstacles. On the 7th he writes to Sackville:[130] 'As the sea officers seem to think that no attack can be made from Quebec nor no diversion up the River St. Lawrence, why we don't send immediate reinforcements to Abercrombie I cannot divine. I have told Mr. Amherst that if Lawrence has any objection to going, I am ready to embark with a brigade or whatever he pleases to send up to Boston or New York. . . .'

Amherst's resolution to go on to Quebec had been much weakened by the news from Abercromby. At the time when Amherst's army first sighted Louisbourg, Abercromby had begun his advance up Lake George towards his first objective, Montcalm's position at Ticonderoga. The British force was overwhelmingly superior to Montcalm's in numbers and equipment and was excellently organized by Lord Howe. Contact was made with the French and Howe, at the head of the leading column, was killed by their first volley. There was no one to replace him. Abercromby—known to his men as 'Mrs. Nabbycromby'—ordered a suicidal frontal attack upon the French position which was defended by an impenetrable abattis. The attackers were driven off with heavy casualties and Abercomby retired to his base at Fort William Henry, where he remained in despondent inactivity until he was recalled by Pitt. Abercromby's army outnumbered Montcalm's by nearly four to one, but it was in order to reinforce him that Amherst finally sacrificed the chance of taking Quebec in 1758.

Wolfe was pining for action. 'We are gathering strawberries & other wild fruits of the Country,' he writes on the 7th to his father, 'with a seeming indifference about what is doing in other parts of the world.' To Amherst, on the 8th, he writes more firmly: 'If the Admiral will not carry us to Quebec, reinforcements should certainly be sent to the continent* without losing a moment's time. The companies of Rangers, and the Light Infantry, would be extremely useful at this juncture; whereas here they are perfectly idle, and, like the rest, of no manner of service to the public. If Lawrence has any objection to going I am ready to embark with four or five battalions, and will hasten to the assistance of our countrymen. I wish we were allowed to address the Admiral, or I wish you yourself, Sir, would do it in form. This d——d French garrison take up our time and attention, which might be better bestowed upon the interesting affairs of the continent. The transports are ready, and a small convoy would carry a brigade to Boston or New York. With the rest of the troops we make an offensive and a destructive war in the Bay of Fundy and in the Gulf of St. Lawrence. I beg pardon for this freedom, but I cannot look coolly upon the bloody inroads of those hell-hounds the Canadians; and if nothing further is to be done, I must desire leave to quit the army.'

Amherst acted on Wolfe's advice, and on the same day, he held a formal meeting with Boscawen. They signed a joint declaration agreeing that to go on to Quebec was no longer a practicable plan, and proposing instead to send six battalions to Boston to join Abercromby, and five others to the St. Lawrence and the Bay of Fundy to create a diversion. Amherst then replied to Wolfe's letter, restating the decisions already made known in the joint declaration. He added a gentle but well-merited rebuke: 'My wishes are to hasten everything for the good of the service and I have not the least doubt but Mr. Boscawen will do the same. Whatever schemes you have, or information that you can give, to

* To reinforce Abercromby.

quicken our motions, your communicating them will be very acceptable, and will be of much more service than your thoughts of quitting the army, which I can by no means agree to, as all my thoughts and wishes are confined at present to pursuing our operations for the good of his Majesty's service, and I know nothing that can tend more to it than your assisting in it.'

Amherst, himself, commanded the six battalions for the relief of Abercromby; Colonel Monckton was to take two battalions to the Bay of Fundy; and Wolfe and Sir Charles Hardy, with three battalions, seven ships of the line, and three frigates, were to lay waste the French settlements in the Gulf of St. Lawrence. Wolfe writes scornfully of this work, on 21st August: 'Sir Charles Hardy & I are preparing to rob the Fishermen of their nets & to burn their Hutts. When the great exploit is at an end (which we reckon will be a month's or five weeks' work) I return to Louisbourg, and from thence to England if no orders arrive in the mean while that oblige me to stay.'

Bell's journal reveals that Wolfe tried to persuade Hardy to go as far as Quebec to destroy the French squadron in the river:[131] 'The General as soon as he found what a small Game he had to play wanted Sir C. Hardy to go to Quebeck, if not so high as that, to go some way up in order to destroy their settlements, but Sir Charles urged many reasons & difficulties which timidity ever suggests & which great souls have a pleasure in encountering and almost always overcome.' He adds, a little unfairly, 'Had Sir Charles pursued Genl. Wolfe's advice, Quebec must certainly have fallen.' This is clearly untrue; but had Hardy agreed to take Wolfe and his regiments far enough up the St. Lawrence for them to land and destroy the crops, the shortage of provisions in Quebec might have been a decisive factor in the following year.

By 30th September Wolfe and Hardy had completed their unenviable operation and were back in Louisbourg. Knox records in his journal: 'Brigadier Wolfe has been also successful at Gaspée, and the N.N.E. parts of this province; he has made some hundreds of prisoners, and burned, among other settlements, a most valuable one called Mont Louis . . . wherever he went with his troops, desolation followed; but he would not suffer the least barbarity to be committed upon any of the persons of the wretched inhabitants.' The enterprise had been worth while: useful information had been gained about the river approaches to Quebec, and valuable stocks of corn and fish destined for Quebec had been captured or destroyed. Wolfe penned lengthy reports to Abercromby and Barrington, and then wrote to Amherst. 'Your orders,' he writes on the 30th, 'were carried into execution as far as troops who were limited in their operations by other powers could carry them. I have made my report to General Abercromby, to which (as it is pretty long) I beg to refer. Our equipment was very unproper for the business, and the numbers, unless the squadron had gone up the river, quite unnecessary. We have done a great deal of mischief,—spread the terror of His Majesty's arms through the whole gulf; but have added nothing to the reputation of them. The Bay of Gaspé and the harbour are both excellent, and now well known to our fleet. By the beginning of the month of July, I hope the river of Quebec will be as well known; although the aversion to that navigation, and the apprehensions about it, are inconceivably great. If you do business up the river, you must have small craft and a number of whale boats, two at least to each transport. Pilots are easily had for sloops and schooners; every fisherman in the river can conduct them up. . . . Mr. Boscawen is in haste to get back. No return to the express of the surrender of Louisbourg. If you will attempt to cut up New France by the roots, I will come back with pleasure to assist.'

Wolfe was, himself, in haste to return to England. His health had suffered in five months of strenuous campaigning, and although the return voyage could not be expected to aid his recovery he hoped for several months in England in which he might have a chance to regain his strength. He was also anxious to see his parents again before he was sent off on another campaign. He therefore embarked with Boscawen in the *Namur* and sailed for England. The voyage was not without excitement as Boscawen fell in with seven French men-of-war off Land's End and gave chase; but they escaped under cover of darkness and on 1st November the British squadron anchored off St. Helen's. Wolfe landed at Portsmouth the same evening.

Apart from Abercromby's disastrous failure at Ticonderoga and the irreparable loss of Howe, the campaign of 1758 had been successful. Amherst had achieved at least the first part of his object by the capture of Louisbourg, and information had been gained which would prove useful for operations against Quebec. In the Ohio valley Forbes had hacked his way through dense forests in snow and torrential rain to capture Fort Duquesne, which he had renamed Pittsburg. But his gallant spirit drove him too hard; he was a sick man and in constant pain, and the strain of the operation proved too great for his tortured body. He had to be carried most of the way on a litter, and he died in the following year at Philadelphia. Abercromby was, in Wolfe's words, 'a man who signalised himself neither before nor after his advancement,' but even his army shared in the successes, for after his ignominious retreat from Ticonderoga he was pursuaded by Colonel Bradstreet to detach a force to attempt the destruction of the French fort at Frontenac at the foot of Lake Ontario. Bradstreet commanded this detachment and conducted the whole movement with speed and brilliance. Reaching the lakes at Oswego, he launched his boats on Lake Ontario, surprised the fort at Frontenac, and captured it intact with its valuable stock of stores and furs. In the harbour lay almost the entire French inland naval force, all of which was captured or destroyed. In May Wolfe had written to Lord George Sackville, 'The position of Oswego manifests its great utility. You secure an interest with the Indians and awe them; share the furr trade with the French; make war upon their colony from thence with great ease, cut off the communication with the Ohio by a squadron of armed vessels upon the lake, and, by obliging them to defend themselves at home, prevent the bloody ravages made upon the frontiers of our colonies.'

If the operations of 1758 had not achieved all that had been hoped of them, they had at least laid a solid foundation for the destruction of the French Empire in America, and they had proved beyond doubt the effectiveness of combined operations under proper leadership.

Writing to his mother on 11th August, Wolfe sets down his thoughts on the future of America. 'This will,' he writes, 'some time hence, be a vast empire, the seat of Power and Learning. They have all the Materials ready, Nature has refus'd 'em nothing, & there will grow a People out of our little spot, (England) that will fill this vast space, and divide this great Portion of the Globe

with the Spaniards, who are possess'd of the other half. If we had
been as lucky this Campaign as we had reason to expect, and had
not lost the great man, (whom I shall ever lament)*—the corner-
stone would probably have been laid of this high Fabrick.' A year
later he was to lay the great stone himself.

* Lord Howe.

CHAPTER XVI

Eccentric Attacks in Europe

PITT had good reason to be satisfied with the development of his strategy. The reverses of 1757—Closterseven, Rochefort, and Fort William Henry—had not shaken his faith in his system; and the success of his plans in 1758, which not only compensated for the previous failures but also cut the pattern for a year of triumph to follow, more than justified that faith. In America, it is true, his hopes had not been fully realized; but a good start had been made and there were reasonable grounds for supposing that one more campaign would put an end to French domination of the hinterland and dreams of an empire in the west. In the east, too, French ambitions had been thwarted: Clive's victory at Plassey in June 1757, had not, in spite of his entreaties, been sufficient to persuade Pitt to give his full support to operations in India; but the small fleet, commanded until his death by Watson, and then by Sir George Pocock, had prevented the French from reinforcing their army and had given valuable assistance to Clive in his conquest of Bengal. Neither America nor India had been conquered but French influence had been weakened and British commerce protected.

Pitt's system had also borne fruit in a number of expeditions—or 'eccentric attacks'—designed to confuse and harass the enemy and exploit the flexibility and mobility of a small army supported by a fleet which had won command of the sea. The first of these expeditions was in answer to Frederick's demand for a secure base in the North Sea, but it was also aimed at a point in the French defences where success would give the greatest assistance to Prince Ferdinand. Ferdinand's and Richelieu's armies faced each other across the line of the River Aller which they had contested during the autumn. The French Army was supplied from magazines in East Friesland and from its main base at Wesel on the Rhine. Ferdinand's army was supplied from Stade. In February 1758 Ferdinand intended to seize Verden, at the junction of the Weser and the Aller, and to force Richelieu back to the line of the Ems. This plan was endangered by the certainty that Richelieu would call for reinforcements from East Friesland. It was an obvious opportunity for one of Pitt's eccentric attacks. If a small British force could threaten Emden from the sea, either the French would decide to defend the port in preference to reinforcing Richelieu, or the garrison would be withdrawn altogether; if the second alternative were chosen, Emden might become a base for British operations on land which would menace the vital lines of communication between Richelieu and his base at Wesel and perhaps force the entire army to withdraw to the Rhine.

The plan was well conceived and brilliantly executed. Command of the North Sea squadron was given to Commodore Charles Holmes. By the time he arrived in the River Ems, the situation had changed: Richelieu had been succeeded in command by Clermont, and the opening moves of Ferdinand's spring campaign had so alarmed the French that Clermont had withdrawn to a line stretching from Osnabrück through Minden to Hameln. Emden was still occupied, but it was doubtful whether the garrison could be left there much longer. Holmes decided the issue by navigating the unbuoyed river with two frigates and an armed cutter and cutting off supplies to the town. The garrison was hastily evacuated (though not before Holmes had captured one of their transports containing several staff officers and hostages) and Minden having fallen to Ferdinand on 14th March, Clermont was in full retreat to the Rhine.

Ferdinand at once sent an urgent request to Pitt for a British garrison to occupy Emden. This would not only secure his own right flank and his outlet to the North Sea, but prove an effective thorn in the side of the French in any future advance into Westphalia. Pitt agreed: the North Sea squadron was withdrawn for operations elsewhere, and Emden was occupied by a battalion of Brudenell's Regiment.

Meanwhile, Pitt had examined the plans of Thomas Cumming,

a Quaker merchant who had tried to interest previous governments in the conquest of the French trading posts at Senegal and
Goree on the West African coast. A small expedition was fitted
out and Senegal was captured in April. The attempt on Goree
failed, but a second expedition under Keppel captured the island
at the end of the year. The immediate gains were small, but they
would have some barter value when the terms of the peace were
agreed upon, and they opened up the possibilities of African trade
and the discovery of unknown sources of wealth in a new continent.

But Pitt had more ambitious projects in mind. At sea the way
had been cleared by Osborne and Saunders in the Mediterranean
and by Hawke in the Channel. In March the French had attempted
to get de la Clue's fleet out of the Mediterranean to Canada and
had reinforced him with a squadron under the Marquis Duquesne.
This attempt had been frustrated by Osborne and Saunders: by
April de la Clue was back in Toulon dismantling his fleet, and
Duquesne's squadron had been captured in a brisk action in
which his flagship, *Foudroyant*, of eighty-four guns, was engaged
and disabled by the *Monmouth*, a little sixty-four commanded by
Captain Arthur Gardiner. Gardiner had been Byng's flag captain
and was determined to retrieve his reputation. He was killed
early in the action, but his first lieutenant, Robert Carkett, was a
man of equal courage and tenacity and held on until both ships lay
dismasted and helpless, waiting for other ships of Osborne's
fleet to catch up with them. At the beginning of April Hawke
drove aground a French convoy destined for Louisbourg and
although no ships were captured all hope of fitting them out
again in time to relieve Louisbourg was lost. With the French
fleets thus crippled the risk of a major amphibious operation was
greatly reduced. Pitt's plan was nothing less than the seizure of
St. Malo, and for this project he ordered seventeen battalions
with transport and artillery to assemble in the Isle of Wight.

The semi-permanent intention of the diversion is made clear in
a letter from Holdernesse to Ferdinand written on 5th May:[132]
'to make the diversion useful it must be lasting, and accordingly
we are seeking a place whence we can seriously hurt the enemy
and maintain ourselves against a superior force, while keeping
open our communications with the sea.' St. Malo was perfectly

situated for such a project: perched on a rock and connected with the mainland only by a narrow causeway a mile long, it could, with adequate support from the sea, be held or evacuated without difficulty. Anson and Pitt had agreed to split the naval command in order to leave the battle fleet under Hawke free to deal with any emergency. The convoy was to be commanded by Howe. Pitt's authoritarian manner, which enabled him to trample down opposition and the delays imposed by official methods, had often angered his political supporters as much as his opponents. He dispatched Howe to the Isle of Wight to take over his command without previously informing Hawke of the reason for the appointment or of the objective. Hawke, who imagined that another attempt was to be made on Rochefort, was justly furious that command should be given to a junior captain and immediately struck his flag. This difficult situation could only be resolved by the self-sacrifice of Anson, who agreed to take command of the battle fleet himself with Hawke as his second. Howe remained in command of the convoy. The troops were to be led by the Duke of Marlborough, whose ability was unfortunately no match for his great name, and Wolfe's old friend Lord George Sackville.*

The expedition, some 34,000 strong, set out from St. Helen's on 1st June: Anson, with the battle fleet, westward to a station off the north coast of Brittany; Howe, with the convoy, straight across the Channel to Cancale Bay where he anchored three days later. The division of forces is significant. Whereas Pitt looked upon the expedition as a means of relieving pressure on Ferdinand and supporting his new offensive which had begun on the day Howe sailed, Anson proposed to use it as a bait for the French fleet in Brest. There was, therefore, no attempt to blockade Brest; on the contrary the way was left open for the French to put to sea; but to attempt to interfere with the landing at St. Malo would be to invite a naval engagement against the superior numbers of Anson's battle fleet. Hawke was ill and had gone home, and Anson, who had expressed himself dissatisfied with the discipline

* News of this concentration had evidently reached Louisbourg, for Boscawen wrote dryly to Amherst on 5th August:[133] 'At the Isle of Wight, all real Lieuten't Generals and Major Generals in Number eight, to sixteen Battalions; in Gabarus bay fourteen Battallions, Rangers equal to another, detachment of Duroures and Cornwallis's another, with only four Lance Generals, and yet we have conquer'd, what won't they do with so much more experience.'

and efficiency of the fleet, had asked for Saunders to succeed Hawke as second-in-command, with Holmes as third.

Howe, with the lessons of Rochefort fresh in his mind, wasted no time in getting the troops ashore. A landing was made almost without opposition, and Cancale was occupied and entrenched. On the 7th, Marlborough advanced towards St. Malo, and that night, the light horse carried out a torch-light raid on the little port of St. Servan where they fired sixty-six ships, including four of the fleet. Galloping on to Solidore, they destroyed twenty vessels and a huge quantity of naval stores. Marlborough then turned his attention to St. Malo and called upon the governor to surrender, a demand which was very properly declined. Marlborough and Sackville had been prepared if necessary to undertake a formal siege, but it was found that no suitable roads existed for the transport of guns, and Howe's attempt to land the siege train at St. Servan as an alternative failed. Meanwhile, reports came in hourly from outposts of the approach of a French army. Marlborough, no doubt with the approval of Sackville, decided to withdraw. This decision has been condemned by historians largely on the dubious ground that Sackville, who was Marlborough's chief adviser and second-in-command, later disgraced himself at Minden. In fact, unless St. Malo could be forced to surrender in a matter of days—and this, in view of the difficulties so far encountered, seemed at least improbable—Marlborough's position must soon become precarious, if not untenable. It is also, perhaps, significant that no protest against this decision appears to have been offered by Howe. Whether from faint-heartedness or necessity the troops were re-embarked on the 12th, but for more than a week the weather kept the convoy in Cancale Bay. When at last it sailed, Howe made for Havre where he made a show of landing. The true objective was Caen, but the sea was too rough to make an attempt possible and the convoy returned to the mouth of the Seine to threaten Honfleur. On the 28th Howe again drew away to reappear two days later at Cherbourg. Here the convoy anchored and the troops were ordered into the boats for a landing; but once again a gale sprang up and they had to be re-embarked. By the following day the gale was so strong that the ships could not remain at anchor. Forage and provisions were running short, and there seemed to be nothing for it but to give up all thoughts of a second landing and return to England. The convoy arrived at Spithead on 1st July.

Small as its local successes had been, the expedition had not failed entirely. Ferdinand had launched his offensive on 1st June and, coolly violating Dutch territory, had started to put his army across the Rhine on the Dutch frontier, outflanking the French left. This movement, which took Clermont completely by surprise, coincided with the sailing of a large convoy and battle fleet from England. The obvious inference was that some secret arrangement had been made with the Dutch to allow British troops to land in Holland, join hands with Ferdinand's army, and roll up the French line from the west. Hurried redispositions of French troops were made to counter such a move. The news of the landing at St. Malo came as a surprise and a relief. Unfortunately, Belleisle was not to be drawn into weakening Clermont's army to deal with Marlborough, and Marlborough's hasty withdrawal removed any serious threat from the south. The real achievement of the expedition lay in the renewed general threat of amphibious operations against the French coast, and the demoralizing realization in France that a substantial British force could be transported across the Channel and set ashore without interference from the French fleet.

Meanwhile Ferdinand's advance had been crowned on 23rd June by a great victory at Crevelt, and Clermont was flung back to Cologne. In London the news was received with fireworks and public celebrations. Pitt, himself, so far forgot his objections to a continental army to propose that five regiments of cavalry and three of foot should be sent at once to Emden to reinforce Ferdinand. General Bligh, a seventy-three-year-old veteran of the late war, was summoned from Ireland to command this force but he was not allowed to take up his command. Marlborough and Sackville had returned from the St. Malo expedition disgusted with the hardships and difficulties of amphibious warfare and determined to have nothing more to do with what Sackville contemptuously described as 'buccaneering'. Sackville sent in his papers as a protest against Bligh's appointment and was only persuaded to withdraw them when Marlborough was appointed in Bligh's place with Sackville as second. The unhappy Bligh, whose age alone proclaimed him to be quite unfitted for such a task, was appointed to command the next expedition to the coast of France.

A new expedition was, in fact, already fitting out. The scale of the operation was to be reduced to a diversionary attack and there was to be no intention of trying to hold captured territory. The expedition sailed on 1st August, and on the 7th a landing was made in strength at Marais Bay, about six miles to the west of Cherbourg. A French force of six battalions with 250 dragoons was brushed aside and early next day Cherbourg was captured. During the following week the fort and guns were destroyed and the harbour blocked with burnt and scuttled ships. This was all very satisfactory, but Bligh was incapable of commanding discipline and the troops sacked the town with brutal thoroughness. But for Howe, who was again in command of the naval convoy, there would have been no proper dispositions for re-embarkation. Realizing the incompetence of Bligh and his staff, Howe took it upon himself to make all necessary arrangements, including the details of rearguard defence in case of attack while the main body was being taken off. The entire force was re-embarked without loss on the 16th and returned to Weymouth.

On the 31st, the expedition set out again, and three days later a landing was made at St. Lunaire near St. Malo. Pitt was under the impression that the expedition was bound for Borlaix, about a hundred miles further west; no one could have anticipated that Bligh or Howe would attempt a second attack on a part of the coast where the defences had already been put on their guard. Whose idea it was is not known; it was certainly unsound, and from the first it showed all the familiar signs of disaster. About 7,000 men were landed, but the weather then became so foul that Howe was obliged to move the fleet to a safer anchorage. It was decided to re-embark the troops, but this could not be done in such weather, and it was clear that a more sheltered place must be found. Eventually the bay at St. Cas was chosen, and Bligh led his men off towards it, pursued by the Duc d'Aiguillon, who was hurrying from Brest at the head of a formidable body of French troops. Bligh, who had already afforded ample evidence of his incapacity at Cherbourg, now gave proof of his incompetence. In spite of the lack of any proper discipline in his army, which was shown in the complete absence of scouts, outposts, or the most elementary precautions, Bligh had by the evening of the 8th succeeded in reaching Matignon, some three miles from St. Cas. There, unbelievably, he decided to make camp. It would be impossible to imagine a more idiotic and ill-timed decision. It is doubtful if anyone shared Bligh's surprise when a deserter informed him during the night that d'Aiguillon was only a few miles off and in overwhelming strength. There was still time for Bligh's army to slip away silently in the darkness to Howe's waiting boats at St. Cas. But even this was too difficult; the drummers beat the *générale* and the weary rabble stumbled away cursing into the night, the French at their heels. They reached the shore in safety, but once more Bligh had made no provision for protecting the embarkation of the main body and they came under heavy fire from d'Aiguillon's guns. For a time Howe's frigates kept the French from pressing home the attack, but at last they broke through on to the beach and although the remaining officers and men fought stubbornly they were overwhelmed. The British losses were about a thousand killed and wounded. Bligh was fortunate to escape with so light a punishment.

Pitt was less fortunate. This reverse at St. Malo condemned for good his 'buccaneering' raids on the French coast and, with the threat of these removed the French were free to concentrate their military strength on the defeat of Ferdinand, who was pushed back across the Rhine. Meanwhile, Frederick had fought a bloody and indecisive battle with the Russians at Zorndorff towards the end of August; and on 14th October he sustained a crushing defeat from the Austrians at Hochkirch.

In the midst of this constant ebb and flow of hope and disappointment, success and disaster, Pitt clung grimly to the rock on which his policy was built: if America could be won, France would be beaten and peace in Europe could be made on favourable terms. To this end he would continue to devote his energy and the greater part of British military strength.

CHAPTER XVII

The Great Opportunity

TOWARDS the end of July an unofficial report from France was received in London; Amherst's army, it was said, had landed on Cape Breton Island. For Pitt this was heartening news indeed. Victory in Canada was the only possible justification for his refusal to send an army to fight in Europe, and the only likely approach to a favourable peace. He did not doubt that once a landing had been made Louisbourg must fall, and without waiting for official confirmation of the rumour he wrote to Boscawen giving orders for the consolidation of this anticipated victory. Ten ships of the line with attendant frigates were to winter in Halifax to be ready for the next campaign 'very early in the spring'. On 18th August definite news was received of the capture of Louisbourg. Pitt shared in the general rejoicing, but his satisfaction was tempered by the knowledge that this conquest could be as much a liability as an asset to his policy. Louisbourg was the key to the French dominions in Canada, but it was also the key to peace. 'This,' wrote the Duke of Newcastle to Hardwicke on 18th August,[134] 'is the greatest & most glorious Event that ever was, & *if proper use be made of it, must do our Business.*' The business he had in mind was the negotiation of peace with France; and Louisbourg would do very well in exchange for Minorca. This, it need hardly be said, was not what Pitt had in mind for Louisbourg, and he was fortunate, surprisingly enough, in having the support of the King. George II, flushed with the thrill of conquest, had announced exuberantly to the shocked Duke of Newcastle that he proposed to keep Cape Breton, drive the French out of America, and raise two large armies for Germany.[135] How he proposed to find either the troops or the money was never explained, but to Pitt the essential fact emerged that the King did not intend to sacrifice Louisbourg and the possibility of the conquest of Canada in order to achieve an early peace and relieve his flustered First Lord of the Treasury of his financial burdens.

Nevertheless, Newcastle was not alone in thinking that the time was approaching when peace might be bought at a fair price. All that appeared to be lacking was some signal victory in Europe. Pitt therefore determined to make certain of his Canadian gains by acquiring another French possession which would have an exchange value equal to that of Minorca. Early in September Newcastle became aware that a scheme was being worked out for an attack on Martinique, the richest of the islands in the French Antilles. At first he showed some enthusiasm for the project, which he considered would strike a useful blow against French trade in the West Indies; soon, however, he was appalled to discover that this was to be no mere raid on enemy commerce but a full-scale expedition of 6,000 men with appropriate naval support, designed to capture the island and hold it against counter-attack. In vain he protested against the expense; in spite of his objections, and the opposition of Anson, who feared that the home fleet would be weakened when it most needed to be strong, the expedition sailed on 12th November.

While plans for the expeditions to Senegal and Goree and to Martinique were being made, Pitt was putting the finishing touches to his plan for the spring campaign in America. He had already ordered part of the fleet to winter in Halifax, and directed the Admiralty to provide the necessary stores to maintain the ships and their crews there. Commodore Philip Durrell, Boscawen's junior flag officer, was appointed to command the squadron, with orders to prevent any French attempt to reinforce or supply Quebec through the St. Lawrence. The entire army also remained in America. Amherst succeeded Abercromby in supreme command, and Wolfe was to be appointed to command in an attack on Quebec as early as possible in the following year.

Pitt's orders to Wolfe did not reach him in Canada: he had already sailed with Boscawen for England. Before he left for the Louisbourg expedition, Wolfe had been promised by Ligonier that he should return to England at the end of the campaign. It was probably also inferred that he would be appointed to a command in Germany. As soon as he arrived in England he wrote to his mother to inform her of his safe return, and then applied to Ligonier for leave. While he waited for a reply he spent his time with his new regiment, the 67th, at Salisbury. About ten days after his arrival in England his leave was granted and he was able to join his parents at Blackheath. The old general had aged rapidly in Wolfe's absence, and had become testy and enfeebled with gout, but both he and Mrs. Wolfe were delighted to see their now famous son. Wolfe's reputation had been much enhanced by his spirited behaviour in the Louisbourg siege, and although, as a subordinate officer, his name was not mentioned in the parliamentary vote of thanks to the commanders, it was already well known throughout the country. His health had suffered in the campaign and, as usual, the long voyage home had been made miserable by sea-sickness. At Blackheath he was able to recuperate. Under the care of his mother, and with the benefit of exercise in the park with his dogs, he soon recovered and felt ready to undertake any service that might be required of him.

From Blackheath he took an early opportunity of visiting London. There he learned that a letter had been sent to America ordering him to remain there with the army in preparation for the new campaign, and that his return with Boscawen was viewed with the gravest displeasure by Pitt. Wolfe wrote to him at once. 'Since my arrival in town,' he writes on 22nd November,[136] 'I have been told that your intentions were to have continued me upon the service in America. The condition of my health and other circumstances, made me desire to return at the end of the campaign; and by what my Lord Ligonier did me the honour to say, I understood it was to be so. General Amherst saw it in the same light. I take the freedom to acquaint you that I have no objection to serving in America, and particularly in the river St. Lawrence, if any operations are to be carried on there. The favour I ask is only to be allowed sufficient time to repair the injury done to my constitution by the long confinement at sea, that I may be the better able to go through the business of the next summer.' His letter did much to make amends. Pitt had already decided to appoint him to command at Quebec. It only remained for the

King to give his assent and in view of the depressing record of failure of his own elderly nominees this was unlikely to be withheld.

At the end of November Wolfe rejoined his regiment at Salisbury. In the few weeks that he served with it, Wolfe instilled into the 67th much of the spirit and discipline that he had created in the 20th, and a commander of the regiment ten years later paid generous tribute to his influence.[137] From Salisbury he wrote to Rickson, setting down with his usual frankness his criticisms of the campaign in America, and in particular of the 'slow and tedious' operations which had destroyed the chance of taking Quebec in the same year. He pays tribute to Lord Howe and to Bradstreet, but his estimate of the Marquis de Montcalm's ability is unflattering and ill-judged. He makes no attempt to disguise his preference for an appointment in Germany but is well aware that his chances are slight. 'When I went from hence,' he writes, 'Lord Ligonier told me that I was to return at the end of the campaign; but I have learned since I came home that an order is gone to keep me there; & I have this day signified to Mr. Pitt that he may dispose of my slight Carcass as he pleases, & that I am ready for any undertaking within the reach of my skill and cunning. I am in very bad condition both with the Gravel & Rheumatism, but I had much rather die than decline any kind of service that offers. If I followed my own taste, it would lead me into Germany; & if my poor talent was consulted, they would place me in the cavalry, because nature has given me good eyes, and a warmth of temper to follow the first impressions. However, it is not our part to choose, but to obey. My opinion is, that I shall join the army in America, where, if fortune favours our force & best endeavours, we may hope to triumph.'

Wolfe had received a letter of congratulation from Captain Parr, who had served under him in the 20th and was now with that regiment, serving under Sackville in Germany, and wrote from Salisbury on 6th September to express his satisfaction at the reports he had received of the good conduct of his old regiment and to ask for news of his friends. He makes no secret of his longing for service in Germany: 'It is my fortune to be cursed with American service, yours to serve in an army commanded by a great and able Prince,* where I would have been if my choice and inclination had been consulted.' He was in constant pain from rheumatism and gravel and the prospect of another campaign in America deepened his depression. On the 7th he reviewed his regiment for the last time. He had decided to try a cure for his ailments, and in the afternoon he bade farewell to his men and climbed stiffly into a post-chaise on the road to Bath.

Wolfe took lodgings in Queen's Square, 'to be more at leisure, more in the Air, & nearer the Country,' as he explains to his father on the 9th. He adds, 'The Women are not remarkable, nor the men neither; however, a man must be very hard to please if he does not find some that will suit him.' He was not bored with the company for long: within a few days of his arrival he discovered that Katherine Lowther and her mother were in Bath, and he wasted no time in calling on them. But his time was short; scarcely a week after he had met the Lowthers, he was summoned by Pitt to Hayes, where he received the command of the Quebec expedition and a full explanation of the Minister's plans for the spring offensive in Canada. He rode over to Blackheath for the night to tell his parents of his appointment and from there he wrote a guarded letter to his old friend George Warde. 'I would not ask you if you desire to serve. I know your inclinations in that respect; but let me know if I may mention you for distant, difficult, and disagreeable service, such as requires all your spirit and abilities. 'Tis not the Indies, which is as much as I can say directly; but if the employment of Adjutant-General, or perhaps Quartermaster-General to a very hazardous enterprise be to your taste, there are people who would be extremely glad of your assistance.' On the following day, the 21st, he was back in Bath.

He had many preparations to make for his departure early in the new year—the most important task being the choice of his subordinate commanders—and he might well have chosen to spend Christmas at home with his parents, where he would be close to London and to Pitt. But he decided instead to return to Bath. No doubt he needed to make the most of his opportunity to repair his broken health, but the real reason for his early return was the presence there of the beautiful Katherine Lowther. Wolfe

* Prince Ferdinand of Brunswick.

had fallen deeply in love with her, and even the promise of a great and independent command could not keep him from her.

But the coming campaign could not be forgotten. While he pursued his courtship, Wolfe had also to consider Pitt's plan for the attack on Quebec and make his own. Command of the naval force had been given to Charles Saunders, with Durrell, who was already in America, as his second. On Christmas Eve Wolfe wrote to Pitt. Consideration of the task before him had shown him with perfect clarity that the key to success lay in denying the St. Lawrence to French ships until the campaign was finished. 'I will add,' he writes,[138] 'from my own knowledge, that the second naval officer in command there is vastly unequal to the weight of business; and it is of the first importance to the country that it does not fall into such hands.' His opinion of Durrell was more than justified by events. The difficulties of navigating the St. Lawrence had become almost a legend, and a previous attempt by a British fleet to enter the river had cost eight ships and most of their crew.* In Wolfe's view the only way to close the St. Lawrence was to enter it as soon as the ice broke and to sail two hundred miles up river to the Isle of Bic where the estuary narrowed to a controllable width. 'A squadron of eight or ten sail stationed there, in the earliest opening of the river would effectually prevent all relief; and it would be a very easy thing for the remainder of that squadron to push a frigate or two, and as many sloops, up the river, even as high as the Isle of Orleans, with proper people on board to acquire a certain knowledge of the navigation, in readiness to pilot such men-of-war and transports as the commanders should think fit to send up, after the junction of the whole fleet at Isle Bic. Nor does there appear any great risk in detaching the North American squadron to that station, as it is hardly probable that a force equal to that squadron could be sent from Europe to force their way up to Quebec, because it is a hundred to one if such a fleet keeps together in that early season, and if they were together, it is next to a certainty that they would be in a very poor condition for action. Besides, it would effectually answer our purpose to engage a French squadron in that river, even with the superiority of a ship or two on their side, seeing

* In 1711.

211

that they must be shattered in the engagement, and in the end destroyed.' He goes on to look further ahead: 'If the enemy cannot pass the squadron stationed in the river, and push up to Quebec, a few ships of war and frigates would do to convoy the transports from the Isle Bic to Quebec, and to assist in the operations of the campaign; and, in this case, the gross of the fleet remaining at the Isle of Bic is at hand to prevent any attempt upon Louisbourg or Halifax; whereas, if the whole went up to Quebec, intelligence would be long in getting to them, and their returns in proportion. You must excuse the freedom I have taken, both in writing and sending the enclosed papers. If you see one useful hint in either, my intent is fully answered; if not, I beg you will burn them without further notice.' This masterly appreciation was accepted both by Pitt and Anson. Within a few days orders were sent to Durrell to put Wolfe's plan into operation.

At the same time, it is clear that Pitt also had doubts about Durrell's reliability, for he sent a copy of Durrell's orders to Saunders and added:[139] 'You will take the earliest opportunity to renew the said orders in the strongest manner, as nothing can be so essential to the success of the important expedition against Quebec as effectually blocking up the river St. Lawrence as early in the year as shall be practicable.'

Pitt then wrote to Amherst, setting out the entire plan of campaign, which, he explained, was designed to consolidate and improve the advantages gained in 1758, and to deal a final blow to French ambitions in Canada. The offensive would be split between Amherst's land operation and Wolfe's attack from the sea. The detailed instructions for the preparation of Wolfe's force cover more than half the dispatch. Amherst was to detach 12,000 men, including a number of units named by Wolfe, to be ready and fully equipped at Louisbourg by April. The remainder of the dispatch deals with Amherst's own campaign which, he cannot but have realized, had been thrust into the backround by the priority accorded to the Quebec expedition. His own task was to advance either by Crown Point and Lake Champlain or by La Galette down to the south bank of the St. Lawrence to Montreal and Quebec. In addition he was to re-establish the inland naval base destroyed by Bradstreet at Oswego and capture the French base at Niagara; but these two assignments were clearly intended to be subsidiary and subordinated to the main objectives of Montreal and Quebec. This part of his instructions Amherst failed to understand with consequences which might have destroyed Pitt's entire plan.

Wolfe, meanwhile, was fully occupied collecting his staff. He writes again to George Warde on 26th December: 'My dear Friend,—I have told the leading men that if they charge a young soldier with weighty matters they must give him the best assistance. I know none better than those I took freedom to mention, & if there be any obstacles on the side of Government I shall desire to be excus'd from taking the first part. . . . The readiness you express encourages me to hope that our united efforts may at least be useful. Nothing shall be press'd upon you, altho' I know of nothing that you need decline. We shall meet in London towards the middle of the next week, & talk the matter over; till then I bid you farewell.' But Warde did not accompany the expedition. He was sent instead to Germany, though whether this was at his own request is not known. Another friend's name was crossed off the list of those Wolfe wished to have with him: he had asked for Guy Carleton as Quartermaster-General, but the King refused to endorse the appointment. Wolfe was unmoved; this was the second time that the King had refused to give his consent to an appointment for Carleton, as punishment for a witty but indiscreet remark about the Electorate; but if the King had made up his mind not to let Carleton go to Canada, Wolfe had decided not to go without him. Twice Ligonier tried to persuade the King, but it was not until Pitt, himself, represented to George II that Wolfe could not be held responsible for the conduct of the expedition unless he was allowed some latitude in the choice of his staff that Carleton's commission was signed.

It remained for Wolfe to fill the three most important appointments to the command of his brigades. For the senior appointment he chose the Hon. Robert Monckton, second son of the 1st Viscount Galway. Monckton, who was a year Wolfe's senior, had already proved himself in America and had considerable experience of colonial troops. He was well known to Wolfe, and his experience and ability, his youth and energy, made him an obvious choice. The third brigade was given to the Hon. James Murray, the fifth and youngest son of Lord Elibank. Murray was also known personally to Wolfe who had a high opinion of his abilities. He had served with distinction at Louisbourg, and had also been with the ill-fated Carthagena expedition of 1740, in the war in Flanders, and under Mordaunt at Rochefort. He was now thirty-eight, autocratic and intolerant, but a man of intrepid courage, passionately determined to win promotion and glory. The second brigade was allotted, at his own request, to the Hon. George Townshend, younger son of the Third Viscount Townshend. George Townshend had been present at Dettingen, Fontenoy, Culloden, and Laffeldt, and had been for a time aide to the Duke of Cumberland; but after differences with him, he had resigned his commission and had turned his talents to politics, with his brother, Charles, who was a privy councillor. He had been very largely responsible for the Militia Bill and was thus favoured by Pitt and had recently become aide-de-camp to the King. He was a man of undoubted courage and a ready wit, which had not deserted him even when, at Dettingen, when he was nineteen, a drummer-boy standing close to him had been struck on the head by a cannon-ball scattering the boy's brains all over him. An old soldier standing nearby tried to reassure the young officer. 'Oh,' said Townshend, 'I am not afraid, I am only astonished that a fellow with such a quantity of brains should be here.' Unfortunately, this wit often found expression in sarcasm and malicious caricature. Even Walpole, who could find little good to say of him, was forced to admit that 'his genius for likenesses in caricatura is astonishing,' but this was not a quality likely to endear him to his fellows.

Townshend's offer to serve under Wolfe was considered an act of great condescension for which Wolfe should feel honoured and grateful. The position is made amply clear in a letter to Townshend from Lieutenant-General Sir Richard Lyttelton, the Adjutant-General at the War Office:[140] 'I congratulate you most sincerely upon the honour this spirited and magnanimous acceptance of yours will do you in the world as soon as it becomes known, and upon the glory you will obtain, and I flatter myself the short time you will be absent and the small risk you will probably run in this enterprise will in some degree reconcile

Lady Ferrers* to it.' This was hardly a sound basis for a satisfactory relationship between the commander of an army and one of his brigadiers.

Wolfe knew little of Townshend as a soldier, but he was prepared to accept his appointment as third in command of the expedition with good grace. On 6th January he writes generously,[141] 'I came to town last night and found the letter you had done me the honour to write. Your name was mentioned to me by the Marshal* and my answer was, that such an example in a person of your rank and character, could not but have the best effects upon the troops in America and, indeed, upon the whole military part of the nations; and I took the freedom to add that what might be wanting in experience was amply made up, in an extent of capacity and activity of mind, that would find nothing difficult in our business. I am to thank you for the good opinion you have entertained of me, and for the manner in which you have taken occasion to express your favourable sentiments. I persuade myself that we shall concur heartily for the public service —the operation in question will require our united efforts and the utmost exertion of every man's spirit and judgment.'

One other matter caused Wolfe serious concern: the expense involved in his new duties. He had been promoted to major-general, but the rank applied only in America; his rank in England was still colonel, and he received only a colonel's pay. Nor did he qualify, as Amherst did, for the special pay of ten pounds a day as commander-in-chief. Fortunately there was provision for a special grant to an officer chosen to lead an expedition, and for this Wolfe applied. Barrington, the Secretary at War, endorsed his application and the King signed a special warrant for five hundred pounds.

The time was approaching for Wolfe to leave. On 29th January he wrote from London one of his most significant letters to his uncle Walter Wolfe:[142] 'You had a right to expect to hear from me sooner and I am to blame that you did not. These omissions of mine are too frequent even with those I love and

* Townshend's wife. He had married in 1751, Lady Charlotte Compton, only daughter of the Earl of Northampton, and Baroness Ferrers of Chartley in her own right.
† Lord Ligonier.

honour most. Mr. Lynch delivered me your letter and proceeded directly to North America, where in the course of the campaign I doubt not he will find an opening. Our force is considerable upon that continent and except the Garrisons of Louisbourg and Halifax will all be employed this year, and as early as possible. If the Marquis de Montcalm finds means to baffle our efforts another summer, he may be deemed an able officer; or the colony has resources that we know nothing of; or our Generals are worse than usual. We had Canada in our hands last year; with common prudence on one side, and a little spirit of enterprise on the other, it appears to me that Abercromby might have cut off the enemy's retreat from Ticonderoga, and in the end forced them to lay down their arms. If the siege of Louisbourg had been pushed with vigour, Quebec would have fallen. The French are arming in all their ports; their object, no doubt, is the defence of Canada; ours to attack it, and the fleet for that service is formidable. I am to act a greater part in this business than I wished or desired. The backwardness of some of the older officers has in some measure forced the Government to come down so low. I shall do my best, and leave the rest to fortune, as perforce we must when there are not the most commanding abilities. We expect to sail in about three weeks. A London life and little exercise disagree entirely with me, but the sea still more. If I have health and constitution enough for the campaign, I shall think myself a lucky man; what happens afterwards is of no great consequence.'

Of his leave-taking from Katherine Lowther nothing is known, though a highly-coloured description appears in Charles Johnstone's *Chrysal*, but at some time in January he asked her to marry him and was accepted. Before he left England she gave him her portrait in miniature, a lock of her hair, and a copy of Gray's *Elegy in a Country Churchyard* which had been published in 1751. It appears that once again Wolfe's choice did not meet with parental approval, for he seems to have spent only one night at Blackheath during his last three months in England, and he did not return there to take leave of his parents. Instead, he wrote a brief note to his mother shortly before he sailed:

'Dear Madam,——The formality of taking leave should be as much as possible avoided; & therefore I prefer this method of offering my good wishes & duty to my Father & to you. I shall carry this business thro' with my best abilities; the event, you know, is in the hands of Providence—to whose care I hope your good life and conduct will recommend your Son.

Saunders talks of sailing on Thursday, if the Wind comes fair. . . . I heartily wish you health & the easy enjoyment of the many good things that have fallen to your share. My best duty to the General.

I am, dear Madam,

Your obedient and affectionate Son,

Jam: Wolfe.'

On the eve of his departure, Wolfe dined with Pitt, the only other guest being Pitt's brother-in-law, Temple. The story of what took place at that dinner rests on the sole evidence of Temple who repeated it to Grenville. Temple was known as an accomplished and malicious liar, and his story, no doubt much embroidered in the telling, was passed on a generation later to Stanhope who printed it in his *History of England*. When the dinner was over, the conversation was of the expedition which was to sail on the following day. Wolfe, we are told, drew his sword, rapped the table with it, and swaggered round the room boasting of the mighty achievements his sword would accomplish. When at last he left in his carriage, Pitt exclaimed to Temple: 'Good God! that I should have entrusted the fate of the country and of the Administration to such hands!' Lack of self-confidence was not among Wolfe's failings even in his worst moods of depression, but it is difficult to relate such behaviour to the modest hopes expressed in his letter to Walter Wolfe. Nor is it easy to believe that a man with such varied experience of the unpredictable fortunes of war could act with such foolishness. From what is known of him, and of Temple, it is probable that Wolfe was excited and over-vehement in his promise that the expedition should not fail, as others had failed, for want of courage to act. This, at least, was a promise which he could fulfil.

It was not long after this episode that Newcastle suggested to George II that Wolfe was mad. 'Mad is he,' retorted the King, no doubt remembering the inglorious performances in the field of

Braddock, Mordaunt, and Abercromby, 'then I hope he will bite some other of my generals.'*

* That this story was well known after Wolfe's death is proved by a collection of manuscript poems written by a brother of Wolfe's friend Kit Mason and dedicated to Mrs. Wolfe, which contains the following lines dated 14th October 1759:

> 'What Time great George who gallant Actions priz'd
> And Cowards from his inmost Soul despis'd
> Was praising Valiant Wolfe his Actions great,
> Whom Death nor Hell could aught intimidate
> Who on the Gauls Britannia's Fury hurl'd
> And at his Death bequeath'd her a new World
> May't please your Majesty (exclaim'd his Foes)
> The Man was mad, which all his Deeds disclos'd
> Mad, then I wish he'd bit, the King reply'd,
> Some of my Generals before he'd died.'

This collection is now in the McCord Museum, McGill University.

CHAPTER XVIII

Quebec: Unexpected Difficulties

On 14th February 1759, sixty transports, with an escort of six sail of the line and nine frigates, sailed from Portsmouth under the command of Rear-Admiral Charles Holmes, who had distinguished himself a year earlier in the Ems. Two days later Wolfe followed with Vice-Admiral Sir Charles Saunders in the ninety-gun three-decker flagship *Neptune* escorted by the rest of the fleet destined for Quebec.

Saunders was known to Wolfe only by reputation: one of the brilliant band of officers who had accompanied Anson on his great voyage round the world in 1744, he had served with distinction under Hawke in the previous war, and had been sent out to the Mediterranean after Byng's failure at Minorca. His reputation was one of courage, energy, and clarity of decision, masked by a forbidding taciturnity. Fourteen years Wolfe's senior in age, he may well have shared the doubts expressed by other senior officers of the ability of so young a general to command an expedition of such strength and importance. The voyage lasted ten weeks; it gave the two commanders ample time to know each other, and they were drawn together by their shared problems. According to their instructions, the fleet was to play a subsidiary part in the expedition: once the troops had been conveyed up the St. Lawrence, little was to be expected of it but the protection of communications; but this, alone, entailed crossing several thousand miles of ocean and seeing the transports safely up a virtually uncharted river through hostile country. Saunders made his own intentions clear as he passed down the coast of Spain. Here he had been instructed to detach two 'sixties' for service with Boscawen's fleet, one of which was to be the *Stirling Castle* of sixty-four guns. On his own authority he detached a 'seventy-four', retaining the *Stirling Castle* which, as he wrote in explanation to Pitt, though small, was 'very handy, on that Account for working in Rivers or Narrow Channels.'[143] This was the ship which later flew his flag before Quebec. Without discussion he had already decided on the use of his smaller ships to support the land attack.

For Wolfe the voyage was, as always, humiliating and miserable. Sea-sickness aggravated his other complaints: he was in constant pain from rheumatism and his old bladder trouble, and there is little doubt that he was suffering from an advanced condition of tuberculosis. He lay in his cabin, exhausted by pain and sickness, weighing the immense problems which he knew would confront him on his arrival in the St. Lawrence.

The destination of the fleet and its convoy of transports was no secret in England, for on 9th February Walpole had written to Horace Mann: 'The expedition, called to Quebec, departs on Tuesday next, under Wolfe and George Townshend, who has thrust himself again into the service, and as far as wrongheadedness will go, very proper for a hero. Wolfe, who was no friend of Mr. Conway last year, has great merit, spirit, and alacrity, and shone extremely at Louisbourg. I am not such a Juno but I will forgive him after eleven more labours.' Townshend sailed with Wolfe on board the *Neptune*, and the wearying weeks of the voyage were little improved by his sarcastic tongue and patronizing manner. Serving as first lieutenant on board the flagship was a promising young officer, John Jervis, for whom Saunders had a high regard. Jervis, who was later to justify Saunders's faith in him and, as Earl St. Vincent, to be regarded as one of Britain's greatest sailors, had been educated at Swinden's school in Greenwich some years after Wolfe had left. The story has been told by Jervis's biographer that Wolfe entrusted to Jervis his will and the miniature of Katherine Lowther shortly before the battle for Quebec, but this is without foundation.*

The concentration of Wolfe's forces at Louisbourg was planned for 20th April, but it was not until ten days later that the

* Jervis wrote on 18th July 1798:[144] 'The memory of the gallant Wolfe is dear to me. . . . He was six years my senior & our careers lay widely apart—I saw him once in the year 1756 & not again until the Quebeck campaign when we met several times before his lamented though glorious death.'

fleet sighted Cape Breton, and then only to find that the winter ice had not yet melted and it was impossible to enter the harbour. Saunders made several gallant attempts to find a way through the ice, but it proved impossible and he was obliged to move on to Halifax. There to his disgust he found Durrell still at anchor. His fleet had been ready for service for more than a month, but he was waiting for news that the melting of the ice would allow him to enter the St. Lawrence. This was a piece of inexcusable indolence worthy of severe punishment; but there was no time for recriminations. Command of the lower reaches of the St. Lawrence, denying to the garrison the possibility of reinforcement and supply by sea, was vital to the success of the whole expedition. Durrell was immediately ordered to sea, but delayed by foul weather, was unable to sail until 5th May. His demand for 300 troops to complete his crews was met without argument by Wolfe, who, as an additional safeguard against more half-heartedness, sent with them his most trusted friend and quarter-master-general, Colonel Guy Carleton.

Wolfe was already faced by unexpected difficulties which threatened his chances of success: he feared that Durrell's inaction might have enabled the French to send reinforcements and provisions to Quebec; and it was clear that the strength of his own army would fall far below that planned by Pitt and Ligonier. Only one of the transports escorted by Holmes had so far arrived in Halifax, and it was reported that the convoy had been widely dispersed by a violent storm. The troops, for whom they were intended, had not benefited in health from their winter in America, and a number had died during a recent epidemic of smallpox.

On 1st May Wolfe wrote both to Pitt and to his commander-in-chief in America, General Amherst. To Pitt he gives a mere outline account of events, mentioning without comment that he granted Durrell's request for men 'that there might be no impediment to his sailing.'[145] He adds that he has 'put the whole under the command of the Quartermaster-General, Colonel Carleton, to assist Mr. Durrell's operations in the river St. Lawrence, where perhaps it may be necessary to land upon some of the islands, and push a detachment of his fleet up the basin of Quebec, that the navigation may be perfectly free from transports. By this early attempt, it is more than probable that the Canadians will not have time to prepare a defence at the Isle aux Coudres and at the Traverse—the two most difficult and rapid parts of the river, and where the pilots seem to think they might and would (if not prevented in time) give us a great deal of trouble. If Mr. Durrell had been at sea, as we imagined, I did intend to have sent Colonel Carleton with this additional force, some artillery and tools, with the first ship that Mr. Saunders might have ordered to reinforce the Rear-Admiral's squadron.' Of his army he says, 'Our troops, indeed, are good and very well disposed. If valour can make amends for want of numbers we shall probably succeed.' To Amherst, Wolfe is more explicit. 'We were,' he writes,[146] 'astonish'd to find Mr. Durrell at an anchor. . . . Our four battalions are at a very low ebb—and I believe, if Mr. Murray, Mr. Howe, & the other Gentlemen, had not taken more than common precaution and been at more than ordinary expense, & pains for the preservation of their men assisted by Mr. Russell's skill & diligence* these Regiments wou'd have been annihilated. Otway's and Bragg's are still worse, as I am informed. So that you see, Sir, what a numerous body of men are here for the conquest of Quebec. I believe they *feel Stout*, and so they had need— seeing there is not a multitude. . . . The least loss in the River, or sickness among the Men, reduces our undertaking to little more than a diversion—& I can assure you that I think we are very *liable* to accidents. It can't be doubted but that the French have thrown succours in, or will do it, before our Squadron gets to its proper station. . . . I wish you health and Success—of the former I have but a small share; of the latter as little hope, unless we get into the River first; however, trust me—they shall feel us.'

While the fleet refitted at Halifax and waited for the arrival of more transports, Wolfe busied himself with preparations for the move from Louisbourg to the St. Lawrence. He issued orders detailing the appointments on his staff, including those of Carleton as Quartermaster-General, Major Isaac Barré as Adjutant-General, and Captains Hervey Smyth and Bell as his aides, and allotting the regiments and brigades to their positions in the fleet and in the line of battle. The men were ordered 'to be

---

* Lawrence in a letter to Amherst dated 10th February 1758 had paid tribute to the 'extraordinary diligence & skill'[147] of Dr. Russell and recommended him for promotion.

as much in the open air as possible, and to eat upon deck.' Saunders also issued his orders designating Gaspée Bay 'at the upper end of the St. Lawrence' as the rendezvous for the fleet after it had left Louisbourg. On 13th May the fleet sailed from Halifax and, falling in with Holmes off Cape Sambro, entered Louisbourg harbour on the 15th.

At Louisbourg Wolfe found a letter waiting for him telling of his father's death on 26th March. The news was not unexpected, for the old general had been in failing health for several years, but it was a sad blow to Wolfe and increased his anxiety for his mother. On the 19th he wrote to Major Walter Wolfe:[148] 'Since our arrival in this country the news of my father's death has reached me. I left him in so weak a condition that it was not probable that we should ever meet again. . . . I am exceedingly sorry that it so fell out that I had it not in my power to assist him in his illness, and to relieve my mother in her distress, and the more so as her relations are not affectionate, and you are too far off to give her help. I have written to Mr. Fisher* to continue the pensions which my father had assigned to his kindred, my easy circumstances enabling me to fulfill all his intentions.' It was characteristic of Wolfe that he should cloak his generosity under the pretence of 'easy circumstances'. He was not drawing the pay for his local rank of major-general and though he had little opportunity for spending his pay while he was in America, he well knew that if he returned to England to command his own regiment again the family pensions could not but prove a financial burden.

In this letter to his uncle, Wolfe gives a penetrating analysis of the tactical situation.

'We are [he writes] ordered to attack Quebec,—a very nice operation. The fleet consists of twenty-two sail of the line and many frigates, the army of 9,000 men; in England it is called 12,000. We have ten battalions, three companies of Grenadiers, some Marines (if the Admiral can spare them), and six new-raised companies of North American Rangers—not complete, and the worst soldiers in the universe; a great train of artillery, plenty of provisions, tools, and implements of all sorts; three Brigadiers under me,—all men of great spirit; some Colonels of reputation,

* His agent.

223

Carleton for Quartermaster-General, and upon whom I chiefly rely for the engineering part. Engineers very indifferent, and of little experience; but we have none better. The regular troops in Canada consist of eight battalions of old Foot—about 400 a battalion—and forty companies of Marines (or colony troops), forty men a company. They can gather together 8,000 or 10,000 Canadians, and perhaps 1,000 Indians. As they are attacked by the side of Montreal by an enemy of 12,000 fighting men, they must necessarily divide their force; but, as the loss of the capital implies the loss of the colony, their chief attention will naturally be there, and therefore I reckon we may find at Quebec six battalions, some companies of Marines, four or five thousand Canadians, and some Indians; altogether, not much inferior to their enemy.

Rear-Admiral Durrell, with ten sail, is gone up the river, and has orders to take such a station as will effectually cut off all succours; but as he sailed late from Halifax (4th May) there is reason to think that some store-ships have already got up. If so, our difficulties are like to increase. I have sent a detachment with Mr. Durrell to assist his first operations, and to seize the islands in those parts of the river where the navigation is most dangerous. The Admiral has positive instructions to watch the first opening of the river St. Lawrence, so as to push with his squadron as high as the Isle de Bic, and from thence to detach some small ships to the basin of Quebec, that all might be free and open behind. The admiral Commander-in-Chief of the fleet is a zealous, brave officer. I don't exactly know what disposition he intends to make in the river after the junction of the two squadrons; but I conclude he will send four or five of his smallest ships of the line to assist us at Quebec, and remain with the rest at an anchor below the Isle aux Coudres, ready to fight whatever fleet the enemy may send to disturb us.

The town of Quebec is poorly fortified, but the ground round about it is rocky. To invest the place, and cut off all communication with the colony, it will be necessary to encamp with our right to the River St. Lawrence, and our left to the river St. Charles. From the river St. Charles to Beauport the communication must be kept open by strong entrenched posts and redoubts. The enemy can pass that river at low water; and it will be proper to establish ourselves with small entrenched posts from the point of

Levi to La Chaudière. It is the business of our naval force to be masters of the river, both above and below the town. If I find that the enemy is strong, audacious, and well-commanded, I shall proceed with the utmost caution and circumspection, giving Mr. Amherst time to use his superiority. If they are timid, weak and ignorant, we shall push them with more vivacity, that we may be able before the summer is gone to assist the Commander-in-Chief. I reckon we shall have a smart action at the passage of the river St. Charles, unless we can steal a detachment up the river St. Lawrence, and land them three, four, five miles, or more, above the town, and get time to entrench so strongly that they won't care to attack. . . . The army under my command is rather too small for the undertaking, but it is well composed.

You may be assured that I shall take all proper care of my own person, unless in case of the last importance, where it becomes a duty to do otherwise. I never put myself unnecessarily in the way of danger. Young troops must be encouraged at first. What appears hazardous sometimes is really not so to people who know the country. The separate corps which I commanded last year, divided as they were into a number of posts—encamped within cannon-shot of the ships or town, and often within the reach of grape-shot—suffered hardly any loss at all, because the ground is so uneven that we could place them everywhere in security. We are every hour in expectation of seeing the regiments arrive which are to compose the army. Most of them are actually at sea, and upon this coast; but the fogs are so frequent and lasting, that ships are obliged to stand out to sea waiting for fair weather. I hope we shall be able to sail in about ten days, and if no accident happens in the river, I hope we shall succeed. I wish you your health; mine is but indifferent. . . .'

The particular significance of this letter lies in Wolfe's first plan of attack, made four months before the final assault. He has been much criticized by biographers, and in particular by one military historian for failing to realize the importance of a landing above Quebec to sever communications with the rest of the French army facing Amherst and cut off the supply routes to the west. This letter proves beyond doubt that he was not only well aware of the vital significance of the upper river, but that he had, before he ever set eyes on Quebec, decided that the town must be invested from the west, and had considered a landing above the town. It remained to be seen whether or not this plan would prove to be practicable.

On the same day he wrote to Brigadier Whitmore, who had been left in command of Louisbourg after the campaign of the previous autumn, applying to him for a company of Light Infantry from the garrison. This company had originally been allotted to Wolfe's command, but by some oversight the necessary instructions had not been sent to Whitmore from England. It was to be replaced by a thousand Boston Militia which would have the effect of increasing rather than depleting the garrison. Anticipating some reluctance from the brigadier whom he had disparaged at Louisbourg as a 'poor old sleepy man', Wolfe added: 'Mr. Lawrence, who has a very bad fortress and a very weak garrison, accepted of the sick and recovering men of the two American battalions as part of the 500 regulars intended for the defence of Nova Scotia, knowing very well that upon the success of our attacks in Canada, the security of the whole continent of North America in a great measure depends.' Whitmore replied with some hauteur that he could take orders only from the commander-in-chief, and the company was withheld.

On the last day of the month, Monckton arrived from Halifax with four battalions and Wolfe's army was completed. It numbered 8,535, some 3,000 less than had been ordered to assemble for the expedition. Pitt's instructions to Wolfe had made it clear beyond doubt that he expected Quebec to be taken before Amherst could force his way through from Montreal and for this purpose he had allotted to Wolfe a force of 12,500 men. It seemed impossible that this object could be achieved by an army already shrunk, even before it set out, to little more than two-thirds of its intended strength. There was little to be done to remedy this want of numbers, but Wolfe was determined at least to see that such troops as he had were fit and well trained. While the fleet took on board provisions, water, and ammunition, he saw to it that the men were landed daily for drill and exercise and issued with as much fresh beef as could be obtained. Orders were given that good quantities of spruce beer should be taken on board the transports as a protection against scurvy, and lines and hooks were distributed to all regiments to encourage the men to supplement their rations with fresh fish. The weather was mainly dark, foggy and cold, but the energy and enthusiasm of their commander spread throughout the troops of his army. He had no time for unnecessary regulations or rigid training methods. On the 25th he reviewed the Louisbourg Grenadiers and seemed well pleased with their performance. Some of the commanding officers, who expected their own regiments to be reviewed in their turn, apologized in advance to Wolfe that their regiments, having been confined through the long winter, had not had any opportunity to learn and practice the new drill exercise. Wolfe's reply was a startling relief:[149] 'New exercise—new fiddlestick; if they are otherwise well disciplined and will fight, that's all I shall require of them.' This practical attitude to many of the accepted canons of military procedure—an attitude mercifully different from the obstinacy of Braddock and the ponderousness of Amherst—was to be the cause of constant friction with Townshend. Wolfe had spent almost his entire service in command of troops, and much of it in battle. He knew that regulations were made as a guide, to be broken according to circumstances. He had read widely among the military textbooks and assimilated all they had to teach him, but he had no belief in their infallibility. Townshend, on the other hand, had spent his entire service on the staff. His naturally overbearing manner derived from his social rank and influence had thus been aggravated by the veneer of superiority adopted by the staff officer towards the regimental officer. This fundamental clash of attitude was to be the root of their mutual dislike and distrust throughout the campaign.

On 1st June, orders were issued that the troops were to land no more for exercise and 'the flat-bottomed boats to be hoisted up, that the ships may be ready to sail on the first signal', and on the following day they were warned that 'the Admiral proposes sailing with the first fair wind.' But thick fog and a strong head-wind prevented any move until the 4th, when some of the warships succeeded in clearing the harbour. At nine o'clock on the morning of the 5th the rest of the fleet weighed anchor, but by noon the wind had veered round and many of the ships had to put back into harbour. At last, before dawn on the 6th, the wind set fair, enabling the transports to sail, and by ten o'clock the entire fleet had joined outside the harbour. Wolfe sailed with Saunders in the *Neptune*, but without Townshend, who had transferred to a ship in the second division, Carleton, who had been sent ahead with Durrell, or Jervis, who had been appointed to command the fourteen-gun sloop *Porcupine*. The fleet sailed in three divisions: the White Division leading with Monckton's brigade consisting of the 15th, 43rd, 58th and 78th Regiments; the Red Division with Townshend's brigade of the 28th and 47th Regiments with the 2nd Battalion of the Royal Americans; and the Blue Division with Murray's brigade of the 35th and 48th Regiments and the 3rd Battalion of the Royal Americans.* The fleet, it is estimated, cannot have consisted of much less than 150 sail without those ships which had been sent with Durrell, and Knox writes that 'imagination cannot conceive a more eligible prospect.' The men were in high spirits at the promise of action after their long winter in garrison, and the popular toast among officers was 'British colours on every French fort, port, and garrison in America.'[150]

A week later the fleet was in the Gulf of St. Lawrence, and on the 18th it came to anchor off the Isle of Bic, about 170 miles from Quebec, where Saunders and Wolfe had arranged to meet a ship of Durrell's squadron bearing the vital news of his success or failure in the river.

---

* 15th Regiment.   The East Yorkshire Regiment.
43rd Regiment.   The Oxfordshire and Buckinghamshire Light Infantry.
58th Regiment.   2nd Battalion The Northamptonshire Regiment.
78th Regiment.   (Franc's Highlanders). Disbanded 1763.
28th Regiment.   The Royal Gloucestershire Regiment.
47th Regiment.   The Loyals.
Royal Americans.   The King's Royal Rifle Corps.
35th Regiment.   The Royal Sussex Regiment.
48th Regiment.   1st Battalion The Northamptonshire Regiment.

CHAPTER XIX

The French Administration

In the autumn of 1758, the Marquis Vaudreuil, Governor-General of Canada, consulted with his commander-in-chief, Montcalm, as to the preparations for the defence of the colony in the following year. The condition of Canada was certainly alarming: a British garrison held Louisbourg, and their fleet lay in the harbour; French supplies of food, arms and ammunition were inadequate and fast dwindling; and the people were nearing starvation. Furthermore, it was known that the British were preparing another attack in strength for the following year, and it was believed that this would take the form of an advance via Lake Champlain by about 50,000 men under Amherst. If Canada were to be saved, it was imperative that reinforcements and great quantities of supplies should be sent without delay from France. The only hope was a direct appeal to the Court, and it was therefore agreed that a deputation should be sent to lay the desperate situation before the King and his ministers. Two men were chosen: Doreil, the Commissary of War, and Bougainville. Louis Antoine de Bougainville was the most brilliant of Montcalm's staff. At the age of twenty-two he had written a treatise on integral calculus which had gained for him a fellowship of the Royal Society in England, and he had then become a secretary at the French Embassy in London under Mirepoix. In 1755, at the beginning of the war, he had returned to France to join the army and, as one of Montcalm's aides-de-camp, he had sailed with him from Brest in 1756. He was known to be a favourite of Madame de Pompadour, and it was hoped that he would be able to persuade her to use her influence in favour of the neglected colony.

Bougainville's mission failed. France needed all her military resources for the coming struggle in Europe, and all her naval strength for the projected invasion of England. Nothing could be spared for America; Montcalm and Vaudreuil must be content with sympathy and decorations, and they must be instructed to concentrate their forces and hold cn at all cost to some part of the colony, however small, so that when peace came French claims to Canada could be supported by right of possession. In answer to his desperate appeal for troops, ships, arms, ammunition and food, Bougainville was told by de Berryer, the Minister of Marine, 'Quand le feu est à la maison on ne s'occupe pas des écuries,' to which he replied in disgust, 'On ne dira pas du moins, monsieur, que vous parlez comme un cheval.' All he was able to obtain was 300 recruits for the regular battalions, a few engineers and artillerymen, and a quantity of arms and ammunition barely sufficient to carry the garrison through the coming campaign. But his mission was by no means wasted: while he was in France a British dispatch was intercepted giving details of the entire campaign in America including those for the attack on Quebec. It was now his urgent duty somehow to evade the blockade of the St. Lawrence and carry this vital information to Montcalm. If he failed Quebec would fall to a *coup de main* before any realistic preparations could be made for its defence.

In theory, in spite of the shortage of essential supplies, the tactical situation favoured the French. They had the immeasurable advantage of defending a country they knew on interior lines, whereas the attacking armies would operate in unfamiliar terrain, supplied, if at all, across three thousand miles of ocean, and their movements restricted almost entirely to predictable lines of approach along rivers or lakes. Quebec, though quite unprepared for defence, was a natural fortress, and it was generally considered that the impossibility of navigating the St. Lawrence without buoys or experienced pilots was sufficient protection against attack from the sea. Numerically there was little to choose between the available forces on both sides; but whereas the French could call upon the entire population capable of bearing arms and the doubtful asset of a horde of undisciplined Indians, the British had no such control over their colonial manpower which far exceeded that of the French. The significant difference between the two armies lay in the fact that the British forces of Amherst and Wolfe included about 15,000 regular troops, against which the French could muster barely 6,000.

The most serious French weakness lay, however, not in numbers or lack of supplies, but in administration and command. Nor is it fair to blame the system which, though unpractical and lifeless, could have been made to work by leaders less unequivocally at loggerheads than Vaudreuil and Montcalm. Vaudreuil was Canadian born, fanatically devoted to the colony which he served with unflagging fervour, jealous of all appointments, supremely conscious of his own importance, and a shameless moral coward. Montcalm, in direct contrast, was a French aristocrat, polished and scholarly, a resolute and experienced general, fiery and impetuous of temper, impatient, proud, intolerant, courageous and incorruptibly devoted to his country. Vaudreuil had bitterly opposed Montcalm's appointment to command in Canada and had since used his superior authority as Governor-General to hamper and undermine Montcalm's actions by constant interference and misrepresentation. His dispatches to the French Government were filled with complaints of Montcalm's inefficiency, lack of co-operation, and disobedience. His only motive appears to have been a malicious jealousy. He even went so far as to demand Montcalm's recall and the promotion of his second-in-command, de Lévis, but his influence in France was not strong enough to obtain agreement. This bitter feud between the Governor-General and the commander-in-chief divided the loyalties of the army: the French regular battalions supported Montcalm, whom they knew and respected as a fine soldier; the colonial troops were for Vaudreuil, who flattered them and exaggerated their achievements at the expense of the regulars. This division would have been of less consequence had it not been for Vaudreuil's insistence on exercising his final authority as Governor-General over military matters of which he had neither knowledge nor experience. Political control over military affairs is a commonplace of national administration: Pitt, as the King's representative, exercised that control over the forces of the Crown, and the system has remained unchanged in this country to the present day. But Pitt, with advice from his military commanders, made the strategic plan and left the handling of tactical situations to his commanders in the field. Vaudreuil was, himself, a political commander in the field, and his lack of experience, his indecisive nature, and abject moral cowardice, constituted a liability overwhelming even to a commander of Montcalm's strength of purpose. If it is true that there was a lack of harmony between Wolfe and one, at least, of his brigadiers, it was, though unpleasant, of little consequence: Wolfe's supreme authority was unquestionable and he was answerable for his actions only to Pitt.

Nor was the dangerous lack of unity in the colony—disastrous as it might prove to be if its military strength were tested—the worst of the administrative evils. The civil government of the country was in the hands of speculators whose treachery and corruption passes belief. Chief among them was the Intendant of Canada, François Bigot. The Intendant was a personage of immense importance in the civil administration of the colony, second only to the Governor-General. He had complete control of all finance, government contracts, public works, and the regulation of prices. To anyone of Bigot's abilities the position offered unrivalled opportunities for fraud and plunder on a gigantic scale and he made good use of them. He was an accomplished rogue, unprepossessing in appearance but with unusual charm of manner and a talent amounting to genius for the misappropriation of public funds. He had learnt his methods as commissary at Louisbourg, a position which he had held from 1739 until its capture by Pepperell six years later, and at the end of the war he had been appointed Intendant. He had gathered around him a motley collection of swindlers, the most notable of whom was Joseph Cadet, to whom he granted in 1756 a contract for the supply of all provisions to French garrisons in Canada. The contract was based on fixed prices which, as costs rose, obliged Cadet to resort to dishonest methods in order to make any profit. Bigot ignored these irregularities in return for a large share of the profits and Cadet's services in other shady transactions. Another devoted follower, Captain Duchambon de Vergor, was tried by court-martial for his too-ready surrender of Beauséjour to Monckton in 1755. The two principal defence witnesses at his trial, at which he was acquitted, were Vaudreuil and Bigot.

It is debatable whether Vaudreuil was a knave or a fool. Surrounded by corrupt officials who made enormous fortunes by defrauding both Government and people, he made nothing for

himself. He was perfectly well aware of the wholesale robbery going on all around him and he condoned it, not only by his failure to take action but by giving his friendship and protection to Bigot and Vergor. The only reasonable explanation is that he was the victim of blackmail: that his silence was bought by silence. Many of Bigot's malpractices were a public scandal, and it is a measure of the lack of interest shown by the French Government in their greatest colony that nothing was done to put an end to them. Even in France, the Government can hardly have been unaware that supplies sent to Canada were bought by Bigot and resold to the King at an immense profit through an organization of merchants in Bordeaux and functionaries at Quebec so infamous that it became known as 'La Friponne'.*
The extent of Bigot's pillage of the colony is best indicated by the sentences imposed on him and his confederates in 1763: Bigot was banished from France for life, fined 1,000 *livres* and ordered to restore 1,300,000 *livres*: Cadet was banished from Paris for nine years, fined 300 *livres*, and ordered to restore 6,000,000.†

Such was the deplorable condition of Canadian administration. It could not be expected that corruption on such a scale would have no effect on the defence of the country: public money intended for defence lined the pockets of Bigot and his friends; money was frittered away on worthless fortifications built by the Intendant's contractors; the farmers, defrauded of their living, abandoned their farms, and the shortage of food became acute. The Canadian peasantry could feel little loyalty to an administration that showed no concern for them. Their resistance to an invader could not be expected to be remarkable for self-sacrifice and devotion to the French cause.

On 10th May Bougainville reached Quebec, after eighteen anxious days locked in the ice in the entrance to the Gulf of St. Lawrence. He found the city undefended. Vaudreuil, Montcalm, and de Lévis were in Montreal, preparing to resist Amherst's advance. Bougainville's news was dispatched at once to them, and Montcalm hastened to Quebec, followed by Vaudreuil and the entire force of the colony except for two strong detachments under Bourlamaque and la Corne which were ordered to make what resistance they could to the threat from the west. A few days

* 'The Cheat.'   † The *livre* was worth a little less than a shilling.

233

after Bougainville's arrival, a fleet of eighteen sail appeared and anchored in the harbour. It was the convoy of supplies. All had come through safely except two store-ships captured in the Gulf by Durrell. 'Had we but sailed at the time so earnestly wished,' wrote one of Durrell's officers to Lawrence at Halifax,[151] 'we had most certainly intercepted them, as they were not more than ten days ahead of us.'

Montcalm arrived in Quebec on 23rd May, and Vaudreuil on the 25th, and no time was lost in preparing the city for a siege. The army was entrenched, as it arrived, along the north bank of the St. Lawrence between the St. Charles and Montmorency rivers, a strong defensive position about seven miles in length. Montcalm made his headquarters in a large stone house at Beauport, about half-way between the two flanking rivers. A boom of logs was drawn across the mouth of the St. Charles guarded by two hulks mounted with cannon, and the mouth of the Montmorency below the falls was protected on the Beauport side by batteries and redoubts on the shore overlooked by the main position on the heights above. The south bank of the St. Charles was also entrenched as a second line of defence, and communication between the city and Beauport was confined to a bridge of boats set across the river about a mile above the boom. More than a hundred cannon were mounted on the walls of the city, and floating batteries, fire-ships and fire-rafts were constructed for the protection of the river. Some of the merchantmen recently arrived from France were sacrificed to make the fire-ships, and the rest, with their attendant frigates, were sent up river to a safe anchorage above the town. Their crews were brought down again to the city to help man the defences.

The army along the Beauport shore numbered nearly 14,000 excluding about 1,000 Indians. In Quebec, itself, under command of the city governor, de Ramezay, there was a garrison of about 1,500. Vaudreuil and Bigot, with much bustle and braggart talk, took up their headquarters with the army. As the days and weeks dragged by without any sign of the British fleet, the French began to wonder if Bougainville's information had been false, or if the St. Lawrence had made their defensive dispositions unnecessary. Those who hoped for action to relieve the boredom of waiting behind their entrenchments were not to be disappointed.

By 6th June, the entire British fleet was clear of Louisbourg harbour, and on the following day a vessel was returned to England with dispatches. Wolfe had urged that these should be delayed until it was possible to include news from Durrell in the St. Lawrence, but Saunders was insistent, and from the *Neptune* on the 6th Wolfe wrote to Pitt. The tone of his dispatch is not optimistic. The foul weather which had delayed him on the Atlantic crossing and in Louisbourg, the reduced strength of the army, Durrell's suspected failure to intercept French reinforcements to Quebec, and his own physical handicaps gave him little cause for hope of an early success. With this dispatch went a letter to the Secretary at War, Lord Barrington. At Louisbourg Wolfe had found Barrington's letter ordering him to stay there through the previous winter. His reply repeats with more than customary bluntness his reasons for his return to England:[152] 'I shall only say, that the Marshal told me, I was to return at the end of the Campaign, and as General Amherst had no other commands than to send me to Winter at Halifax under the orders of an Officer, who was, but a few months before, put over my head, I thought it was much better to get into the way of Service, and out of the way of being insulted; and as the stile of your Lordship's letter is pretty strong, I must take the liberty to inform you, that tho' I shou'd have been very glad to have gone with Genl. Amherst to join the Army upon the Lakes, & offer'd my services immediately after the reduction of Louisbourg to carry a reinforcement to Mr. Abercrombie if Quebec was not to be attack'd; yet rather than receive orders in the Government of an officer younger than myself (tho' a very worthy Man) I shou'd certainly have desir'd leave to resign my commission; for as I neither ask nor expect any favour, so I never intend to submit to any ill usage whatsoever.' Two days later he drew up his will, and it was witnessed by Delaune of the Light Infantry, and Bell, his aide.

The weather was intermittently fair in the Gulf and the fleet anchored on the 18th off the Isle of Bic in the river itself. There Wolfe and Saunders found the frigate *Richmond* and a tender from Durrell's fleet with the news they had feared. Durrell had reached Bic four weeks earlier, having captured on his way two ships bound for Quebec. From them he had learned that three frigates and a fleet of merchantmen had entered the river only a few days ahead of him. What he did not know was that one of the ships that had escaped him carried Bougainville with the detailed plans of the British campaign in Canada.

Durrell had already failed in his assignment; but it must be said for him that he did his utmost to retrieve the situation. Leaving only one small vessel to meet Saunders, he pushed boldly on a hundred miles up the river with the rest of his squadron as far as the Isle aux Coudres, only sixty-five miles from Quebec. Carleton immediately landed and took possession of the island. Durrell was determined to continue the chase. From his two French prizes he had taken some valuable charts of the river and with these he proposed to brave the famous 'Traverse' which the French believed to be unnavigable without a local pilot. After ten days at Coudres he sent forward three ships of the line and a frigate as far as the Isle of Orléans at the entrance to the Quebec basin. The master of the *Pembroke*, James Cook, later to become one of the greatest of British navigators, took soundings of the Traverse and on 13th June the *Centurion* passed safely through, followed next day by *Devonshire*, *Pembroke* and *Squirrel*. Durrell at once set to work to survey and buoy the channel for the rest of the fleet.

Information regarding Durrell's movement up the river had been sent back to the Isle of Bic, and with it a number of French pilots. These he had captured by the simple ruse of hoisting French colours at his masthead. The pilots had rowed out to him only to discover too late their mistake and to be made prisoner. This, according to Knox, was watched with 'inconceivable consternation, rage, and grief' by the French lining the shore, and had such an effect on a priest who was watching through a telescope 'that he dropped down and instantly expired'. Durrell's latest reports were encouraging, but there was no word from Carleton. Wolfe transferred to the *Richmond* and went up river to see for himself. For Saunders this was the moment of decision. He was expected to send a few light vessels up the river and to cruise with the battle fleet where he could cover the entrance to the St. Lawrence and yet be within range of Louisbourg and Halifax. He made a signal for the transports and frigates to move on up the river; as they passed, he brought the ships of his battle fleet into line and signalled to them to follow towards the Traverse and Quebec.

CHAPTER XX

Navigation of the St. Lawrence

HAVING once made the decision to risk his entire battle fleet in the St. Lawrence where no fleet of such strength had been seen before, Saunders lost no time in leading it up river. The country through which they passed rose high on either side and was seen to be thickly forested. Townshend describes it in his journal[153] as 'very beautiful, tho' of a most wild and uncultivated aspect, save where a few straggly French settlements appear.' Another officer writes:[154] 'As you advance higher up, every object appears grand, and sublime, nature here displays, such luxury, and majesty, as commands veneration! Rivers like seas! mountains reaching the clouds, cover'd with lofty trees, such variety, of fish, sporting round, sea-cows, seals, and porpusses, who are white.' The first shots of the campaign were fired from the shore at Rimouski but there were no casualties. Earlier in the month three midshipmen from Durrell's squadron had gone ashore and had been captured by a scouting party. Taken before Montcalm for questioning, they had wildly exaggerated the strength of Wolfe's army, greatly increasing by their assertions the general anxiety among the garrison. The entire fleet could now be seen strung out in line down the river—a cloud of white canvas stretching for several miles—and signal fires were lit along the shore every few hours by the inhabitants to warn the French Army of its approach. After a storm on the 19th, the weather lifted and remained warm and clear as the fleet worked slowly up river, led by a screen of light boats taking soundings as they went. Early on the 23rd the Isle aux Coudres was sighted with Durrell's squadron at anchor there, and by five o'clock the transports had anchored off St. Joseph's.

The most hazardous part of the navigation, the Traverse, was now in sight. Saunders transferred his flag to the *Stirling Castle* and sailed on ahead to supervise the passage, leaving Durrell to command the squadron of heavy ships of the line. On the 24th there was violent thunder and lightning followed by heavy rain, but on the following day wind and weather were favourable for the attempt and preparations were made for all ships to pass the Traverse. At three in the afternoon a French pilot was put on board each of the transports and the signal was made for the fleet to sail. Much of the channel had been buoyed by Durrell's squadron, and marking-boats were placed at intervals on either side. But the masters of the transports were unimpressed. Knox gives a vivid description of the passage through the Traverse in the *Goodwill* transport under her master, Captain Killick, a Thames pilot and one of the younger brothers of Trinity House: 'As soon as the Pilot came on board today, he gave his instructions for the working of the ship, but the Master would not permit him to speak; he fixed his Mate at the helm, charged him not to take orders from any person except himself, and, going forward with his trumpet to the forecastle, gave the necessary instructions. All that could be said by the Commanding-Officer, and the other Gentlemen on board, was to no purpose: the Pilot declared we should be lost, for that no French ship ever presumed to pass there without a Pilot; "aye, aye, my dear" (replied our son of Neptune) "but d—— me I'll convince you, that an Englishman shall go where a Frenchman dare not show his nose." The Richmond frigate being close astern of us, the Commanding Officer called out to the Captain, and told him our case; he enquired who the Master was?—and was answered from the forecastle by the man himself, who told him "he was old Killick, and that was enough." I went forward with this experienced mariner, who pointed out the channel to me as we passed, shewing me, by the ripple and colour of the water, where there was any danger; and distinguishing the places where there were ledges of rocks (to me invisible) from banks of sand, mud or gravel. He gave his orders with great unconcern, joked with the sounding boats who lay off on each side, with different coloured flags for our guidance; and, when any of them called to him, and pointed to the deepest water, he answered, "aye, aye, my dear, chalk it down, a d——d dangerous navigation—eh, if you don't make a sputter about it, you'll get no credit for it in England. . . .'' After we had cleared this remarkable place, where the channel forms a complete zig-zag, the Master called to his Mate to give the helm to somebody else, saying, "D—— me, if there are not a thousand places in the Thames fifty times more hazardous than this: I am ashamed that Englishmen should make such a rout about it." The Frenchman asked me if the Captain had not been here before? I assured him in the negative, upon which he viewed him with great attention, lifting, at the same time, his hands and eyes to heaven with astonishment and fervency.'

By the 26th the last transport was through the Traverse and the leading ships were anchored in the south channel off the Island of Orléans near the parish of St. Laurent. Knox was charmed with his first sight of the country: 'Here we are entertained with a most agreeable prospect of a delightful country on every side; wind-mills, water-mills, churches, chapels, and compact farm-houses, all built with stone, and covered, some with wood, and others with straw. The lands appear to be everywhere well cultivated, and, with the help of my glass, I can discern that they are sowed with flax, wheat, barley, pease, etc. and the grounds are enclosed with wooden pales . . . the country-people on the south shore, are removing their effects in carts, and conducting them, under escorts of armed men to a greater distance.'

Orléans was Wolfe's first military objective in the river. It was essential to secure a firm land base from which to plan and carry out operations against the city, and Orléans was well suited to his purpose. Twenty miles in length, this narrow island divided into two channels the river at the eastern entrance to the basin, and from its western headland there was an excellent view of Quebec and the French defences on the shore of the north channel. On the evening of the 26th Wolfe gave orders from the *Richmond* for a landing at six o'clock the following morning. At midnight a body of about forty Rangers landed without opposition to carry out a preliminary reconnaissance. Inland they were attacked by a superior force of Canadians and Indians and were driven back to the ships, but after this short skirmish the inhabitants deserted the island and the landing the following day was unopposed. Near to the place where the Rangers had been attacked the previous night, the body of one of their number was found 'scalped and butchered in a very barbarous manner'—a foretaste of the treatment to be expected for those who fell into the hands of Indians.

In the morning some of the officers visited the little church of St. Laurent, a compact building with a steeple and spire, from which all the altar ornaments had been removed, 'a few indifferent paintings only remaining.' The curé of the parish had fled, leaving behind him a note addressed to 'The Worthy Officers of the British Army' and praying that 'from their well known humanity and generosity, they would protect that church and its sacred furniture, as also his house and other tenements adjoining to it; and this, if not for his sake, yet for the love and mercy of God, and in compassion to his wretched and distracted parishioners.' He added that 'he wished we had arrived a little earlier, that we might have enjoyed the benefit of such vegetables, viz. asparagus, radishes, etc. etc. as his garden produced, and are now gone to seed.' Knox, who gives this account, adds dryly, 'He concluded his epistle with many frothy compliments, and kind wishes, etc. consistent with that kind of politeness so peculiar to the French.'

Soon after landing, Wolfe, accompanied by his chief engineer, Major McKellar, and an escort of Light Infantry, set off to the western end of the island to reconnoitre. Standing on high ground near the Pointe d'Orléans, with the aid of his telescope Wolfe had a clear view across the four miles of the basin separating him from the rocky promontory that was Quebec. Sweeping eastwards, and stretching from the St. Charles river to the Montmorency, some eight miles down river, lay the steep coast of Beauport, and Montcalm's army entrenched along its heights. It was here that Sir William Phipps had made his landing sixty-nine years earlier in an ambitious but fruitless attempt to surprise the city; and it was here that Wolfe had planned to make his first landing. From this base on the north shore, he would force the St. Charles, and thrusting through to the St. Lawrence on the west side of the city, cut off the defenders from their lines of communication and supply from Montreal. This plan was now obviously impossible, for Montcalm's army, though inferior in quality, was superior in numbers and defended a position of natural strength. Access to the city from the Beauport side required the defeat of this army. Though he had never before seen Quebec and the surrounding country, Wolfe was, as he shows in his letters, already familiar with the main topographical features, and McKellar had furnished him with an accurate plan of the city and assessment of its vulnerability. Wolfe had expected that Montcalm would concentrate his army near to the city, behind the natural barrier of the St. Charles river, and left to himself, this is probably what Montcalm would have chosen to do; but Vaudreuil had insisted on holding the entire coastline as far as the Montmorency. By doing so the French had immeasurably increased Wolfe's difficulties in making a landing on the north shore, but at a cost of which Montcalm was uncomfortably aware: even 14,000 men were none too many to hold a line seven miles in length; and communications with the city, restricted to a single bridge of boats and a few fords across the St. Charles, lengthened dangerously the time it would take to concentrate the army to the west of the city if it became necessary. It was clear to Wolfe that no easy victory could be snatched by a landing on the Beauport shore. It remained to be seen whether the country and defences to the west of the city offered any better opportunity.

On the night of the 27th a severe north-easterly squall hit the fleet at its exposed anchorage in the south channel off St. Laurent. In the confusion caused by dragging anchors and slipped cables several transports ran aground and a large number of smaller craft and flat-bottomed boats used for the landing the previous day were driven on to the rocks and destroyed. Saunders at once decided that a safer anchorage must be found, and he chose the upper part of the south channel where it enters the basin itself between Pointe Lévi on the south shore of the mainland and the Pointe d'Orléans. Tactically, command of this gateway into the basin was essential for offensive operations in the river, and it appeared that the French had done little to prepare Pointe Lévi against attack, though Saunders, who had made a reconnaissance on the river, thought he had seen signs of work in progress. He therefore proposed that Pointe Lévi should be attacked and captured without delay, to forestall any such attempt to defend it and to secure a new and safe anchorage for the battered fleet. Wolfe, who had already planned to establish a series of fortified posts along the south shore of the mainland from Lévi to the Chaudière river, was quick to agree to Saunders's proposal, and

Monckton's brigade was immediately ordered to carry the plan into effect. But the landing of troops on Orléans was not yet completed and it was not possible for Monckton to collect his brigade for the attack until the 30th. As it happened, this delay combined with the precipitate action of the French to save the fleet from disaster.

Among the preparations for defence made by the French after Bougainville's return from France with the unwelcome news of the approach of Saunders's fleet had been the construction and equipment of eight 400-ton fire-ships, of which seven were now ready for action. They had cost more than a million *livres* and, in spite of Montcalm's gloomy foreboding that they would prove to be 'good for nothing after all', Vaudreuil had high hopes of their success. Had they been used to the best advantages his hopes might well have been fulfilled. Command of these '*brûlots*' was given to a Captain Delouche, a braggart friend of Vaudreuil's, and each ship was manned by an officer and a small crew. They were to sail down the river until they were close to the British fleet when Delouche would fire two guns and ignite his ship as a signal to the others to do the same. The ships would then be abandoned to drift among the British fleet.

At about eleven o'clock on the night of the 28th, sentries posted on the Pointe d'Orléans reported the approach of several ships, and the fleet was warned for action. But Delouche, so ready before the event with promises of heroic leadership, was taking no chances with his life when the time came. When fully half a mile from the nearest ship of the British fleet he fired his signal guns, lit the fuses in his ship, and made good his escape. All but one of his gallant captains followed his example. The one exception, Captain Dubois de la Multière, remained at his command until he was surrounded by the blazing inferno of the other ships and, being unable to escape, was burnt to death with his second officer and one of his crew. The British crews behaved with great coolness and gallantry: ignoring the hail of round and grape shot from the guns mounted on the fire-ships, the boats' crews rowed out to them, took them in tow, and beached them out of range of the fleet. In the army, on the other hand, the loud explosions and the sudden rattle of shot among the trees, caused the utmost consternation and confusion and the whole camp was roused.

Knox had a fine view of the scene on the river: 'They were certainly the grandest fire-works (if I may be allowed to call them so) that can possibly be conceived, every circumstance having contributed to their awful, yet beautiful, appearance; the night was serene and calm, there was no light but what the stars produced, and this was eclipsed by the blaze of the floating fires, issuing from all parts, and running almost as quick as light up the masts and rigging; add to this the solemnity of the sable night, still more obscured by the profuse clouds of smoke, with the firing of the cannon, the bursting of the grenado's, and the crackling of the other combustibles; all which reverberated thro' the air, and the adjacent woods, together with the sonerous shouts and frequent repetitions of *All's well*, from our gallant seamen on the water. . . .'

Saunders had been prepared for an attempt of this kind. McKellar's report of 1757* had warned Wolfe of the building of 'radeaux à feu', or fire-rafts of tarred logs, at Quebec, and a similar abortive attempt had been made against Durrell's fleet earlier in the month. It was, however, particularly fortunate that the attempt was made while the fleet lay off St. Laurent. In the constricted waters between the Pointe Lévi and Pointe d'Orléans the damage caused to the fleet might well have been irreparable.

On the following day some of the fire-ships were still burning. An officer who had commanded one of the outposts and whose troops had panicked was arrested but on Monckton's recommendation was pardoned. Wolfe issued orders enjoining the strictest vigilance against ambush or surprise attack. It was possible at any time that the French would send a party across the river to surprise the position on Orleans, and the dangers from snipers and scouting parties would be infinitely greater on the mainland. On the night of the 29th, in cold showery weather, the light troops of Monckton's brigade crossed over to Lévi. They met with some resistance from a party of Canadians and Indians of whom they scalped seven, but there was no sign of the enemy in strength, and at seven o'clock the following morning the rest of the brigade landed unopposed. The brigade halted at the village of Beaumont, and to the door of the church there Monckton

* McKellar had been in Quebec in 1757 and had made a detailed report to the Board of Ordnance on the fortifications and approaches to the city.[155]

nailed a manifesto in French prepared by Barré and signed by Wolfe addressed to the local population. Pompous as it now appears, it deserves to be quoted in full as an example of local propaganda of the period. The translation is that given by Knox, who was with Monckton's brigade at the time.

'*By his Excellency James Wolfe, Esq., Colonel of a Regiment of Infantry Major-General, aud Commander-in-Chief of his Britannic Majesty's Forces in the River St. Lawrence, etc.*

The formidable sea and land armament, which the people of Canada now behold in the heart of their country, is intended by the King, my master, to check the insolence of France, to revenge the insults offered to the British colonies, and totally to deprive the French of their most valuable settlement in North America. For these purposes is the formidable army under my command intended.—The King of Great Britain wages no war with the industrious peasant, the sacred orders of religion, or the defence-less women and children: to these, in their distressful circumstances, his Royal clemency offers protection. The people may remain unmolested on their lands, inhabit their houses, and enjoy their religion in security; for these inestimable blessings, I expect the Canadians will take no part in the great contest between the two crowns.—But if, by a vain obstinacy and misguided valour, they presume to appear in arms, they must expect the most fatal consequences; their habitations destroyed, their sacred temples exposed to the exasperated·soldiery, their harvest utterly ruined, and the only passage of relief stopped up by the most formidable fleet. In this unhappy situation, and closely attacked by another great army, what can the wretched natives expect from opposition?—The unparalleled barbarities exerted by the French against our settlements in America might justify the bitterest revenge in the army under my command. *But Britons breathe higher sentiments of humanity, and listen to the merciful dictates of the Christian religion.* Yet, should you suffer yourselves to be deluded by any imaginary prospect of our want of success, should you refuse those terms, and persist in opposition, then surely will the law of nations justify the waste of war, so necessary to crush the ungenerous enemy; and then the miserable Canadians must in the winter have the mortification of seeing the very families, for whom they have been exerting but a fruitless and indiscreet bravery, perish by the most dismal want and famine. In this great dilemma let the wisdom of the people of Canada show itself; Britain stretches out a powerful, yet merciful hand: faithful to her engagements, and ready to secure her in her most valuable rights and possessions: France, unable to support Canada, deserts her cause at this important crisis, and, during the whole war, has assisted her with troops who have been maintained only by making the natives feel all the weight of grievous and lawless oppression.—Given at Laurent in the island of Orleans, this 28th day of June, 1759.

Ja. Wolfe.'

At ten in the morning the Light Infantry returned to Beaumont and the entire brigade moved forward to occupy Pointe Lévi. Their advance was disputed by a body of about 600 Canadians and forty Indians, but after a brisk engagement, an assault on their position led by Monckton in person routed the enemy and the Lévi position was captured. Monckton's brigade lost about thirty killed and wounded but the position now occupied would fully have justified casualties ten times as large. Whoever held Lévi and Orléans commanded the entrance to the south channel, and it was a short step from Lévi to the Pointe des Pères* on the western tip of the same headland from which it would be possible to bombard the city of Quebec itself. Montcalm had already made urgent representations to Vaudreuil to occupy and defend Lévi, but his advice had been ignored. Now that it was already lost, a feeble attempt to harass Monckton's brigade was made by three floating batteries, one mounting two guns and the others one each, which fired on his position from the river for an hour and a half. Wolfe went at once to the scene of the trouble, taking with him some guns from the siege train which he ordered to be dug in close to the shore to prevent similar attacks. Saunders had also dispatched the frigate *Trent* to their aid, and the floating batteries were driven off. The *Trent* and two other frigates were ordered to anchor off shore to prevent any further attempt to interfere with progress at Lévi or Pointe des Pères.

* The name derived from ownership of this land by the Jesuit Fathers. Similarly the Anse des Mères was the property of the Ursuline Convent.

Meanwhile, Wolfe had lost no time in completing the conquest of the Island of Orléans. Carleton was dispatched the same day with a detachment of Townshend's brigade to seize the western end and set up a battery of guns.

On 2nd July, Wolfe, accompanied by a strong escort from Monckton's brigade, marched to the Pointe des Pères, two miles to the westward of Lévi, to make a reconnaissance. From this position he could see for the first time the full extent of his difficulties. From Quebec to the eastward lay the Beauport position which he had already reconnoitred from Orléans. Quebec, itself, he knew to be impregnable, for, as McKellar's report had made clear, the guns of the fleet could not be used at such an elevation and, even if a footing could be gained in the lower town the ascent to the upper town could be made impossible by a comparatively small garrison. To the west lay the lines of communication and supply by land and river with Montreal, but the cliffs rose almost sheer from the water to a height of three hundred feet, and even to attempt a landing assumed the passage of ships through the channel less than a mile wide between Quebec and the south shore, under the guns on the city walls. Even supposing this apparently impossible feat could be achieved, it would be a valueless manœuvre unless it could be accomplished in perfect secrecy or at such speed that Montcalm had no time to re-deploy his army on the cliffs to the west of Quebec.

While Amherst was pinned down beyond Montreal, Montcalm's safety lay in defence from his impregnable position. Wolfe's only chance of victory lay in tempting Montcalm to leave his defences and come out and fight, and there was little hope of doing this while his army remained concentrated in one camp. To divide his force, already outnumbered by nearly two to one, entailed the risk of having it destroyed piecemeal, but command of the river and the energetic co-operation of Saunders made it possible for Wolfe to regard the entire operation as amphibious and to use his army accordingly.

CHAPTER XXI

Reconnaissance

WOLFE'S reconnaissance to Pointe des Pères on 2nd July had convinced him of the value of the position: it commanded an unrivalled view of the enemy's defences and movements in the upper river, and from there, as he noted that night in his journal, it would be easy to bombard the town. Such a bombardment would have little effect on Montcalm's army, for the garrison left in the city numbered less than 2,000, but Wolfe had noticed the strength of the enemy batteries commanding the entrance to the upper river and it was clear that some at least must be destroyed before Saunders could risk his fleet in the narrow channel between Quebec and the south mainland. Wolfe hoped, also, that the destruction of the town and the consequent demoralization of its inhabitants, would induce Montcalm to attempt an attack on the British batteries. It had in fact already been suggested to Montcalm that a detachment should be sent across the river to drive Monckton from his position at Lévi, and there is little doubt that the attempt would have been made but for intelligence gained from a British prisoner that the occupation of Lévi was a feint to cover an assault on the Beauport shore. By the time Montcalm and Vaudreuil were satisfied that a Beauport landing was no longer imminent, the 28th Regiment had seized the Pointe des Pères, and the Lévi position had been well fortified against attack by entrenchments and batteries mounting six 24-pounder brass cannon.

Wolfe was again suffering from gravel, but although in great pain he was constantly on the move between the Orléans and Lévi positions. On the 3rd he had a meeting with Saunders and they agreed to attempt a landing above the town. Orders were prepared for the army and the fleet, and Murray was sent on a reconnaissance up the south shore towards the Chaudière; but everything depended on the rapid mounting of batteries on the Pointe des Pères to cover the movement of ships through the narrows and into the upper river, and this work, carried out in full view of the garrison in Quebec, was retarded by a steady hail of shot from the guns on the city walls. Fortunately their fire was inaccurate and caused no casualties, but it gave Saunders some measure of the risk of taking his ships through the channel.

Wolfe's army was now divided between his main defensive base on the Isle d'Orléans and Monckton's camp at Lévi and the batteries at Pointe des Pères. He had already decided to attempt a landing above the town, and he now determined to support this attempt by a diversionary attack below the Montmorency falls to pin down the French army in the Beauport lines. On the 4th a warning order was issued to Townshend's brigade to hold itself in readiness for this secondary attack. The following day, Murray reported that a landing would be practicable above the town at St. Michel, and further preparations were made for the Montmorency landing. On the 7th orders were given to Townshend's brigade, with the Light Infantry, Rangers, and three companies of Grenadiers to be ready to march the following morning. Monckton's troops at Lévi were also under orders to move at short notice. Wolfe was recovering from an acute attack of dysentery, and his temper was not improved by a disagreement with one of his subordinate commanders. He writes in his journal,[156] 'Some difference of opinion upon a point termed *slight* and *insignificant* and the Commander in Chief is threatened with Parliamentary Inquiry into his Conduct for not consulting an inferior Officer and seeming to disregard his Sentiments.' This note has always been taken to refer to a quarrel with Townshend, and Townshend's subsequent behaviour seems to bear this out, but in the light of recent research it seems possible that it was to Murray that he referred.

On the 8th the tides were unfavourable and the attack was postponed, but further orders were issued for the landing, though without any indication of its objective. The French kept up a brisk fire on Burton's position at Pointe des Pères, where Wolfe was personally supervising the erection of the batteries, and work was frequently interrupted by the shout of 'Shot' or 'Shell' from the sentry posted to observe the flashes from guns and mortars on the city walls.

Meanwhile Saunders, who had sent for Holmes and four of the line to come up into the basin from Durrell's fleet which lay at anchor down river to the east of Orléans, had ordered soundings to be taken of the northern channel. These were successfully completed, although the *Lowestoft*'s boat was captured, and at about noon on the 8th Jervis in the *Porcupine* led a sloop into the Montmorency channel and anchored off Ange Gardien, a part of the river believed by the French to be unnavigable because of the reefs. From this position he was able to drive the French occupying the forward entrenchments on the extreme left flank of the Beauport defences back from their lines. This movement coincided, conveniently enough, with the arrival at the French headquarters of a deserter with details of a plan to be carried out that night for three simultaneous assaults on Montmorency, Beauport, and the lower town. The arrival in the basin of Holmes with four men-of-war supported this story, and Montcalm was persuaded that the operations off Ange Gardien were a feint. This had, indeed, been Wolfe's intention; but by the 8th he had decided to postpone the landing above the town and to concentrate on gaining a footing on the north shore below the Montmorency. There can be little doubt that this decision was prompted by Saunders. No landing could be made above the town without the help of the fleet, and Saunders could not be blamed if he thought it an unjustifiable risk to attempt to pass ships through the channel and under the guns of the city without fire support from the south shore, and the batteries on the Pointe des Pères were not yet ready.

On the night of 9th July, therefore, in a storm of rain, and covered by Jervis in the *Porcupine*, Wolfe led Townshend's brigade across the north channel between Orléans and Montmorency and landed unopposed at Ange Gardien. By daylight on the 10th the brigade was established in a position to the east of the Montmorency falls where it was joined later in the day by Murray's brigade which was rowed across from Orléans. While Wolfe and Townshend's brigade had been occupied in effecting a landing, Monckton's brigade had withdrawn under cover of darkness and rain to the woods a few miles inland from the Lévi position, leaving the batteries manned only by small detachments.

When daylight came, the French found the British already in possession of a strongly defended position on the high ground to the east of the Montmorency river overlooking their left flank, and Murray's brigade could be seen crossing to reinforce the threat. Lévi and the Pointe des Pères on the other hand had evidently been drained of men to concentrate the maximum force at Montmorency. Montcalm appears to have been deceived by this manœuvre, for he proposed an attack on Lévi to regain control of the vital south channel. It is ironical that it should have been Vaudreuil who by his refusal to act prevented him from falling into Wolfe's carefully baited trap.

The landing at Montmorency was the cause of more friction between Wolfe and Townshend. In his journal Townshend gives a petulant account of the operation, full of complaint and criticism: Wolfe, it appears, left no guides on the shore to welcome Townshend on his arrival, and posted no guards over the baggage, which had been dumped on landing. Townshend wasted valuable time collecting it together and posting guards—an unnecessarily meticulous proceeding considering that the landing was not only unopposed but apparently undetected. Wolfe was rightly critical of Townshend's fussy delays when speed was the first essential, and when, later, Townshend asked for his approval of the dispositions he had made and the defences he had dug round his camp, Wolfe agreed, perhaps unkindly, that he had indeed built himself a fortress. Townshend was severely critical of the first dispositions made by Carleton and of those made later by Wolfe, but as no account of them exists other than that in Townshend's journal it is impossible to decide what justification there was for his criticism. What is made amply clear by Townshend's own account of his actions is his own agitated behaviour: his reports of enemy reconnaissance parties, one of which he said included Montcalm, the feverish fortification of his camp, his constant demands for orders, and his outspoken criticism of the work of other more experienced officers, showed him to be in a state of anxiety bordering on hysteria. This nervousness does not appear to have come from any lack of personal courage, but rather from a fear that his lack of practical experience would become apparent to those to whom he had shown a supercilious over-confidence. Wolfe was too intolerant—and also too occupied—to give Townshend the help he needed; the anxiety of his own heavy responsibilities was enough for him to bear. On the 13th, while Townshend was directing the work of entrenching a new position, he heard that Wolfe was leaving for Orléans and Lévi, 'leaving me,' as he writes in his journal,[157] 'the first officer in the camp, not only without orders but also even ignorant of his departure or time of return. Upon this I ran down as fast as I could to the water-side . . . he received me in a very stately manner, not advancing five steps. I told him that if I had suspected his intentions of going over I had waited on him for his commands which I should be glad to receive and execute to his satisfaction. "Sir," says he very dryly, "the Adjutant-General has my orders—permit me, Sir, to ask are your troops to encamp on their new ground, or not to do it until the enemy's battery begins to play?" '

This was for Wolfe a time of intense anxiety. He was fully aware of the dangers inherent in dispersing his small army among three camps, each separated from the other by a stretch of river. But Wolfe, perhaps alone among the military staff, realized with Saunders that the river, while dividing his forces, also formed a flexible chain between them. He took a calculated risk in exposing any one of the three camps to attack by a superior force; but it was a necessary risk, for if anything was to be achieved Montcalm must be tempted from his impregnable position on the Beauport shore. Deserters from both armies crossed almost daily to the other side, and the movements of both armies could be observed by their enemies. Wolfe, therefore, kept his own counsel. Only those required immediately to act upon orders were given any idea of his plans: false rumours were circulated, orders were issued and countermanded without explanation. If Montcalm could not be lured from his stronghold, he should be so mystified by the movements of his enemy as to enable Wolfe to concentrate his striking force, when the time came, at the most vulnerable point.

Meanwhile there were signs that the bait at Lévi would be effective. On the 12th the batteries at the Pointe des Pères opened fire on the city, causing much damage and confusion, and at the same time the French could see more batteries being erected on the Montmorency position to harass their left flank. It seemed certain that Montcalm intended to attack the Pointe des Péres and Lévi positions, and Wolfe crossed the river to conduct the defence. He remained with Monckton's brigade until the 14th, when a deserter reported that the attack had failed and that the French detachment concerned had recrossed the river to the north bank. Knox noted that 'the General was greatly disappointed.'

The French attack on Lévi was indeed a pathetic fiasco. On the 9th, the very night that Wolfe crossed with Townshend's brigade to Montmorency, M. Charrier, Lord of the Manor of Lévi, and M. Dumas, the town major, crossed to the south mainland with a mixed force of 500 armed civilians, 300 students, 100 Indians, and 600 militia. They made a reconnaissance of the batteries and redoubts, but finding them too strong, sent for reinforcements of 300 colonial troops who crossed to join them without delay. The attack was planned for the night of the 12th, but for some reason it had to be postponed. On the night of the 13th they formed into two columns, one of which advanced confidently towards the British position. Passing through a coppice on the way to the objective, the first column was put to flight by the sound of movement which the men took to be an ambush. According to Foligné* the movement was nothing more than a detachment of the second column, impatient for action, attempting to overtake the vanguard. The first column fell back in disorder on the second, who, taking them for the enemy, fired upon them and there were a number of casualties. The survivors abandoned the attempt and withdrew ignominiously to Quebec. Even if they had continued, it seems unlikely that such inexperienced troops could have succeeded against Monckton's seasoned brigade in its strong defensive positions.

The Montmorency camp was being strengthened, and patrols were sent up river to see whether it was fordable to the north. Vaudreuil urged Montcalm to attack across the Montmorency, but Montcalm was unruffled by the presence of two enemy brigades on the north shore. While they remained there he knew they could do little damage and he could see for himself every movement made by them.

The proposed British attack on the north shore above the town had been postponed until the batteries at the Pointe des Pères were

* De Foligné commanded one of the batteries on the ramparts of the city.

ready, and held up again while Wolfe waited for Montcalm's attack on Lévi. There was now no reason for further delay, and plans were once more prepared. Major Scott and the Rangers had been sent up the south shore to reconnoitre, but Wolfe was not satisfied with their report. On the 8th he had written to Monckton,[158] 'Major Scott's scout did not answer my expectations; the Pow-wow and paint, and howl operate too strongly upon the Rangers—either they must make themselves useful in their way, or I shall leave 'em to lounge away the campaign in their present Posts.' On the 12th he wrote again to Monckton at Lévi,[159] 'Our works here once finish'd, our Artillery ready and the Radeaux &c. made, Wind and Tide permitting we will attack them. I think it the greatest misfortune that so much water business interferes with us.' He was having some trouble with Saunders who resented his blunt criticism of the looting by seamen of churches on the south side of Orléans. Wolfe was also dissatisfied with the arrangements made to secure river communications between the Montmorency and Orléans camps—a vital link in the chain which had been threatened by a French attack on the 14th. In a conference on the 16th Wolfe and Saunders composed their differences and made their detailed plans for the assault. The Grenadiers of three regiments, and a battalion of the Royal Americans were assembled on the Isle d'Orléans, and on the evening of the 16th they embarked under the command of Guy Carleton on board a squadron of seven ships led by Captain Rous in the *Sutherland*. This squadron was to make the first attempt to slip through the channel between Quebec and the south mainland and on into the upper river. But Rous, it seems, was not anxious to distinguish himself in so hazardous a service. Wolfe writes disgustedly in his journal:[160] 'The wind fair, night exceedingly favourable to their wish, but yet Capt. Rous did not go there.' Bell's journal confirms this, and Saunders sent another captain on board the following day to inquire into the reasons for delay. On the 18th, at ten o'clock at night, the *Sutherland*, with the frigate *Squirrel*, three armed transports and two provision sloops, passed the town. The French fired thirty-one shots at the ships as they passed but failed to do any damage, though the frigate *Diana*, which had been among the squadron, ran aground and had to be floated off two days later.

Wolfe had, meanwhile, sent instructions to Monckton to prepare for the attack, and on the 16th had written,[161] 'I only wait the naval preparations—everything is ready on our side.' On the 19th he reconnoitred westward along the south shore to examine possible landing-places in the upper river. Captain Goreham with a detachment of Rangers had already established a forward post on the south shore above the town opposite to Sillery, and on the 20th Wolfe wrote to Monckton giving him detailed orders for the embarkation of his brigade for the attack. This letter, the significance of which has previously been overlooked, proves beyond doubt Wolfe's intention to land, as early as July, at or near to the very point on the north shore above the town where the final assault was made in September, and therefore merits particular attention.

'You will [he writes [162] 'be pleased to embark a part of your Brigade in 16 or more flat-bottom'd Boats; & row along the South Shoar, until you perceive 3 Lanthorns, hanging a breast, upon that side of the Sutherland which is opposite to the shoar. I shall have these People ready to push ashoar just as your Boats come up, to attack the Houses, and such Posts as the Enemy has thought proper to take. It is of consequence that we get to a rising ground over the village, where the Road leading to Quebec runs; and where we must begin an abbatis, with the utmost expedition; it is woody, & a little Steep—for which reason—it may not be amiss to bring one or two Companies of light infantry with you—to attach themselves to this single point. Hatchets, bill-hooks, & axes, will be our principle instruments of defence at first—till by Dint of Artillery we can extend ourselves. Delaune knows of a place, where, a Body of men, with an hours work of 100 Pioneers, can fall down from the upper road to the Sea-side— Goreham's post, or somewhere thereabouts, is the properest place for the rest of your Brigade to embark at, in order to join us. Goreham has my orders, to go himself, or send some proper Persons to Guide the Troops, which must be march'd in silence, & secrecy, & conceal'd among the brush till they embark—All that march are to bring either a Pick Axe, or a spade per man; the six field Pieces must be forwarded, by the Marines or Sea-men, along the upper road so as to be ready to fall down upon the shoar when the water rises again. If you cou'd be here, a little before the high Water, we shou'd have time to fetch another load of Troops, before the Tide ebbs. . . . I need not recommend silence & good order upon your march by land & by water—the officers will take all due care upon that Point—Goreham must be reinforced to 100 men, & must stay at his present post to keep open our communication until our fleet increases. . . .

'Bring Deruvine and Bentzel* in the boat with you. If we can take four or five good Posts, & keep 'em till our friends arrive, it may bring on a very decisive affair. . . .'

Three days earlier Vaudreuil had written complacently to de Bourlamaque,[163] 'Il paroit que le G[nl]. Wolfe est aussi indecis qu'embarrassé sur le parti qu'il doit prendre, il fait dependre son succéss de sa jonction à l'armée du general Lamers.' On the 18th Townshend had noted in his journal[164] that the enemy seemed 'to have Neglected above the Town intirely'.

Wolfe wrote also to Townshend to acquaint him with the plan and to make arrangements for the withdrawal of all but a detachment from the Montmorency camp to follow up the attack above the town if it proved successful. After giving him detailed instructions for the withdrawal of men and artillery† and for the posting of the detachment to be left behind, he continues,[165] 'The Tide is about to turn (I hope in our favour) so I must be short, and the more so, as I am sure you will do what is most proper to be done. If we get a firm footing—it will cost a multitude to drive us out again.' He adds, as a postscript, 'The French may perhaps think this is a feint attack, and keep their stations, if so they will give me as much time as we want.' Montcalm was deceived, as Wolfe hoped; but as a precaution he dispatched Dumas with 900 Canadians to guard the heights above the town.

At one o'clock on the 20th, Wolfe wrote again to Monckton,[166] 'Particular circumstances make it necessary to delay our attempt for a few days, & to keep it Secret. In the meanwhile we

---

* Deruvine was a captain of Marines and Bentzel an officer of the Royal Americans. Both were acting as engineers for the Quebec campaign.

† By the 18th the artillery at Montmorency consisted of 1 heavy brass 24-pounder, 4 iron ships' cannon, 12 brass 12-pounders, 4 light brass 24-pounders, 5 light brass 12-pounders, 8 light brass 6-pounders, 4 eight-inch howitzers, 6 Royal howitzers, and 6 Royal mortars.

shall make all the diversion we possibly can—It will be in my power to receive Dalling's light Infantry with the squadron previous to our attack. You will countermand the embarkation & the march for a day or two. . . .' It is not known what these particular circumstances were, but it was on that day that he made a personal reconnaissance to Sillery, La Chaudière, and Cap Rouge, and it is probable that he observed the movements of Dumas and his troops on the north shore and decided to postpone his attack until the enemy were less alert. Carleton had, meanwhile, landed at Pointe aux Trembles with a small detachment, and after a brief skirmish, had withdrawn with a number of prisoners.

If Montcalm was confident that the British manœuvres above the town could be disregarded as feints to draw troops away from Beauport, his opinion was not shared by Vaudreuil or the citizens of Quebec. The presence of British ships and troops in the upper river, even in such slender strength, embodied a threat not only to the lines of communication with Montreal, but also to the vital lines of supply with their provision ships further up river. The Canadians who had joined Montcalm's army were already cut off from their farms to the east and south, supplies of grain in the town were dwindling, and the harvest would soon be ready for reaping. Montcalm's problem was to defeat the British without leaving his defensive positions. To achieve this he must either tempt Wolfe into an ill-considered attack in strength or hold out until the autumn weather put an end to operations for the year. The second alternative became daily less practicable, for it was already clear that the provisions in the city, quantities of which had been destroyed under the bombardment, would be insufficient without considerable assistance from Montreal.

On the 21st and 22nd there was rain and thick fog and all operations were suspended. On the following day the *Lowestoft* and *Hunter* attempted to pass the town, but a head-wind and falling tide prevented them from leaving the basin. Wolfe sums up their deliberations in two curt sentences in his journal: 'Resolution to attack the French Army. Debate about the method.'

Wolfe was still determined to attack the town, but it is evident that his proposal met with opposition from the subordinate commanders. On the 25th Barré was sent under a flag of truce to Vaudreuil to inquire after three Grenadiers who had been

captured by Indians and were, according to reports from Beauport, to be burnt alive. Wolfe wrote to Monckton,[167] 'If this
be true, the Country shall be but one universal blaze.' At the same
time he gave orders for sick and pregnant women prisoners to be
set free, and added, 'It would be right to preserve some of the
Milch cows for the young children.'

That night Wolfe took a detachment to reconnoitre the Montmorency ford. Three days later the admiral and the generals met
again. Wolfe records in his journal, 'difficulties arising about our
attack & assault on the Town.' As an alternative he proposed an
attempt on the most advanced redoubt on the extreme left of the
Beauport lines, to be covered by fire from two armed transports
'thrown on Shoar near enough to cannonade the Redoubt & if
possible within muskett shot.' This plan was evidently accepted,
for on the same day instructions were sent to Monckton to hold
his brigade in readiness to embark in the men-of-war's boats and
to order Webb's to march towards Goreham's post to 'give the
Enemy some Jealousy above the Town.'

Wolfe was not confident, and he did not intend to risk his whole
army in this attack. He and Colonel Burton were to lead it with the
Grenadiers, and, if a footing could be gained and the redoubt
captured, the remaining regiments would follow. Wolfe writes in
his journal, 'It seems better to receive the Enemy superior in
numbers with the advantage of a small Intrenchment than to
attack them behind their lines with such a body of Troops as can
be landed at once & by so doing put all to the hazard of one
Action.' That the original intention of landing above the town
was not abandoned was made clear by orders to Holmes to go up
by land to take command of the naval detachment in the upper
river.

On the night of the 28th the French, believing that an attempt
was to be made against the Sillery batteries, sent down a formidable fire-raft to engage the fleet in the basin. It consisted, according
to Knox, of 'a parcel of schooners, shallops, and stages, chained
together; it could not be less than a hundred fathoms in length,
and was covered with grenadiers, old swivels, gun and pistol
barrels loaded up to their muzzles, and various other inventions
and combustible matters. . . . Our gallant seamen, with their usual
expertness, grappled them before they got down above a third

part of the bason, towed them safe to shore, and left them at anchor, continually repeating "*All's Well*". A remarkable expression from some of these intrepid souls to their comrades on this occasion I must not omit, on account of its singular uncouthness, viz. Damn-me, Jack, did'st thee ever take hell in tow before?' For the second time in the campaign, the fleet had been saved from damage by the cool and resourceful behaviour of Saunders's seamen. But both Saunders and Wolfe took a serious view of these incidents, realizing the extent of the damage that could be caused by fire-ships among the fleet. Wolfe effectively put a stop to their use by sending a message to Vaudreuil that any fire-ships sent down in future would be made fast to the two transports in which the French and Canadian prisoners were kept under guard.

In the afternoon, Saunders in *Centurion* edged in towards the north shore and bombarded the advanced shore batteries and redoubts below the Montmorency falls. Wolfe's intentions were now clear, and on the 29th orders were issued for the attack.

CHAPTER XXII

Failure at Montmorency

By the end of July it seemed clear to Wolfe that his plan to lure Montcalm from his defences at Beauport had failed. No attempt had been made to attack any of the three British camps with troops from Beauport; and the only major excursion from the north shore had been an uncoordinated venture executed by amateurs. It was useless to suppose that Montcalm, having failed to take advantage of this dispersal of forces when the camps were preparing their defences, would be tempted to do so when they were well entrenched. Little help could be expected from Amherst, who was conducting his affairs with characteristic and even ponderous thoroughness, and over all Wolfe's plans hung the shadow of shortening daylight and the autumn frosts and storms that would drive the fleet back to Halifax and put an end to operations at Quebec. If Montcalm could not be brought out to battle, he must be attacked; but it was not easy to see where the attack could be made. The decision to postpone the attempt above the town may well have been influenced by Saunders. Though seven of his ships had passed through the narrow channel from the basin, they had been fortunate to escape unharmed, and the French would be better prepared against similar attempts in the future. The guns on the city walls had been so far little affected by the bombardment from the Pointe des Pères, and were capable of causing havoc among a fleet in the narrow waters between the city and the south shore, and a change of wind to the westward might leave the fleet open to total destruction. Saunders was a commander of vigour and daring, but the risk was great, and no full-scale attack could be mounted with the support of seven ships, of which five were transports and provision boats.

The only alternative was an attack on the Beauport defences, either from the Montmorency flank or as a frontal assault from the St. Lawrence. Either plan gave little hope of success, but something must be attempted and it was possible that the enemy could be surprised by a sudden concentration.

The greatest problem was to achieve any element of surprise against an enemy who, from his cliff defences, could observe every movement of Wolfe's army in the camps at Montmorency and Lévi. Moreover both camps were mere footholds in country still held by the enemy, and parties of Canadians and Indians were constantly attacking the outposts, ambushing patrols, and spying on the defences. The strictest vigilance, and severe penalties for those who failed to maintain it, could not prevent the frequent scalping of sentries and raids into the British camps. Scalping was not confined to the Indians: the French colonial troops, and the British Rangers, took scalps without mercy, though they seldom mutilated their victims in the manner approved by what both armies called 'the Savages'. Wolfe was obliged to issue an order in July forbidding 'the inhuman practice of scalping, except when the enemy are Indians or Canadians dressed as Indians.' The exception is significant, for it was a frequent occurrence for an 'Indian' to be captured who was found on examination to be a Canadian in disguise. Knox describes one who was captured taking part in an Indian raid: 'he was quite naked, painted red and blue, with bunches of painted feathers fastened to his head.' There was also a continuous interchange of deserters, with information of varying accuracy, some of them evidently sent as spies to convey false intelligence and return as soon as possible with whatever information they could glean in the enemy camp.* Security was therefore of first importance, and it was observed by Wolfe both by his silence regarding his intentions and by the profusion of contradictory orders which he issued to his troops. James Gibson, an officer in the *Vanguard*, wrote in July,([169] 'within the space of five hours we received at the General's

---

* The writer of a contemporary French journal notes in August:[168] 'This was not the first time that Deserters had given intelligence which proved in the event, directly contrary to their report—it was therefore naturally inferred, that the English Generals, more secret than ours in their deliberations, often spread rumours among their Troops of designs, never seriously intended to be realized, and of which we had more than once been the dupes.'

request three different orders of consequence, which were contradicted immediately after their reception; which indeed has been the constant practice of the General ever since we have been here, to the no small amazement of every one who has the liberty of thinking. Every step he takes is wholly his own. . . .' Knox notes in his journal at about the same time, 'Many new projects are talked of; but I believe from no other motive than to amuse the enemy, in order that false intelligence may be circulated throughout their camps, should any of our soldiers desert. . . .' Montcalm's note in his journal for 29th July is even more explicit: 'deserteurs, verbiage, aucune lumière'.

On the 30th a sergeant of the Royal Americans deserted to the French with information that an assault was to be launched against Sillery. More frigates were, he declared, to pass the town, and sixty barges stood ready to embark troops and pass along the south shore to a point above the town. Whether he was in fact ignorant of the new plan or sent over to the French with false information to mislead Montcalm is not known. Whatever his motives, the information he carried did not affect Montcalm's resolve to keep his main strength for the defence of the coast below the town.

On 31st July the attack was launched. The plan was simple: Monckton's brigade was to embark from Lévi and cross the river to a point on the Beauport shore about three-quarters of a mile to the west of the Montmorency falls, where it would land, protected by the guns of two light vessels which would run as close in shore as possible and engage the forward French batteries. Townshend and Murray would leave the camp on the north shore, ford the Montmorency below the falls,* and march along the beach to join Monckton. To distract Montcalm's attention from these activities, one regiment and a body of light infantry were to march north from the Montmorency camp as if to ford the river above the falls, and a regiment from the Lévi camp was to march westward along the south shore as if to threaten a landing at Sillery. The point of attack was a redoubt on the extreme left of the French lines which was not, as far as could be seen, com-

* By some freak of nature the water from the falls does not run straight out into the St. Lawrence. It is thought to run through an underwater cavern and rise in the main stream of the river.

manded by the defences on the crest above. It was, moreover, held by troops of the militia, Montcalm having reserved his regulars for the defence of the centre, where Phipps had tried to land in 1690. Once the redoubt was taken, Montcalm would be forced to leave his entrenchments to recapture it. The whole movement was to be covered by the two armed transports which would be run close inshore and if necessary grounded, and by Saunders in the *Centurion*.

At ten o'clock on the morning of the 31st, Monckton, with thirteen companies of Grenadiers, the 15th and 78th Regiments, and a detachment of the Royal Americans, embarked from Lévi and made for the north shore at the centre of Montcalm's line. But half-way across the channel, they altered course and began to row up and down in front of the Beauport defences. At eleven the armed transports moved in, supported by the *Centurion*, and opened up a heavy cannonade on the French lines. An hour later a French detachment was seen to be making for the upper ford of the Montmorency to attack the camp on the north shore, and the 48th Regiment was immediately moved with speed and ostentation westward along the south shore as if to attack above Quebec. This had the desired effect of inducing the French to withdraw their detachment from the Montmorency ford to march hurriedly westward above the town. While these manoeuvres were being carried out, the troops from Lévi and Orléans rowed up and down under the broiling sun. Soon after three o'clock they made a dash for their true objective on the extreme left of the French position. Wolfe, who had spent the morning under heavy fire in one of the grounded 'cats', now made the signal to Townshend and Murray to cross the ford below the falls, and took a boat to join Monckton on the beaches. Some of the boats stuck on hidden ledges of rock close to the redoubt, and, while the troops struggled to get them off, Montcalm rushed reinforcements to the threatened flank. It was not until about five-thirty that the Grenadiers, who had waded through water up to their waists, struggled ashore on the muddy river bank. Wolfe ordered the drummers to beat the Grenadiers' march which, according to one officer, 'animated our men so much that we could scarce restrain them.'[170] Under a dark sky, heavy with rain clouds, they quickly overran the redoubt and batteries below the cliff. The 15th and 78th Regiments followed in good order, and Townshend and Murray advanced with their brigades along the beach to join them.

At this point in the assault it became unpleasantly obvious that the redoubt was not in dead ground from the cliffs above as had been thought, and the French poured down a mutilating fire on the attackers. Without waiting for orders or reinforcements, the Grenadiers, galled by the fire from the crest, began a frontal assault on the cliff top entrenchments. The ascent was rocky and precipitous, and as they scrambled gallantly towards the crest they were drenched by a heavy rainstorm which damped their powder and in the space of minutes made the cliff face so slippery that it was impossible to continue. They retired in disorder to the shelter of the redoubt on the beach, where the rest of Monckton's brigade had formed under the personal command of Wolfe.

The situation was now desperate: the Grenadiers had suffered heavy casualties in their attempt on the cliff; the sudden storm of rain had drenched the army and made its powder unusable; and Townshend and Murray were moving in towards the vulnerable redoubt position. Wolfe acted quickly. Sending a signal to Townshend and Murray to withdraw at once to the Montmorency camp, he ordered Monckton to abandon the redoubt and make for the boats. The brigade was re-embarked in good order in the flat-bottomed boats used for the landing, and many of the wounded were brought off safely. But the attack had been a miserable and costly failure, more than four hundred of Monckton's brigade having been killed or wounded. Vaudreuil wrote exultantly to de Bourlamaque, 'I have no more anxiety about Quebec.'[171]

Wolfe, with the Highlanders, had covered the withdrawal of Townshend's and Murray's brigades across the lower ford, and from that camp on 1st August he issued his orders: 'The check which the grenadiers met with yesterday will, it is hoped, be a lesson to them for the future. They ought to know that such impetuous, irregular, and unsoldier-like proceeding destroys all order, and makes it impossible for the commander to form any disposition for an attack, and puts it out of the general's power to execute his plan. The grenadiers could not suppose that they alone could beat the French army, and therefore it was necessary that the corps under brigadiers Monckton and Townshend should have time to join, that the attack might be general. The very first fire of the enemy was sufficient to repulse men who had lost all sense of order and military discipline. Amherst's and the Highland Regiment alone, by the soldier-like and cool manner in which they formed, would undoubtedly have beat back the whole Canadian army, if they had ventured to attack them: the loss however is inconsiderable; and may, if the men shew a proper attention to their officers, be easily repaired when a favourable opportunity offers.' The rebuke was merited, but it was thought by many to be too severe. The attack had failed not so much through the indiscipline of the Grenadiers as through an error of judgement and a jumble of unfavourable circumstances which combined to make an unpromising plan impossible. The mistaken assumption that the shore redoubt was in dead ground from the cliff defences, the serious delay in landing occasioned by the ledges of rock in the river, and the heavy rainstorm, had all contributed to the failure of the attack. But it was the plan itself which was most seriously at fault. It had proved in practice impossible to co-ordinate the movements of troops from three separate camps, and this had resulted in a complete loss of any element of surprise. Only Wolfe's decision to abandon the attempt while there was yet time had prevented the set-back from becoming a major disaster.

The Grenadiers, with the Light Infantry and Highlanders, * were Wolfe's favourite regiments, reserved always, because of his faith in their courage and discipline, for the most difficult tasks and he may therefore be forgiven if his criticism of their behaviour seemed unduly harsh. But he knew that the plan itself was much at fault; it had, indeed, only been proposed by him when it became clear that the attack above the town must be postponed. On the night before the battle he had written in his journal, 'Dislike of the Gen[l.] Officers & others to this Business—but nothing better propos'd by them.' Anxious to criticize and oppose his schemes for attacking the enemy, his subordinate commanders were far from forming any constructive proposals of their own. More serious, they allowed their views to be known in the army, for James Gibson wrote to Lawrence the following day,[173] 'the

---

* The Highlanders were greatly feared by the French who called them 'Les Sauvages sans Culottes'.[172]

attempt was, I had almost said, impracticable; which some Genl. Officers scarcely hesitate to say. One of them of Knowledge, Fortune and Interest I have heard has declar'd the attack *then* and *there*, was contrary to the advice and opinion of every officer; and when things are come to this, you'l judge what the event may be!' Wolfe, in his disappointment, had not even the support of loyal officers; even his close friend, Carleton, temporarily deserted him, for Bell records briefly in his diary on the 31st 'Carleton's abominable behaviour to ye General.'

To Saunders, who had supported the attack to the best of his ability, and had taken personal command of the *Centurion* during the covering bombardment, Wolfe did less than justice. He criticized the handling of the 'cats' which, although they had been run aground and had to be burnt when the attack was called off to prevent their falling into enemy hands, he considered had not been driven close enough in to the shore. In his journal that night he writes a bald account of the day's failures, concluding bitterly, 'Two hundred & 10 killed, 230 wounded—Many excellent Officers lost in this foolish Business.'

His difference with Saunders was to be revived at the end of August when Wolfe drafted his dispatch to Pitt, but in the meantime they were both concerned to patch up their quarrel so that the conduct of the campaign should not suffer. Wolfe was more than ever determined to revert to his original plan of attacking Quebec from the upper river. By 1st August, after a night's rest at Montmorency, his old resilience of spirit had reasserted itself and he wrote to Monckton,[174] 'This check must not discourage us. The loss is not great . . . prepare for another & I hope more successful attempt.'

On the 5th he sent Murray up river with 1,200 men. With the ships under Holmes already above the town, Murray was to reconnoitre the north shore and create a diversion by landing to destroy the French magazines above Quebec. Saunders readily agreed to this plan and instructed Holmes to make every endeavour to reach and destroy the enemy ships which had been withdrawn far up river when the British fleet appeared before Quebec. The store-ships now lay seventy miles above the town, and the supplies they had brought from France were ferried down to the garrison in small boats. The move of Murray and Holmes into the upper river cut this line of supply. Montcalm was not unduly worried about the ships, which were safely above the junction with the Jacques Cartier river where navigation became too difficult without local pilots for Holmes to risk his small squadron, but he was acutely anxious about his land communications with Montreal, which might be severed if Murray were allowed to land and gain a secure foothold. Although the wind had blown obstinately from the west for several days making it impossible to reinforce Holmes, twenty flat-bottomed boats had slipped past the town on the night of the 5th, and Murray's striking force was superior to the French detachment above the town. Bougainville was therefore sent at once to take over command from Dumas, and his detachment was increased to 1,600. Montcalm would have liked to increase this reinforcement, but news had been received from de Bourlamaque that he had withdrawn from Ticonderoga, and this was immediately followed by intelligence that Amherst had detached from his army a force under Prideaux which had captured Niagara. It was obvious that de Bourlamaque's army must be strengthened without delay, and there was no alternative but to send de Lévis, Montcalm's second-in-command, to Montreal with a thousand men. This was a grievous blow to Montcalm's army but, if the thousand men could ill be spared, events were to show that the loss of de Lévis was irreparable.

Meanwhile, Amherst was anxious for news of Wolfe. No communication had passed between them since the beginning of the campaign, and there is no evidence that either had tried to send any message through by land.[175] Wolfe heard of Amherst's movements from French prisoners and deserters and it was already plain to him that he could expect no help that year from the west. His time was running out: already the days were shortening and he had achieved nothing. But there was another reason for urgency: the strain of the campaign had proved too much for his enfeebled constitution; his strength was ebbing away, and only his indomitable spirit kept him from collapse.

CHAPTER XXIII

Consultation with the Brigadiers

THE month of August was comparatively uneventful. Indifferent health and the defeat the army had suffered on 31st July prevented Wolfe from considering any major assault, though it is clear from all his movements that he was turning his attention once more to the upper river. Murray's expedition with the squadron under Holmes above the town might alert the French in that area, but Bougainville's small force was quite inadequate to cover the thirty-five miles of vulnerable coastline, and, while the greater part of Wolfe's army remained at Montmorency and Lévi, Montcalm could not afford to spare more troops from the Beauport lines.

Wolfe, it is clear, had at this time no definite plan of attack, but hoped rather that Murray, by cutting the French lines of river communication and supply with the west, would force Montcalm to attack the weakened Montmorency or Lévi camps. On 5th August Wolfe wrote to Monckton,[176] 'I have thought of your situation, when Murray is detached, & heartily wish you may be attacked—you have more than enough to beat the whole French army . . . with a single battalion of 700 men, & the Rangers to look out, I shou'd think myself in certain security.' Again, he wrote on the 6th,[177] 'I hope they will attack you—because I'm sure you'll put an end to the war.' Monckton was evidently less confident, and Wolfe's withdrawal of a detachment of troops from Lévi without informing him led to such ill-feeling that on the 15th Wolfe was obliged to write to reassure him: 'If you had been upon the spot I shou'd have taken the freedom to have desir'd you to make the change; & certainly in that or in any other military point, I never mean to disoblige. I am too well convinc'd of your upright Sentiments, & zeal for the publick service, not to set the highest value upon your friendship. . . . With regard to your Situation & ours, I must desire you to consider that the Enemy has two ways of coming at us, if they chuse it, & may when they like fall upon this body with their whole Army, without its being possible to prevent it, or to cut off their retreat—this is widely different from your position the Enemy must cross the River, between the Squadrons, land amongst your posts, and that with a Corps inferior to your own, well entrench'd with artillery. The least of your redoubts well man'd wou'd repulse an Army so compounded as theirs is. I mention these things, that you may not think I weaken you too much by the detachments that I am obliged to send or call away in this Service.'

Meanwhile, Murray and Holmes had struck their first blow. The point selected for their landing on the 8th was Pointe aux Trembles, about twenty-five miles above Quebec. The first attempt was hampered by a concealed reef and, though a landing was made by the advance guard, Murray was forced to withdraw to regroup his force. The second attempt fared still worse, as by the time it could be launched, Bougainville, who had been keeping pace on the north shore with the movements of the British squadron, had arrived to command the defences. Murray was driven back to the boats with the loss of more than eighty killed and wounded. He withdrew to St. Nicholas, on the south shore, and entrenched his camp as a base for further operations. The Canadians having paid scant attention to Wolfe's manifesto issued in June and recently proclaimed a second time in even plainer terms, orders had been given for the wholesale destruction of buildings and crops, churches only being spared. This instruction, harsh as it appears, was a necessary part of Wolfe's plan to deny supplies to the enemy. The harvest was due, and Wolfe knew that nothing would so encourage the defection of Canadians from Montcalm's army as the destruction of their farms and crops. Murray began at once to put these orders into execution.

Murray's presence in the upper river now began to be a matter of acute anxiety to Montcalm and Vaudreuil. Not only had they lost control of the south shore from Lévi to St. Nicholas, but stores from the supply ships could no longer come down by river further than Jacques Cartier and little or no provision had been made for transporting them thence to Quebec by land. Bougain-ville was urged by Vaudreuil to attack Murray across the river, but this was plainly impossible with his inadequate force and without any ships to guard his troops against the squadron under Holmes which commanded that part of the river. Nor was it any consolation to Montcalm to know that the British were trying to reinforce the squadron above the town: on the night of the 9th the *Lowestoft*, the *Hunter* and a small schooner, tried to pass through the channel, but the wind dropped and only the schooner succeeded in reaching the upper river. Wolfe was impatient for reinforcements to reach Holmes and wrote irritably to Monckton on the 13th,[178] 'What reason is given for the delay of the Ships and for their not attempting it yesterday, when the weather was so favourable?'

Wolfe was, in fact, less concerned with the reinforcement of Holmes and Murray than with strengthening the squadron and troops above the town for a major assault. Already he was pre-paring to abandon the Montmorency camp by transferring some of his artillery to the Pointe des Pères. On the 12th he had in-structed Monckton to prepare platforms to increase his batteries to twenty-four to thirty pieces of cannon, and to 'Talk to William-son about this, & let me know if everything will be ready in 10 days or a fortnight.'[179] The next day he wrote,[180] 'You may have 6 or 8 of our Brass 12 Pounders, but they must be carried off quietly; give me notice when you propose to send for them. . . . I shou'd imagine 10 12 Pounders, & 8 24 Pounders wou'd with the aid of Ships calm the fire of the Artillery of Quebec.' He was naturally anxious that the French should not know of these movements; but that he was prepared to weaken the artillery of the north camp at a time when Murray was absent with 1,200 men shows beyond reasonable doubt that he had in mind a with-drawal from Montmorency. Furthermore his insistence on the destruction of the batteries on the citadel is a clear indication of an intention either to attack the city itself—a project which McKellar had already informed him was out of the question—or to send more ships into the upper river to support a new attack.

On the 15th Wolfe made known to Townshend[181] his plan for future operations, which appears to have included a landing on the 24th. The details of that plan will probably never be known, but every move made after the failure of the Beauport assault indicates his intention to go above the town. He was impatient for news of Murray, and needed him to return before he could put his plan into operation: 'I wish we had Murray's corps back,' he wrote to Monckton on the 19th,[182] 'that we might be ready to decide it with them.' Three days later he wrote, 'Murray, by his long stay above and by detaining all our boats, is actually master of the operations—or rather puts an entire stop to them. I have writ twice to recall him.' The plain fact was that communication with Murray had been lost. Two French armed boats had slipped between Holmes and the channel into the basin, and the wind had blown continuously from the west precluding any attempt to send ships into the upper river. Monckton had dispatched a messenger westward along the south shore but he had returned without having made contact with Murray. Wolfe could only wait for his return and hope that it would not be long delayed.

Meanwhile, on the 17th, Murray had carried out a brilliant raid on the north shore. On the night of the 16th, leaving about two hundred Marines at the St. Nicholas camp with orders to keep the tents standing and light the usual fires, Murray and the rest of his detachment embarked in flat-bottomed boats and were carried on the tide to Portneuf. This move was covered by Holmes who made a feint with his squadron towards the Pointe aux Trembles. While Bougainville was following the movements of the naval squadron and watching the camp on the south shore, news was brought to him of Murray's unopposed landing at Portneuf and the destruction of the entire magazine of stores and equipment valued at £90,000 at Deschambault. By the time Bougainville could reach the area Murray had re-embarked his force without the loss of a man. When an orderly brought news of this catastrophe to Montcalm he hurried to the scene with reinforcements to take personal command; but Murray had slipped away, and while Montcalm remained above the town the Beauport army was left without its commander.

Both Holmes and Murray were hoping to destroy the French ships further up river. They had learned that Amherst was in possession of Ticonderoga and Niagara, and it seemed possible that they might be able to open communications with him by river. Holmes took a schooner up river to try to find a safe channel but without success. The project was abandoned and Murray began to march his men back towards the Etchemin, burning and destroying as he went.

At Montmorency Wolfe had sent out orders for rockets to be fired from Goreham's post to recall Murray. 'This,' wrote Barré,[183] Wolfe's Adjutant-General, 'will be a hint to the people above that we want something.' Wolfe was no longer able to exercise his customary control of operations: he had fallen desperately ill and was confined to his bed with a high fever. It seems to have been tubercular and his condition was critical. His impatience to see Murray and put into effect his new plan merely added to his suffering. Knox records on the 22nd, 'It is with the greatest concern to the whole army, that we are now informed of our amiable General's being very ill of a slow fever: the soldiers lament him exceedingly, and seemed apprehensive of it, by his not visiting this camp for several days past.' On the 24th Knox visited Montmorency from Lévi to receive orders for Monckton's brigade but he did not see Wolfe, who was still 'above stairs'. The following day Knox wrote, 'His Excellency General Wolfe is on the recovery, to the inconceivable joy of the whole army.' At nine o'clock the same evening Murray arrived from the upper river.

On the 27th the brigadiers met Saunders on board his flagship. What was decided at that meeting is not known, but the French had a story that Saunders issued an ultimatum saying that he would take his fleet back to England if no new plan of attack was proposed. Wolfe had suffered a relapse and he was once more confined to his bed; but on the 28th he was able to dictate to Barré a letter for the brigadiers. It proved to be a letter of particular significance, as it has been the cause of much of the confusion and controversy which has for so long prevented any clear understanding of the final weeks of the campaign. It was a bitter decision for him to ask the advice of his subordinates, whose criticism of his conduct of the campaign had been no secret. Until then he had made his own plans, kept his own counsel, and taken full responsibility for his actions. Unable now to lead them, he could only guide their deliberations and it seemed that he was condemned to personal failure without even attempting the plan to which he was already half committed. His letter was delivered by Barré on the 29th:[184]

271

'To the Brigadiers,

That the public service may not suffer by the General's indisposition, he begs the Brigadiers will be so good to meet, and consult together for the public utility and advantage, and to consider of the best method of attacking the Enemy.

If the French Army is attacked and defeated, the General concludes the town would immediately surrender, because he does not find they have any provisions in the place.

The General is of opinion the army should be attacked in preference to the place, because of the difficulties of penetrating from the lower to the upper Town; in which attempt, neither the guns of the shipping nor our own batteries could be much use.

There appears three methods of attacking this Army.

1st, In dry weather a large detachment may march in a day and a night so as to arrive at Beauport (fording the Montmorency 8 or 9 miles up) before day in the morning—it is likely they could be discovered upon this march on both sides the River. If such a detachment penetrates to their intrenchment and the rest of the Troops are ready, the consequence is plain.

2dly, If the troops encamped here passed the ford with the falling water and in the night march on directly towards the point of Beauport, the Light Infantry have a good chance to get up the Woody Hill, trying different places and moving quick to the right, would soon discover proper places for the rest. The upper redoubts must be attacked and kept by a company of Grenadiers. Brigadier Monckton must be ready off the point of Beauport to land when our people have got up the hill; for which signals may be appointed.

3dly, All the chosen troops of the Army attack at the Beauport at low water—a division across the ford an hour before the other attack.

N.B. For the 1st it is enough if the water begins to fall a little before day light or about it. For the other two it would be best to have it low water about half an hour before day. The General thinks the country should be ruined and destroyed, as much as can be done consistent with a more capital operation.

N. There are guides in the Army for the detachment in question.'

Assuming that Barré's interpretation of Wolfe's message as

dictated to him was reasonably accurate, what Wolfe's motives can have been for proposing three such unlikely plans it is hard to guess. He clearly thought little of either the first or third alternatives, and the second was merely a variant on the disastrous attempt of 31st July with the additional complication and hazard of a night march. For the past three weeks he had been urging the strengthening of the Pointe des Pères batteries, which now mounted no less than thirty-nine guns, and had noticeably weakened the Montmorency defences in order to do so. This was a movement quite at variance with any attempt on the Beauport lines. Furthermore, the *Lowestoft*, *Hunter* and *Seahorse* had passed the town on the 27th to reinforce Holmes in the *Sutherland*. If Wolfe had been intending to land at Beauport he would surely have countermanded the order for these ships to go above the town; they had already waited nearly three weeks for a favourable wind. It may be, as Waugh* suggests, that Wolfe wished to test the value of the proposals and to discover whether any of his commanders still favoured the old plan, but it seems far more likely that he intended, by proposing three altogether impracticable plans for attacks on the Beauport defences, to force the brigadiers—and, with them, Saunders—to suggest and support an assault above the town.

The brigadiers met Saunders aboard his flagship on the evening of the 29th and again on the 30th. Townshend drafted their reply which was handed to Wolfe on the 30th:[185]

'Having met this day in consequence of General Wolfe's desire, to consult together for the public utility and advantage, and to consider of the best method of attacking the enemy; and having read His Majesty's private instructions which the General was pleased to communicate to us; and having considered some propositions of his with respect to our future operations, we think it our duty to offer our opinion as follows—

The natural strength of the enemy's situation between the rivers St. Charles and Montmorenci, now improved by all the art of their engineers, makes the defeat of their army, if attacked there, very doubtful. The advantage which their easy communication along the shore gives over our attack from boats, and by the ford

* W. T. Waugh: *James Wolfe, Man and Soldier*. Toronto, 1928.

of the river Montmorenci, is evident from late experience; and it appears to us that that part of the army which is proposed to march through the woods nine miles up to Montmorenci, to surprise their camp, is exposed to certain discovery, and consequently to the disadvantage of a constant wood fight. But allowing that we could get a footing on the Beauport side, the Marquis de Montcalm will still have it in his power to dispute the passage of the river St. Charles, till the place is supplied with provisions from the ships and magazines above, from which it appears they draw their subsistence.

We are therefore of opinion that the most probable method of striking an effectual blow is to bring the troops to the south shore, and to carry the operations above the town. If we can establish ourselves on the north shore, the Marquis de Montcalm must fight us on our terms; we are between him and his provisions, and between him and the army opposing General Amherst. If he gives us battle and we defeat him, Quebec, and probably all Canada, will be our own, which is beyond any advantage we can expect by the Beauport side; and should the enemy pass over the river St. Charles with force sufficient to oppose this operation, we may still, with more ease and probability of success, execute the General's third proposition (which is, in our opinion, the most eligible), or undertake anything else on the Beauport shore, necessarily weakened by the detachments made to oppose us from the town.

With respect to the expediency of making an immediate attack or the postponing it, more effectually to prevent the harvest and otherwise destroy the colony, or with a view to facilitate the operations of General Amherst's armys now advancing into the heart of the country, we cannot presume to advise, although we are fully convinced that the progress of his troops hath, and must still depend upon the detention of, the greatest part of the enemy's force on this side, for the defence of their capital.

We cannot conclude without assuring the General that whatever he determines to do, he will find us most hearty and zealous in the execution of his orders.'

Evidently the brigadiers had some trouble with the wording of their reply. The original draft ended very differently:

'With respect to the expediency of making an immediate attack, or the postponing it to be able the more effectually to prevent the harvest and destroy the Colony; or with a view of facilitating the operations of our armies now advancing into the heart of the country, we cannot take upon us to advise, altho' we cannot but be convinced that a decisive affair to our disadvantage must enable the enemy to make head against the army under the command of General Amherst already far advanced by the diversion this army has made on this side.'

If Wolfe's intention had been to induce the brigadiers to propose a landing above the town he had succeeded admirably. Each of them had good reason to favour such an attack: Monckton and Townshend because they knew of Wolfe's plan in July; and Murray because he had led expeditions up river and knew from experience that a landing was possible. Saunders now agreed, and the brigadiers made their plan accordingly. Montmorency was to be abandoned during the next three days, and the entire army transported to a position west of the Etchemin river, leaving defensive garrisons of 1,000 men at the Pointe des Pères, 600 at Orléans, and 600 at Lévi. From there they would carry out a landing by night at any suitable point on the north shore from Cap Rouge to Les Ecureuils.

From the brigadiers' letter and plan it is plain that they had little conception of the fundamental essentials of a successful landing. Vaudreuil's letter of 6th September shows Bougainville to have been in command of more than 2,300 men including over a hundred cavalry, nearly half of whom were organized into a 'flying column' to be moved at speed to any threatened point. It was quite unreasonable to suppose that an army of the size proposed by the brigadiers could be transported to Cap Rouge and landed without opposition from Bougainville; and even if it had been able to land and overcome his detachment, it would still have been at least fifteen miles from Quebec, giving Montcalm ample time to assemble his entire army from Beauport to protect the city from the west. To suggest that this manœuvre, if unsuccessful, might still be followed by an attack on the Beauport shore was muddled thinking verging on lunacy and quite unworthy of officers of their experience. It is, moreover, painfully apparent from the last paragraph of their original draft that they were far from being convinced that the attempt should be made at all, preferring, evidently, the destruction of crops to an attack on the enemy which might risk defeat.

But Wolfe had achieved his object. Once above the town he would have the opportunity for which he had been waiting. He agreed to the brigadiers' plan, for, as he confided to Saunders,[186] 'My ill state of health hinders me from executing my own plan; it is of too desperate a nature to order others to execute. The Generals seem to think alike as to the operations, I, therefore, join with them, and perhaps we may find some opportunity to strike a blow.' He was still seriously ill, and it is probable that he knew he was dying. Success, he knew beyond doubt, depended on his personal leadership, and it was imperative that he should recover sufficient strength to put his own plan into operation. To his surgeon he is believed to have said, 'I know perfectly well you cannot cure my complaint; but patch me up so that I may be able to do my duty for the next few days, and I shall be content.' Whether as a result of his surgeon's skill or of his own courage and tenacity, Wolfe was on his feet again by the beginning of September and able to direct preparations for the final attack.

CHAPTER XXIV

In the Upper River

IT is not difficult to imagine Wolfe's feelings as he gave his consent to the brigadiers' plan. His campaign of three months had failed to bring Montcalm's army to action, and the one attempt at a landing in strength had ended near disaster. Physically he was on the brink of final collapse, and it was at least arguable whether he would be strong enough to continue in command until another attack could be launched. His brigadiers had shown themselves to be lacking both in resolution and ideas. Murray, it is true, had carried out a successful raid during his expedition to the upper river, displaying courage and resource, but he was too much concerned with his personal glory and aggrandizement to be a good subordinate; Monckton had given no indication of the qualities he had shown in previous campaigns which would have fitted him to succeed Wolfe as commander of the army; and Townshend seemed content to criticize the moves of others and to draw obscene and libellous caricatures of his general.* One of these drawings is said to have been passed round the mess at Montmorency until it reached Wolfe, who crumpled it angrily to the ground saying that if he survived the campaign the incident should be made the subject of an inquiry.†

Wolfe's relations with Saunders were hardly more cordial. A ship was due to sail to England with dispatches, and the draft of Wolfe's letter to Pitt was severely censured by the Admiral, who considered the account of the Navy's part in the Beauport landing unjust and inaccurate. Wolfe wrote to him on the 30th,[187] 'I

* Two are shown in the illustrations facing pp. 240 and 241.
† The caricature illustrated facing p. 240 shows creases which indicate that this may have been the drawing concerned.

shall leave out that part of my letter to Mr. Pitt which you object to, although the matter of fact to the best of my recollection, is strictly as I have stated it. I am sensible of my own errors in the course of the campaign; see clearly wherein I have been deficient; and think a little more or less blame to a man that must necessarily be ruined of little or no consequence.' He discusses in detail the action of the *Centurion* and the 'cats' grounded on the shore, and it is clear that he is dissatisfied with their handling, but throughout the letter he underlines his own responsibility for failure, and the inadequacies of his plan.

An uncharacteristic lack of confidence, obvious in his letter to Saunders, is even more apparent in his dispatch to Pitt, completed on 2nd September. In this he gives an account of the entire campaign to date and holds out little hope for future operations. It is a document of outstanding interest and importance and one of the most famous of its kind. It is therefore reprinted here in its entirety.[188]

'Sir,

I wish I could upon this occasion have the honour of transmitting to you, a more favourable Account of the Progress of His Majesty's Arms; But the Obstacles we have met with in the Operations of the Campaign are much greater than we had reason to expect or could foresee, Not so much from the numbers of the Enemy (tho superior to us) as from the natural strength of the Country, which the Marquis de Montcalm seems wisely to depend upon.

When I learn't that succours of all kinds had been thrown into Quebec, That five Battalions of regular Troops compleated from the best of the Inhabitants of the Country, Some of the Troops of the Colony, And every Canadian that was able to bear Arms, besides several Nations of Savages, had taken the Field in a very advantagious situation; I could not flatter myself that I should be able to reduce the Place: I sought however an occasion to attack their Army, knowing well that with these Troops I was able to fight, And hoping that a Victory might disperse them.

We found them incamp'd along the Shore of Beauport, from the River St. Charles to the Falls of Montmorenci, & intrenched in every accessible part. The 27th of June we landed upon the

278

Isle of Orleans; But receiving a Message from the Admiral, that there was Reason to think the Enemy had Artillery & a Force upon the Point of Levi, I detach'd Brigadier Monckton with four Battalions to drive them from thence. He pass'd the River the 29th, at Night, & march'd the next Day to the Point; He obliged the Enemy's Irregulars to retire & possess'd himself of that Post: The advanced Partys upon this occasion had two or three Skirmishes with the Canadians and Indians with little loss on either side. Colonel Carleton march'd with a Detachment to the Westermost point of the Isle of Orleans, From whence our Operations were likely to begin.

It was absolutely necessary to possess these two Points & fortify them; Because from either the one or the other, the Enemy might make it impossible for any Ship to lye in the Bason of Quebec, or even within two miles of it.

Batterys of Cannon & Mortars were erected with great dispatch, on the Point of Levi, to bombard the Town, and Magazines, and to injure the Works and Batteries: the Enemy perceiving these Works in some Forwardness, pass'd the River with 1600 men to attack & destroy them: Unluckily they fell into Confusion, fired upon one another, & went back again, By which we lost an Opportunity of defeating this large Detachment. The Effect of this Artillery has been so great, (tho' across the River) that the Upper Town is considerably damaged, & the Lower Town entirely destroy'd.

The works for the security of our Hospitals and Stores on the Isle of Orleans being finish'd; on the 9th July at night we pass'd the North Channel & encamp'd near the Enemy's left, the River Montmorenci between us. Capt. Dank's Company of Rangers posted in a wood, to cover some Workmen, were attack'd & defeated by a Body of Indians, And had so many killed and wounded as to be almost disabled for the rest of the Campaign. The Enemy also suffer'd in this Affair & were in their turn driven off by the nearest Troops.

The Ground to the Eastward of the Falls, seem'd to be (as it really is) higher than that on the Enemy's side, & to command it in a manner which might be made useful to us: There is besides a Ford below the Falls, which may be pass'd for some hours in the latter part of the Ebb & beginning of the Flood Tide; And I had hopes that possibly means might be found of passing the river above, so as to fight the Marquis de Montcalm upon terms of less disadvantage than directly attacking his Intrenchments. In reconnoitring the River Montmorenci, we found it fordable at a Place about three miles up, But the opposite Bank was intrench'd & so steep & woody, that it was to no purpose to Attempt a Passage there; The Escort was twice attack'd by Indians, who were as often repulsed, But in these Rencounters we had forty (Officers & Men) kill'd & wounded.

The 18th of July, two Men of War, two arm'd Sloops, & two Transports with some Troops on board, pass'd by the Town without any Loss, & got into the Upper River; this enabled me to reconnoitre the Country above, where I found the same attention on the Enemy's side & great difficultys on ours, Arising from the Nature of the Ground, & the Obstacles to our Communication with the Fleet. But what I feared most, was, that if we should land between the Town & the River Cap Rouge, the Body first landed could not be reinforced before they were attack'd by the Enemy's whole Army. Notwithstanding these difficultys, I thought once of attempting it at St. Michels, about three miles above the Town; But perceiving that the Enemy were jealous of the design, were preparing against it, and had actually brought Artillery & a Mortar (which, being so near to Quebec, they could increase as they pleased) to play upon the Shipping; And as it must have been many hours before we could attack them (even supposing a favourable night for the Boats to pass by the town unhurt) It seem'd so hazardous that I thought it best to desist.

However, to divide the Enemy's force, & to draw their Attention as high up the River as possible, And to procure some intelligence, I sent a detachment under the Command of Colonel Carleton, to land at the Point de Trempe,* to attack whatever he might find there, bring off some Prisoners, & all the usefull Papers he could get. I had been inform'd, that a Number of the Inhabitants of Quebec had retired to that Place, and that probably we should find a Magazine of Provisions there.

The Colonel was fired upon by a Body of Indians, the Moment he landed, but they were soon dispersed, & driven into the Woods: He search'd for Magazines, but to no purpose, brought

* Pointe aux Trembles.

off some Prisoners, & return'd with little loss. After this business I came back to Montmorenci, where I found that Brigadier Townshend had by a superior fire prevented the French from erecting a Battery on the Bank of the River, from whence they intended to cannonade our Camp. I now resolved to take the first Opportunity which presented itself, of attacking the Enemy, tho' posted to great advantage, & everywhere prepared to receive us.

As Men of War cannot (for want of a sufficient depth of Water) come near enough to the Enemy's Intrenchments to annoy them in the least, the Admiral had prepar'd two Transports (drawing but little water) which upon Occasions could be run aground to favour a Descent, With the help of these Vessels, which I understood would be carry'd by the Tide close in shore, I proposed to make myself Master of a detach'd Redoubt near to the Water's Edge, & whose situation appear'd to be out of Musquet Shot of the Intrenchment upon the Hill: If the Enemy supported this detach'd piece, it would necessarily bring on an Engagement, what we most wish'd for; And if not, I should have it in my Power to examine their Situation, so as to be able to determine where we could best attack them.

Preparations were accordingly made for an Engagement. The 31st July, in the forenoon, the boats of the Fleet were fill'd with Grenadiers & a part of Brigadier Monckton's Brigade from the Point of Levi; The two Brigades under Brigadiers Townshend & Murray were order'd to be in readiness to pass the Ford when it should be thought necessary. To facilitate the passage of this Corps, the Admiral had plac'd the Centurion in the Channel, so that she might check the fire of the lower Battery, which commanded the Ford; This Ship was of great use, as her fire was very judiciously directed. A great Quantity of Artillery was placed upon the Eminence, so as to batter & enfilade the left of their Intrenchments.

From the Vessel which run aground nearest in I observed that the Redoubt was too much commanded, to be Kep't without very great loss, And the more as the two arm'd Ships could not be brought near enough to cover both with their Artillery & Musquetry, which I at first conceived they might. But as the Enemy seem'd in some Confusion, and we were prepared for an Action, I thought it a proper time to make an attempt upon their

Intrenchment. Orders were sent to the Brigadiers General, to be ready with the Corps under their Command, Brigadier Monckton to land, And the Brigadiers Townshend & Murray to pass the Ford. At a proper time of the Tide, the signal was made. But in rowing towards the Shore, many of the Boats grounded upon a Ledge that runs off a considerable distance. This accident put us into some Disorder, lost a great deal of time & obliged me to send an Officer to stop Brigadier Townshend's march, whom I then observed to be in motion. While the Seamen were getting the Boats off, the Enemy fired a number of Shells & Shot, but did no considerable damage. As soon as this Disorder could be set a little to Rights, & the Boats were ranged in a proper Manner, some of the Officers of the Navy went in with me to find a better place to land; we took one Flat-bottom'd Boat with us to make the Experiment, & as soon as we had found a fit part of the Shore, the Troops were ordered to disembark; thinking it, not yet too late, for the attempt.

The thirteen Companys of Grenadiers & 200 of the second Royal American Battalion got first on shore; the Grenadiers were order'd to form themselves into four distinct bodys & to begin the Attack, supported by Brigadier Monckton's Corps, As soon as the other Troops had pass'd the Ford, & were at hand to assist. But whether, from the Noise & Hurry at landing, or from some other Cause, the Grenadiers, instead of forming themselves as they were directed, ran on impetuously towards the Enemy's Intrenchments in the utmost Disorder & Confusion, without waiting for the Corps which were to sustain them, & join in the Attack:—Brigadier Monckton was not landed, & Brigadier Townshend was still at a considerable Distance, tho' upon his march to join us, in very good Order.

The Grenadiers were check'd by the Enemy's Fire, & obliged to shelter themselves, in, or about the Redoubt, which the French abandon'd upon their approach. In this Situation they continued for some time, unable to form under so hot a fire, & having many gallant officers wounded who (careless of their Persons) had been solely intent upon their Duty: I saw the Absolute Necessity of calling them off, that they might form themselves behind Brigadier Monckton's Corps, which was now landed, & drawn up upon the Beach in extream good Order. By this new Accident & this second Delay, It was near Night; a sudden Storm came on, & the Tide began to make, so that I thought it most advisable not to persevere in so difficult an Attack, least (in Case of a Repulse) the Retreat of Brigadier Townshend's Corps might be hazardous, & uncertain.

Our Artillery had a great Effect upon the Enemy's left, where Brigadiers Townshend & Murray were to have attack'd, And it is probable that, if those Accidents I have spoke of, had not happen'd, We should have penetrated there, Whilst our left & center, more remote from our Artillery, must have bore all the violence of their Musquetry.

The French did not attempt to interrupt our March; some of their Savages came down to murder such wounded as could not be brought off, And to scalp the Dead, as their Custom is.

The place where the Attack was intended, has these Advantages over all others hereabout—Our Artillery could be brought into use—the greatest Part, or even the whole of the Troops might act at once—And the Retreat (in case of a Repulse) was secure, at least for a certain time of the Tide. Neither one, nor other of these Advantages can anywhere else be found.—The Enemy were indeed posted upon a commanding Eminence—the Beach upon which the Troops were drawn up, was of deep Mud, with Holes, and cut by several Gullys—the Hill to be ascended, very steep, & not every where practicable—The Enemy numerous in their Intrenchments & their fire hot—If the Attack had succeeded, our loss must certainly have been great, and their's inconsiderable from the shelter which the neighbouring woods afforded them. The River St. Charles still remained to be pass'd, before the Town was invested—All these Circumstances I considered, But the Desire to act in Conformity to the King's intentions induced me to make this Trial, Persuaded that a victorious Army finds no Difficultys.

The Enemy have been fortifying ever since with Care, so as to make a second Attempt still more dangerous.

Immediately after this Check, I sent Brigadier Murray above the Town with 1200 men, Directing him to assist Rear Admiral Holmes in the Destruction of the French Ships (if they could be got at) in order to open a Communication with General Amherst. The Brigadier was to seek every favourable Opportunity of fighting some of the Enemy's Detachments, provided he could do it upon tolerable Terms, And to use all the Means in his Power to provoke them to attack him. He made two different attempts to land upon the North Shore, without success; but in a third was more fortunate—He landed unexpectedly at Dechambaud & burnt a Magazine there, in which were some Provisions, some Ammunition, And all the spare Stores, Cloathing, Arms, & Baggage of their Army. Finding that their Ships were not to be got at, & little Prospect of bringing the Enemy to battle, He reported his Situation to me, & I order'd him to join the Army. The Prisoners he took informed him of the Surrender of the Fort of Niagara, And we discovered by intercepted Letters, that the Enemy had abandoned Carillon & Crown Point, were retired to the Isle aux Noix, And that General Amherst was making Preparations to pass the Lake Champlain, to fall upon Monsieur de Bourlamaques's Corps, which consists of three Battalions of Foot, & as many Canadians as make the whole amount to 3000 men.

The Admirals Dispatches & mine would have gone eight or ten days sooner, If I had not been prevented from writing by a Fever; I found myself so ill, & am still so weak, that I begg'd the General Officers to consult together for the Publick Utility. They are all of Opinion, that, (as more Ships & Provisions have now got above the Town) they should try, by conveying up a Corps of 4 or 5000 Men, (which is nearly the whole Strength of the Army, after the Points of Levi and Orleans are left in a proper State of Defence) to draw the Enemy from their present Situation, & bring them to an Action. I have acquiesced in their Proposal & we are preparing to put it in Execution.

The Admiral and I have examin'd the Town, with a view to a general Assault, but after consulting with the Chief Engineer who is well acquainted with the interior parts of it, and after viewing it with the utmost Attention, we found, that tho' the Batterys of the lower Town might be easily silenced by the Men of War, Yet the Business of an Assault would be little advanced by that, since the few Passages that lead from the lower to the upper Town are carefully intrench'd, And the upper Batterys cannot be affected by the Ships which must receive considerable Damage from them & from the Mortars.

The Admiral would readily join in this or in any other Measure for the Publick Service, But I could not propose to him an undertaking of so dangerous a Nature & promising so little Success.

At my first coming into the Country, I used all the Means in my Power to engage the Canadians to lay down their Arms, by offers of Protection, &c. I found that good treatment had not the desired Effect, so that of late I have changed my Measures, and laid waste the Country, partly to engage the Marquis de Montcalm to try the Event of a Battle to prevent the Ravage, And partly in Return for many Insults offer'd to our People by the Canadians, As well as the frequent Inhumanitys exercised upon our own Frontiers. It was necessary also to have some Prisoners as Hostages for their good Behaviour to our People in their Hands, whom I had reason to think they did not use very well. Major Dalling surprized the Guard of a Village & brought in about 380 prisoners, which I keep not proposing any Exchange till the end of the Campaign.

In case of a Disappointment, I intended to fortify Coudres & leave 3000 Men for the Defence of it; But it was too late in the Season, to collect Materials sufficient for covering so large a Body.

To the uncommon strength of the Country, the Enemy have added (for the Defence of the River) a great Number of Floating Batteries & Boats. By the vigilance of these, and the Indians round our different Posts, it has been impossible to execute anything by surprise. We have had almost daily skirmishes with these Savages, in which they are generally defeated, But not without Loss on our Side.

By the List of Disabled officers (many of whom are of Rank) you may percieve, Sir, that the Army is much weaken'd—By the Nature of the River, the most formidable part of this Armament is deprived of the Power of Acting; Yet we have almost the whole force of Canada to oppose.—In this situation, there is such a Choice of Difficultys that I own myself at a Loss how to determine. The Affairs of Great Britain, I know, require the most vigorous Measures; But then the Courage of a Handfull of brave Men should be exerted, only where there is some Hope of a favourable Event. However, you may be assured, Sir, that the small part of the Campaign which remains, shall be employ'd (as far as I am able) for the Honour of His Majesty & the Interest of the Nation, In which I am sure of being well seconded by the

Admiral & by the Generals. Happy, if our Efforts here can contribute to the success of His Majesty's arms in any other Parts of
America.

> I have the honour to be with the greatest Respect Sir,
> Your most obedient and most humble Servant,
> Jam: Wolfe.'

Whatever Wolfe's fears, it was now time for the plan of the
brigadiers to be put into operation, starting with the withdrawal
from Montmorency; but Wolfe, who was steadily regaining his
strength, was already preparing in secret to solve his 'Choice of
Difficultys' by executing his own plan. His intention was confided
to no one. 'Desperate' was his own description of the plan, and its
success depended on absolute secrecy. Meanwhile, the preliminary
moves to put it into execution suited the brigadiers' plan for a
landing above Cap Rouge, and the first requirement for both was
the evacuation of the Montmorency camp. This hazardous
operation was planned and executed with such skill that it was
completed in two days without the loss of a man or a gun.

At midnight on the 31st the *Seahorse* with two armed sloops and
a couple of provision boats had passed the town into the upper
river. Rous, in the *Sutherland,* who had been left in command of
the squadron above the town, moved down river from the Pointe
aux Trembles to Cap Rouge. Meanwhile the activity at Montmorency convinced the French that the camp there was either to
be evacuated or used once more as a base for an attack on Beauport. Montcalm remained stubbornly on the defensive at his
Beauport headquarters, but Vaudreuil was in a fever of anxiety
which was displayed in a series of contradictory orders to Bougainville, whose troops were recalled, reinforced, and made to march
hither and thither above the town in resentful bewilderment.

On 2nd September Wolfe issued his orders for the final withdrawal from Montmorency. Tents were to be struck at dusk and
carried down to the waiting boats which would unload at Lévi
and return with the ebb tide to pick up the troops who would
embark the following morning. The signal for embarkation was
to be the firing of Townshend's headquarters barn. Wolfe hoped
that Montcalm would attack at dawn, and had therefore instructed
his men to lie concealed in their normal defensive positions until

the signal was given. Knox notes in his journal, 'General Wolfe is endeavouring to draw the flower of the French Army from their strong intrenched camp, to an engagement on his own ground before he abandons it.' But Montcalm was too experienced a tactician to be caught in the trap: obstinately refusing the advice of his officers, he waited until Wolfe began to move his men to the boats. This was the opportunity to strike a crushing blow at the Montmorency brigades and Montcalm seized it: two columns of French troops were rushed to the upper ford to take the withdrawing army in the rear. But Wolfe and Saunders had prepared for this, and demonstrated once again their complete understanding of the value of the river as a flexible chain linking their divided forces. Saunders had already laid buoys opposite the Beauport shore, and, as soon as the French began to move, Monckton embarked his brigade from Lévi while Wolfe formed his remaining troops at Montmorency as if to cross that river below the falls. Montcalm was now threatened with an attack on identical lines to that of 31st July and hastily withdrew from the upper ford to defend the vulnerable Beauport shore. Monckton's regiments remained in their boats for four hours, until the withdrawal from Montmorency had been safely completed, and then rowed back to Lévi where they entertained their commander-in-chief at dinner.

The following day was spent in reorganization of the army in the two camps at Lévi and Orléans, and in drafting orders for the advance into the upper river. There was no secret of the intention to take the army above the town, and orders were given out for the boats containing the light baggage of the army to pass through the channel that night. The Light Infantry under Colonel William Howe,* with the 28th, 35th, 47th and 58th Regiments and the Louisbourg Grenadiers, were ordered to march under Murray's command at two o'clock on the afternoon of the 5th. This was a crucial time for the operation of the plan, the anxiety and his exertions of the previous day brought on another bout of Wolfe's fever. Knox reports on the 5th, 'General Wolfe was much indisposed

* The youngest of the three brilliant brothers. The eldest was killed at Ticonderoga in 1758, and the second brother, Richard, served with Wolfe at Rochefort. Richard Howe succeeded his brother as fourth Viscount and subsequently became an admiral and first Earl Howe. Colonel William Howe became a general, was knighted in 1775, and succeeded his elder brother to the Irish viscountcy in 1799.

last night; he is better today; but the army are, nevertheless, very apprehensive, lest his ill state of health should not permit him to command this grand enterprise in person.' News on the 5th of the safe passage of the boats helped to restore Wolfe's spirits, but he was fighting a losing battle against his illness and it was as much as he could do to stay on his feet. That day Murray led his regiments westward above the town by land. In the evening the boats picked them up and conveyed them to the waiting ships in the upper river. The 6th was showery, after a heavy storm at night, and in the afternoon Monckton and Townshend set out with the 15th, 43rd and 78th Regiments to join Murray. By evening they had arrived at Goreham's post and as night fell they forded the Etchemin river, wading some fifty yards through two feet of water and over a stony, uneven and slippery river bed across a rapid current. That night they embarked on board the ships in the river and there they were joined by Wolfe.

Apart from two detachments left to guard the bases at Orléans and Lévi, and the Rangers, who had been sent on a raid down river, the entire army numbering about four thousand was now in the upper river with sufficient boats to support a landing anywhere on the north bank above the town. As soon as all the men were embarked the squadron moved up river to Cap Rouge, followed closely on the north bank by the ever watchful Bougainville with his flying column. Montcalm and Vaudreuil were undecided: as Vaudreuil wrote to Bougainville on the 6th,[189] 'Il est certain que la conduite des ennemis est aussi embarrassante qu'equivoque.' Eventually they concluded that the move up river could foreshadow one of two plans: an attack on the communications with Montreal and thus a landing above Cap Rouge, or a feint above the town followed by a swift move by river to double back on Beauport. Montcalm therefore drew in his left flank from Montmorency and remained with the bulk of his army at Beauport. Above the town, in detached positions stretched from the Anse du Foulon to Jacques Cartier were some 2,200 men, of whom 1,100 were organized into a flying column under the personal command of Bougainville.

The justification for Montcalm's apparent inactivity is plain. The steep, rocky cliffs stretching along the north shore above the town made a landing in force impracticable much below Cap

Rouge, and any such attempt would be strongly opposed by Bougainville's flying column which could keep pace with any movement by the British squadron in the upper river. By the time any opposed landing could gain a foothold, Montcalm could transfer his army across the St. Charles to cover Quebec and use his superior strength to destroy the attacking force before it had time to entrench across his lines of communication with the west. To leave Beauport undefended, on the other hand, in favour of taking up a new defensive position above the town, was to court disaster. Wolfe's army could be transported very quickly down river to Beauport, and the greater part of the fleet with detachments of the army at Lévi and Orléans were already there to provide support for any attack below the town. By putting his army on board the squadron in the upper river Wolfe was exploiting to the full the advantage of extreme mobility afforded by command of the St. Lawrence. For the first time in the campaign Wolfe dominated the situation.

Townshend chose this inopportune moment to write to his wife,[190] 'Gen¹. Wolfe's Health is but very bad. His Generalship in my poor opinion—is not a bit better, this only between us. He never consulted any of us till the latter end of August, so that we have nothing to answer for I hope as to the Success of this Campaign, which from the Disposition the French have made of their force must chiefly fall to Gen¹. Amherst & Gen¹. Johnson. . . . I never served so disagreeable a Campaign as this. Our unequal Force has reduced our Operations to a Sceene of Skirmishing Cruelty & Devastation. It is War of the worst Shape. A Sceene I ought not to be in.'

A week earlier, Wolfe, who was just recovering from his illness, wrote his last letter to his mother. Written before he had formulated his plan for the final attack, and when his health and spirits were at their lowest ebb, it provides an instructive comparison with Townshend's.[191]

'Dear Madam,

My writing to you will convince you that no personal Evils (worse than defeats & disappointments) have fallen upon me. The enemy puts nothing to risk & I can't in conscience put the whole army to risk. My antagonist has wisely shut himself up in inaccessible intrenchments, so that I can't get at him without spilling a torrent of blood, and that perhaps to little purpose. The Marquiss de Montcalm is at the head of a great number of bad soldiers and I am at the head of a small number of good ones, that wish for nothing so much as to fight him—but the wary old fellow avoids an action doubtful of the behaviour of his army. People must be of the profession to understand the disadvantages and difficulties we labour under arising from the uncommon natural strength of the country. I approve entirely of my father's disposition of his affairs, tho' perhaps it may interfere a little with my plan of quitting the service which I am determined to do the first opportunity.—I mean so as not to be absolutely distressed in circumstances nor burdensome to you nor any body else.

I wish you much health and am

Dear Madam,

Your obedient & Affectionate Son

Jam: Wolfe

Banks of the river St. Lawrence
31st of August 1759

if any sums of money are paid to you of what is due to my father from the Government let me recommend to you not to meddle with the Funds but keep it for your support until better times.'

CHAPTER XXV

Prelude to Battle

FROM the time when Wolfe succeeded in transferring the greater part of his army into the upper river, there is hardly a moment in the campaign that has not been subsequently the subject of controversy. His own diary ceases on 16th August, for he personally destroyed the last pages before the final battle. Carleton's papers were destroyed on his instructions after his death. Of the senior commanders only Townshend kept a journal that has survived, and his relations with Wolfe were not such as could make him either Wolfe's trusted confidant or an unbiased witness. The mass of evidence from other sources is formidable and conflicting, and the wealth of circumstantial detail and the prejudgements of family historians have all but obscured the framework of undisputed fact upon which any account of these events must be built. Fortunately this framework exists in the journals of more junior officers, the logs of the ships engaged, letters of the French commanders, and dispatches to England; the rest is in their interpretation.

On the morning of 7th September, off Cap Rouge, Wolfe issued his orders for a landing. These were extremely detailed as to the order of regiments and distribution of boats but gave no hint of the landing place. It was simply stated that 'when the coasts have been examined, and the best landing place is pitched upon, the troops will be ordered to disembark, perhaps this night's tide.' The squadron was anchored off the cove, described by Knox as 'spacious' and strongly entrenched by the enemy who 'appear very numerous and may amount to about one thousand six hundred men, besides their cavalry, who are cloathed in blue, and mounted on neat light horses of different colours; they seem very alert. . . .' Early in the afternoon the *Seahorse* and two captured floating batteries edged in towards the shore and engaged the enemy armed boats guarding the approaches. Meanwhile, the troops put into their boats and rowed up and down as if intending to land. Thinking that this was the start of an attack, they were much disappointed when they were ordered back to the ships. That this was not the intention was made clear by Wolfe who left with his brigadiers on a reconnaissance up river to Pointe aux Trembles and did not return until after nightfall. Knox astutely guessed that this feint landing was 'calculated to fix the attention of the enemy on that particular part, while a descent is meditated elsewhere, perhaps lower down. . . .'

The following day was windy and wet, but early in the morning six more vessels succeeded in passing the town under heavy fire from the guns on the walls. Orders were issued for Monckton's brigade to lead a landing early next morning, and the sloop *Hunter* and a transport went up river to create a diversion. Meanwhile Wolfe went alone on a reconnaissance *down* river.[192] Immediately on his return the orders for landing were cancelled. The reason given was that the weather was unfavourable.

The troops had now been crowded in the transports for three days, the greater number of them above deck and without cover in stormy weather. On the 9th, Wolfe issued further orders postponing the landing: 'As the weather is so bad that no military operations can take place, and as the men are so extremely crowded in the transports, and in the men of war, so as to endanger their health; it is ordered that the undermentioned troops be landed at the mill upon the south shore, and that they may be cantoned in the village and church of St. Nicholas, in readiness to embark at the first signal.' The signal by day was to be 'two guns fired fast, and two slow, from the Sutherland;' the signal by night, three lights at the main-top-gallant masthead and two guns. That day Barré arrived from Goreham's post after a narrow escape from two Canadian canoes which pursued his boat up river. Holmes at once ordered the *Seahorse* to a position below Chaudière to keep open communications with Goreham's post and the garrisons left below the town.

Wolfe had secretly made a detailed plan of action, but it was confided to no one. No mention of any cause for hope is made in his last dispatch to England, addressed to Lord Holdernesse and dated 9th September. He gives a brief account of events from the arrival of the fleet in the St. Lawrence to the move to Cap Rouge and ends on a note of pessimism. 'The weather,' he writes,[193] 'has been extremely unfavourable for a day or two, so that we have been inactive. I am so far recovered as to do business, but my constitution is entirely ruined, without the consolation of having done any considerable service to the State, or without any prospect of it.'

On the 10th Wolfe called for an officer and thirty men from the 43rd Regiment to escort a reconnaissance party down river. He took with him Monckton, Townshend, McKellar, and Holmes, thinly—and, as it turned out, ineffectively—disguised in coats borrowed from the Grenadiers to hide their rank. They were accompanied by Captain Chads of the *Vesuvius* and Captain Delaune of the Light Infantry, both of whom were to play a vital part in the forthcoming attack. From the composition of the party it is clear that Wolfe had already formed his plan in detail, and subsequent correspondence with the brigadiers shows that he did little more than show them the place where he intended to land and allow them to examine the area. Holmes was probably more fully in the secret, for his part in the operation required preparation of the fleet, and his dispatch written a week later indicates that he knew of the plan well in advance. Before he returned to the *Sutherland* Wolfe met Burton and took him into his confidence, and later that day he wrote to confirm the plan to him. Burton was not only a trusted friend but also in command at Lévi, and it was essential that he should make his preparations to support the assault. Wolfe writes,[194] 'You perfectly understood my meaning in every particular. Goreham's first post is under the point of a hill, where there is a little road running from Dalling's old quarter up to the river; the way down is very steep, but I believe the troops can march at low water all along the beach from the Point of Lévi. . . . Sixteen hundred of our men are upon the south shore, to clean and refresh themselves and their transports; and indeed to save the whole army, which must have perished if they had continued forty-eight hours longer on board. Tomorrow the troops re-embark, the fleet sails up the river a little higher, as if intending to land above upon the north shore, keeping a convenient distance for the boats and armed vessels to fall down to the *Foulon*; and we count (if no accident of weather or other prevents) to make a powerful effort at that spot about *four* in the morning of the 13th. At ten or eleven, or twelve at night, sooner or later, as it may be necessary, of Wednesday, the 12th, we get into our boats. If we are forced to alter these measures, you shall know it; if not, it stands fixed: be you careful not to drop it to any, for fear of desertion; and it would not be amiss for Carleton to pass his troops in the beginning of Wednesday night. . . . If we succeed in the first business, it may produce an action, which may produce the total conquest of Canada; in all cases it is our duty to try the most likely way, whatever may be the event.'

The point on the coast chosen by Wolfe for his landing and shown to the brigadiers on the 10th was the Anse du Foulon, a small cove about a mile and a half above the town from the head of which a winding track led up a steep, wooded gully to the heights above. The way was barred by an abattis and guarded by a small outpost under the command of Captain Duchambon de Vergor, an officer of suspect loyalty and proven lack of resolution. A protégé of the notorious Bigot, he had already shown his unworthiness for command in his capitulation of Beauséjour to Monckton in 1755. The credit of Wolfe's choice of the Anse du Foulon has been the subject of much speculation and argument. Some have ascribed it to a Major Stobo, while others have ridiculed this theory, correctly asserting that Stobo left the St. Lawrence on the 7th and could not, therefore, have been with Wolfe on his reconnaissance down river on the 8th. Stobo had been taken by the French as a hostage at Fort Necessity and held as a prisoner at Quebec. He escaped by breaking his parole and joined the British at Louisbourg.* He was thoroughly familiar with Quebec and the surrounding countryside and could therefore have drawn Wolfe's attention to the cove at Foulon early in the campaign, and perhaps during the reconnaissance in July which preceded Wolfe's first plan for an assault above the town. It seems most probable that it was Stobo who first directed Wolfe to the area immediately above Quebec and that it was, therefore,

* Captain Henry Pringle, who was a prisoner with Stobo at Quebec, writes:[195] 'About the first of May last Cap^n. Stobo . . . made his escape with an Officer of Rangers, down the River, from Quebec; this put the Town in a ferment, & the Commanding Officer (Mr. Ramezay) put us all, English Officers, into prison.'

294

to Goreham's post that Wolfe went on reconnaissance on the 8th. Mahon* denies the possibility of this asserting that it would have been too dangerous for the General to go down river without escort and that he was already fully occupied with plans for an assault on Pointe aux Trembles; but the only shred of evidence he produces to support this is the negative fact that there is no record of Wolfe's departure in the log of the *Sutherland*. This theory rests on the assumption that Wolfe intended to follow the brigadiers' plan to land at Pointe aux Trembles. On the contrary, the evidence indicates that he was considering a landing much further down river, and Townshend's statement in his journal for the 8th:[196] 'General Wolfe went a reconnoitring down the river,' is positive confirmation.

Whatever may be the truth about this reconnaissance, it is certain that by the 10th Wolfe had made his final plan. Townshend records in his diary for that day,[197] 'By some intelligence the General has had he has changed his mind as to the place he intended to land; heard we had some deserters from the enemy's camp at Beauport.' It seems less likely that Wolfe had changed his mind than that certain intelligence he had received had strengthened and confirmed his resolve to act on a plan already made. Three significant events may have helped to confirm Wolfe in his decision: Barré's arrival on the 9th, though it is not known what information he brought with him; the arrival on board the sloop *Porcupine* off the Beauport shore of a French deserter, who was quickly transferred to the *Stirling Castle*; and the signal made at four o'clock on the morning of the 10th from Goreham's post for a boat to be sent to collect letters for the general. What was in the 'packet' addressed to Wolfe will probably never be known, but it must have been of singular urgency to be dispatched through the night from Lévi to Goreham's post, and it is not impossible that it came from Saunders who would, by then, have had time to interrogate the deserter from Beauport.

Wolfe's second reconnaissance of the Anse du Foulon carried out on the 10th was observed by de Remigny, the officer commanding the French post at Sillery. In a letter to Bougainville dated 11th September he tells of three boats which rowed to the

* Major-General R. H. Mahon, C.B., C.S.I.: *Life of General The Hon. James Murray*. London, 1921.

295

south shore opposite to his position:[198] 'La premiere pouvait porter 30[hmes], des deux auxtres n'en n'avait que 14 chacune sous officiers mais la plus chargée était composé de 50[hmes] armés et beaucoup d'officiers vetus de plusieurs couleurs, il y en avait un qui dessous un sourtout bleu était fort galonné le dit surtout avait ses boutonnières en or un chapeau à point d'Espagne tous ses messieurs monteront jusqu'a la plus haute des maisons qui sont sur le grand chemin.' From this vantage point Wolfe and his staff had a clear view of the Foulon and the track leading up the wooded slope. The ground had been broken up and an abattis built near the summit; on the crest a number of tents gave warning of the presence of a detachment about a hundred strong guarding the approach. The reconnaissance party was joined on the south shore by Carleton, who was commanding the garrison at Orléans, and probably by Burton from Lévi. This underlined one of the major advantages of a landing near the city: that the entire army including the Lévi and Orléans garrisons and part at least of their artillery could be concentrated for the assault. Any attempt between Cap Rouge and Pointe aux Trembles would have had to be made without their support. Only the Rangers, sent on a raid down river, could not be recalled in time to take part in the attack. Murray was not with the party, having been left to command the troops on shore at St. Nicholas. At about six o'clock Wolfe and his staff rejoined the squadron above the town, Carleton and Burton returning to Orléans and Lévi.

The following day orders were given for the troops at St. Nicholas to be ready to embark on the morning of the 12th, and detailed instructions were issued for the distribution of men to the boats for a landing. The first wave consisted of thirty flat-bottomed boats and five ships' boats containing about 1,700 men of Howe's Light Infantry, and the 28th, 43rd, 58th and 47th Regiments with a detachment of fifty of Monckton's second 60th and two hundred Highlanders. These were to be followed by the *Lowestoft, Squirrel, Seahorse* and *Hunter* with a number of armed vessels and transports carrying the remainder of the army less Burton's contingent of about 1,200 which was to be ferried across from Lévi when the two larger forces had landed. The total number to be landed was a little less than 4,600.

Although three hours had been spent in reconnaissance on

the 10th it is clear that the brigadiers were far from certain of the plan. In a letter dated the 12th and signed by Monckton, Townshend and Murray they ask for instructions:[199]

'Sir,

As we do not think ourselves sufficiently informed of the several parts which may fall to our share in the execution of the descent you intend to-morrow, we must beg leave to request from you, as distinct orders as the nature of the thing will admit of, particularly to the place or places we are to attack. This circumstance (perhaps very decisive) we cannot learn from the public orders, neither may it be in the power of the naval officer who leads the Troops to instruct us. As we should be very sorry no less for the public than our own sakes, to commit any mistakes, we are persuaded you will see the necessity of this application which can proceed from nothing but a desire to execute your orders with the utmost punctuality.'

The formal phrasing of the letter fails to disguise the underlying antagonism to the plan, and Wolfe was not slow to make a suitable reply. His letter is addressed to Monckton who, as senior brigade commander, was charged with leading the first assault with Wolfe.[200]

Sutherland 8½ *o'clock*

'Sir,—My reason for desiring the honour of your company with me to Goreham's post yesterday was to shew you, as well as the distance would permit, the situation of the enemy, and the place where I meant they should be attacked; as you are charged with that duty, I should be glad to give you all further light and assistance in my power.—The place is called the *Foulon* distant upon two miles or two miles and a half from Quebec, where you remember an encampment of 12 or 13 tents and an abattis below it.—You mentioned today that you had perceived a breastwork there, which made me imagine you as well acquainted with the place as the nature of things will admit of. I took Capt. Shads with me also and desired the Admiral's attendance, that as the former is charged by Mr. Saunders with conducting of the boats, he might make himself as much a master of his post as possible; and as several of the Ships of War are to fall down with the

Troops, Mr. Holmes would be able to station them properly after he had seen the place. I have desired Mr. Holmes to send the boats down, so that we may arrive about half an hour before day, as you desired; to avoid the disorder of a night attack; and I shall be present myself, to give you all the aid in my power. The officers who are appointed to conduct the divisions of boats have been strictly enjoined to keep as much order and to act as silently as the nature of the service will admit of, and Capt. Shads will begin to land the men a little of this side of the naked rock, which you must remember to have seen, within which (to the eastward) the enemy is posted. It is not a usual thing to point out in the public orders the direct spot of an attack, nor for any inferior Officer not charged with a particular duty to ask instructions upon that point. I had the honour to inform you today, that it is my duty to attack the French Army. To the best of my knowledge and abilities I have fixed upon that spot where we can act with most force and are most likely to succeed. If I am mistaken I am sorry for it and must be answerable to his Majesty and the public for the consequences. I have the honour to be, Sir,

Your most obedient and most humble servant,
Jam: Wolfe.'

Murray was to land with the first brigade and could therefore be expected to see Wolfe's letter to Monckton, but to Townshend, who was to lead the second landing, Wolfe sent a separate answer:[201]

'Sir,—General Monckton is charged with the first landing and attack at the Foulon, if he succeeds you will be pleased to give directions that the troops afloat be set on shore with the utmost expedition, as they are under your command, and when the 3600 men now in the fleet are landed, I have no manner of doubt but that we are able to fight and beat the French Army; in which I know you will give your best assistance.'

In his letter to Monckton dated the 12th Wolfe refers to the reconnaissance as having been carried out the previous day, but this is evidently an error as both the brigadiers' letter and his replies to Monckton and Townshend are dated the 12th and they were clearly written in the morning; the evidence of Knox, de Remigny, and the ships' logs bears this out. That afternoon Murray and Townshend went on board the *Sutherland*. Probably Monckton was already there to receive his final orders from Wolfe and it must have been at this meeting that the last instructions were given to the brigadiers for the landing the following day. Wolfe's last orders to his troops had already been issued. As an example of brevity, clarity, and confidence they will stand comparison with any battle orders in history and it is hardly possible to read the third paragraph without wondering if Nelson had seen it before he made his famous signal of 21st October 1805.

'The Enemy's force is now divided, great scarcity of provisions now in their camp, and universal discontent among the Canadians; the second officer in command is gone to Montreal or St. John's, which gives reason to think that General Amherst is advancing into the colony; a vigorous blow struck by the army at this juncture may determine the fate of Canada. Our troops below are in readiness to join us; all the light artillery and tools are embarked at the point of Levi, and the troops will land where the French seem least to expect it.

The first body that gets on shore is to march directly to the enemy and drive them from any little post they may occupy; the officers must be careful that the succeeding bodies do not, by mistake, fire upon those who go on before them. The battalions must form on the upper ground with expedition, and be ready to charge whatever presents itself. When the artillery and troops are landed, a corps will be left to secure the landing place, while the rest march on and endeavour to bring the French and Canadians to battle.

The officers and men will remember what their country expects from them, and what a determined body of soldiers, inured to war, is capable of doing against five weak French battalions, mingled with a disorderly peasantry.

The soldiers must be attentive and obedient to their Officers and resolute in the execution of their duty.'

There was still no public mention of the landing place, and this secrecy was amply justified when, on the 12th, a man from the Royal Americans deserted to the French.

At eleven o'clock that night two deserters arrived on board the *Hunter*, which had replaced *Seahorse* off Sillery, bringing information that a French convoy of provisions was expected by river from Cap Rouge that night. Remembering Wolfe's orders of 4th August concerning the examination of prisoners, there can be little doubt that the deserters were seen by him shortly after their arrival and that he was able to make use of this information. Some two hours earlier the troops for the first landing began to embark in their boats to wait for the tide to carry them down to their objective.

Meanwhile, in the French camp the loss of initiative and the indications of an approaching crisis served only to underline the weakness of a divided command. Confident in the ability of Bougainville and the strength of his detachment above the town, Montcalm determined to maintain the greater part of his army at Beauport. Beyond writing to Bougainville to stress the importance of constant vigilance, he paid little attention to the frequent and accurate reports from de Remigny giving detailed information of British movements in the Sillery area. On 5th September Montcalm had written,[202] 'Le mouvement des ennemis, mon cher Bougainville, est si considerable que je crains qu'il ne passe la rivière des Etchemins et qu'il ne cherche a nous derober une marche pour nous couper la communication,' and on the same day Vaudreuil had warned Bougainville,[203] 'Je n'ay besoin de vous dire, monsieur, que la salut de la colonie est en vos mains que certainement le projet des ennemis est de nous couper la communication en faisant des debarquements au Nord.' But Montcalm was convinced that no landing could be made below Cap Rouge, and any attack above that point could be contained by Bougainville's force until his own arrival with the army from Beauport. His plans relied on the watchfulness and vigour of Bougainville and his own ability to take command in an emergency.

Vaudreuil, on the other hand, as Governor-General, was not prepared to allow military dispositions to be made by a mere soldier; he meddled with them, countermanding Montcalm's orders and creating confusion and unrest in the army. As early as the 5th, Montcalm had given orders for the Guienne Regiment which was encamped in reserve at the St. Charles bridgehead to be moved to the road behind Sillery to give support at any nearby point on the coast that might be attacked, but this did not meet with the Governor-General's approval and he wrote on the 6th to countermand the order. The wretched Montreuil, Montcalm's Adjutant-General, was obliged to reverse the orders he had issued only the day before. On the 12th, according to the Abbé Recher, Montcalm again ordered the Guienne Regiment to move—this time to the Foulon itself; but his order was again revoked by Vaudreuil. According to his own account written after the battle, Vaudreuil was counting on the Guienne Regiment which he imagined was at the Foulon, but Montcalm recalled it on the night of the 12th without informing him. With the evidence of Montreuil, Recher, and the Chevalier Johnstone before us, it is quite impossible to believe this statement. In fact his entire story, related after the battle to dissociate himself from the blame of losing Quebec, is clearly an intricate web of lies woven to strangle the reputations of the military commanders, and, in so doing, to cloud the evidence of corruption and incompetence in his administration.

Another circumstance favoured the British attack. On 12th September Cadet wrote to Bougainville to arrange for a convoy of boats with supplies for Quebec to pass down the river that night:[204] 'Je vous prie, monsieur, de vouloix bien passer les batteaux cette nuit s'il y a de la possibilité, sans quoi je serai oblige de faire passer demain des charettes pour aller chercher ces vivre parceque j'en ai absolument besoin, mais s'ils venoient par eau, cela nous epargnerai bien de la peine.' It was information of this convoy that was brought to Wolfe the same night by deserters and he made good use of it. Considering the strength of the British squadron at Cap Rouge, it was an inopportune time to choose, and it is hardly possible that Cadet could not have waited a few days for his provisions. It may be that Bougainville thought the risk too great, for the convoy was not sent. It seems, however, that his outposts were warned to let it pass.

Much has been made of the appointment of Vergor to command at the Foulon post, the movements of the Guienne Regiment, and Cadet's request for the convoy, in an effort to prove that Quebec was not conquered but betrayed. There is no possible justification for this theory which is based on pure supposition unsupported by the smallest shred of evidence. Suspicion has been centred round the Intendant, Bigot, and his colleague, Cadet, but it has been suggested that Vaudreuil may have been implicated and even that Montcalm was a party to the betrayal of the city he had defended with such tenacity. Against Vaudreuil and Montcalm there is no case: one loved Canada and the other France too much, and both were too jealous of their honour and reputation, ever to have considered surrender except in defeat. Of Bigot and Cadet it is possible to believe anything but that they would be party to any action detrimental to their own interests, and nothing would more surely destroy their infamous organization and put an end to their plundering than a British victory at Quebec. Had it been that their speculation was about to be exposed, they might have turned to treachery in the hope that all evidence against them would be destroyed in the British capture of the city; but there is no reason to suppose that this was so, for both continued in positions of influence, responsibility and trust until the city was taken. The efforts of historians to uncover evidence of betrayal would have been the more praiseworthy had they sprung as much from an honest desire for the truth as from a determination to detract at whatever price from the greatness of the British achievement.

In one vital respect Wolfe's plan differed from all others: the boats were above their objective and would drift down in silence with the tide. This made it possible to deceive Bougainville, and to keep him engaged elsewhere Holmes was to send a few vessels up river as soon as the boats put off from the squadron. The remaining ships carrying the second brigade under Townshend would follow the boats after about three-quarters of an hour. This would bring both brigades to the objective at the same time and thus minimize the interval between the two landings. It required precise timing and the direction was entrusted to Holmes. Captain Chads was detailed to marshal the boats as they put off from the ships. The first landing was to be made by Colonel Howe, Captain Delaune, and twenty-four volunteers of the Light Infantry.

At nine o'clock the troops for the first landing began to scramble into the boats waiting under the lee of the ships. The tide was not due to turn until half-past one the next morning, but the noisy embarkation of 1,700 men could not be carried out in darkness when it would be certain to alarm the enemy sentries. At last the general entered his own barge. There, under the shadow of the *Sutherland* swinging at anchor, he listened as one of his officers quietly recited part of Gray's Elegy, the poem given to him by Katherine Lowther before he left England and read by him so often during the long voyage to the St. Lawrence. As the officer finished Wolfe turned to him and said, 'I would rather have been the author of that piece than beat the French tomorrow.'[205]

By midnight all was ready for the attack. In the boats the British troops huddled together, cold and impatient. At Beauport Montcalm strode anxiously round the trenches while Vaudreuil slept fitfully in his headquarters, disturbed by the thunder of the batteries at Pointe des Pères. All along the coast from Quebec to Pointe aux Trembles Bougainville's detachments waited for the dawn. Soon after half-past one the tide began to turn and a single light shining from the top-mast of the *Sutherland* gave the signal for the boats to assemble under the directions of Captain Chads between the *Sutherland* and the south shore. Wolfe's boat took up its position in the lead, and at about two o'clock two lights from the *Sutherland* conveyed to the boats the order to leave for the Foulon.

CHAPTER XXVI

'The Inevitable Hour'

THE passage of the boats down the St. Lawrence as far as Sillery was accomplished without incident. The night was cloudy but fine, and there was no moon to disclose the presence of the convoy to the sentries on the shore. The stars cast a thin light upon the dark water as the boats were rowed with muffled oars down river, hugging the safety of the south bank. The men huddled together, the stiff following breeze blowing coldly on their backs. A three-knot current lent strength to the oarsmen and soon after three o'clock the black mass of the sloop *Hunter*, swinging at anchor off Sillery, loomed above them.* Slowly the line of boats turned across the stream of the river and headed towards the north shore.

The danger of discovery was now acute. The crossing to the north had been left as late as possible, but from Sillery the boats must pass within a few yards of the French outposts where sentries stood staring out across the river, straining their ears for the sound of any movement. The first post was passed in safety, but as the convoy drifted noiselessly past the second the loud challenge of a sentry sounded across the water. There was a moment's startled hesitation. The men crouched tensely in their boats waiting for the rattle of musketry that must follow their discovery. Then Simon Fraser answered quietly from one of the leading boats,[206] 'La France'. 'A quel régiment?' Again Fraser answered: 'De la reine'. 'Pourquoi est-ce que vous ne parlez pas plus haut?' Fraser cut the sentry short: 'Tais-toi,' he ordered curtly, 'Nous serions entendus.' Thinking them to be the

* The story that they were challenged by the *Hunter* can be discounted, for the sloop was commanded by Captain Adams who had been directed in the orders issued by Admiral Holmes the previous day to take over command of the boats 'should any accident happen to Capt. Chads.'

304

French provision boats or a river patrol the sentry let them pass. The convoy glided on into the darkness and in a few minutes the first boat was beached at the Anse du Foulon. One by one the rest came in, and soon the whole of Wolfe's division, apart from the complements of three or four craft which had been carried downstream beyond the landing-place, was formed up in readiness for the assault on the cliff.

The ascent was led by Wolfe's friend, Captain Delaune, with twenty-four volunteers, followed closely by Colonel Howe and the rest of the Light Infantry. The zigzag path to the summit had been broken up by the French and obstructed near the top by a formidable abattis. Any attempt to climb the path would lead to discovery and expose Wolfe's division to the fire of the French outpost on the cliff. Delaune therefore led his men up a spur to the east of the cove pointed out to him by Wolfe as soon as they had landed. The ascent was one of incredible difficulty: the curtain of night that had hidden the boats from the sentries, only increased the hazard of climbing a wooded, unexplored cliff face, made slippery by the rains of previous days. That the climb could be completed in silence without giving the alarm to the sentries posted at the head of the path a few yards to the left seemed impossible; but Delaune and his small party of volunteers succeeded. Clutching at roots and the boughs of trees, they pulled themselves slowly up to the top, and pausing only to form up with the Light Infantry which had followed, they led the attack on the French outpost. Surprise was complete: after one ragged volley the French took to their heels, leaving their commander, Vergor, who had been wounded in the foot, and several of their company, to be taken prisoner. The Light Infantry were soon joined by the Highlanders and a company of Grenadiers, and while a detachment cleared the abattis an attack was launched against the Samos battery which had opened fire on the boats. This was captured and the remaining regiments of the first division climbed the path to the crest.

To the modern observer the climb does not appear remarkably difficult or perilous; but it must be remembered that the coastline has been much changed in two hundred years by frequent landslides, and there can be no doubt that it was then far more precipitous than it is today. We have the evidence of Saunders and numerous other witnesses that the cliff was not only steep and slippery, but that the ascent without previous reconnaissance and in darkness was considered by many to be impossible. Wolfe was aware of the difficulties of the task and of the danger that the first troops to attempt the climb would alert the French post on the crest. As soon as his first division was landed he went forward to reconnoitre, sending Barré back to the boats to hold up the landing of more troops until he could be satisfied that the risk of committing his entire force was justified. Barré ran down to the shore to find that the boats had already left to bring in the second division. By the time he could return to report that the landings were continuing according to the original plan, Wolfe had penetrated eastward to within a mile of the city and was astonished to find no sign that the alarm had been raised in the French camp at Beauport. By six o'clock the entire army had landed and was assembled on the crest.

Wolfe returned to his army and, leaving the 3rd Battalion of the Royal Americans to guard the landing place and his rear, marched down to the St. Foy road and on to an open piece of ground little more than twelve hundred yards from the city walls. There the army was deployed in line of battle, the right on a knoll close to the cliffs over the river, and the left extended towards the St. Foy road. The right, commanded by Monckton, was held by the 35th Regiment, the Louisbourg Grenadiers under Carleton, and the 28th and 43rd Regiments. On their left the 47th Regiment, the Highlanders, and the 58th Regiment under Murray's command extended to the left flank—the 15th Regiment and Light Infantry—thrown back to face the road and commanded by Townshend. In reserve were Webb's 48th Regiment under Colonel Burton and the 2nd Battalion of the Royal Americans. The half-mile length of front and the necessity of guarding its vulnerable flanks persuaded Wolfe to use a formation previously advocated by Amherst and himself but so far untried: a line only two deep, the famous 'thin red line' of the British Army, was thus seen for the first time on any battlefield. The army was now in its chosen position, though as yet without artillery, and Wolfe ordered his men to lie down and load with double shot while they waited for the first appearance of the French Army.

In the French camp there was the utmost confusion. Contemporary accounts by de Lévis and de la Pause are of little value as neither was present, and the account left by the Jacobite Chevalier Johnstone, Montcalm's senior aide-de-camp, is much coloured by their friendship. On the night of the 12th Vaudreuil was quartered near the bridge of boats over the St. Charles river. Montcalm's headquarters were in the centre of the Beauport camp. At about midnight Montcalm received reports of movements by the fleet under Saunders which seemed to threaten a landing from Lévi and Orléans. The tents at these camps had been left standing when the army was marched to join the squadron in the upper river and the French had no accurate reports of the strength of the army remaining below the town. Montcalm, in fact, believed that the greater strength was concentrated at Lévi and Orléans and that the force above the town would therefore be used for diversionary attacks on the north shore. Bougainville's mobile detachment would be sufficient to repulse any such attempt, and Montcalm was rightly confident that his repeated orders to Bougainville to follow closely any movements of the British squadron above the town would be carried out to the letter. An attack on the Beauport shore therefore still seemed the most likely danger. The entire Beauport army was ordered into the trenches, and Montcalm's aide-de-camp, Marcel, was sent to Vaudreuil's headquarters with a messenger who could return to Montcalm with any urgent news from the Governor-General.

Montcalm walked the lines of trenches with Johnstone and Poularies, commander of the Royal Roussillon, until dawn. By then he could see no sign of threatening movement in the British camps on the south shore, and the troops at Beauport were ordered back to their tents to rest. The firing from the Samos battery could be heard plainly in the Beauport lines and Montcalm feared that the provision boats had been attacked by the British squadron under Holmes, but no news came from Vaudreuil and it was concluded that it was a false alarm. Montcalm retired to his tent for a hot drink while horses were being saddled. He then set out with Johnstone to visit Vaudreuil.

At his headquarters by the St. Charles, Vaudreuil had spent a restless night. The first official news of the landing had come from one of Vergor's men who had escaped from the French outpost above the Foulon when it was attacked by the Light Infantry.

His report was quickly conveyed to Vaudreuil and must have reached him soon after five o'clock. He appears to have taken no action whatever until the arrival of Montcalm, soon after six. By that time Montcalm already knew that a landing had been made above the town for he had seen British troops moving about on the heights above the St. Charles valley. To his consternation he learnt from Vaudreuil that the landing was in strength and that the heights to the east of the town were already occupied by a considerable British force. Johnstone was dispatched at once to the Beauport headquarters to order the entire army except 200 men to cross the St. Charles and join Montcalm on the heights. At Beauport Johnstone found de Sennezergues, one of Montcalm's brigadiers, under orders from Montreuil not on any account to stir from the Beauport lines. These orders, dictated by Vaudreuil, had been delivered less than an hour earlier. Johnstone urged de Sennezergues to obey Montcalm's order, explaining the urgency of the demand for troops and the desperate emergency that had prompted it. He left de Sennezergues undecided, but shortly afterwards the troops from Beauport began to stream across the bridge of boats towards the city and the heights beyond. There they were deployed under the orders of Montcalm and Montreuil behind a ridge of broken ground called Buttes-à-Neveu about six hundred yards from Wolfe's line. On the arrival of three pieces of artillery from the city, the French troops moved up onto the ridge in full view of the British. While Montcalm was thus engaged in assembling his army to cover the city from the east, Vaudreuil, the boastful Governor-General whose responsibility it was to conduct the defence of Quebec and, indeed, of the whole colony, sat down to write a dispatch to Bougainville. He succeeded in arriving on the field of battle too late to influence events in any way.

Wolfe's deployment had been completed by about half-past seven, and Montcalm finished assembling his force behind the Buttes-à-Neveu about an hour later. Indian and Canadian snipers had harried the British flanks, and Montcalm sent 1,500 more to the right flank to pin down Townshend's troops. There some skirmishing took place for possession of a house held by the Light Infantry, but the Canadians were beaten off. The British had succeeded in dragging up two small brass cannon, and these had opened a brisk fire in reply to those brought out of the city by Montcalm. The British battle strength was 3,826, but little more than half this number was in the front line, the remainder guarding the flanks and rear or being held in reserve. Montcalm's strength is difficult to assess with accuracy, but taking into account the detachments with de Lévis and Bougainville, the garrison in Quebec, and the troops from the extreme left of the Beauport lines which never arrived for the battle, it seems that he had gathered a total force of about 4,500 including Indians. The numerical disparity between the two armies was therefore small. Wolfe had the advantage of having achieved surprise, and of commanding a force of disciplined regular troops on ground of his own choosing against a French army composed partly of regulars and partly of militia and Indians. Montcalm believed that Bougainville with more than 2,000 men including cavalry threatened the rear of Wolfe's army. By the slight dispositions made to guard his communications with the shore, it is plain that Wolfe knew Bougainville to have been drawn far up river to the east by the movement of the ships of Holmes's squadron the previous night.

Montcalm was faced with a terrible and fascinating decision. Should he attack at once, or should he wait for more troops from Beauport and for the arrival of Bougainville? He knew little of the numbers of the British force in the St. Lawrence, the strength of which had been wildly exaggerated in reports reaching him on its arrival, and he did not know, therefore, to what extent Wolfe's army on the plains could be reinforced. If he waited for Bougainville, Wolfe might have time to entrench his army and to bring up reinforcements of men and artillery. It might then be impossible to dislodge him from his position across the lines of communication and supply with Montreal. If Montcalm attacked at once without his full strength he risked defeat and the piecemeal destruction of his entire army; and all Canada must inevitably fall. Montcalm was confident that Bougainville could not be far away for he must have heard the firing from the Samos battery. It therefore seemed to him that his only chance of a decisive victory lay in an attack before the British position could be established.

Wolfe, on the other hand, knew that he must draw Montcalm

into battle before Bougainville could return, for a siege supplied from the river held little hope of success before winter. When the French appeared over the Buttes-à-Neveu he knew that his plan had succeeded.

A little after nine o'clock Montcalm led his army over the crest of the ridge and began to deploy from three columns into line. Captain York, who was directing the fire of one of the brass cannon, immediately ran it out near the St. Foy road and began to pour down a steady and accurate enfilading fire on the French line.

Wolfe now roused his troops and advanced them a hundred paces. There they halted and watched the French deployment. Light rain, which had fallen steadily since the landing, stopped, and the sun shone palely upon the two armies as they faced each other in line.

Through the ranks of the French, where the white uniforms of the regulars mingled with the grey of the militia and the blue of the Royal Roussillon Regiment, Montcalm rode on his great black charger, supervising the work of Montreuil and de Sennezergues. The British stood motionless; Townshend, Murray, and Monckton in front of their brigades, while Wolfe, a familiar, tall, lean figure resplendent in a new scarlet coat, strolled easily, cane in hand, up and down the line. The French skirmishers on the flanks kept up a steady harassing fire but the British reserved their powder. As a man in the front rank fell, his place was instantly taken and the ranks closed. It was while Wolfe was with Murray's brigade on the left that he was struck in the wrist by a bullet, but he quickly bound his handkerchief round the wound and continued his tour of the line.

Soon after ten o'clock the French began to advance. Almost at once Wolfe was wounded again by a bullet that struck him in the groin, but he scarcely seemed to feel it and continued to walk to and fro in front of his army encouraging his men and repeating the order to hold their fire. The French advanced rapidly until at a distance of about a hundred and thirty yards they opened fire, shooting irregularly, their line wavering and breaking as the colonial troops fell to reload and then came on again. The British line stood unbroken, awaiting the order to fire. Only the cries of the wounded and the sharp commands of the officers broke the silence in the ranks. Wolfe had taken up his position on the right, between the Louisbourg Grenadiers and the 28th Regiment, and, according to one witness, observed the French as they advanced 'with a countenance radiant and joyful beyond description'. At seventy yards the French shooting became more accurate and there was a continuous ripple in the British ranks as men from the second line stepped forward to replace those who had fallen. Some of the officers and men began to look questioningly at their commander, standing motionless on the right, anticipating his order to fire; but no order came from him.

At last, as the French came within forty yards, Wolfe gave the command. There was a single deafening crash like the report of a monstrous gun as more than 2,000 muskets poured their hail of double shot at point-blank range into the advancing French line. As the smoke gradually cleared it was possible to see the extent of its effect. Nearly every man in the French front rank was down, and the attempts of the survivors to re-form and close their shattered ranks were pitiful to see. They were given no time for recovery, for as the smoke cleared the British had reloaded, and they now advanced twenty paces and poured a series of deadly volleys into the remains of the French line. The right of the line wavered, broke and then fled before the bayonet charge of Murray's brigade, and the rest soon followed. The gallant Royal Roussillon on the left fought on under Montcalm until they were at last forced to retire before the charge of the Grenadiers and the rest of the British right, and the entire British line was hurled forward in pursuit, led by Murray's shouting Highlanders. From the right, a messenger ran to find Townshend. Wolfe and Monckton had been hit, and Townshend was now in command.

Monckton had been severely wounded in the chest and lungs and was carried quickly to the rear. Wolfe received his third wound as the smoke cleared from the first British volley. A musket ball struck him in the right breast and he was supported as he fell by Lieutenant Browne and a volunteer, James Henderson, of the Louisbourg Grenadiers. They carried him to the rear and laid him down about three hundred yards from the line, but it was plain that he had only a few minutes to live. Hewit, a surgeon's mate from the 28th Regiment, ran with another soldier to help them, but there was little he could do. Wolfe had closed his eyes and appeared to be in a coma. His breathing was painful and shallow. Blood flowed freely from the wounds in his chest and groin, and the handkerchief bound round his wrist was scarlet as his coat. The four men with him watched helplessly in stricken silence until one of them, moving away for a moment to a low ridge from which he could see the battle, cried suddenly in great excitement,[207] 'They run! see how they run!' At this Wolfe opened his eyes and struggled to rise: 'Who runs?' he asked. 'The Enemy, Sir, Egad they give way everywhere.' For one last moment, as the shouts of his victorious army echoed across the plain, Wolfe was again in full command. Summoning his last reserves of strength he gave his last order: 'Go one of you, my lads, to Colonel Burton; tell him to march Webb's regiment with all speed down to Charles's river to cut off the retreat of the fugitives from the bridge.' Then, turning on his side, he murmured, 'Now, God be praised, I will die in peace.'

Happy at last in the victory of the army he had led with such determination and courage, Wolfe died in the arms of the soldiers he loved. Caring for his men, he was loved by them, and there were many who, like James Henderson, wept unashamedly at his death.

On the battlefield, Townshend had assumed command of the army which, in headlong pursuit of the enemy, had split into brigades, losing all semblance of order. Murray led his brigade in a determined attempt to cut off the French from their last safe line of retreat across the St. Charles, while Monckton's brigade had pursued the enemy almost to the gates of the city. Townshend immediately recalled both brigades and reformed them on the battlefield. At eleven o'clock Bougainville appeared with his detachment from the west and finding the British drawn up to receive him and the French army nowhere to be seen, prudently withdrew to Ancienne Lorette about seven miles away. Entrenching tools had been brought up from the Foulon, and the Navy had succeeded in landing some cannon which they had dragged up the cliffs, and on Townshend's orders the British began to entrench and fortify their position. According to Knox every bush was cut down and it is clear that Townshend expected to have to withstand a concentrated assault. Meanwhile the scattered and demoralized remnants of the beaten French Army escaped in confusion across the St. Charles river. Vaudreuil and Bigot, deciding that all was lost, deserted their army and fled to Jacques Cartier where they were soon joined by the rest of the army from the Beauport lines. The inadequacy of the garrison in Quebec made its capture inevitable unless a counter-attack could be launched at once, and Vaudreuil left a message for the Governor, de Ramezay, authorizing the surrender of the city in forty-eight hours. It is much to his credit that de Ramezay held out until the 17th when it was at last clear that he could no longer expect help to arrive in time.

The late arrival of Bougainville on the battlefield has been for many years one of the unsolved mysteries of the campaign. It is plain from correspondence addressed to him from the French headquarters at Beauport that on the night of the 12th he was expected to be at Cap Rouge with his flying column of more than 1,100 men. The rest of his force was distributed among fortified posts above and below Cap Rouge. The Samos battery began to fire at the British boats landing at the Foulon soon after four o'clock on the morning of the 13th, but it was not until seven hours later that Bougainville arrived on the Plains, only six miles away from his headquarters. Mahon* has suggested that the presence of a certain Madame de Vienne in the district may have had something to do with Bougainville's late arrival; but it is now certain that he was deceived by the movement of some of Holmes's fleet up the river shortly before the landing into following them westward towards the landing-place at Pointe aux Trembles. In a letter to de Bourlamaque on the 18th, Bougainville states that he knew nothing of the landing until eight o'clock on the morning of the 13th. This could not be possible if he were at Cap Rouge, only four miles from the outpost at Sillery where the watchful de Remigny must have known of the landing as soon as it was made. If Bougainville was on his way to Pointe aux Trembles, he might not have heard news of the landing for several hours and his failure to join Montcalm is explained.

The precipitate flight of the French army, and the failure of Vaudreuil to make any attempt to rally it and join with Bougain-ville's force to relieve the city, leads to a consideration of Town-shend's recall of the pursuing army and his decision to entrench on the Plains. It is only fair to say of this decision that it was from

* *Life of General The Hon. James Murray*, 1921.

a textbook point of view correct and prudent, and the action to be expected of a well-trained staff officer. The pursuit of the beaten French army was out of control; the lines of communication and supply from the Foulon—and thus with the fleet—were insecure; only a few cannon had arrived from the shore; and Bougainville with a force of 2,000 or more might be expected to appear at any moment in the rear of the British position. Any attempt to continue the pursuit must jeopardize all that had been gained. On the other hand it may be argued that the prize—the capture of Quebec and the destruction of the French army that had at last been brought to battle—justified the risk, for if the remnants of the French army were allowed to escape and regroup with the Beauport garrison and Bougainville's brigade, the capture of Quebec might well be prevented until de Lévis could be recalled with reinforcements to drive the British back into the river.

It is easy to be wise or unwise after the event, and it is perhaps unwise to quarrel with the weight of informed military opinion that has endorsed Townshend's decision; but if the accounts of Wolfe's last words are true there can be no doubt that his decision would have been different. He would not have been content with the eventual capture of Quebec, for he had made it plain throughout the campaign that his aim was the destruction of the French army by bringing it to battle on any reasonable terms. The capture of Quebec itself must inevitably follow. He had realized, as his staff had not, that the campaign, and thus Canada itself, was to be won not by the capture of cities but by the destruction of armies, and it is this fact that was overlooked by Townshend and has escaped the attention of his admirers. To make Townshend's action unassailable, it has been argued that Wolfe's plan was in itself ineffectual: that a landing at Pointe aux Trembles would have achieved more; that a set-piece siege from entrenchments across the French line of communication would have led to the capture of Quebec. These arguments presuppose complete control of the St. Lawrence above and below the town by Holmes and Saunders; a landing undetected and unopposed at Pointe aux Trembles; the starvation and capitulation of the Quebec garrison and the French army at Beauport under siege; and the inactivity of de Lévis and the French army to the west, pinned down by pressure from Amherst. None of these suppositions can be upheld. Nor does the plan encompass more than the taking of Quebec. The French army would still be free to escape to fight again. Wolfe's plan, on the other hand, by making the fullest use of mobility and surprise could achieve both objects. That it failed in its primary object was due not to a faulty plan but to unimaginative and faint-hearted command after his death. It is too often forgotten that it was from Townshend, not from Wolfe, that the French army escaped to fight for Quebec again in 1760.

De Ramezay held out in Quebec until the 17th. Deserted by Vaudreuil and the army, he had no choice but surrender. Montcalm, mortally wounded on the 13th, had died on the following day, and both his brigadiers, de Sennezergues, and St. Ours, had been killed in the battle. Townshend had brought up his artillery to batter the upper town, and the lower town had already been reduced to rubble by the guns on the Pointe des Pères. On the 18th Townshend received the capitulation of the city and composed his dispatch to Pitt, announcing the victory. The dispatch is less remarkable for its contents which, though poorly expressed, are in the main accurate, than for the indignation it caused on its arrival and publication in England by the omission of any expression of regret at Wolfe's death. It was hardly to be expected that a factual dispatch should express sentiments which it is doubtful if Townshend felt, though the arid 'it was there that our General fell at the Head of Braggs and the Louisbourg Grenadiers' was certainly less than just tribute to his dead commander-in-chief. In England it gave the impression that he was preparing to snatch the laurels of victory for himself.

Saunders wrote his dispatch about the 20th. The account it gives is brief and accurate and understates the essential part played by the Navy. His co-operation and daring use of his fleet made an indispensable contribution to the success of the campaign at every stage. If, from time to time, he had disagreed with Wolfe, he had never failed to give his immediate and loyal support to any plan that was made.

The brigade commanders had not chosen to give Wolfe such undivided loyalty and their behaviour is open to the severest censure. Perhaps a commander less headstrong and uncertain of temper might have found them less troublesome and more loyal, but it could be that a weaker character might have been broken by their jealousy and disloyalty. The troops, it is clear from their letters, loved and respected Wolfe and had complete confidence in his ability as a commander. With the exception of the Grenadiers at Montmorency whose failure had been from excess of unrestrained zeal, the regiments had shown exemplary discipline, courage and fortitude in a long and arduous campaign, and the artillery in particular had been used with distinction under its commander, Colonel George Williamson, who was later to become a lieutenant-general and commandant at Woolwich. It was the accuracy of the fire directed against the city from the Pointe des Pères batteries which enabled Saunders to pass the squadron under Holmes through the narrow channel leading to the upper river and upon this movement of the fleet had hinged the fate of the entire campaign. Knox writes, 'The admirable service performed by the artillery, under that experienced master of his profession, Colonel, now Major-General, Williamson, exceeds everything that can possibly be said in their behalf: and, for the honour of that corps, it may, with the strictest justice, be acknowledged, that not any other country can boast of greater proficients in the art of gunnery, than those produced by that excellent academy at Woolwich.'

On the 23rd Wolfe's embalmed body was taken on board the *Royal William*, and two days later Bell and Delaune sailed with it for Spithead.

Saunders and Townshend sailed with the fleet, leaving Murray as Governor of Quebec. Monckton went to New York to recover from his wound. After a winter of appalling severity, Murray and his sickly garrison faced in the spring a new attack by de Lévis which was only driven off by the arrival of a British squadron in the St. Lawrence. In September 1760, Vaudreuil surrendered the rest of Canada to Amherst at Montreal.

CHAPTER XXVII

'Impute to these the fault'

ON 14th October, Wolfe's gloomy dispatch of the 2nd September reached England. Walpole wrote to Sir Horace Mann, 'You must not be surprised that we have failed at Quebec, as we certainly shall. . . . Two days ago came letters from Wolfe, despairing, as much as heroes can despair. The town is well victualled, Amherst is not arrived, and fifteen thousand men encamped defend it. We have lost many men by the enemy, and some by our friends—that is, we now call our nine thousand only seven thousand. How this little army will get away from a much larger, and in this season in that country, I dont guess—yes, I do.' The news was a bitter blow to Pitt, for in Europe and the West Indies the tide had begun to turn in England's favour. At the beginning of the year Guadeloupe, the richest of the French West-Indian sugar-islands, had been captured; and though Frederick had sustained a crushing defeat in August at Kunersdorf, the brilliant victory of Ferdinand of Brunswick at Minden had redressed the balance. In the Mediterranean Boscawen and Brodrick fell upon de la Clue as he ventured out of Toulon in August and captured or drove ashore most of his fleet. But to Pitt the American issue was paramount. Amherst's painful progress against negligible opposition held no immediate prospect of conquest. Only to Quebec could Pitt look with hope, and he waited impatiently for news that would justify the bold choice of Wolfe to command there.

He did not have long to wait. Two days after the arrival of Wolfe's dispatch came news from Townshend of the fall of Quebec. To a people prepared for news of a costly failure, the story of Wolfe's triumph—the scaling of the heights of Abraham and Wolfe's glorious death at the moment of victory—came as a dramatic and thrilling shock. There was public rejoicing on a scale not seen since the Aix-la-Chapelle celebrations ten years earlier. The Prince of Wales and the rest of the Royal Family waited upon the King at Kensington on the 17th to offer their congratulations on the success of His Majesty's arms in Canada, the park and Tower guns were fired, flags were flown, 'and the greatest illuminations were made throughout the city and suburbs that were ever known.' 'Can one easily leave the remains of such a year as this?' wrote Horace Walpole to George Montagu on 21st October,[208] 'It is still all gold. I have not dined or gone to bed by a fire till the day before yesterday. Instead of the glorious and ever-memorable year 1759, as the newspapers call it, I call it this ever warm and victorious year. We have not had more conquest than fine weather: one would think we had plundered East and West Indies of sunshine. Our bells are worn threadbare with ringing for victories. . . . One thing is very fatiguing; all the world is made knights or generals. Adieu! I don't know a word of news less than the conquest of America. P.S. You shall hear from me again if we take Mexico or China before Christmas.'

For Henrietta Wolfe, now a lonely widow in Blackheath, the deaths of her husband and only surviving son had extinguished the last flames of interest in life and left her world in darkness. She had been a stern mother, but she had loved her sons, watching over their health and interests with a jealous devotion, apprehensive of their ambitions, yet proud of their achievements. She drew little comfort from the glory of Wolfe's last hours: the knowledge of his immortality in history could not console her for his death. She shut herself up in her house, refusing to see anyone, and all correspondence was answered for her by friends. Katherine Lowther set aside her own grief to write to Mrs. Wolfe; but Wolfe's parents had never approved of his engagement, and the reply written by a Miss Aylmer was cold. She wrote again and was answered by Miss Scott, a cousin of Mrs. Wolfe's: Miss Lowther should have her portrait returned to her as soon as it was set according to the instructions in Wolfe's will. Sadly Katherine Lowther realized that she could neither comfort nor be comforted. She wrote once again to Miss Scott,[209] 'not that I shall ever attempt intruding my Company since (tho' I feel for her more than I can express; & shall if it was given me to alleviate

318

her Grief Gladly exert every power which nature or Compassion has bestow'd)—Yet I think we are the last people in the World who ought to meet.' Of her portrait, she added, 'I can't as a Mark of his Affection Refuse it, otherwise I wou'd willingly spare my Self the pain of seeing a Picture given with such far different Hopes & expectations.' Six years later she married the Duke of Bolton. She lived for fifty years after Wolfe's death, and it seems that she destroyed all her letters from him.

The people of Blackheath sympathized with Mrs. Wolfe in her desolation and 'unanimously agreed to admit no illuminations or firing, or any other sign of rejoicing whatsoever near her house, lest they should seem by an ill-timed triumph to insult over her grief.'[210]

The news of Wolfe's victory and death was received in London with mixed feelings. While sharing in the general rejoicing, many believed that victory had been extravagantly bought. On 27th October Lady Hervey wrote to her sailor son, Augustus,[211] 'The K—— told Mr. Pitt publicly at his levée, the day the news came of taking Quebec, "All your plans have succeeded". Quebec is certainly a great acquisition, but 'tis gold bought too dear. Woolfe is an irreparable loss, such an head, such an heart, such a temper and such an arm are not easily to be found again. He was an excellent scholar, knew all the advantages of the Roman Phalanx and Grecian Discipline, had a memory that made all the past present to him and he could therefore profit by all the battles fought and sieges laid either by ancients or moderns: with all these public virtues he had also all private ones, was the most tender, most dutiful son in the world and the most humane benevolent master: he has left a young lady to whom he was to have been married at his return inconsolable—'tis a sister of Sir James Lowther's. His poor mother does not feel his loss, she has been insensible since she heard the certain news of his death—but what must that first feeling have been to have worked such an effect so immediately, poor, poor, miserable woman. I pity her from my soul. . . .'

On 16th November the *Royal William* anchored at Spithead and the next morning Wolfe's body was lowered into a barge and rowed ashore at Portsmouth escorted by twelve ships' boats. To the solemn music of minute guns and muffled bells the body was handed over to a regiment of Invalids and a company of artillery which escorted the hearse through streets lined by thousands of silent spectators to the outskirts of the city. From there the hearse was driven slowly to Blackheath without escort and the coffin laid in the hall of the Wolfes' house, where it remained, covered by its velvet pall and heaped with laurel wreaths, until the 20th when Wolfe's body was at last laid beside that of his father in the family vault at St. Alfege's, Greenwich.

Wolfe's possessions had been sorted by Captain Bell, his aide-de-camp, who had accompanied the body to England in the *Royal William*, and these were now delivered to Blackheath. Among them was Wolfe's will. Anticipating that by the time of his death he would have inherited from his father, Wolfe had made a number of generous bequests to his friends including a thousand pounds each to Colonels Oughton, Carleton, Howe, and Warde, and a hundred guineas each to Barré, Delaune, Hervey Smyth, Bell, Leslie and Caldwell. His miniature of Katherine Lowther was to be set in jewels to the value of five hundred guineas and returned to her. In a codicil added in September he had left a thousand pounds each to his uncle, Major Walter Wolfe, and his cousin Edward Goldsmith. After various bequests of his plate to Saunders, camp equipment to Monckton, books and papers to Carleton, and clothing and money to François, Ambrose, and his other servants, the remainder of his property was left to his mother 'entirely at her disposal'. Altogether his bequests amounted to more than £7,000. Wolfe's father had been generous in his gifts and allowances to his sons and had certainly given Wolfe the impression that he was a man of considerable means, but in his will he had left his wife a life interest in his estate, which was not large. Wolfe's own assets were negligible and it was painfully clear that the major bequests in his will could not be found from his estate. The gifts to his servants were evidently made, and Mrs. Wolfe herself paid for the setting of Katherine Lowther's miniature in diamonds. The remainder of the legacies were included by Mrs. Wolfe in her own will. Remembering the enormous sums of money voted by Parliament to the commanding generals in comparable victories, it is curious that Wolfe received only the thanks of the House and a monument in Westminster Abbey.

More curious still was the behaviour of the Government to Wolfe's mother. Realizing that the bequests in her son's will far exceeded his assets, Mrs. Wolfe sought a method of obtaining some at least of the money. She embarked on a lengthy correspondence with the War Office in an attempt to prove that Wolfe was entitled to the extra pay of ten pounds a day due to commanders-in-chief from the period of his commission to the date of his death, a sum of nearly £2,500. This submission was rejected successively by Barrington and by Charles Townshend, brother of Wolfe's brigadier, who succeeded him as Secretary at War, on the ground that Amherst was commander-in-chief in America and that Wolfe's command was subordinate. There can be no doubt that technically the War Office was right. Whether the Duke of Newcastle was also technically right to refuse Mrs. Wolfe's appeal for a pension to assist her in the fulfilment of her son's bequests is less easily decided. Finally in desperation, and on the advice of her friends, Lord Shelburne and Sir Robert Rich, Mrs. Wolfe addressed a memorial to George III. Her answer, stolidly accurate and unsympathetic, from Welbore Ellis, Townshend's successor at the War Office, arrived only a few months before her death on 26th September 1764. It is reasonable to add that Barrington's acceptance of Mrs. Wolfe's contention would have set a precedent for the payment of many other similar claims, but there was no ground but lickpenny parsimony for refusing a special grant in memory of a general who, had he lived to gather the harvest of his endeavours, must certainly have received a special vote of money from Parliament. George II would not have been so forgetful of his services. Better by far would it have been to have given Mrs. Wolfe the money voted by Parliament for the monument in Westminster Abbey than to have squandered it on Wilton's pretentious edifice unveiled in 1773.

Public acclaim of Wolfe as conqueror of Quebec was not constrained by any doubt of his responsibility for the victory. There was, however, a small but influential party which considered that the glory should be Townshend's. As early as 30th October Horace Walpole had written that Townshend's mother had 'covered herself with more laurel leaves than were heaped on the children in the wood'. This was probably fair comment. Townshend's dispatch had caused resentment on its publication in

England by its curt dismissal of Wolfe's death and failure to pay tribute to his responsibility for victory, but there was never any active attempt by Townshend to claim the victory for himself. He merely accepted with becoming gratitude, and in discreet silence, the official thanks of the nation. Had he taken that opportunity to make it clear that he accepted them on behalf of his dead commander-in-chief and all those who had served with him at Quebec the affair might have ended there; but he did not, and, with the publication by an unknown author of *A letter to an Honourable Brigadier-General* and the refutation issued shortly afterwards, the rivalry between the Townshend and Wolfe factions became public scandal.

Wolfe had been loved and respected by his army. Letters from his men recounting his death at Quebec are filled with expressions of sincere grief. Townshend's behaviour to him had not passed unnoticed and it had aroused great indignation. Reports of this reaching England might have been suppressed but for the determination of Townshend's family and friends to bask in reflected glory. He thus fell a victim to the demands of a self-seeking few who sought to create a live conqueror from the laurels of a dead hero. The *Letter to an Honourable Brigadier-General*, a scurrilous and unjust attack by an anonymous author, circulated publicly the charges of cowardice and disloyalty until then only whispered by those who had returned from Quebec. Townshend suspected Lord Albemarle to be the author and challenged him to a duel; but friends of both parties intervened and prevented a meeting. The letter of refutation, probably written by Charles Townshend, failed to answer the charges or satisfy public opinion. The rancour against Townshend created by this bitter controversy has lasted to the present day. Wolfe's biographers, like well-trained circus dogs following each other through a familiar hoop, have repeated the charge that Townshend returned to England intent on robbing Wolfe of his laurels and gathering them for himself. There is no evidence whatever to support this. Mahon tells the story in his biography of Murray, asserting that the 'same malicious tongues which commenced the intrigue against Townshend also involved Murray'. Recent research shows that there was good reason for doing so. A series of letters passing between Townshend, Murray, and Amherst as late as 1774 cast a revealing light on the true feelings of two of Wolfe's brigadiers.

Wolfe, it will be remembered, had been threatened with an inquiry into his conduct of the Quebec campaign. In Bell's copy of Wolfe's journal the following note is added: 'The Journal destroyed by the Gen¹. on board the Neptune contained a careful account of the Officers' ignoble conduct towards him in case of a Parliamentary enquiry.' That the last pages of Wolfe's journal contained evidence to the discredit of his subordinate commanders must be beyond doubt. Soon after his death rumours of their disloyalty and antagonism to his final plan began to circulate in his army. On 5th October 1759 Murray wrote to Townshend,[212] 'I shall look for the letter you mention, take a copy of it, and deposit the original with you. Since so black a lye was propagated I think myself very happy, that you will be on the spot to contradict whatever Ignorance or Faction may suggest. I have no copy of the paper I sent by you to Gen¹. Wolfe concerning his Scheme of landing betwixt point au Tremble and St. Augustin, but the publick orders are a sufficient proof of his intention to do it, and likewise of the suddenness of the thought of landing where we did. Indeed his orders through out the campaign shews little stability, stratagem, or fixt resolution; I wish his friends had not been so much our Enemys, his memory would probably have been dearer to his Country than now it can be, we are acting on the defensive, you may have the Execution of the plan, and I am well persuaded you will manage it with as much tenderness to the memory of the poor Gen¹. as the nature of things will admit of.' Two days later Townshend thought it necessary to write to Amherst:[213] 'Before I take my leave I must beg one favour of you; which is: should any Idle & malicious Reports reach your Ears concerning any Negative the Brigadiers gave to Poor Mr Wolfe's carrying the operations above the Town, or to his making the Descent at Foulon which has proved so successful; that you will not believe any such thing. . . . If we receive as little justice in your army as I'm told we have met with from some in this, Brigadier Monckton has the Papers which will explain our Conduct ready to lay before you tho' it is a subject we both wish that no more may be said upon.'

This prudent wish was not shared by Murray. The last evidence relating to this deplorable intrigue is found in correspondence between Murray, Townshend, and Amherst written in 1774. They do much to obliterate the discredit associated with Townshend, and give the clearest possible picture of the scheming, mean and obdurate malice of Murray.[214]

Murray to Townshend, 25th October 1774.

'... I think it right to communicate the enclosed paper. It may not be very interesting to you tho' a very strong proof that the alacrity you showed the 13th September, 1759, at Quebec, contributed greatly to the success of the day: As I have never yet seen a true account of our American Campaigns, I am attempting to throw the Events of three of them together, in this attempt I thought it necessary to know the Truth of what was reported relative to Coll. Barré's assertions. . . .'

The enclosure[215] related to a story that Barré, while dining with the historian, Hume, at the table of a nobleman in France, had told how on 13th September 1759, after the first ascent of the cliffs, Wolfe had sent him to countermand the orders to disembark the rest of the troops, saying that there were enough already landed to be sacrificed; but that he had deliberately ignored this order and 'hurried the remainder of the Troops on shore by which the victory was gained'. When questioned by Caldwell, who had been his assistant Quartermaster-General at Quebec, Barré had hotly denied this story and had said that 'after the first Debarkation had taken place, and that just as Mr. Wolfe had got on the hights, he order'd him to return to the Boats, & stop them a little 'till he had an Opportunity of knowing the Ennermys Strength, there, and whether they might not be in numbers sufficient to prevent his establishing himself; That he accordingly went to the Shore, and found but very few Boats there, the remainder being along side the transports that had fallen down the River, and actually full of troops, ready to come on shore. That he, Col. Barré, knowing how much General Wolfe was desirous to bring the Ennemy to an engagement, & thinking from the knowledge he had of Mr. Wolfe's Intentions, that the orders he had received were in consequence of his not expecting the Troops could be got landed so soon, took the Liberty seeing Things thus situated, not to deliver the Orders . . . & Reported it to Gen¹. Wolfe, who

324

was much pleased to find himself established on Shore with his Army sooner than he expected. Col. Barré further Remarks that it was notorious to every Body, who had any the least knowledge of Mr. Wolfe's wishes, and Intentions, that Campaign that they were most ardently bent on bringing the Enemy to an Action, on any Thing like equal terms, & that his ordering him to stop the boats, could be only a temporary Measure 'till he learnt the Ennemy's Force in the Neighbourhood of the landing Place.'

To anyone but Murray, Townshend's reply would have been sufficient to deter him from pressing the matter further.

'You have,' Townshend wrote on 29th October, 'communicated your intentions so frankly and fully to me . . . that I feel I ought not to be under any reserve to you, upon the occasion.

The orders which Colonel Barré appears by that Letter you have enclosed, to have given, at that critical time, seem to me, *tho' not* strictly correspondent with those of Mr. Wolfe, to have sprung from a Zeal for the Service, and from affection for the Success of his General;—they corresponded with the general view of his Chief, tho' not with his precise words, at the Moment he doubted (and with great reason) of the Success of the Enterprise—The General's view was to support the experiment, if he found it practicable:—the Colonel, from the State of things on the Beach, found it more so than the *General advanced* could determine; and therefore in a state of great responsibility he seconded the efforts of Mr. Wolfe; as every one else did to the best of their abilities, on that important day. . . . You must recollect, besides Sir, the doubts the conducting Naval Officer had, of bringing us in that rapid current to our proper Landing;—which must have rendered Mr. Wolfe's calculations still more uncertain; but which Mr. Barré found, I suppose, fortunately beyond expectation. . . .

. . . I own I could wish . . . that this letter were made no matter of public discussion. Moreover the public admire Mr. Wolfe, for many eminent qualities, and revere his Memory; and therefore any distinction that may be made, upon the Merits of a Field, where he fought, and died, will be but ill-received and deemed an irreverence to a Tomb, where it is to be wished, the Laurels may ever sprout.

I have lived long enough to see people not only divided in

their opinions upon those who served there; but even *upon the utility of the Service itself*, and of that important acquisition: And as my love of fame has in this capricious Age (when Individuals, nay Kings, and Nations, are occasionally proscribed) expired sooner than some other passions, which might well have faded earlier, with a better grace, I will confess to you, that if the Expedition of Quebec, lay upon my Table, with that of Tanjour, (which I certainly know less of) I should naturally be led to take up the latter, the first.'

Four days later Townshend wrote to Amherst to warn him of Murray's intended attack on Wolfe's reputation. He ends his letter,[216] 'In what light Mr. Murray will receive my opinion, I do not know, but I thought his unsollicited Communication of the Materials authorised me to endeavour to prevent a publication of a circumstance productive in my opinion of more personality, than utility to the public—& at a time when it will be much more difficult to discover who will preserve America than who conquer'd Canada.'

Murray's reply was written on 5th November. It reveals not only his inflexible animosity but also his astonishing failure to grasp the first essentials of the strategy required for victory:[217]

'Your Lordship has been much further upon Major Calldwell's letter than I expected; it is needless for me to Say more on that Subject, Nothing shall deter me from publishing to the World, every matter of fact relative to the Campaigns I have mentioned. Men will think differently, being actuated *by different Motives*, on all Subjects: Truth must prevail at last.

It does not appear to me that it ever was Mr. Wolfe's intention to bring the Enemy to a general Action; His Rejection of landing above the Town, by means of the Redans, before our Ships passed the place; His refusing to Execute Mr. Pallisiers plan of assaulting Quebec, His absurd visionary, attack of the Enemy's Lines at Beauport; and at last his desertion of the Sensible, well conserted, Enterprise to land at the point Au Tremble, where without opposition, with his whole Army, and Artillery, he might have taken Post, and entrenched himself betwixt the Enemy and their Provisions, with the almost impossible, tho' successful attempt

326

thanks to Providence at the Foulon, and many many &cs. are evident proof to me that my Conjecture is well founded.

God forbid my Lord that I should interrupt your Amusements: Tanjoure you may quickly Enjoy, while I am knocking my obstinate Scotch head, against the Admiration, and Reverence of the English Mob for Mr. Wolfe's memory.'

It is difficult to believe, and harder still to understand, Murray's unremitting malice fifteen years after the capture of Quebec. He had become a lieutenant-general and had been for three years Governor of Canada. In 1759 he had resigned his commission and, but for Wolfe's intervention, his career would have ended before the campaign for Quebec had begun. There is no evidence that Wolfe had at any time given him cause for such hatred, and it is impossible to attribute his extraordinary behaviour to anything but boundless ambition and a frustrated desire for glory. Townshend, it appears, was guilty only of silence.

Of Wolfe's other officers, Monckton became a lieutenant-general and Governor of Portsmouth; Townshend, a field-marshal and first Marquis; and Carleton, a general, first Baron Dorchester, and Governor of Quebec. Barré lost an eye at Quebec but remained with the Army, becoming a colonel and, in 1772, Treasurer to the Navy.

It would be idle to speculate to what heights Wolfe himself might have risen had he lived, for it is impossible to know how his military capabilities would have developed. Great achievement requires great endeavour and great opportunity, and it may justly be said that Wolfe owed much to the genius of Pitt, and to the ignorance and lethargy of his contemporaries; but it is well to remember that while young naval commanders were trained under Anson, one of the ablest men ever to hold office at the Admiralty, the Army had no comparable leader to follow. Wolfe learnt his profession from experience and from a meticulous study of military history, and the thoroughness of his training methods was unexampled in England. Had he lived he might have created for the Army what Anson built for the Navy, a nucleus of highly trained, courageous, and energetic young officers who would, in their turn, train commanders to succeed them. It was then generally supposed—as it has been in more recent times—that experience in war was all the training needed for a soldier, and it was not until the turn of the century that a commander was found, in Sir John Moore, to lay down for the Army the principles of training it so clearly needed.

Wolfe's death, following so soon that of the eldest of the three brilliant Howe brothers, robbed the Army of the last of its young commanders of promise. There was no one to take their place. The capture of Quebec, by striking at the roots of French domination in America, laid the foundation for the Declaration of Independence; Wolfe's death in the battle ensured that there was no British general of comparable ability to face Washington. Had Wolfe failed at Quebec in 1759, Canada and the United States of America as we know them today might never have come into being.

These issues lie beyond the measure of Wolfe's life and achievement. His claim to greatness lies in the success of a single campaign in which he was killed. He had never before commanded an army in the field. But if greatness lies in the ability to surmount all obstacles, then Wolfe was great indeed. Throughout his life he fought against continuous ill-health and pain, and the growth of a deadly disease; in the campaign for Quebec he overcame incredible difficulties and outwitted one of the most skilful and experienced French generals of his time. His reward was a great victory. He would have wanted no other.

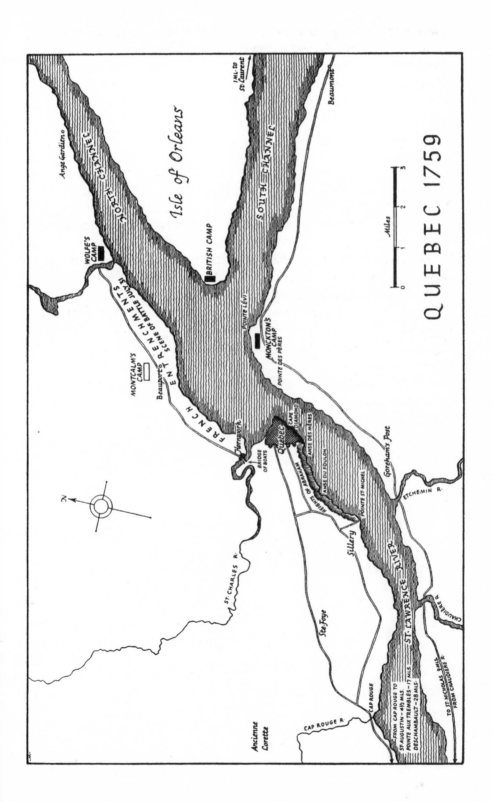

QUEBEC 1759

Miles
0   1   2   3

N

Ange Gardien

NORTH CHANNEL

WOLFE'S CAMP

ENTRENCHMENTS

MONTCALM'S CAMP

Beauport

FRENCH

SCENE OF BATTLE JULY 31

Hornwork

BRIDGE OF BOATS

ST. CHARLES R.

Isle of Orleans

BRITISH CAMP

POINTE LÉVI

MONCKTON'S CAMP

POINTE DES PÈRES

SOUTH CHANNEL

1 MI. to St. Laurent

Beaumont

CAPE DIAMOND

QUEBEC

ANSE DES MÈRES

ANSE DU FOULON

HEIGHTS OF ABRAHAM

POINTE ST. MICHEL

Sillery

Ste. Foye

CAP ROUGE

CAP ROUGE R.

Ancienne Lorette

Gorcham's Post

ETCHEMIN R.

ST. LAWRENCE RIVER

CHAUDIÈRE R.

FROM CAP ROUGE TO
ST. AUGUSTIN – 4½ MLS.
POINTE AUX TREMBLES – 17 MLS.
DESCHAMBAULT – 28 MLS.

TO ST. NICHOLAS 9 MLS.
FROM CHAUDIÈRE R.

APPENDIX I

Notes and References

General

Unless otherwise specified, the quotations in the text from Wolfe's letters are taken from the following sources:

1. MS. Letters from Wolfe to his parents and to his brother Edward, in the possession of Major J. R. O'B. Warde, Squerryes Court, Westerham.
2. MS. Letters to William Rickson in the National Library of Scotland.
3. Letters to Lord George Sackville in the Sackville Papers, Historic Manuscripts Commission Ninth Report, Appendix to Part III.

In this Appendix reference is made to Wolfe's letters only where the date has not been made clear in the text or where the source is not one of those listed above. For all references I have followed the accepted custom of giving the title of the book in full the first time and citing the author's name or an abbreviated title thereafter.

Chapter I CHILDHOOD: WESTERHAM AND GREENWICH

1. Snail tea recipe. Mrs. Wolfe's MS. recipe book at Squerryes Court.
2. Pitt's speech 8 March 1739. *Parliamentary History*, Vol. X.
3. Pitt's speech 8 March 1739. *Parliamentary History*, Vol. X.
4. Cathcart to Newcastle. Major-General R. H. Mahon: *Life of General The Hon. James Murray*, 1921.
5. Tobias Smollett: *Roderick Random*.
6. Coxe: *Memoirs of Sir Robert Walpole*, 1816, Vol. IV, p. 202.

Chapter I (cont.)

7. Wolfe to William Weston. MS. letter, McCord Museum, McGill University, Montreal.

Chapter II ACTIVE SERVICE IN FLANDERS

8. Sir John Fortescue: *History of the British Army*, Vol. II, p. 28.
9. *Private Correspondence of Chesterfield and Newcastle*, 1744–6. Ed. by Sir R. Lodge, 1930.
10. *The Gentleman's Magazine,* 1742.
11. Pitt's speech 10 Dec. 1742. *Gent. Mag.* Feb. 1744.
12. 12 Sept. 1742.
13. 12 Sept. 1742.
14. Stair to Carteret 9 Feb. 1743. Fortescue.
15. Lt.-Col. C. V. F. Townshend: *The Military Life of Field-Marshal George First Marquess Townshend*, 1901.
16. *Letters of Horace Walpole*, Ed. by Mrs. Paget Toynbee, 1903–5. Walpole to Mann, 16 Aug. 1744.
17. 21 Aug. 1743 (dated 1st Sept. N.S.)
18. 21 March 1744.
19. Carteret to Wade, 13 and 17 July, 1744.
20. 18 Oct. 1744.

Chapter III THE 'FORTY-FIVE'

21. Pitt's speech 1 December 1743. John Almon: *Anecdotes of the Life of William Pitt*, 1793, Vol. I, p. 144.
22. Pitt's speech 10 Dec. 1744. *Gent. Mag.* 1744.
23. *Walpole Letters*, Walpole to Mann, 27 Sept. 1745.
24. *Historic Manuscripts Commission*, 14th Report. Appendix to Part IX.
25. MS. Letter McCord Museum.
26. 20 Jan. 1746. Beckles Willson: *The Life and Letters of James Wolfe*, 1909, p. 56.
27. J. T. Findlay: *Wolfe in Scotland*, 1928.
28. H.M.C. 14th Report, Appx. to Pt. IX. Sir Everard Fawkener (Secretary to Cumberland) to Robert Trevor (H.B.M. Minister Plenipotentiary to the Hague).
29. *The Genealogist*, 1883, Vol. VII, pp. 225–9.

Chapter III (cont.)

30. Willson, p. 65.
31. *H.M.C.* 14th Report, Appx. to Pt. IX. Edward Weston to Robert Trevor.
32. *Walpole Letters.*
33. Allanton story. *Anti-Jacobin Review*, Vol. XIII, p. 125.
34. 19 May 1746. Willson, p. 68.
35. *Correspondence of John, Fourth Duke of Bedford 1842–6*, Vol. I, p. 123.

Chapter IV LAFFELDT

36. 17 Sept. 1751.
37. *Walpole Letters.*
38. *Walpole Letters.*
39. 17 Apr. 1748.
40. *The Grenville Papers*, 1852, Vol. I, p. 73.
41. *Walpole Letters*, 3 May 1749.
42. Aug. 1748.
43. 10 Nov. 1748.

Chapter V SCOTLAND: COMMAND OF A REGIMENT

44. *Walpole Letters.* To Horace Mann, 5 May 1747.
45. 2 Apr. 1749.
46. 2 Apr. 1749.
47. 2 Aug. 1749.
48. 13 Aug. 1749.
49. MS. letter. McCord Museum. MS. 1218.
50. 6 Feb. 1750.
51. 17 Sept. 1751.
52. 16 Jan. 1750.
53. 6 Feb. 1750.
54. 19 Feb. 1750.
55. 13 Aug. 1750.

Chapter VI 'PASSION AND DISAPPOINTMENT'

56. 23 Sept. 1750.
57. 9 June 1751.
58. 19 July 1751.

Chapter VI (cont.)

59.   9 June 1751.
60.   9 June 1751.
61.   12 Aug. 1751.
62.   17 Sept. 1751.
63.   Oct. 1751.

Chapter VII   SCOTLAND: INVERNESS

64.   3 Oct. 1751.
65.   6 Nov. 1751.
66.   1 Feb. 1752.
67.   12 Jan. 1752.
68.   1 Feb. 1752.
69.   6 March 1752.
70.   6 Nov. 1751.
71.   20 March 1752.
72.   16 May 1752.

Chapter VIII   ON LEAVE IN PARIS

73.   26 June 1752.
74.   13 July 1752.
75.   25 Nov. 1752.
76.   19 Jan. 1753.
77.   19 Jan. 1753.
78.   13 Feb. 1753.
79.   29 Jan. 1753.
80.   22 Apr. 1753.

Chapter IX   A MOVE SOUTH

81.   *Old Berkshire Memories,* 1827.
82.   19 Nov. 1753.

Chapter X   RIVALRIES IN AMERICA

83.   British Museum Additional Manuscripts 32836. Newcastle
      to Albemarle, 24 May 1751.
84.   B.M. Add. MSS. 32851. Newcastle to Albemarle, 10 Oct.
      1754.

Chapter XI WAR WITH FRANCE

85. MS. Letter, 15 Sept. 1755. McCord Museum MS. 1290.
86. B.M. Add. MSS. 32860–4.
87. B.M. Add. MSS. 32865.
88. 19 July 1756. B.M. Add. MSS. 32866.
89. Horace Walpole: *Memoirs of the Reign of George II*, 2nd Ed. 1847.
90. Voltaire: *Candide*, Ch. 23.
91. Walpole: *George II*.
92. 18 July 1756. Willson.
93. Undated. Willson.
94. A War Office Minute dated 25 August provided for the addition of second battalions of 780 men.
95. *Scots Magazine*, May, 1756.

Chapter XII THE ROCHEFORT EXPEDITION

96. Walpole: *George II*.
97. *Bedford Correspondence*, Vol. II, p. 259.
98. Walpole: *George II*.
99. B.M. Add. MSS. 6815.
100. B.M. Add. MSS. 6815.
101. B.M. Add. MSS. 32866.
102. Walpole: *George II*.
103. B.M. Add. MSS. 32872.
104. Walpole: *George II*.
105. 23 Sept. 1757.
106. Willson.
107. Willson.

Chapter XIII DESIGN FOR CONQUEST IN AMERICA

108. MS. Letters in the possession of the Marquis of Lansdowne, Bowood, Wiltshire.
109. *Grenville Papers*, Vol. I, p. 230.
110. B.M. Add. MSS. 32876.
111. There is in the Public Archives of Canada, in Ottawa, an unpublished letter from Wolfe to his friend, Captain Parr, referring to the same incident: 'You have heard by this of our sudden Orders for North America of which

Chapter XIII (*cont.*)

> I was appriz'd at Exeter a fortnight ago & cover'd the distance pretty fast (170 miles in 20 Hours) stumbling in the darkness over Salisbury Plain. We won't speak of rewards for this heroick Achievement. . . .'

112. Walpole: *George II.*
113. Willson.
114. Willson.

Chapter XIV LOUISBOURG

115. *An Authentic Account of the Reduction of Louisbourg in June and July 1758 by a SPECTATOR*, London, 1758.
116. *H.M.C.* IX. Appx. to Pt. III (Stopford-Sackville Papers)
117. Waldo to Pitt, 7 Nov. 1757, Public Records Office, P.A.C. C.O. 5/52.
118. For further information see 'The Assault Landing at Louisbourg, 1758', an excellent article by J. Mackay Hitsman with C. C. J. Bond in the *Canadian Historical Review*, XXXV, No. 4, December 1954.
119. *H.M.C.* IX Appx. to Pt. III.
120. *An Authentic Account*, etc.
121. P.R.O. C.O. 5/213 and Canadian Archives. M.S. Group 18 N.16(2).
122. Captain John Knox: *Historical Journal of the Campaigns in North America . . . 1757–60*, 1769.
123. Willson.
124. *An Authentic Account*, etc.
125. A number of modern writers have stated that it was the *Célèbre* which was set on fire, but contemporary accounts do not bear them out.

Chapter XV IN THE GULF OF ST. LAWRENCE

126. Willson.
127. Canadian Archives. MS. Group 18, Northcliffe Collection M 1(10). *Journal of the Siege of Louisbourg.*
128. *H.M.C.* IX Appx. to Pt. III.
129. Canadian Archives. MS. Group 18. Amherst Papers (20). *Diaries 1756-63.*

Chapter XV (cont.)

130. H.M.C. IX Appx. to Pt. III.
131. Canadian Archives. MS. Group 18 N 3(24). Bell's *Journal of the Gaspée Expedition* 1758.

Chapter XVI ECCENTRIC ATTACKS IN EUROPE

132. Sir Julian Corbett: *England in the Seven Years' War*, 1907.
133. Canadian Archives. MS. Group 18. Amherst Papers (4).

Chapter XVII THE GREAT OPPORTUNITY

134. B.M. Add. MSS. 32882.
135. B.M. Add. MSS. 32883. Newcastle to Hardwicke.
136. Willson.
137. *Memoirs of Sir James Campbell of Ardkinglass.*
138. Willson.
139. Corbett, Vol. I, p. 403.
140. H.M.C. Townshend Papers.
141. Willson.
142. Willson.

Chapter XVIII QUEBEC: UNEXPECTED DIFFICULTIES

143. P.R.O., S.P. Colonial (America & West Indies) 51. 13 Feb. 1759.
144. MS. letter. McCord Museum. MS. 1431.
145. Willson.
146. P.R.O. W.O. 34/46B.
147. P.R.O. W.O. 34/46B.
148. Willson.
149. Knox. 25 May 1759.
150. Knox. 6 June 1759.

Chapter XIX QUEBEC: THE FRENCH ADMINISTRATION

151. Doughty, Vol. V, p. 62.
152. P.R.O. W.O. 1/1.

Chapter XX QUEBEC: NAVIGATION OF THE ST. LAWRENCE

153. C. V. Townshend 158.

Chapter XX (cont.)

154. Canadian Archives. MS. Group 18. Amherst Papers (54).
155. Canadian Archives. MS. Group 18. Northcliffe Collection, Townshend Papers (9), and McCord MS. 1423.

Chapter XXI   QUEBEC: RECONNAISSANCE

156. Wolfe's Journal. Canadian Archives. MS. Group 18. Northcliffe Collection 3 (24).
157. C. V. Townshend.
158. Canadian Archives MS. Group 18. Northcliffe Collection, (Monckton Papers) 1 (22).
159. Monckton Papers (22).
160. Bell's Journal. Canadian Archives, Northcliffe Collection, 3 (24).
161. Monckton Papers (22).
162. Monckton Papers (22).
163. Canadian Archives. MS. Group 18. Bourlamaque Papers.
164. Canadian Archives. MS. Group 18. Townshend Papers (9).
165. MS. Letter in possession of Colonel R. Campbell Preston, Ardchattan Priory, Connel, Argyll.
166. Monckton Papers (22).
167. Monckton Papers (22).

Chapter XXII   QUEBEC: FAILURE AT MONTMORENCY

168. Monckton Papers (29).
169. Doughty. Vol. V, p. 65.
170. Canadian Archives. MS. Group 18. Military 15 (2).
171. Bourlamaque Papers.
172. Amherst Papers (20).
173. Doughty, Vol. V, p. 65.
174. Monckton Papers (22).
175. Amherst eventually dispatched Ensign Hutchings of the Rangers on 6th August (Amherst Papers, 21). Hutchings reached Wolfe's army and returned on 9th October with Major Stobo having left Wolfe more than a month earlier. On their return journey by sea their sloop had been boarded by pirates and Stobo had thrown all Wolfe's dispatches to Amherst into the sea. Amherst

Chapter XXII (*cont.*)

> writes, 'I am not a whit the wiser except that he says
> M. Gen¹. Wolfe had got with his allmost whole Army
> above the Town, & he thinks he will not take it.'

Chapter XXIII   QUEBEC: CONSULTATION WITH THE BRIGADIERS
176. Monckton Papers (22).
177. Monckton Papers (22).
178. Monckton Papers (22).
179. Monckton Papers (22).
180. Monckton Papers (22).
181. Townshend Papers (9).
182. Monckton Papers (22).
183. Monckton Papers (22).
184. Townshend Papers (1).
185. P.R.O. Chatham Papers (50). (Original draft in Townshend
     Papers (11).) Copy in B.M. Add. MSS. 32895, but this is
     incomplete.
186. Willson.

Chapter XXIV   QUEBEC: IN THE UPPER RIVER
187. Willson.
188. P.R.O. C.O. 5/51.
189. Bougainville Papers.
190. C. V. Townshend.
191. Canadian Archives.

Chapter XXV   QUEBEC: PRELUDE TO BATTLE
192. Townshend Papers (9).
193. G. S. Kimball, *Correspondence of William Pitt*, 1906, p. 610.
194. Willson.
195. Canadian Archives. MS. Group 18. MS. Letter Book of
     Captain Henry Pringle.
196. Townshend Papers (9).
197. Townshend Papers (9).
198. Canadian Archives. MS. Group 18, Bougainville Papers.
199. Townshend Papers (12).
200. Townshend Papers (1).

Chapter XXV (cont.)

201. Townshend Papers (1).
202. Bougainville Papers.
203. Bougainville Papers.
204. Bougainville Papers.
205. The story of the repetition of Gray's *Elegy* has been re-peated in various forms in almost every account of the Quebec campaign, though a number of modern writers have questioned its authenticity. All versions are based on one of three sources—Professor John Playfair's account of the life of John Robison read to the Royal Society of Edinburgh; a letter from William Wallace Currie written in 1804; and a letter from Sir Walter Scott to Robert Southey dated 1830. These three accounts are themselves founded on their writers' varying memories of John Robison's verbal testimony.

Robison was tutor to Admiral Knowles's son and accompanied him on the Quebec expedition with the honorary rating of midshipman. He was present in one of the boats very close to Wolfe's on the night before the final assault. Later he became Professor of Natural Philosophy at Edinburgh University. The earliest written account of his story appears in William Currie's letter to his father in 1804 (reprinted in his *Memoir of the Life, Writings, and Correspondence of James Currie*). Currie was then a student at Edinburgh University and gives, in his letter, a detailed account of Professor Robison's conversation one night at dinner when this story was told. When Playfair recounted his version, Robison had been dead for ten years, and Scott's version appeared fifteen years after that. In short, Currie's account appears far the most likely to be reliable. That Wolfe's words, as they are repeated by Currie, refer to taking Quebec 'tomorrow' is easily explained by the fact that the men entered the boats well before midnight on the 12th.

Wolfe's own copy of Gray's *Elegy*, which was found some forty years ago, contains brief annotations in his own hand which bear witness to his familiarity with the poem. That he would have recited it himself on such an

Chapter XXV (cont.)

occasion seems unlikely, but its repetition in his hearing by another officer would certainly have aroused his interest and comment.

Chapter XXVI   QUEBEC: 'THE INEVITABLE HOUR'

206.   Knox. This is also confirmed by Foligny.
207.   Knox.

Chapter XXVII   'IMPUTE TO THESE THE FAULT'

208.   Walpole Letters.
209.   MS. Letter in the possession of Major J. R. O'B. Warde.
210.   *A New Military Dictionary or The Field of War* by a Military Gentleman, London, 1760.
211.   *Augustus Hervey's Journal,* Ed. David Erskine.
212.   Townshend Papers.
213.   Amherst Papers (15).
214.   Amherst Papers (15).
215.   Amherst Papers (15).
216.   Amherst Papers (15).
217.   Amherst Papers (15).

APPENDIX II

Wolfe Portraiture

Wolfe's sudden fame and heroic death at Quebec created an unusual public demand for his portraits which has been undiminished by the passing of two centuries. It has been satisfied to some extent by the production of a number of posthumous portraits—most of them by artists who had obviously never seen him—and, more recently, by the 'discovery' of many more.

Of all the supposed portraits of James Wolfe, only three are likely to have been painted during his lifetime: the oil painting of Wolfe as a boy (facing p. 48) has apparently been in the possession of the Warde family since it was painted, and there seems to be no reason to suppose that it was not painted from life; the Townshend watercolour (frontispiece) was probably painted at Quebec, where the caricatures were drawn, and as a portrait by Wolfe's most notorious personal enemy (who was also noted for his draughtsmanship) for one of his closest friends, it is perhaps the best likeness in existence; the famous Highmore portrait (facing p. 80) was handed down through succeeding generations of the Rev. Samuel Swinden's descendants and may have been commissioned when Wolfe was with the 20th Regiment, but it bears such a striking resemblance to the Warde family's portrait that it is at least possible that it was commissioned after Wolfe's death and the likeness taken from the earlier portrait.

In addition, there are several sketches, notably by Hervey Smyth and Delaune, and the Townshend caricatures, which are valuable because they were drawn by men who knew their subject intimately. Of the rest of the portraits, which include work by Gainsborough, Romney, Ramsay, and West, none can be described with certainty as contemporary, and many of them bear as little resemblance to the authenticated portraits as they do to each other.

A detailed study of this difficult subject has recently been completed by Mr. J. F. Kerslake, Assistant Keeper of the National Portrait Gallery, and his conclusions are to be published under the title *Wolfe: portraiture and genealogy*. I am indebted to him for his expert advice.

APPENDIX III

Letter from Henry Browne

Letter from Henry Browne to his father, 17 November 1759.

I am indebted to Lord Kilmaine for drawing my attention to a previously unpublished letter from Lieutenant Henry Browne to his father, John Browne (later Earl of Altamont), which gives a vivid contemporary account of Wolfe's death. The letter was, unfortunately, discovered too late to be included in the main narrative, and the relevant extracts are, therefore, published by kind permission of the owner, Sir George Mahon, Bt., in this Appendix.

From Henry Browne, Lieutenant the 22nd Regiment and the Louisbourg Grenadiers, to his father, John Browne, dated 'Louisbourg November the 17th 1759':

Dr Father,

I writ a letter to my Dr Mother the 29th of last Month, two Days after my arrivall here from Quebeck, which I hope she has rec^d before now. I was in hopes upon my arrivall here to have heard from you, or some of my Bro^s but am sorry my Expectations were not answered. I take this Opportunity to write to you, which I believe is the last I shall have till Spring as the Ice hinders our having any communications with even our friends on ye Continent, except very rarely during the winter. . . . I writ you a letter the 19th September & another to my brother Peter the 1st October both which letters I hope have arrived safe. I gave you Dr Father as distinct an account in your's as I could of our Action of the 13th Sep^r & of the taking of the town of Quebeck. I must add a little to it by Informing you that I was

343

the Person who carry'd Genl Wolf off the field & that he was wounded as he stood within a foot of me. I thank God I escaped, tho' we have had out of our Comp^y which consisted but of 62 men at the beginning of the Engagement an officer & 4 men killed & 25 wounded—the Genl did our Comp^y & Bray's Regt the honour to head us in Person as he said he knew he could depend upon our behaviour, & I think we fully answered his expectations as did indeed the whole front Line consisting at most but of 2500 by beating according to their accounts 8000 men 2500 of which were regulars our second line consisting of 1500 men did not Engage nor fire a shot—the poor Genl after I had had his wounds dressed died in my arm's, before he died he thanked me for my care of him & asked me whether we had totally defeated the Enemy, upon my assuring him we had killed numbers taken a number of Officers & men Pris^{rs} he thanked God & begged I would let him die in Peace, he expired in a minuit afterwards without the least struggle or Groan. You can't imagine Dr Father the sorrow of every Individual in the Army for so great a Loss. Even the Soldiers dropt tears, who were but the minuet before driving their Bayonets through the French. I cant compare it to anything better than to a family in tears & sorrow which had just lost their father, their friend & their whole Dependance. We have not a word of any kind of news here, nor do we know anything how Genl Amherst has finished his Camp^n. . . .

I beg my sincere love & Duty to my Dr Mother & Love to all my Bro^s & Sisters & remain Dr Father

Your truly most Dutifull & Aff^{te} Son

Hen: Browne

BIBLIOGRAPHY

I. Manuscript Sources

British Museum

Carteret Papers	Add. MSS. 22511–22545
Hardwicke Papers	Add. MSS. 35349–36278
Intercepted Dispatches	Add. MSS. 32271–32288
Newcastle Papers	Add. MSS. 32679–33201

Lansdowne MSS. MSS. Letters in the possession of the Marquess of Lansdowne, Bowood, Calne, Wiltshire.

McCord Museum McGill University, Montreal.
MS. Letters.
Wolfe's Journal 10 June–7 August 1759.

National Library of Scotland Wolfe's letters to Rickson.

Public Archives of Canada, Ottawa MS. Group 18 (Pre-Conquest Papers).
especially Division G 2 Vaudreuil Papers
J 9 Memoirs of the Chevalier de la Pause (Photostat)
10 Memoirs of the Chevalier de Johnstone (Copy)
K 7 Montcalm Papers
8 de Lévis Papers. 11 Vols.
9 de Bourlamaque Papers
10 de Bougainville Papers (Transcript)
12 de la Grandville Papers (Photostat)
L 1 Colville Papers (Photostat)
2 Alexander Murray Papers
4 Amherst Papers. 77 Vols. (MSS., Transcripts & Photostat)

5   Wolfe Papers
7   Townshend (Fakenham) Papers
(Transcript)
M Northcliffe Collection
1   Monckton Papers
2   Townshend Papers
3   Separate Items (Esp. Item 24 Wolfe's
Journal)

Public Record Office Chatham MSS
Colonial Office Papers Esp. 5/51.
War Office Papers. Esp. 1/1 and 34/46B

Warde MSS. Letters in the possession of Maj. J. R. O'B.
Warde, Squerryes Court, Westerham, Kent.

II. PRINTED SOURCES

Biographical Material

Aylward, A. E. Wolfe: *The Pictorial Life of Wolfe.* Plymouth, 1924.

Bradley, A. G.: *Wolfe.* Macmillan, 1923

Casgrain, H. R.: *Wolfe and Montcalm (Makers of Canada).* 1905.

Findlay, J.T., *Wolfe in Scotland.* Longmans Green, 1928.

Parkman, Francis: *Wolfe and Montcalm.* 2 Vols. Boston, 1922.

Salmon, Edward: *General Wolfe.* Pitman, London, 1909.

Waugh, W. T.: *James Wolfe, Man and Soldier.* Macmillan, Canada,
1928.

Webster, J. C.: *Wolfe and the Artists.* Toronto, 1950.

Whitton, F. E.: *Wolfe and North America.* Benn, 1929.

Willson, Beckles: *The Life and Letters of James Wolfe.* Heinemann,
1909.

Wright, R.: *The Life of Major-General James Wolfe.* London, 1864.

General Material

Almon, John: *Anecdotes of the Life of William Pitt, Earl of Chatham,*
3 Vols., 1797.

Amherst, Field Marshal Jeffery, Baron: Journal Ed. J. C. Webster. Chicago, n.d.

Bedford: *Correspondence of John, fourth Duke of Bedford.* 3 Vols. 1842–6.

Blaikie, W. B.: *Itinerary of Prince Charles Edward Stuart, 1745–6.* Edinburgh, 1897.

Bland, H.: *Treatise on Military Discipline.* 1727.

Bradley, A. G.: *The Fight with France for North America.* Constable, 1905.

British Diplomatic Instructions 1689–1789, Vol. VII. France Pt. IV, 1745–1789. Ed. L. G. Wickham Legg. Camden Series Vol. XLIX. Royal Historical Society, 1934.

Cambridge Modern History, Vol. VII. The Old Regime 1713–63. C.U.P., 1957.

Casgrain, H. R.: *Guerre du Canada,* 1756–60. Quebec, 1891.

Chesterfield: *Private Correspondence of Chesterfield and Newcastle.* Ed. Sir R. Lodge. Royal Historical Society, 1930.

Clode, C. M.: *Military Forces of the Crown,* 2 Vols. 1869.

Corbett, Sir Julian S.: *England in the Seven Years' War.* Longmans, 1907.

Coxe, William: *Memoirs of Sir Robert Walpole.* 4 Vols., 1816.

Creswell, John: *General and Admirals.* Longmans, 1952.

Doughty, A. and Parmelee, G. W.: *The Siege of Quebec and the Battle of the Plains of Abraham.* 6 Vols. Quebec, 1901.

English Historical Documents, Vol. X. 1714–1783. Eyre & Spottiswoode, 1958.

Entinck, J.: *The General History of the Late War.* London, 1775.

Fortescue, Hon. J. W.: *History of the British Army*, Vols. I & II. Macmillan, 1899–1917.

George, M. D.: *London Life in the Eighteenth Century.* Kegan Paul, 1930.

Grenville: *The Grenville Papers.* Ed. W. J. Smith, 4 Vols. London, 1853.

Hervey: *Augustus Hervey's Journal.* Ed. David Erskine. William Kimber, 1953.

Historical Manuscripts Commission
                      esp. Ninth Report & Appx. Pt. III
                             Eleventh Report, Appx. Pt. IV
                             Fourteenth Report, Appx. Pt. IX

Ketton-Cremer, R. W.: *Thomas Gray*, C.U.P., 1955.

Kimball, G. S.: *Correspondence of William Pitt*. 2 Vols., 1906.

Knox, Captain John: *An Historical Account of the Campaigns in North America*. London, 1769.

Lecky, W. E. H.: *History of England in the Eighteenth Century*. 8 Vols. Longmans, 1883.

Levinge, Sir Richard, Bt.: *Historical Records of the 43rd Regt.* London, 1868.

Louisbourg, *An Authentic Account of the Reduction of Louisbourg in June and July* 1758 *by a SPECTATOR*. London, 1758.

Macleod: *Memoirs of Sergeant Donald Macleod*. London, 1791.

Mahon, Maj.-Gen. R. H.: *The Life of General The Hon. James Murray*. Murray, 1921.

Mante, T.: *History of the Late War in North America*. 1772.

Marshall, Dorothy: *English People in the Eighteenth Century*. Longmans, 1956.

Martin, Le R. F. P.: *Le Marquis de Montcalm*. Paris, 1898.

Montcalm: *Journal du Marquis de Montcalm*, 1756–59. Ed. H. R. Casgrain. Quebec, 1895.

Newspapers & Periodicals   *The Gentleman's Magazine*
                                    The London Gazette
                                    The Monitor

Notes and Queries: 1st Series Vols. IV–VII, X–XII
                      2nd „   Vols. I, IV, V, VII, VIII
                      3rd „   Vols. V, VI
                      4th „   Vols. IV, V, VII
                      5th „   Vol. VII
                      6th „   Vols. VI, IX
                      7th „   Vols. I, V
                      8th „   Vols. VI–VIII, XII

Plant, Marjorie: *The Domestic Life of Scotland in the Eighteenth Century*. Edinburgh, 1952.

Plumb, J. H.: *England in the Eighteenth Century*. Penguin Books, 1950.

Powell, Rosamond Bayne: *Housekeeping in the Eighteenth Century*. Murray, 1956.

Quebec: *An Accurate and Authentic Journal of the Siege of Quebec by a Gentleman in an Eminent Station on the Spot*. London, 1759.

Robertson, Sir C. Grant: *Chatham and the British Empire*. Eng. U.P. 1946.

Rochefort: *A Journal of the Campaign*. London, 1758.
    A Letter by a Country Gentleman. London, 1758.
    A Letter to the Author of Candid Reflections on the Report of the General Officers. London, 1758.
    An Authentic Account of our Last Attempt upon the Coast of France. London, 1758.
    Report of the General Officers on the Causes of Failure. London, 1757.

Samuel, Sigmund: *The Seven Years War in Canada*. Toronto, 1934.

Seeley, Sir J. R.: *The Expansion of England*. Macmillan, 1931.

Sherrard, O. A.: *Lord Chatham*. 3 Vols. Bodley Head, 1955–8.

Smollett, Tobias: *An Account of the Expedition against Cartagena*. London, 1756.

Smyth, Maj. B.: *History of the Lancashire Fusiliers*. 2 Vols. Dublin, 1903.

Smythies, Capt. R. H. Raymond: *Historical Records of the 40th Regiment*. A. H. Swiss, 1894.

Townshend, Lt.-Col. C. V. F.: *The Military Life of the Marquis Townshend*. Murray, 1901.

Trimen, Richard: *Records of the 35th Regiment*. 1873.

Tucker, J. S.: *Memoirs of the Earl St. Vincent*. 2 Vols. London, 1844.

Tunstall, Brian: *William Pitt, Earl of Chatham*. 1938.

Walpole, Horace: *Letters*. Ed. Mrs. Paget Toynbee. 19 Vols. O.U.P. 1903–5.

—— *Memoirs of the Reign of George II*. 2nd Ed. 3 Vols. 1847.

Warburton, G.: *The Conquest of Canada*. 2 Vols. London, 1849.

Webb, Lt.-Col. E. A. H.: *History of the 12th (The Suffolk) Regiment*. Spottiswoode, 1913.

Whitworth, Rex: *Field-Marshal Lord Ligonier*. Oxford, 1958.

Williams, B.: *The Life of William Pitt, Earl of Chatham*. 2 Vols. 1913.

—— *The Whig Supremacy*. O.U.P., 1952.

Wood, W.: *The Fight for Canada*, Constable, 1905.

Wright, J.: *A History of the Late War*. London, 1765.

Wrong, G. M.: *The Fall of Canada 1759–60*. Oxford, 1914.

—— *The Rise and Fall of New France*. 2 Vols. Macmillan, 1928.

Young, Maj. W.: *Manœuvres* (Contains Wolfe's orders and his Instructions to Young Officers). c. 1788.

Useful material is also to be found in the fiction of the period and particularly in Smollett's *Roderick Random* and *Humphrey Clinker*; Thackeray's *The Virginians*; Defoe's *Moll Flanders*; and Charles Johnstone's *Chrysal, or the Adventures of a Guinea*.

INDEX

351